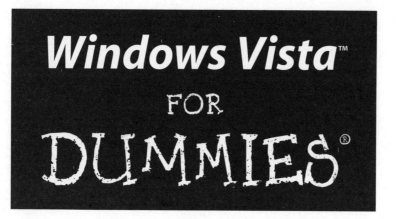

Windows Vista™ FOR DUMMIES®

by Andy Rathbone

BICENTENNIAL
1807
WILEY
2007
BICENTENNIAL

Wiley Publishing, Inc.

Windows Vista™ For Dummies®

Published by
Wiley Publishing, Inc.
111 River Street
Hoboken, NJ 07030-5774
www.wiley.com

Copyright © 2007 by Wiley Publishing, Inc., Indianapolis, Indiana

Published by Wiley Publishing, Inc., Indianapolis, Indiana

Published simultaneously in Canada

For general information on our other products and services, please contact our Customer Care Department within the U.S. at 800-762-2974, outside the U.S. at 317-572-3993, or fax 317-572-4002.

For technical support, please visit www.wiley.com/techsupport.

Wiley also publishes its books in a variety of electronic formats. Some content that appears in print may not be available in electronic books.

Library of Congress Control Number: 2006934815

ISBN-13: 978-0-471-75421-3

Manufactured in the United States of America

10 9 8 7

1B/SZ/RR/QW/IN

WILEY

About the Author

Andy Rathbone started geeking around with computers in 1985 when he bought a 26-pound portable CP/M Kaypro 2X. Like other nerds of the day, he soon began plying with null-modem adapters, dialing computer bulletin boards, and working part-time at Radio Shack.

He wrote articles for various techie publications before moving to computer books in 1992. He's written the *Windows For Dummies* series, *Upgrading and Fixing PCs For Dummies, TiVo For Dummies, PCs: The Missing Manual,* and many other computer books.

Today, he has more than 15 million copies of his books in print, and they've been translated into more than 30 languages. You can reach Andy at his Web site, www.andyrathbone.com.

Author's Acknowledgments

Special thanks to Dan Gookin, Matt Wagner, Tina Rathbone, Steve Hayes, Kelly Ewing, Colleen Totz, Dave Diamond, Joyce Nielsen, Kristie Rees, Jodi Jensen, and Amanda Foxworth. Thanks also to all the folks I never meet in editorial, sales, marketing, proofreading, layout, graphics, and manufacturing who work hard to bring you this book.

Publisher's Acknowledgments

We're proud of this book; please send us your comments through our online registration form located at www.dummies.com/register/.

Some of the people who helped bring this book to market include the following:

Acquisitions, Editorial, and Media Development

Project Editor: Kelly Ewing

Senior Acquisitions Editor: Steve Hayes

Technical Editor: Joyce Nielsen

Editorial Manager: Jodi Jensen

Media Development Manager: Laura VanWinkle

Editorial Assistant: Amanda Foxworth

Sr. Editorial Assistant: Cherie Case

Cartoons: Rich Tennant
(www.the5thwave.com)

Composition Services

Project Coordinator: Kristie Rees

Layout and Graphics: Carl Byers, Denny Hager, Barry Offringa, Heather Ryan, Rashell Smith

Proofreaders: Melanie Hoffman, Jessica Kramer, Dwight Ramsey, Techbooks

Indexer: Techbooks

Publishing and Editorial for Technology Dummies

Richard Swadley, Vice President and Executive Group Publisher

Andy Cummings, Vice President and Publisher

Mary Bednarek, Executive Acquisitions Director

Mary C. Corder, Editorial Director

Publishing for Consumer Dummies

Diane Graves Steele, Vice President and Publisher

Joyce Pepple, Acquisitions Director

Composition Services

Gerry Fahey, Vice President of Production Services

Debbie Stailey, Director of Composition Services

Contents at a Glance

Table of Contents

Introduction

Welcome to *Windows Vista For Dummies,* the world's best-selling book about Windows Vista!

This book's popularity probably boils down to this simple fact: Some people want to be Windows whizzes. They love interacting with dialog boxes. Some randomly press keys in the hope of discovering hidden, undocumented features. A few memorize long strings of computer commands while washing their hair.

And you? Well, you're no dummy, that's for sure. But when it comes to Windows and computers, the fascination just isn't there. You want to get your work done, stop, and move on to something more important. You have no intention of changing, and there's nothing wrong with that.

That's where this book comes in handy. Instead of making you a whiz at Windows, it merely dishes out chunks of useful computing information when you need them. Instead of becoming a Windows Vista expert, you'll know just enough to get by quickly, cleanly, and with a minimum of pain so that you can move on to the more pleasant things in life.

About This Book

Don't try to read this book in one sitting; there's no need. Instead, treat this book like a dictionary or an encyclopedia. Turn to the page with the information you need and say, "Ah, so that's what they're talking about." Then put down the book and move on.

Don't bother trying to memorize all the Windows Vista jargon, such as Select the Menu Item from the Drop-Down List Box. Leave that stuff for the computer enthusiasts. In fact, if anything technical comes up in a chapter, a road sign warns you well in advance. Depending on your mood, you can either slow down to read it or speed on around it.

Instead of fancy computer jargon, this book covers subjects like these, all discussed in plain English:

- ✔ Keeping your computer safe and secure
- ✔ Finding, starting, and closing programs
- ✔ Locating the file you saved or downloaded yesterday
- ✔ Setting up a computer for the whole family to use
- ✔ Copying information to and from a CD or DVD
- ✔ Working with your digital camera's photos and making slide shows
- ✔ Scanning and printing your work
- ✔ Creating a network between PCs to share an Internet connection or printer
- ✔ Fixing Windows Vista when it's misbehaving

There's nothing to memorize and nothing to learn. Just turn to the right page, read the brief explanation, and get back to work. Unlike other books, this one enables you to bypass the technical hoopla and still get your work done.

How to Use This Book

Something in Windows Vista will eventually leave you scratching your head. No other program brings so many buttons, bars, and babble to the screen. When something in Windows Vista leaves you stumped, use this book as a reference. Look for the troublesome topic in this book's table of contents or index. The table of contents lists chapter and section titles and page numbers. The index lists topics and page numbers. Page through the table of contents or index to the spot that deals with that particular bit of computer obscurity, read only what you have to, close the book, and apply what you've read.

If you're feeling spunky and want to find out more, read a little further in the bulleted items below each section. You can find a few completely voluntary extra details, tips, or cross-references to check out. There's no pressure, though. You aren't forced to discover anything that you don't want to or that you simply don't have time for.

If you have to type something into the computer, you'll see easy-to-follow bold text like this:

Type **Media Player** into the Search box.

In the preceding example, you type the words *Media Player* and then press the keyboard's Enter key. Typing words into a computer can be confusing, so a description follows that explains what you should be seeing on the screen.

Whenever I describe a message or information that you see on-screen or a Web address, I present it this way:

```
www.andyrathbone.com
```

This book doesn't wimp out by saying, "For further information, consult your manual." Windows Vista doesn't even *come* with a manual. This book also doesn't contain information about running specific Windows software packages, such as Microsoft Office. Windows Vista is complicated enough on its own! Luckily, other *For Dummies* books mercifully explain most popular software packages.

Don't feel abandoned, though. This book covers Windows in plenty of detail for you to get the job done. Plus, if you have questions or comments about *Windows Vista For Dummies,* feel free to drop me a line on my Web site at www.andyrathbone.com.

Finally, keep in mind that this book is a *reference.* It's not designed to teach you how to use Windows Vista like an expert, heaven forbid. Instead, this book dishes out enough bite-sized chunks of information so that you don't *have* to learn Windows.

And What about You?

Chances are you already own Windows Vista or are thinking about upgrading. You know what *you* want to do with your computer. The problem lies in making the *computer* do what you want it to do. You've gotten by one way or another, hopefully with the help of a computer guru — either a friend at the office, somebody down the street, or your fourth-grader.

But when your computer guru isn't around, this book can be a substitute during your times of need. (Keep a doughnut or Pokémon card nearby in case you need a quick bribe.)

How This Book Is Organized

The information in this book has been well sifted. This book contains seven parts, and I divide each part into chapters relating to the part's theme. With an even finer knife, I divide each chapter into short sections to help you figure out a bit of Windows Vista's weirdness. Sometimes, you may find what you're looking for in a small, boxed sidebar. Other times, you may need to cruise through an entire section or chapter. It's up to you and the particular task at hand.

Here are the categories (the envelope, please).

Part I: Windows Vista Stuff Everybody Thinks You Already Know

This part dissects Windows Vista's backbone: its opening screen and user-name buttons, the mammoth Start button menu that hides all your important stuff, and your computer's desktop — the background where all your programs live. It explains how to move windows around, for example, and click the right buttons at the right time. It explains the Windows Vista stuff that everybody thinks that you already know.

Part II: Working with Programs and Files

Windows Vista comes with bunches of free programs. Finding and starting the programs, however, often proves to be a chore. This part of the book shows how to prod programs into action. If an important file or program has vanished from the radar, you discover how to make Windows Vista dredge your computer's crowded cupboards and bring it back.

Part III: Getting Things Done on the Internet

Turn here for a crash course in today's computing playground, the Internet. This part explains how to send e-mail and globetrot across Web sites. Best yet, an entire chapter explains how to do it all safely, without viruses, spyware, and annoying pop-up ads.

A section explains Internet Explorer's security toolbar. The toolbar stops evil phishing sites from tricking you and keeps Web parasites from attaching themselves to your board as you Web surf.

Part IV: Customizing and Upgrading Windows Vista

When Windows Vista needs a jolt, fix it by flipping one of the switches hidden in its Control Panel, described here. Another chapter explains computer maintenance you can easily perform yourself, reducing your repair bills. You discover how to share your computer with several people in a family or shared apartment — without letting anybody peek into anybody else's information.

And when you're ready to add a second computer, head to the networking chapter for quick instructions on linking computers to share an Internet connection, files, and a printer, as well.

Part V: Music, Movies, Memories (and Photos, Too)

Turn here for information on playing music CDs, DVDs, digital music, and movies. Buy some cheap CDs and create your own greatest hits CDs from your favorite tunes. (Or just copy a CD so that your favorite one doesn't get scratched in the car.)

Digital camera owners should visit the chapter on transferring pictures from your camera to your computer, organizing the pictures, and e-mailing them to friends. Bought a camcorder? Head to the section that explains how to edit out the dopey parts and save your completed masterwork onto a DVD the relatives will *enjoy* for a change.

Part VI: Help!

Although glass doesn't shatter when Windows crashes, it still hurts. In this part, you find some soothing salves for the most painful irritations. Plus, you find ways to unleash the Windows Vista program's team of troubleshooters.

Stuck with the problem of moving your files from an old computer to a new one? You can find help here, as well. (If you're ready to upgrade your Windows XP computer to Windows Vista, check out the Appendix, too, which holds complete instructions.)

Part VII: The Part of Tens

Everybody loves lists (except during tax time). This part contains lists of Windows-related trivia, such as ten aggravating things about Windows Vista (and how to fix them). As a bonus for the laptoppers, I've collected Windows Vista's most useful laptop tools and placed them into one chapter, complete with step-by-step instructions for most laptopping tasks.

Icons Used in This Book

It just takes a glance at Windows Vista to notice its *icons,* which are little push-button pictures for starting various programs. The icons in this book fit right in. They're even a little easier to figure out:

Watch out! This signpost warns you that pointless technical information is coming around the bend. Swerve away from this icon to stay safe from awful technical drivel.

This icon alerts you about juicy information that makes computing easier: A tried-and-true method for keeping the cat from sleeping on top of the monitor, for example.

Don't forget to remember these important points. (Or at least dog-ear the pages so that you can look them up again a few days later.)

The computer won't explode while you're performing the delicate operations associated with this icon. Still, wearing gloves and proceeding with caution is a good idea.

Are you moving to Windows Vista from Windows XP? This icon alerts you to places where Vista works significantly differently from Windows XP.

Where to Go from Here

Now, you're ready for action. Give the pages a quick flip and scan a section or two that you know you'll need later. Please remember, this is *your* book — your weapon against the computer nerds who've inflicted this whole complicated computer concept on you. Please circle any paragraphs you find useful, highlight key concepts, add your own sticky notes, and doodle in the margins next to the complicated stuff.

The more you mark up your book, the easier it will be for you to find all the good stuff again.

Part I

Windows Vista Stuff Everybody Thinks You Already Know

The 5th Wave   By Rich Tennant

"How do you like that Aero glass interface on Vista? Nice, huh?"

In this part . . .

Most people are dragged into Windows Vista without a choice. Their new computers probably came with Windows Vista already installed. Or maybe the office switched to Windows Vista, where everyone has to learn it except for the boss, who doesn't have a computer. Or maybe Microsoft's marketing hype pushed you into it.

Whatever your situation, this part gives a refresher on Windows Vista basics and buzzwords like dragging and dropping, cutting and pasting, and tugging at vanishing toolbars.

It explains how Vista's changed Windows for the better, and it warns you when Vista's messed things up completely.

Chapter 1

What Is Windows Vista?

Chances are, you've probably heard about Windows: the boxes and windows and mouse pointer that greet you whenever you turn on your computer. In fact, millions of people all over the world are puzzling over it as you read this book. Almost every new computer sold today comes with a copy of Windows preinstalled — cheerfully greeting you when first turned on.

This chapter helps you understand why Windows lives inside your computer and introduces Microsoft's latest Windows version, called *Windows Vista*. It explains how Windows Vista differs from previous Windows versions, whether you should upgrade to Vista, and how well your faithful old PC will weather the upgrade.

What Is Windows Vista, and Why Are You Using It?

Created and sold by a company called Microsoft, Windows isn't like your usual software that lets you write term papers or send angry e-mails to mail-order companies. No, Windows is an *operating system,* meaning it controls the way you work with your computer. It's been around for more than 20 years, and the latest whiz-bang version is called *Windows Vista.*

Windows gets its name from all the cute little windows it places on your monitor. Each window shows information, such as a picture, a program that you're running, or a baffling technical reprimand. You can put several windows on-screen at the same time and jump from window to window, visiting different programs. You can also enlarge a window to fill the entire screen.

Like the mother with the whistle in the lunch court, Windows controls every window and each part of your computer. When you turn on your computer, Windows jumps onto the screen and supervises any running programs. Throughout all this action, Windows keeps things running smoothly, even if the programs start throwing food at each other.

In addition to controlling your computer and bossing around your programs, Windows Vista comes with a bunch of free programs. Although your computer can run without these programs, they're nice to have. These programs let you do different things, like write and print letters, browse the Internet, play music, and even whittle down your camcorder's vacation footage into a three-minute short — automatically.

And why are you using Windows Vista? If you're like most people, you didn't have much choice. Nearly every computer sold since early 2007 comes with Windows Vista preinstalled. A few people escaped Windows by buying Apple computers (those nicer-looking computers that cost more). But chances are, you, your neighbors, your boss, your kids at school, and millions of other people around the world are using Windows.

- ✔ Microsoft took pains (and several years of work) to make Windows Vista the most secure version of Windows yet. (Just ask people who upgraded from previous versions.)

- ✔ Windows makes it easy for several people to share a single computer. Each person receives his or her own user account. When users click their name at the Windows opening screen, they see their *own* work — just the way they left it. Vista adds new controls for parents to limit how their kids use the PC, as well as how much of the Internet they can view.

- ✔ A new, automated version of Backup makes it easier to do what you should have been doing all along: Make copies of your important files every night. (Vista Home includes the Backup program, but it's not automatic: You must remember to run the program each night.)

- ✔ Finally, Vista's powerful new search program means that you can forget about where you stored your files. Just click the Start menu and type what that file contained: a few words in a document, the name of the band singing the song, or even the date you took that picture of Kelly at the office party.

Yes, Microsoft is sneaky

Microsoft may tout Windows as your helpful computing companion, always keeping your best interests in mind, but that's not really true. Windows always keeps *Microsoft's* interests in mind. You'll find that out as soon as you call Microsoft for help on making Windows work right. Your first two questions are free if you pick up the long distance charges to Redmond, Washington. The third call (and all the rest) cost $35 a piece, but prices may change at any time.

Microsoft also uses Windows to plug its own products and services. Sometimes you click a menu item that touts something helpful, but

Windows simply leads you to a Web site where you can purchase additional items from Microsoft or its business partners. For example, the Start menu, normally your launch pad for programs, sports an entry for Windows Marketplace. The Order Prints option in Windows Photo Gallery doesn't let you enter your own favorite print shop; it just lists printers who've partnered with Microsoft.

Simply put, Windows not only controls your computer, but also serves as a huge Microsoft advertising vehicle. Take Microsoft's advertising flyers with the traditional grain of salt.

Should I Bother Switching to Windows Vista?

Microsoft releases a new version of Windows every few years. If you bought your PC between 2001 and 2006, you've probably grown accustomed to the mechanics of Windows XP. That leaves the nagging question, why bother upgrading to Windows Vista when Windows XP works just fine?

Actually, if Windows XP's running just fine, then you probably won't need Windows Vista. But Microsoft hopes the following improvements in Vista will push your hand toward your credit card.

Improved security

Windows Vista's tougher new exterior helps make it more difficult for evil programs to louse up your PC. For example, Vista's built-in Windows Defender program constantly searches your PC for any *spyware* — small programs that spy on your activities, often showing you pop-up ads and slowing down your PC in the process. Microsoft constantly trains Windows

Defender, shown in Figure 1-1, to recognize and squash the newest breeds of spyware.

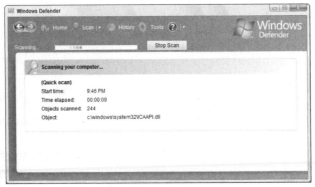

The other parts of Vista's security regime aren't as simple, unfortunately. See, PCs recognize programs as mere strings of numbers, and they can't tell a good string — a word processor, for example — from a bad string, such as a virus. To solve the identification problem, Vista simply dumps the decision onto *your* shoulders: Whenever a particularly powerful program tries to run on your PC, Vista states, "Windows needs your permission to run this program." Then it leaves you with two choices: Allow or Cancel.

To ease you through this admittedly difficult new responsibility, I cover Vista's new security features in Chapter 10.

And although Windows Defender keeps you covered from spyware, Vista doesn't include a free antivirus program. Instead, Microsoft invites you to subscribe to its new Live OneCare antivirus program (www.windowsonecare. com) for $49 dollars a year.

New Internet Explorer version

Vista's new Internet Explorer 7 (which I cover in Chapter 8) lets you surf the Web more easily and securely with the following new features:

✔ **Tabbed browsing:** In the past, keeping two Web sites open on-screen meant running *two* copies of Internet Explorer. With Vista, Internet Explorer displays several Web sites simultaneously, each running in a separate page with a clickable tab at the top for easy switching. That tab makes it easier to compare prices from several different shopping sites, for example, or read one Web site while others load in the background. You can even save a group of Web sites as your home page: Whenever you load Internet Explorer, your favorite sites will already be waiting for you, each living in its own tab.

✔ **Phishing filter:** An evil new industry called *phishing* sends e-mails that pretend to be from finance-related companies, such as banks, PayPal, eBay, and others. The realistic-looking e-mails pretend to alert you to some security problem as they try to trick you into entering your name and precious password. Internet Explorer's new Phishing Filter, shown in Figure 1-2, sniffs out the phishing Web sites before you enter your information, keeping your name and password safe.

✔ **Built-in Search box:** Tired of racing off to Google to find a Web site? The top of Internet Explorer 7 sports a tiny Search box for on-the-fly searches. Although it's programmed to search on Microsoft's own MSN search, Chapter 8 shows you how to make it search Google, instead.

✔ **RSS feeds:** Short for Really Simple Syndication, this feature lets you see headlines from your favorite Web sites in a short drop-down box. By ogling the RSS box, you can catch up on the latest news headlines, for example, without stopping to visit your favorite news site. RSS feeds also let you know if your favorite sites have any new articles, sparing you a wasted visit. RSS feeds speed up your browsing and, conveniently, leave out the ads.

Figure 1-2:
Internet Explorer's new Phishing Filter alerts you to fake Web sites that try to trick you into entering your name, password, or credit-card information.

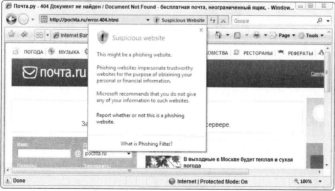

New Media Player and Media Center

Vista's new version of Media Player sports streamlined, easier-to-use controls. The big star, however, is Vista's Media Center, which not only plays DVDs and music but lets you watch TV on your PC and even record shows onto your hard drive for later viewing.

Recording TV shows requires two important things, however: a TV tuner in your PC and the proper version of Vista. (Vista comes in a startling *five* versions, all described at this chapter's end.) Installing a TV tuner can be as simple as plugging a box into your PC's USB port or sliding a card inside your PC. I describe both tasks in one of my other books, *Upgrading and Fixing PCs For Dummies,* published by Wiley Publishing, Inc.

DVD burning

More than five years after DVD burners hit the market, Windows can finally take advantage of them without third-party software. Windows Vista lets you copy files and movies to DVDs as well as CDs.

In fact, Vista's updated version of Movie Maker (described in Chapter 16) lets you turn your camcorder footage into DVDs that play back on a normal DVD player and TV. Mail them to your friends and prepare for a deluge of incoming vacation DVDs, as well.

Calendar

For the first time, Windows now sports a calendar, shown in Figure 1-3, for keeping track of your appointments. You can even publish your calendar to other PCs or Web sites, keeping your appointments synchronized with the calendars of your friends and coworkers.

Easier searching for files

Windows XP really drags its feet when searching for files. Searching for a filename takes several minutes on a crowded hard drive, and if you're searching your files for a particular word or phrase, you're in for a long weekend. Vista, by contrast, spends its idle time fine-tuning an index of every word on your hard drive.

Figure 1-3:
The built-in Calendar program in Vista tracks your tasks and appointments, as well as synchronizes your calendar with others to coordinate meetings.

Instead of sending you on a constant search for your files, Vista automatically remembers your files' locations. For example, search for every document mentioning "Celery," and Vista instantly lists those files' names, ready for opening with a double-click. Whenever you create new documents mentioning "Celery," Vista automatically remembers their locations, too, making for quick and easy retrieval.

Vista places a Search box on the Start menu, atop every folder, in the Help and Support window, and in a few other key spots. The handy Search box and Vista's up-to-date index make it faster than ever to find the files and programs you want.

Vista even updates its index with words on Web sites you've visited recently, letting you quickly reread that headline you scrolled through last week.

I explain how to put the Search box to work in Chapter 6.

Vista looks prettier

Microsoft spent some time decorating Vista with a three-dimensional look, a treat available only to PCs with powerful graphics capabilities. When you can't find an open window, for example, press the Windows and Tab keys: All the windows appear on your PC in a Flip 3D view, shown in Figure 1-4.

Figure 1-4: To see a 3D view of your currently open windows, press Tab while holding down the Windows key. Press Tab or spin your mouse's scroll wheel to flip through the windows and then let go of the Windows key when your window is on top.

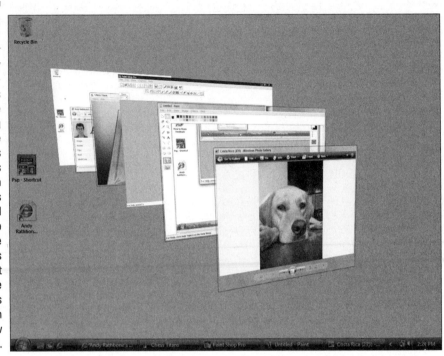

Hover your mouse pointer over any name listed on your desktop's taskbar, and Vista displays a thumbnail picture of that window's current contents, making your window much easier to retrieve from the sea of programs.

Can My PC Still Run Vista?

If your PC already runs Windows XP well, it will probably run Vista, but not at its best. However, upgrading your PC with a few things will help Vista run better, a job I tackle in *Upgrading and Fixing PCs For Dummies,* 7th edition. Here's the shopping list:

✔ **Video:** Vista requires powerful graphics for its fanciest 3D features, such as Flip 3D (see Figure 1-4). Upgraded video cards can cost more than $100, and they're not available for laptops. But if your PC's video lacks the muscle and your wallet lacks the cash, don't despair. Vista simply slips into more casual clothes, letting your PC run without the 3D views.

- **Memory:** Vista loves memory. For best results, your PC should have 1GB of memory or more. Memory's easy to install and relatively cheap, so don't skimp here.

- **DVD drive:** Unlike Windows XP, which comes on a CD, Windows Vista comes on a *DVD*. That means your PC needs a working DVD drive to install it. That probably won't rule out many PCs these days, but it may rule out some older laptops.

Windows Vista should be able to run most of your current programs without problems. Some, however, won't work, including most security-based programs, such as antivirus, firewall, and security programs. You'll need to contact the program's manufacturer to see whether it'll give you a free upgrade.

Shopping for a new PC to run Vista? Visit any store, and you'll find plenty of PCs running Vista. To see how well a particular PC handles Vista, click the Start button, choose Control Panel, and open the System and Maintenance category. There, select Performance Information and Tools. Vista displays that particular PC's Windows Experience Index, which ranges from 1 (dismal) to 5 (excellent).

Not sure what version of Windows your PC has? Right-click Computer from the Start menu and choose Properties. That screen states your Windows version.

Can I Make Windows Vista Look and Feel Like Windows XP?

Some people crave Vista's new interface; others feel like they're looking at a rental car's unfamiliar dashboard. Follow these steps to make Vista look *almost* like Windows XP:

1. **Start by changing the Start menu: Right-click the Start button, choose Properties, select Classic Start Menu, and click OK.**

2. **Next, bring back the desktop: Right-click a blank part of the desktop and choose Personalize. Choose Theme and then choose Windows Classic from the Theme pull-down menu. Click OK.**

3. **Finally, put the menus back on top of each folder: Open your Documents folder from the Start menu. Then click the Organize button, choose Folder and Search Options, and choose Use Windows Classic Folders. Click OK.**

These steps not only bring back the look of previous Windows versions, but speed up an older PC that's struggling to keep up with Vista's fancy layers of graphics.

The Five Flavors of Vista

Windows XP came in two easy-to-understand versions: One for home, and one for business. Microsoft confuses things in Vista by splitting it into five different versions, each with a different price tag.

Luckily, only three versions are aimed at consumers, and most people will probably choose Windows Vista Home Premium. Still, to clear up the confusion, I describe all five versions in Table 1-1.

Table 1-1: The Five Flavors of Windows Vista

The Version of Vista	What It Does
Windows Vista Home Basic	Reminiscent of Windows XP Home Edition, this version leaves out Vista's fancier media features, such as DVD burning, HDTV, TV recording, and other similar features.
Windows Vista Home Premium	This version is Windows Vista Home Basic, but with the media features tossed back in. It targets people who watch TV on their PC or who want to create DVDs from their camcorder footage.
Windows Vista Business	Just as with its brethren, Windows XP Professional, this aims at the business market. It includes a fax program, for example, but lacks the media-related features found in Vista Home Premium.
Windows Vista Enterprise	This business market version contains even more tools, such as support for additional languages and larger networks.
Windows Vista Ultimate	A combination of the Home and Business versions, this version aims at the wallets of hard-core PC users, such as gamers, people in the video industry, and similar people who spend their lives in front of their keyboards.

Although five versions may seem complicated, choosing the one you need isn't that difficult. And because Microsoft stuffed all the versions on your Vista DVD, you can upgrade at any time simply by whipping out the credit card and unlocking the features in a different version. Here are some guidelines for choosing the version you need:

- ✔ If your PC can't display or record TV shows, and you don't want to make DVDs from your camcorder footage, then save a few bucks by sticking with **Windows Vista Home Basic.** It's fine for word processing, e-mail, and the Internet.

- ✔ If you want to burn DVDs and/or record TV shows on your PC, then pony up the cash for **Windows Vista Home Premium.**

- ✔ People who run Web servers on their PCs — and you'll know if you're doing it — will want **Windows Vista Business.**

- ✔ Dedicated gamers and computer industry professionals will want **Windows Vista Ultimate** because it includes *everything* found in the other versions.

- ✔ Computer techies who work for businesses will argue with their bosses over whether they need **Windows Business** or **Windows Enterprise** versions. They'll make their decision based on whether they're a small company (Windows Business) or a large company (Windows Enterprise).

That inexpensive **Vista Starter** version you may have heard about isn't sold in the United States. It's sold at reduced prices in developing nations like Malaysia. (It's not really a goodwill gesture as much as it's an attempt to reduce software piracy.)

Vista's Service Pack 1

Whenever a problem pops up in Windows Vista, Microsoft releases a small piece of software called a *patch* for a quick fix. After a long year of patches, Microsoft rolled them all into one megapatch called a *Service Pack.*

Vista's Service Pack 1, automatically delivered and installed on your PC by Windows Update, doesn't change the way Vista works on the surface. But when the service pack arrived on your PC in early 2008, it made Vista run more smoothly under the hood. After Service Pack 1 is installed, the words Service Pack 1 appear in Vista's System window, shown in the following figure. To see whether your PC has Service Pack 1 installed, click the Start menu, right-click Computer, choose Properties, and then look for the words Service Pack 1 as shown.

For more information about Windows Update and its automatic downloading of patches, visit Chapter 10.

(continued)

(continued)

Service Pack 1 is installed.

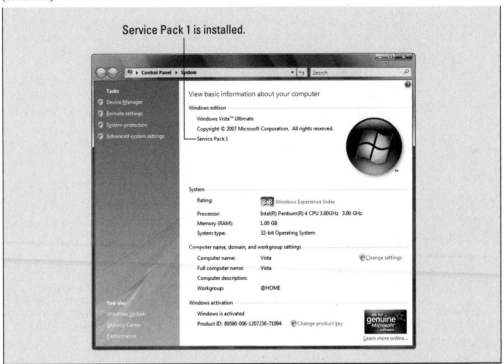

Chapter 2

The Desktop, Start Menu, and Other Windows Vista Mysteries

*T*his chapter provides a drive-by tour of Windows Vista. You'll turn on your computer, start Windows, and spend a few minutes gawking at Vista's various neighborhoods: the desktop, the taskbar, the Start menu, and the environmentally correct (and compassionate) Recycle Bin.

The programs you're using hang out on the Windows *desktop* (a fancy word for the Windows background). The taskbar serves as a head turner, letting you move from one program to another. To invite yet more programs onto the desktop, drop by the Start menu: It's full of push buttons that let you add other programs to the mix.

Want to get rid of something? Dump it into the Recycle Bin, where it either fades away or, if necessary, can be safely revived.

Being Welcomed to the World of Windows Vista

Starting Windows Vista is as easy as turning on your computer — Windows Vista leaps onto the screen automatically with a futuristic flourish. But before you can start working, Windows Vista may throw you a fastball with its first screen: Windows wants you to *log on,* as shown in Figure 2-1, by clicking your name.

I've customized my Welcome screen. Yours will look different. If you don't see a username listed for you on the Welcome screen, then you have three options:

- ✔ **If you just bought the computer, use the account named Administrator.** Designed to give the owner full power over the computer, the Administrator account user can set up new accounts for new users, install programs, burn CDs, start an Internet connection, and access all the files on the computer — even those of other users. Windows Vista needs at least one person to act as administrator, even if your computer isn't connected to other computers. Hit Chapter 13 if you care about this stuff.

- ✔ **Use the Guest account.** Designed for household visitors, this account lets guests, such as the babysitter or visiting relatives, use the computer temporarily. (It's turned on or off in the Add or Remove User Accounts area, described in Chapter 13.)

- ✔ **No Guest account *and* no user?** Then find out who owns the computer and beg that person to set up a username for you. (If they don't know how, show them Chapter 13, where I explain how to set up a user account.)

Don't *want* to log on at the Welcome screen? These hidden Welcome screen buttons control other options:

- ✔ The little blue button in the screen's bottom-left corner, seen in Figure 2-1 and the margin, customizes Windows Vista for people with physical challenges in hearing, sight, or manual dexterity, all covered in Chapter 11. If you push this button by mistake, press Cancel to remove the option menu from your screen without changing any settings.

- ✔ To turn off your PC from this sparse opening screen, click the little red button in the screen's bottom-right corner, seen in Figure 2-1. (If you've accidentally clicked it and turned off your PC, don't panic. Press your PC's power button, and your PC will return to this screen.)

- ✔ Click the little arrow next to the red button, and Vista will end your session by either going to sleep, turning off your PC, or restarting — options all explained at this chapter's end.

Figure 2-1:
Windows
Vista wants
all users to
log on so
that it knows
who's using
the com-
puter at all
times.

Windows Vista dashes back to this Welcome screen whenever you haven't touched your PC for ten minutes. To stop this scurrying, right-click on the desktop and choose Personalize. Choose Screen Saver and remove the check mark next to the On Resume, Display Logon Screen option. Then you'll have to log on only when you start up Windows — not throughout the day.

Fiddling around with user accounts

Windows Vista allows several people to work on the same computer, yet it keeps everybody's work separate. To do that, it needs to know who's currently sitting in front of the keyboard. When you *log on* — introduce yourself — by clicking your *username,* as shown in Figure 2-1, Windows Vista presents your personalized desktop, ready for you to make your own personalized mess.

When you're through working or just feel like taking a break, log off (explained at this chapter's end) so that somebody else can use the computer. Later, when you log back on, your messy desktop will be waiting for you.

Running Windows Vista for the first time

If you've just installed Windows Vista or you're turning on your computer for the first time, you're treated to a few extra Windows Vista spectacles. The Welcome Center leaves you with the following buttons customized to your particular PC:

- **View Computer Details:** The Welcome Center starts at this page, which lists (yawn) technical details about your PC: its particular version of Vista, as well as your PC's processor, memory, and video adapter, and other arcana.

- **Transfer Files and Settings:** Just turned on your *new* Vista PC? This helpful area lets you lug all your old PC's files to your new one, a chore I walk you through in Chapter 19.

- **Add New Users:** Ignore this one unless other people will be sharing your PC. If that's the case, click here to introduce those people to Windows. This area also lets you control what your kids (or roommates) can do on your PC, covered in Chapter 13.

- **Connect to the Internet:** Ready to surf and check e-mail? This feature introduces Vista to your Internet connection, a process I describe in Chapter 8.

- **Windows Ultimate Extras:** Owners of Vista's Ultimate version find downloadable add-ons here.

- **Windows Anytime Upgrade:** Owners of any other Windows versions can click here to upgrade to a more powerful version.

- **What's New in Windows Vista:** Handy for Windows XP upgraders, this button introduces you to the new features in your particular version of Vista.

- **Personalize Windows:** Head here to splash a new screen across your desktop, change Vista's colors, or tweak your monitor (all covered in Chapter 11).

- **Register Windows Online:** Head here to, uh, sign up for Microsoft's e-mail marketing blurbs.

- **Windows Media Center:** This button starts you on the process of revving up Windows Media Center to record TV shows, covered in Chapter 15.

- **Windows Basics:** Designed for owners of their first PC, this tutorial explains how to use the mouse and keyboard, as well as files and folders.

- **Ease of Access Center:** People with physical challenges will enjoy Vista's variety of accessibility tools, described in Chapter 11.

- **Back Up and Restore Center:** I describe how to back up your files in Chapter 10.

- **Windows Vista Demos:** These little movies in Vista's Help program, covered in Chapter 20, help you with different Vista tasks.

- **Control Panel:** The nerve center of your PC, the Control Panel lets you tweak how Vista interacts with your PC, covered in Chapter 11.

Vista initially shows only a few buttons, but to see them all, click Show All 14 Items along the Welcome Center's bottom.

To see more information about any of these tasks, click the button once. Or double-click a button to move directly to that particular chore. To make the Welcome Center stop welcoming you every time you turn on your PC, remove the check mark from the window's Run at Startup box. Missing it already? Retrieve it by clicking the Start button, choosing All Programs, clicking Accessories, and clicking Welcome Center.

Although you may turn your desktop into a mess, it's your *own* mess. When you return to the computer, your letters will be just as you saved them. Jerry hasn't accidentally deleted your files or folders while playing Widget Squash. Tina's desktop contains links to her favorite Web sites. And all of Jim's John Coltrane MP3s stay in his own personalized Music folder.

Of course, the first big question boils down to this: How do you customize the picture next to your username, like my face in Figure 2-1? After you've logged on, open the Start menu and click the little picture at the top of the Start menu. Windows conveniently opens a menu where you can choose Change Your Picture. (For ideas, click Browse for More Pictures and look through the digital photos you've saved in your Pictures folder. I explain how to crop photos to the appropriate square size in Chapter 16.)

Keeping your account private with a password

Because Windows Vista lets bunches of people use the same computer, how do you stop Rob from reading Diane's love letters to Henry Rollins? How can Josh keep Grace from deleting his *Star Wars* movie trailers? Windows Vista's optional *password* solves some of those problems.

By typing a secret password when logging on, as shown in Figure 2-2, you enable your computer to recognize *you* and nobody else. If you protect your username with a password, nobody can access your files (except for the computer's administrator, who can peek anywhere — and even delete your account).

Figure 2-2:
With a password, nobody else can access your files.

To set up or change your password, follow these steps:

1. **Click the Start button, click Control Panel, click User Accounts and Family Safety, and then choose Change Your Windows Password.**

   If your Control Panel shows the "Classic View," choose the User Accounts icon and choose "Create a Password for your account."

2. **Choose Create a Password for Your Account or Change Your Password.**

   The wording changes depending on whether you're creating a new password or changing an old one.

3. **Type a password that will be easy for you — and nobody else — to remember.**

   Keep your password short and sweet: the name of your favorite vegetable, for example, or your dental floss brand.

4. **In the last box, type a hint that reminds you — and only you — of your password.**

5. **Click the Create Password button.**

6. **When the User Accounts screen returns, choose Create a Password Reset Disk from along the screen's left side.**

   Vista walks you through the process of creating a Password Reset Disk from a floppy, CD, DVD, memory card, or USB thumbdrive, a process I describe fully in Chapter 17.

Make Windows stop asking me for a password!

Windows asks for your name and password only when it needs to know who's tapping on its keys. And it needs that information for any of these three reasons:

- Your computer is part of a network, and your identity determines what goodies you can access.

- The computer's owner wants to limit what you can do on the computer.

- You share your computer with other people and want to keep others from logging on with your name and changing your files and settings.

If these concerns don't apply to you, purge the password by following the first two steps in the section "Keeping your account private with a password," but choose Remove Your Password instead of Change Your Password.

Without that password, anybody can now log on using your user account and view (or destroy) your files. If you're working in an office setting, this setup can be serious trouble. If you've been assigned a password, it's better to simply get used to it.

Windows Vista begins asking for your password whenever you log on.

✔ Passwords are *case-sensitive. Caviar* and *caviar* are considered two different passwords.

✔ Forgotten your password *already*? When you type a password that doesn't work, Vista automatically displays your "hint," hopefully reminding you of your password. Careful, though — anybody can read your hint, so make sure that it's something that makes sense only to you. As a last resort, insert your Password Reset Disk, a job I cover in Chapter 17.

I explain lots more about user accounts in Chapter 13.

Working on the Desktop

Normally, people want their desktops to be horizontal, not vertical. Keeping pencils from rolling off a normal desk is hard enough. But in Windows Vista, your monitor's screen is known as the Windows *desktop,* and that's where all your work takes place. You can create files and folders right on your new electronic desktop and arrange them all across the screen. Each program runs in its own little *window* on top of the desktop.

Windows Vista starts with a freshly scrubbed, empty desktop. After you've been working for a while, your desktop will fill up with *icons* — little push buttons that load your files with a quick double-click of the mouse. Some people leave their desktops strewn with icons for easy access. Others organize their work: When they finish working on something, they store it in a *folder,* a task covered in Chapter 4.

The desktop boasts four main parts, shown in Figure 2-3.

Taskbar: Resting lazily along the desktop's bottom edge, the taskbar lists the programs and files you're currently working on. (Point at any program's name on the taskbar to see a name or thumbnail photo of that program, shown in Figure 2-3.)

Start menu: Seen at the taskbar's left edge, the Start menu works like the restaurant's waiter: It presents menus at your bidding, letting you choose what program to run.

Sidebar: Windows Vista's desktop newcomer, the *Sidebar,* clings along the right edge, offering a plethora of customized gadgets such as weather forecasters, search boxes, and Sudoku games.

Recycle Bin: The desktop's *Recycle Bin,* that little wastebasket-shaped icon, stores your recently deleted files for easy retrieval. Whew!

✔ You can start new projects directly from your desktop: Right-click the desktop, choose New, and select the project of your dreams from the pop-up menu, be it adding a new Contact or loading a favorite program. (The menu lists most of your computer's programs for quick 'n' easy access.)

✔ Are you befuddled about some object's reason for being? Timidly rest the pointer over the mysterious doodad, and Windows will pop up a little box explaining what that thing is or does. Right-click the object, and ever helpful Windows Vista usually tosses up a menu listing nearly everything you can do with that particular object. This trick works on most icons found on your desktop and throughout your programs.

✔ All the icons on your desktop may suddenly disappear, leaving it completely empty. Chances are, Windows Vista hid them in a misguided attempt to be helpful. To bring your work back to life, right-click on your empty desktop and choose View from the pop-up menu. Finally, make sure Show Desktop Icons has a check mark so everything stays visible.

The Recycle Bin   Taskbar   Sidebar

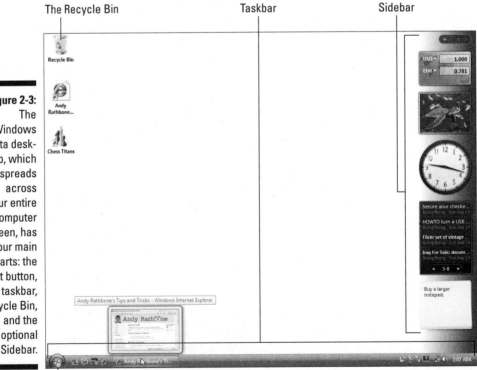

Figure 2-3: The Windows Vista desktop, which spreads across your entire computer screen, has four main parts: the Start button, taskbar, Recycle Bin, and the optional Sidebar.

Click here to open the Start menu

Cleaning up a messy desktop

When icons cover your desktop like a year's worth of sticky notes, Windows Vista offers several ways to clean up the mess. If you just want your desktop clutter to look more organized, right-click the desktop, choose Sort By from the pop-up menu, and choose any of these choices:

- ✔ **Name:** Arrange all icons in alphabetical order using neat, vertical rows.

- ✔ **Size:** Arrange icons according to their size, placing the smallest ones at the top of the rows.

- ✔ **Type:** This lines up icons by their *type*. All Word files are grouped together, for example, as are all links to Web sites.

- ✔ **Date Modified:** Arrange icons by the date you or your PC last changed them.

Right-clicking the desktop and choosing the View option lets you change the icons' size, as well as play with these desk-organizing options:

- ✔ **Auto Arrange:** Automatically arrange everything in vertical rows — even newly positioned icons are swept into tidy rows.

- ✔ **Align to Grid:** This option places an invisible grid on the screen and aligns all icons to the grid to keep them nice and tidy — no matter how hard you try to mess them up.

- ✔ **Show Desktop Icons:** Always keep this option turned on. When turned off, Windows hides every icon on your desktop. If you can remember in your frustration, click this option again to toggle your icons back on.

Most View options are also available for any of your folders by clicking the folder's Views menu.

Jazzing up the desktop's background

To jazz up your desktop, Windows Vista covers it with pretty pictures known as a *background*. (Most people refer to the background as *wallpaper*.)

When you tire of the Vista's normal scenic garb, choose your own picture — any picture stored on your computer:

1. **Right-click a blank part of the desktop, choose Personalize, and click the Desktop Background option.**

2. **Click any of the pictures, shown in Figure 2-4, and Vista quickly places it onto your desktop's background.**

Found a keeper? Click the Save button to keep it on your desktop. Click the Picture Location menu to see more pictures. Or, if you're still searching, move to the next step.

3. **Click the Browse button and click a file from inside your Pictures folder.**

   Most people store their digital photos in their Pictures folder. (I explain browsing folders in Chapter 4.)

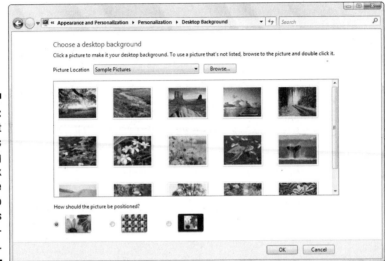

Figure 2-4:
Try different backgrounds by clicking them; click the Browse button to see pictures from different folders.

4. **Found a good picture?**

   Exit the program, and your chosen photo stays stuck to your desktop as the background.

Here are some tips for sprucing up your desktop:

✔ As you browse through different pictures, Windows Vista automatically decides whether the image should be *tiled* repeatedly across the screen, *centered* directly in the middle, or *stretched* to fill the entire screen. To override Windows' automatic choice, select your own preference from the How Should the Picture Be Positioned? area along the window's bottom. Feel free to experiment to see each effect.

✔ You can easily borrow any picture on the Internet for a background. Right-click on the Web site's picture and select Set as Background from the pop-up menu. Microsoft sneakily copies the image onto your desktop as its new background. (You can also right-click any photo in your Pictures folder and choose Set as Background — handy for quick background changes.)

✔ To change Windows Vista's entire *look,* right-click on the desktop, choose Personalize, and choose Theme. Aimed at heavy-duty procrastinators, different themes splash different colors across Windows' various buttons, borders, and boxes. I explain more about Themes in Chapter 11. (If you download any Themes offered on the Internet, check them with antivirus software, covered in Chapter 10.)

Dumpster diving in the Recycle Bin

The Recycle Bin, that little wastebasket icon in the corner of your desktop, works much like a *real* recycle bin. Shown in the margin, it lets you retrieve Sunday's paper when somebody has pitched the comics section before you had a chance to read it.

You can dump something — a file or folder, for example — into the Windows Vista Recycle Bin in one of two ways:

✔ Simply right-click on it and choose Delete from the menu. Windows Vista asks cautiously if you're *sure* that you want to delete the item. Click Yes, and Windows Vista dumps it into the Recycle Bin, just as if you'd dragged it there. Whoosh!

✔ For the ultimate deletion rush, click the unwanted object and poke your keyboard's Delete key.

Want something back? Double-click the Recycle Bin icon to see your deleted items. Right-click the item you want and choose Restore. The handy little Recycle Bin returns your precious item to the same spot where you deleted it. (You can also resuscitate deleted items by dragging them to your desktop or any other folder; drag 'em back to delete them.)

The Recycle Bin can get pretty crowded. If you're searching frantically for a recently deleted file, tell the Recycle Bin to sort everything by the date and time you deleted it: Click the words Date Deleted from the Recycle Bin's top menu. (Click the downward pointing arrow by the word Views and choose Details to see the deletion dates.)

To delete something *permanently,* just delete it from inside the Recycle Bin: Click it and press the Del key. To delete *everything* in the Recycle Bin, right-click on the Recycle Bin and choose Empty Recycle Bin.

To bypass the Recycle Bin completely when deleting files, hold down Shift while pressing Delete. Poof! The deleted object disappears, ne'er to be seen again — a handy trick when dealing with sensitive items, such as credit-card numbers.

  ✔ The Recycle Bin icon changes from an empty wastepaper basket to a full one as soon as it's holding a deleted file.

  ✔ How long does the Recycle Bin hold onto deleted files? It waits until the garbage consumes about 10 percent of your hard drive space. Then it begins purging your oldest deleted files to make room for the new. If you're low on hard drive space, shrink the bin's size by right-clicking on the Recycle Bin and choosing Properties. Decrease the Custom Size number to automatically delete files more quickly; increase the number, and the Recycle Bin hangs onto them a little longer.

  ✔ The Recycle Bin only saves items deleted from your own computer's hard drive. That means it won't save anything deleted from a floppy, CD, memory card, MP3 player, or digital camera.

  ✔ If you delete something from somebody else's computer over a network, it can't be retrieved. The Recycle Bin only holds items deleted from your *own* computer, not somebody else's computer. (For some awful reason, the Recycle Bin on the other person's computer doesn't save the item, either.) Be careful.

The Start Button's Reason to Live

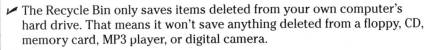

The bright-blue Start button lives in the bottom-left corner of the desktop, where it's always ready for action. By clicking the Start button, you can start programs, adjust Windows Vista's settings, find help for sticky situations, or, thankfully, shut down Windows Vista and get away from the computer for a while.

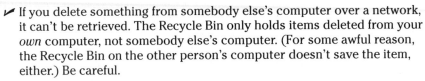

Click the Start button once, and the first layer of menus pops out, as shown in Figure 2-5.

Your Start menu will change as you add more programs to your computer. That's why the Start menu on your friend's computer is probably arranged differently than the Start menu on your computer.

- ✔ Your Documents, Pictures, and Music folders are always one click away on the Start menu. These folders are specially designed for their contents. The Pictures folder, for example, displays little thumbnails of your digital photos. The biggest perk to these three folders? Keeping your files in these folders helps you remember where you stored them. I cover file organization in Chapter 4.

- ✔ Windows thoughtfully places your most frequently used programs along the left side of the Start menu for easy point 'n' click action.

- ✔ See the words *All Programs* near the Start menu's bottom left? Click there, and yet another menu opens to offer more options. (That new menu covers up the first, though; to bring back the first, click the word Back.)

- ✔ Spot something confusing on the Start menu? Hover your mouse pointer over the mysterious icon. Windows responds with a helpful explanatory message.

- ✔ Strangely enough, you also click the Start button when you want to *stop* using Windows. (You click one of the Off buttons along the Start menu's bottom right, a decision-wrought process described at this chapter's end.)

Figure 2-5: The Start button in Windows Vista hides dozens of menus for starting programs.

The Start menu's prime real estate

When the Start menu pops up (refer to Figure 2-5), it always shows you the items listed in the upcoming list, from top to bottom. You'll use these things constantly in Windows, so if you're already bored with this Start button section, please feign interest through the following explanations.

If you find Start menus exciting, you'll love the upcoming "Customizing the Start menu" section, which explains how to rearrange your entire Start menu.

 Internet Explorer: This option lets you visit the Internet, covered in Chapter 8.

 E-mail: Choose this command to send or receive e-mail with Vista's new Windows Mail program, covered in Chapter 9.

Recently Used Programs: The Start menu's left side constantly updates to list your most frequently used programs' icons for quick launches.

Search box: Conveniently placed directly above the Start button, this area lets you find files by typing a bit of their contents — a few words in an e-mail, a document, a band name, a program's name, or anything else. Press Enter, and Vista quickly dredges it up for you. I cover Search more thoroughly in Chapter 6.

Username: The name of your user account appears at the Start menu's top-right corner. Click here to see a folder containing all your files, as well as your Documents, Pictures, and Music folders.

Documents: This command quickly opens your Documents folder, making it more imperative than ever to always store your work here.

Pictures: Keep your digital pictures in this folder. Each picture's icon is a tiny thumbnail image of your photo.

Music: Store your digital music in here so that Media Player can find and play it more easily.

Games: Windows Vista offers several new games, including a decent chess game. Finally!

Search: The word Search on the Start menu, removed by Vista's Service Pack 1, lets you search for files in precise terms — say, all files created in the last two months containing the word "oyster." Stick with the easier-to-use Search box, along the Start menu's bottom.

Recent Items: Viewed a file within the past few hours? Chances are, it will appear here for quick access.

Computer: This option displays your computer's storage areas: folders, disk drives, CD drives, digital cameras, and other attached goodies.

Network: If your computer connects with other computers through a network, click here to visit them.

Connect To: This area lets you connect to different networks, which I cover in Chapter 14. It's a quick way for laptoppers to connect to a wireless network, for example, as well as a one-click Internet entrance for people with dialup Internet connections.

Control Panel: This area lets you adjust your computer's oodles of confusing settings, all described in Chapter 11.

Default programs: Click here to control which program steps in when you open a file. Here's where you tell Windows to let iTunes handle your music instead of Media Player, for example.

Help and Support: Befuddled? Click here for an answer. (Chapter 20 explains the stoic Windows Help system.)

Sleep/Power: Clicking here either puts your PC to sleep or turns it off, options explained in this chapter's last section.

Lock: This command locks your user account, letting other people log on without accessing your files.

I explain how to assign different tasks to the Sleep button, including making it simply turn off your PC, in Chapter 11.

Starting a program from the Start menu

This task's easy. Click the Start button, and the Start menu pops out of the button's head. If you see an icon for your desired program, click it, and Windows loads the program.

If your program isn't listed, though, click All Programs, near the bottom of the Start menu. Yet another menu pops up, this one listing the names of programs and folders full of programs. Spot your program? Click the name, and Windows kicks that program to the front of the screen.

If you *still* don't see your program listed, try pointing at the tiny folders listed on the All Programs menu. The menu fills with that folder's programs. Don't spot it? Click a different folder and watch as its contents spill out onto the Start menu.

Making Windows start programs automatically

Many people sit down at a computer, turn it on, and go through the same mechanical process of loading their oft-used programs. Believe it or not, Windows Vista can automate this task. The solution is the Startup folder, found lurking in the Start button's All Programs menu. When Windows Vista wakes up, it peeks inside that Startup folder. If it finds a program lurking inside, it immediately tosses that program onto the screen.

To make your favorite programs wake up along with Windows Vista, follow these steps:

1. **Click the Start button and choose All Programs.**

2. **Right-click the Start menu's Startup icon and choose Open.**

   The Startup icon, which lives in the Start menu's All Programs area, opens as a folder.

3. **Drag and drop any of your favorite programs or files into the Startup folder.**

   Windows Vista automatically places shortcuts to those programs inside the Startup folder.

4. **Close the Startup folder.**

   Now, whenever you turn on your PC and log onto your user account, Vista automatically loads those programs or files so that they'll be waiting for you.

When you finally spot your program's name, just click it. That program hops onto the desktop in a window, ready for action.

- ✔ Still don't see your program listed by name? Then head for Chapter 6 and find the section on finding lost files and folders. Windows Vista can track down your missing program.

- ✔ There's another way to load a lost program — if you can find something you created or edited with that program. For example, if you wrote letters to the tax collector using Microsoft Word, double-click one of your tax letters to bring Microsoft Word to the screen from its hiding place.

- ✔ If you don't spot a program listed, type the program's name into the Start menu's Search box. Type **Windows Mail**, for example, press Enter, and Windows Mail pops to the screen, ready to send e-mail.

- ✔ If you don't know how to navigate through your folders, visit Chapter 4. That chapter helps you move gracefully from folder to folder, decreasing the time it takes to stumble across your file.

Customizing the Start menu

The Windows Vista Start menu works great — until you're hankering for something that's not listed on the menu, or something you rarely use is just getting in the way.

✔ **To add a favorite program's icon to the Start button's menu,** right-click on the program's icon and choose Pin to Start Menu from the pop-up menu. Windows copies that icon to your Start menu's left column. (From there, you may drag it to the All Programs area, if you want.)

✔ **To purge unwanted icons from the Start menu's left column,** right-click on them and choose either Unpin from Start Menu or Remove from This List. (Removing an icon from the Start menu doesn't remove the actual program from your computer; it just removes one of many push buttons that launch it.)

When you install a program, as described in Chapter 11, the program almost always adds itself to the Start menu *automatically.* Then the program boldly announces its presence, as shown in Figure 2-6, by displaying its name with a different background color.

You can customize the Start menu even more by changing its properties. To start playing, right-click the Start button, choose Properties, and click the Start menu's Customize button. Place a check mark by the options you want or remove check marks to remove the options. Messed up your Start menu somehow? Click the Use Default Settings button, click OK, and click OK again to start from scratch.

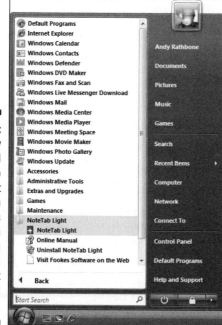

Figure 2-6: The newly installed NoteTab Light program announces its presence by showing up in a different background color.

Bellying Up to the Taskbar

This section introduces one of Windows Vista's handiest tricks, so pull in your chair a little closer. Whenever you run more than one window on the desktop, there's a big problem: Programs and windows tend to cover up each other, making them difficult to locate.

Windows Vista's solution is the *taskbar* — a special area that keeps track of all your open programs. Shown in Figure 2-7, the taskbar normally lives along the bottom of your screen, although you can move it to any edge you want. (***Hint:*** Just drag it from edge to edge. If it doesn't move, right-click on the taskbar and click Lock the Taskbar to remove the check mark by its name.)

Figure 2-7:
Click buttons
for currently
running
programs on
the taskbar.

Rest your mouse pointer over any of the taskbar's programs to see a thumbnail image of that program, shown in Figure 2-7, even if that program's currently covered by other windows on your desktop. (This trick only works if your PC has powerful enough graphics.)

See how the button for Paint Shop Pro looks darker than the other taskbar buttons in Figure 2-7? That's because Paint Shop Pro is the currently *active* window on the desktop: It's the program currently waiting for you to start working. One of your taskbar's buttons always look darker unless you close or minimize all the windows on your desktop.

From the taskbar, you can perform powerful magic on your open windows, as described in the following list:

- ✔ To play with a program listed on the taskbar, click its name. The window rises to the surface and rests atop any other open windows, ready for action.

- ✔ To close a window listed on the taskbar, *right-click* on its name and choose Close from the pop-up menu. The program quits, just as if you'd chosen its Exit command from within its own window. (The departing program gives you a chance to save your work before it quits and walks off the screen.)

✔ If the taskbar keeps hiding below the screen's bottom edge, point the mouse at the screen's bottom edge until the taskbar surfaces. Then right-click the taskbar, choose Properties, and remove the check mark from Auto-hide the Taskbar.

Shrinking windows to the taskbar and retrieving them

Windows spawn windows. You start with one window to write a letter of praise to the local opera house. You open another window to check an address, for example, and then yet another to see whether you've forgotten any upcoming shows. Before you know it, four more windows are crowded across the desktop.

To combat the clutter, Windows Vista provides a simple means of window control: You can transform a window from a screen-cluttering square into a tiny button on the *taskbar,* which sits along the bottom of the screen. The solution is the Minimize button.

 See the three buttons lurking in just about every window's top-right corner? Click the *Minimize button* — the button with the little line in it, as shown in the margin. Whoosh! The window disappears, represented by its little button on the taskbar at your screen's bottom.

 To make a minimized program on the taskbar revert into a regular, on-screen window, just click its name on the taskbar. Pretty simple, huh?

✔ Each taskbar button shows the name of the program it represents. And if you hover your mouse pointer over the taskbar button, Vista displays a thumbnail photo of that program. (If your PC's graphics aren't up to snuff, Vista displays only the program's name.)

✔ When you minimize a window, you neither destroy its contents nor close the program. And when you click the window's name on the taskbar, it reopens to the same size you left it, showing its same contents.

 ✔ Whenever you load a program, its name automatically appears on the taskbar. If one of your open windows ever gets lost on your desktop, click its name on the taskbar to bring it to the forefront.

Clicking the taskbar's sensitive areas

Like a crafty card player, the taskbar comes with a few tips and tricks. For example, here's the lowdown on the icons near the taskbar's right edge, shown in Figure 2-8, known as the *notification area:*

Figure 2-8:
These
taskbar
icons help
with specific
tasks.

- ✔ **Clock:** Hold the mouse pointer over the clock, and Windows Vista shows the current day and date. Click the clock to see a handy monthly calendar. If you want to change the time, date, or even add a second time zone, click the clock and choose Change Date and Time Settings, a task I cover in Chapter 11.

- ✔ **Arrow:** Sometimes the taskbar hides things. Click the little arrow on the far left (shown in Figure 2-8), and a few hidden icons may slide out. (Check out the "Customizing the taskbar" section, later in this chapter, for tips and tricks affecting these icons.)

- ✔ **Speaker:** Click the little speaker to adjust the sound card's volume, as shown in Figure 2-9. Or double-click the word Mixer to bring up a mixing panel. *Mixers* let you adjust separate volume levels for each program, letting you keep Media Player's volume louder than your other program's annoying beeps.

- ✔ **Other icons:** These often appear next to the clock, depending on what Windows Vista is up to. When you print, for example, a little printer icon appears. Laptops often show a battery-power-level gauge, and a network icon shows when you're connected to the Internet. As with all the other icons down there, if you double-click the printer or battery gauge, Windows Vista brings up information about the printer's or battery's status.

- ✔ **Blank part:** The empty portions of the taskbar also hide a menu. Want to minimize all your desktop's open windows in a hurry? Right-click on a blank part of the taskbar and choose Show the Desktop from the pop-up menu.

To organize your open windows, right-click on a blank part of the taskbar and choose one of the tile commands. Windows Vista scoops up all your open windows and lays them back down in neat, orderly squares. (I cover tiling in more detail in Chapter 3.)

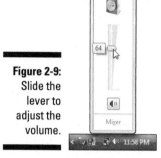

Figure 2-9:
Slide the
lever to
adjust the
volume.

Customizing the taskbar

Windows Vista brings a whirlwind of options for the lowly taskbar, letting you play with it in more ways than a strand of spaghetti and a fork. Right-click on the Start button, choose the Properties option, and click the Taskbar tab to start playing. Table 2-1 explains the options, as well as my recommendations for them. (You need to remove the check mark by Lock the Taskbar before some of these options will work.)

Table 2-1	Customizing the Taskbar
Setting	*My Recommendations*
Lock the Taskbar	Clicking here makes Windows Vista lock the taskbar in place, keeping you from changing its appearance. You can't drag it upward to make it larger, for example. Lock it, but only after the taskbar is set up the way you like.
Auto-Hide the Taskbar	Selecting this option makes the taskbar *automatically* hide itself when you're not near it. (Point at the taskbar to bring it back up.) I leave this option unchecked to keep the taskbar always in view.
Keep the Taskbar on Top of Other Windows	This option keeps the taskbar always visible, covering up any windows that may be low on the screen. I leave this checked.
Group Similar Taskbar Buttons	When you open lots of windows and programs, Windows accommodates the crowd by grouping similar windows under one button: All open documents in Microsoft Word stack on one Microsoft Word button, for example. This option protects the taskbar from overcrowding, so keep it checked.

(continued)

Table 17-1 *(continued)*

Setting	My Recommendations
Show Quick Launch	This setting shows your Quick Launch toolbar, that collection of handy icons hanging out by your Start button. (I cover it and other toolbars later in this chapter.)
Show Windows Previews (Thumbnails)	This option tells the taskbar to show a thumbnail photo of a program when you hover your mouse pointer over the program's taskbar button. Leave this option turned on to make it easier to locate misplaced windows. (This option remains unavailable unless your PC packs powerful graphics.)

Feel free to experiment with the taskbar until it looks right for you. It won't break. After you set it up just the way you want, select the Lock the Taskbar check box described in Table 2-1.

The taskbar's crazy toolbars

Your taskbar won't always be a steadfast, unchanging friend. Microsoft lets you customize it even further, often beyond the point of recognition. Some people enjoy this toolbar gadgetry, sculpting extra buttons and bars onto their taskbars. Others accidentally turn on a toolbar and can't figure out how to get rid of the darn thing.

To turn a toolbar on or off, right-click on a blank part of the taskbar (even the clock will do) and choose Toolbars from the pop-up menu. A menu leaps out, offering the toolbars described in the following list:

- ✔ **Address:** Choose this toolbar, and part of your taskbar becomes a place for typing Web sites to visit. It's convenient, but so is Internet Explorer, which does the same thing.

- ✔ **Windows Media Player:** When turned on, this toolbar in Figure 2-10 turns into a handy button panel for controlling your minimized Windows Media Player.

- ✔ **Links:** This toolbar adds quick access to your favorite Web sites. Click it to visit any Web site listed in Internet Explorer's Favorites menu.

- ✔ **Desktop:** Techies who find the Start menu burdensome add this toolbar for quick access to all their PC's resources. It lets you browse through files, network locations, and Control Panel menus by snaking your way through all the menus.

- ✔ **Quick Launch:** The only toolbar Vista displays when first installed, this places a handful of handy icons, as shown earlier in Figure 2-6, next to your Start button: the Shrink Everything from the Desktop icon, shown in the margin, and the Flip 3D icon, which helps you track down missing windows. (Add your own icons to this toolbar by dragging and dropping them.)

✔ **New Toolbar:** Click here to choose *any* folder to add as a toolbar. For example, choose your Documents folder for quick browsable access to all its files and folders.

Figure 2-10:
The
Windows
Media Player
toolbar.

Toolbars fall into the love 'em or hate 'em category. Some people find toolbars to be timesavers; others feel they consume too much real estate to be worth the effort. And some toolbars, like the Tablet PC Input Panel, only work when you attach an expensive, touch-sensitive pad to your PC. Feel free to experiment until you decide which camp you fall into.

Toolbars are *supposed* to be dragged around with the mouse. When the taskbar is unlocked, grab the toolbar by its *handle,* a vertical line by the toolbar's name. Drag the handle to the left or right to change a toolbar's size.

The taskbar's two sides

Like boys and girls at a school dance, the taskbar's two groups of icons hang out on opposite ends. On the left lives the Quick Launch toolbar; on the right, you'll find the taskbar's Notification Area. What's the difference between the two?

The Quick Launch toolbar is simply a group of shortcuts to frequently used programs. They're no different from shortcuts that live in your folders or your desktops. They don't represent running programs; they're mere push buttons that call programs into action.

The Notification Area, on the other hand, represents *currently running* programs that don't live inside open windows. You'll spot an icon for

Windows Defender, for example, as it runs in the background, constantly scanning for spyware. Another controls Vista's sound, and yet another may show the status of your Internet connection or your printer. You may see one for Apple's iTunes and other third-party programs.

Who cares? Well, because the icons in the Notification Area represent *running* programs, they can bog down your PC if that area grows too crowded. If you spot an unused program's icon in the Notification Area, speed up your PC a bit by firing up the Control Panel and uninstalling that unused program. Or, for a quick, temporary close to a Notification Area program, right-click its icon and choose Exit.

The Sidebar

People who can afford enormous monitors love Vista's new Sidebar, that gadget-packed strip along the desktop's right edge. People with small monitors find it a bothersome waste of space.

 If your Sidebar doesn't grace your desktop, fire it up: Right-click the little icon (shown in the margin) in the taskbar's Notification Area — that icon-packed area next to the desktop's clock — and choose Show Sidebar. The Sidebar springs to life, shown in Figure 2-11.

Figure 2-11: The Sidebar displays *Gadgets,* minuscule programs that snap on and off their panel.

To see Windows Vista's collection of built-in *Gadgets* (minuscule programs that snap on and off their panel), click the little plus sign near the Sidebar's top. A window pops up offering a calendar and stock ticker, among others. Click Get More Gadgets Online to visit Gadget nirvana: A Web site packed with Gadgets, ready for the picking.

- ✔ Prefer your Sudoku game gadget on top? Drag it up there. You can even drag Gadgets off the Sidebar and onto the desktop — if you have a huge enough monitor to sacrifice the space.

- ✔ To change a Gadget's settings — choose which photos appear in your slide show, for example — point at the Gadget and click the tiny wrench icon that appears. To remove a Gadget completely, click the little X, instead.

Logging Off from Windows

Ah! The most pleasant thing you'll do with Windows Vista all day could very well be to stop using it. And you do that the same way you started: by using the Start button, that friendly little helper you've been using all along. (And if the Start menu is hiding, hold down Ctrl and press Esc to bring it back from behind the trees.) You want the one of the two buttons resting at the bottom of the Start menu:

- ✔ **Sleep/Power:** Sleep mode (margin, top) comes in handy when you won't be using your PC for several hours but want to start up where you left off. Designed for impatient desktoppers, this option memorizes your currently open windows, and then turns off your PC. When you turn on your PC, your open programs and documents appear on the desktop where you left them. On laptops, this option is a Power button (margin, bottom) that simply turns off your PC.

- ✔ **Lock:** Meant for short trips to the water cooler, this option locks your PC and places your user account picture on the screen. When you return, type your password, and Vista instantly displays your desktop, just as you left it. This option appears on both laptops and desktop PCs.

Windows Vista offers several other ways to close your session. Look closely at the arrow to the right of the Lock button. Click the arrow to see up to seven options, shown in Figure 2-12.

- ✔ **Switch User:** If somebody else just wants to borrow the computer for a few minutes, choose Switch User. The Welcome screen appears, but Windows keeps your open programs waiting in the background. When you switch back, everything's just as you left it.

- ✔ **Log Off:** Choose this option when you're through working at the PC and somebody else wants a go at it. Windows saves your work and your settings and returns to the Welcome screen, ready for the next user.

- ✔ **Lock:** For some reason, Microsoft offers the Lock option again, described earlier in the main section.

- ✔ **Restart:** Only choose this option when Windows Vista screwed something up: Several programs crashed, or Windows seems to be acting awfully weird. Windows Vista turns off and reloads itself, hopefully feeling refreshed.

✔ **Sleep:** New to Vista, this option saves a copy of your work in your PC's memory *and* its hard drive and then slumbers in a low power state. When you turn your PC back on, Vista presents your desktop, programs, and windows as if you'd never left. (On a laptop, Sleep saves your work only to memory; should the battery life grow threateningly low, Sleep dumps it onto the hard drive and turns off your laptop.)

✔ **Hibernate:** Found on some laptops, this option copies your work to your hard drive and then turns off your PC — a process requiring more battery power than Sleep mode.

✔ **Shut Down:** Choose this option when nobody else will be using the computer until the next morning. Windows Vista saves everything and turns off your computer.

Figure 2-12:
Click the little arrow to see more options for wrapping up work on your PC.

When you tell Windows Vista that you want to quit, it searches through all your open windows to see whether you've saved all your work. If it finds any work you've forgotten to save, it lets you know so that you can click the OK button to save it. Whew!

You don't *have* to shut down Windows Vista. In fact, some people leave their computers turned on all the time, saying it's better for their computer's health. Others say that their computers are healthier if they're turned off each day. Still others say Vista's new Sleep mode gives them the best of both worlds. However, *everybody* says to turn off your monitor when you're done working. Monitors definitely enjoy cooling down when not in use.

Don't just press your PC's Off button to turn off your PC. Instead, be sure to shut down Windows Vista through one of its official Off options: Sleep, Hibernate, or Shut Down. Otherwise, Windows Vista can't properly prepare your computer for the dramatic event, leading to future troubles.

Chapter 3

Basic Windows Mechanics

*T*his chapter is for curious Windows anatomy students. You know who you are — you're the ones who see all those buttons, borders, and balloons scattered throughout Windows Vista and wonder what would happen if you just clicked that little thing over there.

This rather gruesome chapter tosses an ordinary window (your oft-used Documents folder, to be precise) onto the dissection table. I've yanked out each part for thorough labeling and explanation. You'll find the theory behind each one and required procedures for making each piece do your bidding.

A standard field guide follows, identifying and explaining the buttons, boxes, windows, bars, lists, and other oddities you may encounter when you're trying to make Windows Vista do something useful.

Feel free to don any protective gear you may have lying about, use the margins to scribble notes, and tread forcefully into the world of Windows.

Dissecting a Typical Window

Figure 3-1 places a typical window on the slab, with all its parts labeled. You might recognize the window as your Documents folder, that storage tank for most of your work.

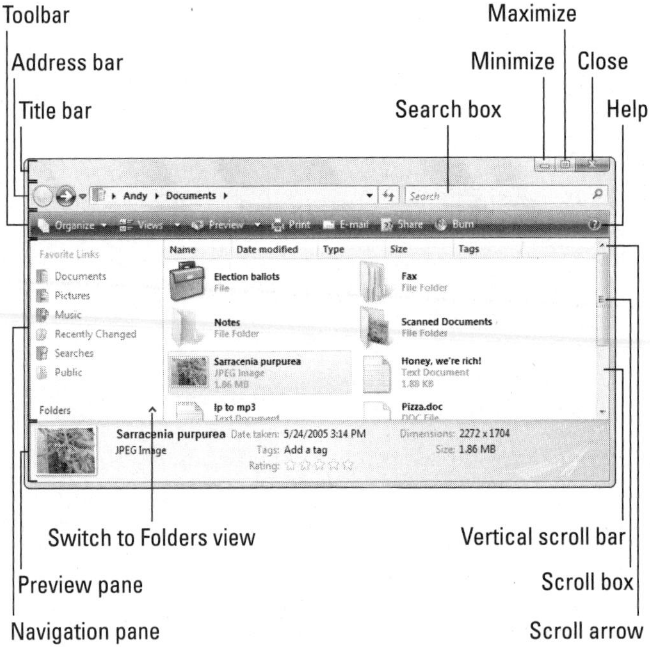

Toolbar   Maximize

Address bar   Minimize | Close

Title bar   Search box   Help

Figure 3-1:
Here's how
the ever-
precise
computer
nerds
address the
different
parts of a
window.

Switch to Folders view   Vertical scroll bar

Preview pane   Scroll box

Navigation pane   Scroll arrow

Just as boxers grimace differently depending on where they've been punched, windows behave differently depending on where they've been clicked. The next few sections describe the main parts of the Documents folder's window in Figure 3-1, how to click them, and how Windows jerks in response.

✔ Windows XP veterans remember their My Documents folder, that stash for all their files. Vista drops the word My to create the Documents folder. (You're still supposed to stash your files inside it.) Other My hatchet jobs include the Pictures and Music folders.

✔ Windows Vista is full of little weird-shaped buttons, borders, and boxes. You don't need to remember all their names, although it would give you a leg up on figuring out Windows' scholarly Help menus. When you spot an odd portion of a window, just return to this chapter, look up its name in Figure 3-1, and read its explanation.

✔ You can deal with most things in Windows by simply clicking, double-clicking, or right-clicking, a decision explained in the nearby sidebar, "Clicking, double-clicking, and right-clicking strategies." (Spoiler: *When in doubt, always right-click.*)

✔ After you click a few windows a few times, you realize how easy it is to boss them around. The hard part is finding the right controls for the *first* time, like figuring out the buttons on that new cell phone.

Tugging on a window's title bar

Found atop nearly every window (see examples in Figure 3-2), the title bar usually lists the program name and the file it's currently working on. For example, Figure 3-2 shows the title bars from Windows Vista's WordPad (top) and Notepad (bottom) programs. The WordPad title bar lists the file's name as Document because you haven't had a chance to save and name the file yet. (It may be full of notes you've jotted down from an energetic phone conversation with Ed McMahon.)

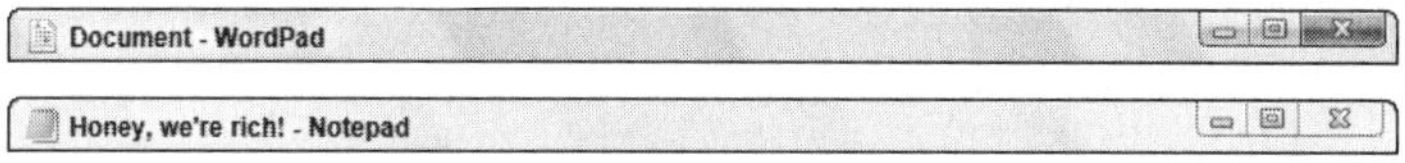

Figure 3-2:
A title bar
from
WordPad
(top) and
Notepad
(bottom).

Document - WordPad

Honey, we're rich! - Notepad

Clicking, double-clicking, and right-clicking strategies

Clicking or double-clicking your mouse controls nearly everything in Windows, yet Microsoft seems befuddled when defining the difference between the two finger actions. Microsoft says to click when *selecting* something, and double-click when *choosing* something. Huh?

You're *selecting* something when you're highlighting it. For example, you click in a box, on a window, or on a filename to *select* it. That click usually *highlights* the item, preparing it for further action.

Choosing something, by contrast, is much more decisive. An authoritative double-click on a file convinces Windows to open it for you immediately.

Microsoft's theoretical hierarchies bore me, so I almost always take the third option and *right-click* on things. Right-click on nearly anything to see a little menu listing everything it can do. I click the option I want, and Windows does my bidding.

The moral? *When in doubt, right-click.*

Although mild-mannered, the mundane title bar holds hidden powers, described in the following tips:

✔ Title bars make convenient handles for moving windows around your desktop. Point at the title bar, hold down the mouse button, and move the mouse around: The window follows along as you move your mouse. Found the right location? Let go of the mouse button, and the window sets up camp in its new spot.

✔ Double-click the title bar, and the window leaps to fill the entire screen. Double-click it again, and the window retreats to its original size.

✔ In Windows XP, every title bar carried a, uh, title of what you were viewing. Vista, however, leaves its folders' names *off* their title bars, preferring an empty strip (refer to Figure 3-1). But although many of Vista's title bars lack titles, they work like regular title bars: Feel free to drag them around your desktop, just as you did in Windows XP.

✔ The right end of the title bar contains three square buttons. From left to right, they let you Minimize, Restore (or Maximize), or Close a window, topics all covered in this chapter's "Maneuvering Windows Around the desktop" section.

✔ In Windows XP, the window you're currently working with always sports a *highlighted* title bar — it's a different color from the title bars of any other open windows. Vista's title bars, by contrast, are much the same color. To find the window you're currently working on, look for a red Close button in its top, right corner (Figure 3-2, top). That distinguishes it from windows you *aren't* working on (Figure 3-2, bottom). By glancing at the corner of all the title bars on the screen, you can tell which window is awake and accepting anything you type.

Dragging, dropping, and running

Although the term *drag and drop* sounds as if it's straight out of a *Sopranos* episode, it's really a nonviolent mouse trick used through-out Windows. Dragging and dropping is a way of moving something — say, an icon on your desktop — from one place to another.

To *drag,* put the mouse pointer over the icon and *hold down* the left or right mouse button. (I prefer the right mouse button.) As you move the mouse across your desk, the pointer drags the icon across the screen. Place the pointer/icon where you want it and release the mouse button. The icon *drops,* unharmed.

Holding down the *right* mouse button while dragging and dropping makes Windows Vista toss up a helpful little menu, asking whether you want to *copy* or *move* the icon.

Helpful Tip Department: Started dragging some-thing and realized midstream that you're drag-ging the wrong item? Don't let go of the mouse button — instead, press Esc to cancel the action. Whew! (If you've dragged with your right mouse button and already let go of the button, there's another exit: Choose Cancel from the pop-up menu.)

Typing in a Window's Address Bar

Directly beneath every folder's title bar lives the *Address Bar,* shown atop the Documents folder in Figure 3-3. Internet veterans will experience déjà vu: Vista's Address Bar is lifted straight from the top of Internet Explorer and glued atop every folder.

Figure 3-3:
Each folder sports an Address Bar, much like the one in Internet Explorer.

The Address Bar's three main parts, described from left to right in the following list, perform three different duties:

- ✔ **Backward and Forward buttons:** These two arrows keep track as you forage through your PC's folders. The Backward button backtracks to the folder you just visited. The Forward arrow brings you back. (Click the miniscule arrow to the right of the Forward arrow to see a list of places you've visited previously; click any entry to zoom right there.)

- ✔ **Address Bar:** Just as Internet Explorer's Address Bar lists a Web site's address, Vista's Address Bar displays your current folder's address — its location inside your PC. For example, the Address Bar shown in Figure 3-3 shows three words: *Andy, Documents,* and *Stuff.* Those words tell you that you're looking inside the *Stuff* folder inside the *Documents* folder of *Andy's* User account. Yes, folder addresses are complicated enough to warrant an entire chapter: Chapter 4.

Feel free to type a Web site's address — something like www.andy rathbone.com — into any folder's Address Bar. Your folder will summon Internet Explorer, which opens to that particular site.

- ✔ **Search box:** In another rip-off from Internet Explorer, every Vista folder sports a Search box. Instead of searching the Internet, though, it rummages through your folder's contents. For example, type the word **carrot** into a folder's Search box: Vista digs through that folder's contents and retrieves every file mentioning *carrot.*

To expand your search beyond that particular folder, click the arrow next to the Search box's magnifying glass icon. A drop-down menu lets you route your search to your entire PC or even the Internet. I cover Vista's new search features in Chapter 6.

Several other areas of the Address Bar deserve mention:

✓ In the Address Bar, notice the little arrows between the words Andy, Documents, and Stuff? The arrows offer quick trips to other folders. Click any arrow — the one to the right of the word Documents, for example. A little menu drops down from the arrow, letting you jump to any other folder inside your Documents folder.

✓ When sending a search to the Internet, the Search box normally routes entries off to Microsoft's *own* Search Provider. (That arrangement lets Microsoft get kickbacks from the ads.) To send the search to Google or any other search engine, fire up Internet Explorer, click the little arrow next to the Search box's magnifying glass, and choose Find More Providers, a task I detail in Chapter 8.

Finding Vista's hidden menu bar

Windows Vista has more menu items than an Asian restaurant. To keep everybody's minds on computer commands instead of seaweed salad, Windows hides its menus inside the *menu bar* (see Figure 3-4).

In fact, Vista even hides every folder's menu bar. To bring them back, press Alt, and they drop into place. To keep the menu bars permanently affixed there, follow these steps:

1. **Click the Organize button (shown in the margin), then choose Folder and Search Options from the menu.**

    The Folder options dialog box appears, opened to the General tab.

2. **In the Tasks section, select Use Windows Classic Folders.**

3. **Click OK.**

Figure 3-4:
The menu bar.

File   Edit   View   Tools   Help

The menu bar sports a different menu for each word. To reveal the secret options, click any word — Edit, for example. A menu tumbles down, as shown in Figure 3-5, presenting options related to editing a file.

Just as restaurants sometimes run out of specials, a window sometimes isn't capable of offering all its menu items. Any unavailable options are *grayed out,* like the Cut, Copy, Paste, Delete, and Go To options in Figure 3-5.

Figure 3-5:
Click any
menu to
see its
associated
commands.

If you accidentally click the wrong word in a menu bar, causing the wrong menu to jump down, simply click the word you *really* wanted. A forgiving soul, Windows retracts the mistaken menu and displays your newly chosen one.

To back out of Menu Land completely, click the mouse pointer back down on your work in the window's *workspace* — the area where you're supposed to be working.

For the convenience of keyboard lovers, Vista underlines one letter on every menu item. (Press Alt to see them.) Mouse haters can press the Alt key followed by an underlined letter — the *F* in F̲ile, for example — to make Windows display the File menu. (Pressing Alt, then F, and then X closes a window.)

Choosing the Right Button for the Job

Many Windows XP veterans fondly remember their folders' *task pane,* a handy strip along a folder's left side that displayed handy buttons for common chores. Vista no longer sports a task pane. Instead, those common chores are relegated to a thin strip of buttons called the *toolbar.* The Computer folder's toolbar, for example, appears in Figure 3-6.

Figure 3-6:
The
Computer
folder's
toolbar.

You don't need to know much about the toolbar, because Vista automatically places the right buttons atop the folder that needs them. Open your Music folder, for example, and the toolbar quickly sprouts a Play All button for marathon listening sessions. Open the Pictures folder, and the friendly toolbar serves up a Slide Show button.

If a button's meaning isn't immediately obvious, hover your mouse over it; a little message explains the button's *raison d'être*. My own translations for the most common buttons are in the following list:

- **Organize:** Found on every folder's toolbar, the Organize button lets you change a folder's layout by toggling those thick informational strips along the window's edges. You can turn on or off the *Navigation Pane,* that strip of shortcuts along the left edge, for example. You can also turn off the *Preview Pane,* that strip along every folder's bottom that displays information about the selected file.

- **Views:** The second button to live atop every folder window, the Views button may be the most useful: It makes the window display your files in different ways. Keep clicking it to cycle through different icon sizes; stop clicking when one looks good. To jump to a favorite view, click the button's adjacent arrow to see a list of every available view. Choose Details, for example, to view everything you want to know about a file: its size, creation date, and other minutia. (Photos look best when shown in Large or Extra Large Icons view.)

Are your folder's icons too big or small? Hold down the Ctrl key and spin your mouse wheel. Spin one direction to enlarge them and the reverse direction to shrink them.

- **Share:** Click here to share the selected file or files with somebody on another computer, provided they already have a User account and password on your PC. You won't see or need this button until you set up a network (which I describe in Chapter 14) to link this PC with others.

- **Burn:** Click here to copy your selected items to a blank CD or DVD. If you haven't yet clicked on anything in the folder, this copies the entire folder's contents to your CD — a handy way to make quick backups.

- **Help:** Click the little blue question mark icon in any folder's top-right corner for help with whatever you happen to be viewing at the time.

Quick shortcuts with the Windows Vista Navigation Pane

Look at most "real" desktops, and you'll see the most-used items sitting within arm's reach: The Inbox, the stapler, and perhaps a few crumbs from the coffee room snacks. Similarly, Vista gathers up your PC's most frequently used items and places them in the new Navigation Pane, shown in Figure 3-7.

Figure 3-7:
The
Navigation
Pane's top
half (right)
offers
shortcuts to
folders you
visit fre-
quently; click
the word
Folders to
see your
folders in a
branching
tree view
(left).

Found along the left edge of every folder, the Navigation Pane contains two main parts. The top half contains a list of words called the Favorite Links section; beneath them awaits a mysterious door called Folders. Here's a more detailed description of both halves of the Navigation Pane:

✔ **Favorite Links:** Not to be confused with the Favorite links in Internet Explorer (Chapter 8), the Favorite Links in the Navigation Pane are words serving as clickable shortcuts to your most frequently accessed folders *inside* your PC:

• **Documents:** Click this shortcut to return straight to the mother of all folders, your Documents folder.

• **Recently Changed:** You guessed it: Clicking this shortcut lists every file that's changed in the past 30 days. They're sorted by date, with the most recent file at the top, making it a handy way to locate your latest work.

• **Pictures:** This shortcut opens your Pictures folder, living quarters to all your digital photos.

• **Music:** Yep, this shortcut jumps straight to your Music folder, where a double-click on a song starts it playing through your PC's speaker.

• **Searches:** Click this shortcut to see Vista's collection of *Saved Searches:* Things you've searched for in the past. Several handy searches already live here: every piece of e-mail you've received in the last seven days, for example.

• **Public:** Drop a file in here to share it with everybody using your PC.

✔ **Folders:** The Navigation Pane's hidden door hides behind a single word called Folders. See the word Folders at the bottom of the Navigation Pane? Click anywhere on that folder bar, and the Navigation Pane displays a "branching tree" view of your folders, covered in Chapter 4. It's an easy way to jump to any folder or drive on your computer.

The following tips let you wring the most value from the Navigation Pane:

✔ Feel free to customize your Navigation Pane by dragging and dropping folders or shortcuts onto it. That setup keeps them within reach of any folder you happen to be working in. To remove an item, right-click it and choose Remove Link.

✔ If you accidentally delete some of the Favorite Links in your Navigation Pane, tell Vista to repair the damage. Right-click anywhere inside the Navigation Pane and choose Restore Default Favorite Links.

Working with the Details pane

Vista's new *Details pane,* shown in Figure 3-8, hovers like a low-lying cloud along the bottom of every folder. Just as the Details pane's name implies, the little strip lists arcane details about the item you're currently viewing, a treat drooled over by techies.

Figure 3-8:
The Details
pane lists
details
about the
folder or file
you've just
clicked.

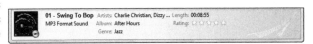

Open a folder, for example, and its Details pane dutifully lists the number of files that folder contains. It even says whether the files live on your own PC, or through a network.

The real information comes when you click a file. For example, click a music file, and the Details pane shows a thumbnail of the album cover, the song's title, artist, length, size, and even any rating you've given it through Vista's Media Player. Click a photo file to see a thumbnail preview, the date you pressed your camera's shutter button, and the photo's size.

✔ The Details pane knows more than it first reveals. Because it's resizable, drag its top border up a bit. As the Details pane grows larger, it starts to reveal more information about your highlighted file: its size, creation date, the date it was last changed, and similar tidbits. A quick upward tug offers a quick peek at information; drag it back down when you're through.

✔ If you think the Details pane consumes too much screen space, drag its top border down a bit. Or, turn it off: Click the Organize button on the toolbar's leftmost corner, click Layout from the drop-down menu, and click Details Pane. (Repeat those steps to revive a missing Details pane.)

✔ While editing a file's properties, feel free to add a *tag* — a keyword that lets you relocate that particular file more quickly. (I cover tags in Chapter 6.)

Moving inside a window with its scroll bar

The scroll bar, which resembles a cutaway of an elevator shaft (see Figure 3-9), rests along the edge of all overstuffed windows. Inside the shaft, a little elevator (technically, the *scroll box*) rides up and down as you page through your work. In fact, by glancing at the elevator's position in the shaft, you can tell whether you're viewing the top, middle, or bottom of a window's contents.

Figure 3-9:
A scroll bar.

You can watch the little box travel up or down as you press the PgUp or PgDn key. (Yes, it's easy to get distracted in Windows Vista.) But nudging the elevator around with the mouse is more fun. By clicking in various places on the scroll bar, you can quickly move around inside a document. Here's the dirt:

✔ Clicking in the shaft *above* the elevator shifts your view up one page, just as if you'd pressed the PgUp key. Similarly, clicking *below* the elevator shifts the view down one page. The larger your monitor, the more information you can see on each page.

- To move up your view line by line, click the little arrow (the *scroll arrow*) at the top of the scroll bar. Similarly, clicking the little arrow at the bottom moves your view down one line with each click.

- Scroll bars occasionally hang out along a window's bottom edge. Handy for viewing spreadsheets and other wide documents, scroll bars let you move your view sideways for peeking at the totals in the spreadsheet's last column.

- No little scroll box in the bar? Then you're already seeing all that the window has to offer.

- To move around in a hurry, drag the scroll box up or down the bar. As you drag, you see the window's contents race past. When you see the spot you want, let go of the mouse button to stay at that viewing position.

- Using a mouse that has a little wheel embedded in the poor critter's back? Spin the wheel, and the list moves up or down, just as if you were playing with the scroll bar.

Boring borders

A *border* is that thin edge surrounding a window. Compared with a bar, it's really tiny.

To change a window's size, drag the border in or out. (Dragging by the corner gives the best results.)

Some windows, oddly enough, don't have borders. Stuck in limbo, their size can't be changed — even if they're an awkward size.

Except for tugging on them with the mouse, you won't be using borders much.

Filling Out Bothersome Dialog Boxes

Sooner or later, Windows Vista will lapse into surly clerk mode, forcing you to fill out a bothersome form before carrying out your request. To handle this computerized paperwork, Windows Vista uses a *dialog box.*

A dialog box is a window displaying a little form or checklist for you to fill out. These forms can have bunches of different parts, all discussed in the following sections. Don't bother trying to remember each part's name. It's much more important to remember how they work.

Poking the correct command button

Command buttons may be the simplest part of a form to figure out — Microsoft labeled them! Command buttons usually require poking after you've filled out a form. Based on the command button you click, Windows either carries out your bidding (rare) or sends you to another form (most likely).

Although Vista eliminated most forms, Table 3-1 identifies the command buttons you'll still come across.

Table 3-1	Common Windows Vista Command Buttons
Command Button	**Description**
OK	A click on the OK button says, "I've finished the form, and I'm ready to move on." Windows Vista reads what you've typed and processes your request.
Cancel	If you've somehow loused things up when filling out a form, click the Cancel button. Windows whisks away the form, and everything returns to normal. Whew! (*Tip:* The little red X in a window's top corner makes pesky windows go away, as well.)
Next	Click the Next button to move to the next question. (Change your mind on the last question? Back up by clicking the Back arrow near the window's top left.)
Browse...	If you encounter a button with dots (...) after the word, brace yourself: Clicking that button brings yet *another* form to the screen. From there, you must choose even more settings, options, or toppings.
Default	When you change a setting that louses things up, click the Default (or Restore Defaults) button with full force. That brings back Vista's freshly installed look.

✔ The OK button usually has a slightly darker border than the others, meaning it's *highlighted.* Just pressing Enter automatically chooses the form's highlighted button, sparing you the inconvenience of clicking it. (I usually click it anyway, just to make sure.)

✔ If you've clicked the wrong button but *haven't yet lifted your finger from the mouse button,* stop! Command buttons don't take effect until you release your finger from the mouse button. Keep holding down the mouse, but scoot the pointer away from the wrong button. Move safely away and then lift your finger.

✔ Did you stumble across a box that contains a confusing option? Click the question mark in the box's upper-right corner (it will look like the one in the margin). Then click the confusing command button to see a short explanation of that button's function in life. Sometimes merely resting your mouse pointer over a confusing button makes Windows take pity, sending a helpful caption to explain matters.

Choosing between option buttons

Sometimes, Windows Vista gets ornery and forces you to select a single option. For example, you can play some games at either a beginner or intermediate level. You can't do *both,* so Windows Vista doesn't let you select both of the options.

Windows Vista handles this situation with an *option button.* When you select one option, the little dot hops over to it. Select the other option, and the little dot hops over to it instead. You find option buttons in many dialog boxes, such as the one in Figure 3-10.

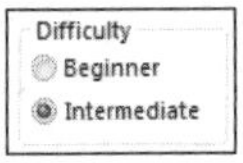

Figure 3-10: Select an option.

Difficulty
◯ Beginner
◉ Intermediate

If you *can* select more than one option, Windows Vista won't present you with option buttons. Instead, it offers the more liberal *check boxes,* which are described in the "Check boxes" section, later in this chapter.

Some programs refer to option buttons as *radio buttons,* after those push buttons on old car radios that switch from station to station, one station at a time.

Typing into text boxes

A *text box* works like a fill-in-the-blanks test in history class. You can type anything you want into a text box — words, numbers, passwords, or epithets. For example, Figure 3-11 shows a dialog box that pops up when you want to search for words or characters in some programs. The text box is where you type the words you want to search for.

✔ When a text box is *active* (that is, ready for you to start typing stuff into it), either the box's current information is highlighted or a cursor is blinking inside it.

✔ If the text box *isn't* highlighted or there *isn't* a blinking cursor inside it, it's not ready for you to start typing. To announce your presence, click inside it before typing.

✔ If you need to use a text box that already contains words, delete any text you don't want before you start typing new information. (Or you can double-click the old information to highlight it; that way, the incoming text automatically replaces the old text.)

✔ Yes, text boxes have way too many rules.

Figure 3-11:
This dialog box contains a text box.

Find

Find what: a good cigar...   Find Next

                    Direction   Cancel
☐ Match case   ⚪ Up ⚫ Down

Choosing options from list boxes

Some boxes don't let you type *anything* into them. They simply display lists of things, letting you pluck the items you want. Boxes of lists are called, appropriately enough, *list boxes.* For example, some word processors bring up a list box if you're inspired enough to want to change the *font* — the style of the letters (see Figure 3-12).

✔ See how the Comic Sans MS font is highlighted in Figure 3-12? It's the currently selected item in the list box. Press Enter (or click the OK button), and your program begins using that font when you start typing.

✔ See the scroll bar along the side of the list box? It works just as it does anywhere else: Click the little scroll arrows (or press the up or down arrow) to move the list up or down, and you can see any names that don't fit in the box.

✔ Some list boxes have a text box above them. When you click a name in the list box, that name hops into the text box. Sure, you could type the name into the text box yourself, but it wouldn't be nearly as much fun.

✔ When confronted with zillions of names in a list box or folder, type the first letter of the name you're after. Windows Vista immediately hops down the list to the first name beginning with that letter.

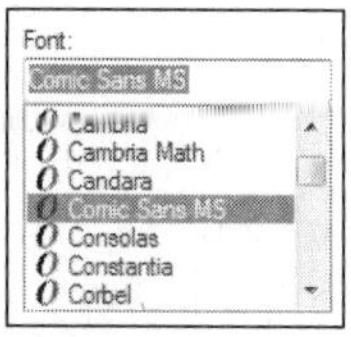

Figure 3-12:
Select a font from the list box.

Font:
Comic Sans MS

𝑂 Cambria
𝑂 Cambria Math
𝑂 Candara
𝑂 Comic Sans MS
𝑂 Consolas
𝑂 Constantia
𝑂 Corbel

When one just isn't enough

Because Windows Vista can display only one background on your desktop at a time, you can select only one file from the list box of available backgrounds. Other list boxes, like those in Windows Explorer, let you select a bunch of names simultaneously. Here's how:

✔ To select more than one item, hold down the Ctrl key and click each item you want. Each item stays highlighted.

✔ To select a bunch of adjacent items from a list box, click the first item you want. Then hold down Shift and click the last item you want. Windows Vista immediately highlights the first item, last item, and every item in between. Pretty sneaky, huh? (To weed out a few unwanted items from the middle, hold down Ctrl and click them; Windows unhighlights them, leaving the rest highlighted.)

✔ Finally, when grabbing bunches of items, try using the "lasso" trick: Point at an area of the screen next to one item, and, while holding down the mouse button, move the mouse until you've drawn a lasso around all the items. After you've highlighted the items you want, let go of the mouse button, and they remain highlighted.

Drop-down list boxes

List boxes are convenient, but they take up a great deal of room. So, Windows Vista sometimes hides list boxes, just as it hides pull-down menus. When you click in the right place, the list box appears, ready for your perusal.

So, where's the right place? It's that downward-pointing arrow button, just like the one shown next to the box beside the Alignment option in Figure 3-13. (The mouse pointer is pointing to it.)

Figure 3-13:
Click the arrow next to the Alignment box to make a drop-down list box display available alignments.

Figure 3-14 shows the drop-down list box after it's been clicked by the mouse. To make your choice, click the option you want from the drop-down list.

Figure 3-14:
A list box
drops down
to display
the available
alignments.

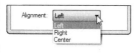

✔ To scoot around quickly in a long drop-down list box, press the first letter of the item you're after. The first item beginning with that letter is instantly highlighted. You can press the up- or down-arrow key to see nearby words and phrases.

✔ Another way to scoot around quickly in a drop-down list box is to click the scroll bar to its right. (I cover scroll bars earlier in this chapter, if you need a refresher.)

✔ You can choose only *one* item from the list in a drop-down list box.

Check boxes

Sometimes you can choose several options in a dialog box simply by clicking in the little square boxes next to their names. For example, the check boxes shown in Figure 3-15 let you pick and choose options in the game FreeCell.

Clicking in an empty square chooses that option. If the square already has a check mark inside, a click turns off that option, removing the check mark.

You can click next to as many check boxes as you want. Option buttons (those similar-looking but round buttons) restrict you to one option from the pack.

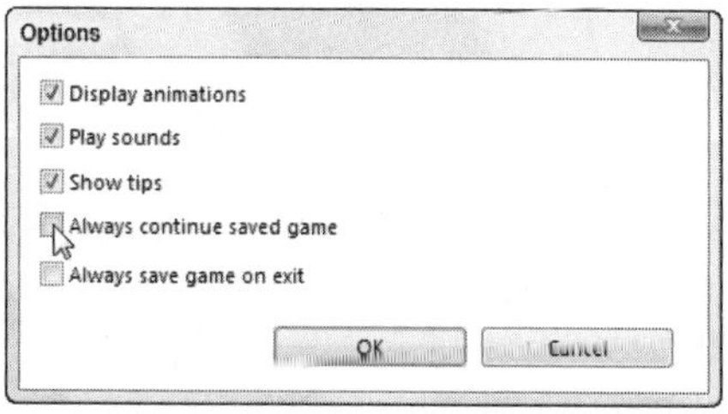

Figure 3-15:
Click to
check a box.

Sliding controls

Rich Microsoft programmers, impressed by track lights and sliding light switches in their luxurious new homes, use sliding controls in Windows Vista. These virtual light switches are easy to use and don't wear out nearly as quickly as the real ones do.

Some levers slide to the left and right; others move up and down. None of them move diagonally — yet. To slide a control in Windows Vista — to adjust the volume level, for example — just drag and drop the sliding lever, like the one shown in Figure 3-16.

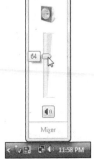

Figure 3-16:
A sliding
lever.

Sliding works like this: Point at the lever with the mouse and, while holding down the mouse button, move the mouse in the direction you want the sliding lever to move. As you move the mouse, the lever moves, too. When you've moved the lever to a comfortable spot, let go of the mouse button, and Windows Vista leaves the lever at its new position.

Maneuvering Windows Around the Desktop

A terrible dealer at the poker table, Windows Vista tosses windows around your desktop in a seemingly random way. Programs cover each other or sometimes dangle off the desktop. This section shows you how to gather all your windows into a neat pile, placing your favorite window on the top of the stack. If you prefer, lay them all down like a poker hand. As an added bonus, you can change their size, making them open to any size you want, automatically.

Moving a window to the top of the pile

Windows Vista says the window at the top of the pile getting all the attention is called the *active* window. I won't argue. The active window is also the one that receives any keystrokes you or your cat happen to type.

You can move a window to the top of the pile so that it's active in one of two ways:

✔ Sometimes you can recognize a tiny portion of the window you're after. If so, you're in luck. Move the mouse pointer until it hovers over any portion of the desired window and click the mouse button. Windows Vista immediately makes the clicked-on window active.

✔ On the taskbar, click the button for the window you want. Chapter 2 explains what the taskbar can do in more detail.

Repeat the process when necessary to bring other windows to the front. (And if you want to put two windows on the screen at the same time, read the "Placing two windows next to each other" section, later in this chapter.)

Moving a window from here to there

Sometimes you want to move a window to a different place on the desktop. Perhaps part of the window hangs off the edge, and you want it centered. Or maybe you want one window closer to another.

In either case, you can move a window by dragging and dropping its *title bar*, that thick bar along its top. (If you're not sure how dragging and dropping works, see the sidebar "Dragging, dropping, and running," earlier in this chapter.) When you *drop* the window in place, the window not only remains where you've dragged and dropped it, but also stays on top of the pile.

Making a window fill the whole screen

Sooner or later, you'll grow tired of all this multiwindow mumbo jumbo. Why can't you just put one huge window on-screen? Well, you can.

To make any window grow as big as it can get, double-click its *title bar*, that topmost bar along the window's top edge. The window leaps up to fill the screen, covering up all the other windows.

The Alt+Tab and ⊞+Tab tricks

Sometimes your desktop becomes so cluttered with windows that you lose track of a particular window. To cycle through every open window, hold down the Alt key while pressing Tab: A little window appears in the middle of the screen, listing every open window by name. Keep holding down Alt and pressing Tab until you see the name of the window you're after. Found it?

Release both keys, and Windows brings the currently listed window to the forefront.

When run on PCs with powerful graphics (I explain the requirements in Chapter 1), Vista can show a three-dimensional view of the windows: Hold down the ⊞ (the key with the Windows logo) and press Tab to see the full-blown graphics shown in Chapter 1's Figure 1-4.

To bring the pumped-up window back to its former size, double-click its title bar once again. The window quickly shrinks to its former size, and you can see things that it covered.

✔ If you're morally opposed to double-clicking a window's title bar to expand it, you can click the little Maximize button. Shown in the margin, it's the middle of the three buttons in the upper-right corner of every window.

✔ When a window is maximized to fill the screen, the Maximize button turns into a Restore button, shown in the margin. Click the Restore button, and the window returns to its smaller size.

Closing a window

When you're through working in a window, close it: Click the little X in its upper, right corner. Zap: You're back to an empty desktop.

If you try to close your window before finishing your work, be it a game of Solitaire or a report for the boss, Windows cautiously asks whether you'd like to save your work. Take it up on its offer by clicking Yes and, if necessary, choosing a name so that you can find your work later.

Making a window bigger or smaller

Like big, lazy dogs, windows tend to flop on top of one another. To space your windows more evenly, you can resize them by *dragging and dropping* their edges inward or outward. It works like this:

1. **Point at any corner with the mouse arrow. When the arrow turns into a two-headed arrow, pointing in the two directions, you can hold down the mouse button and drag the corner in or out to change the window's size.**

2. **When you're done yanking and the window looks about the right size, let go of the mouse button.**

   As the yoga master says, the window assumes the new position.

Placing two windows next to each other

The longer you use Windows, the more likely you are to want to see two windows side by side. For example, you may want to copy and paste text from one document into another document. By spending a few hours with the mouse, you can drag and drop the windows' corners until they're in perfect juxtaposition.

Or you can simply right-click on a blank part of the taskbar (even the clock will do) and choose Show Windows Side by Side to place the windows next to each other, like pillars. Choose Show Windows Stacked to align them in horizontal rows. (If you have more than three open windows, Show Windows Stacked tiles them across your screen, handy for seeing just a bit of each one.)

 If you have more than two windows open, minimize the ones you *don't* want tiled. Then use the Show Windows Side by Side command to align the two remaining windows.

Making windows open to the same darn size

Sometimes a window opens to a small square; other times, it opens to fill the entire screen. But windows rarely open to the exact size you want. Until you discover this trick, that is: When you *manually* adjust the size and placement of a window, Windows memorizes that size and always reopens the window to that same size. Follow these three steps to see how it works:

1. **Open your window.**

   The window opens to its usual, unwanted size.

2. Drag the window's corners until the window is the exact size and in the exact location you want. Let go of the mouse to drop the corner into its new position.

Be sure to resize the window *manually* by dragging its corners or edges with the mouse. Simply clicking the Maximize button won't work.

3. Immediately close the window.

Windows memorizes the size and placement of a window at the time it was last closed. When you open that window again, it should open to the same size you last left it. But the changes you make apply only to the program you made them in. For example, changes made to the Internet Explorer window will only be remembered for *Internet Explorer,* not other programs you open.

Most windows follow these sizing rules, but a few renegades from other programs may misbehave. Feel free to complain to the manufacturers.

Chapter 4

Flipping Through Files, Folders, Floppies, and CDs

*T*he Computer program is where people wake up from Windows' easy-to-use computing dream, clutching a pillow in horror. These people bought a computer to simplify their work — to banish that awful filing cabinet with squeaky drawers.

But click the little Computer icon from the Start menu, start poking around inside your new PC, and that old filing cabinet reappears. Folders, with even more folders stuffed inside of them, still rule the world. And unless you grasp Windows' folder metaphor, you may not find your information very easily.

This chapter explains how to use Vista's filing program, called *Computer*. (Windows XP called the program My Computer.) Along the way, you ingest a big enough dose of Windows file management for you to get your work done. Windows may bring back your dreaded file cabinet, but at least the drawers don't squeak, and files never fall behind the cabinet.

Browsing Your Computer's File Cabinets

To keep your programs and files neatly arranged, Windows cleaned up the convenient file cabinet metaphor with light and airy Windows icons. You can see your new, computerized file cabinets in the Start menu's Computer program. Computer displays all the storage areas inside your computer, allowing you to copy, move, rename, or delete your files before the investigators arrive.

To see your own computer's file cabinets — called *drives* or *disks,* in computer lingo — click the Start menu and click the word Computer. Although your PC's Computer window will look slightly different from the one shown in Figure 4-1, it has the same basic sections, each described in the upcoming list.

Figure 4-1:
The
Computer
window dis-
plays your
computer's
storage
areas, which
you can
open to see
your files.

Windows can display its Computer window in many ways. To make your Computer window look more like the one in Figure 4-1, click the little arrow to the right of the Views button from the menu bar (shown in the margin). Then choose Tiles from the menu that squirts out. Finally, right-click a blank part of the Computer window, choose Group By, and select Type.

These are the basic sections of the Computer window:

✔ **Navigation Pane:** That strip along the left side of most windows, the handy Navigation Pane lists shortcuts to folders carrying your most valuable computerized possessions: your Documents, Pictures, and Music folders. (It tosses in a few other convenient items, covered in Chapter 3.)

✔ **Hard Disk Drives:** Shown in Figure 4-1, this area lists your PC's *hard drives* — your biggest storage areas. Every computer has at least one hard drive, and this PC has two. You may also see a *USB thumbdrive* here — those little sticks that plug into a USB drive to provide portable storage. Double-clicking a hard drive icon displays its files and folders, but you'll rarely find much useful information. Instead of probing your hard drive, open your Start menu to find and start programs.

✔ Notice the hard drive bearing the little Windows icon (shown in the margin)? That means Windows lives on that drive.

✔ **Devices with Removable Storage:** This area shows detachable storage gadgetry attached to your computer. Here are some of the more common ones:

✔ **Floppy Drive:** A dying breed, these drives still appear on some older PCs. But because these 20-year-old disks are too small to hold many files, most people now store files on CDs or DVDs instead.

✔ **CD and DVD drives:** As seen in Figure 4-1, Vista places a short description after each drive's icon to say whether it can only *read* discs or *write* to discs, as well. For example, a DVD burner (shown in the margin) is labeled *DVD-RW,* meaning that it can both *R*ead and *W*rite to DVDs, as well as to CDs. A drive that can burn CDs but not DVDs is labeled *CD-RW.*

Writing information to a CD or DVD is called *burning.*

✔ **Memory card reader:** Memory card readers add a little slot to your PC for inserting memory cards from your camera, MP3 player, or similar gadget. Their icons, shown in the margin, look like an empty slot — even after you insert the card to see your files.

✔ **MP3 players:** Although Vista displays a nice icon like this for a few MP3 players, it coughs up a generic thumbdrive or hard drive icon for the ultra-popular iPod. (I cover MP3 players in Chapter 15.)

✔ **Cameras:** Digital cameras usually appear as icons in the Computer window. Be sure to turn on the camera and set it to View Photos mode rather than Take Photos. To grab the camera's pictures, double-click the camera's icon. After Vista walks you through the process of extracting the images (Chapter 16), it places the photos in your Pictures folder.

✔ **Network Location:** This icon in the margin, seen only by people who've linked groups of PCs into a *network* (see Chapter 14), represents a folder living on another PC.

If you plug a digital camcorder, cell phone, or other gadget into your PC, the Computer window will sprout a new icon representing your gadget. Double-click the new icon to see the contents of your gadget; right-click the icon to see what Vista allows you to do with that gadget. No icon? Then you need to install a *driver* for your gadget, a journey detailed in Chapter 12.

Click almost any icon in Computer, and the Preview Pane along the screen's bottom automatically displays information about that object, ranging from its size or the date it was created, for example, or how much space a folder or drive can hold. To see even more information, enlarge the Preview Pane by dragging its top edge upward. The more room you give the pane, the more info it dishes out.

Getting the Lowdown on Folders

This stuff is dreadfully boring, but if you don't read it, you'll be just as lost as your files.

A *folder* is a storage area on a drive, just like a real folder in a file cabinet. Windows Vista divides your computer's hard drives into many folders to separate your many projects. For example, you store all your music in your Music folder and your pictures in your Pictures folder. That lets both you and your programs find them easily.

Any type of drive can have folders, but hard drives need folders the most because they contain *thousands* of files. By dividing a hard drive into little folder compartments, you can more easily see where everything sits.

Windows' Computer program lets you probe into different folders and peek at the files stuffed inside each one. To see the folders Vista created for *you* to play with, click your user account's name at the top of the Start menu, covered in Chapter 2. The following folders, shown in Figure 4-2, appear:

Figure 4-2: Vista provides every person with these same folders, but keeps everybody's folders separate.

✔ **Your Account Name:** A click on your user account's name at the top of the Start menu opens your User Account folder, shown in Figure 4-2. Your home base, this folder holds all the files you create, all sorted into several important folders.

In Windows XP, your My Documents folder contained everything in your user account, including your My Music and My Pictures folders. In Vista, however, your User Account folder — the one you see when you click your name on the Start menu — now holds all your folders, including your Documents, Music, and Pictures folders, and these new ones:

 ✔ **Contacts:** Have you sent e-mail to somebody with Vista's built-in Mail program? (I cover Mail in Chapter 9.) Vista automatically places that person's name in the Contacts folder, listed on a little business card that opens with a double-click. Right-click a contact's name, choose Action, and select Send E-mail to open a preaddressed e-mail, ready for your message. Right-clicking is often a quicker way to send an e-mail while you _remember,_ as opposed to opening Mail and then getting lost in your Inbox deluge.

 ✔ **Desktop:** Here's a secret: Vista considers your desktop to be one large folder, and everything you place on your desktop really lives inside this folder. Because your desktop's a larger target for pointing and clicking, you probably won't use this folder much.

 ✔ **Documents:** Please, _please_ store all your work inside this folder, and for several reasons. By keeping everything in one place, you can find your files easier. Plus, it's something only _you_ can find; other people using the computer can't fiddle with it. Create as many new folders inside here as you want.

 ✔ **Downloads:** Downloaded something from the Internet? Internet Explorer stashes most downloaded files in this folder, making it easier than ever to find.

 ✔ **Favorites:** Internet Explorer lets you save your favorite Web sites as, er, _Favorites._ That places them all on the program's Favorites menu for easy, one-click access. Those favorite sites also appear in this folder, where a double-click on a site's icon launches Internet Explorer and brings the site to your screen.

 ✔ **Links:** This folder lists all the places listed on Vista's Navigation Pane, which appears along the left side of most folders. Dragging and dropping icons here also adds them to your Navigation Pane.

 ✔ **Music:** When you copy music from CDs to your PC with Media Player, the songs end up in here, stored in a folder named after the CD's title.

 ✔ **Pictures:** Store all your pictures in here, whether they're photos from a digital camera, images from a scanner, or images filched from a Web site. Covered in Chapter 16, the Pictures folder displays thumbnails of your photos, and lets you grab pictures from an attached camera, create slide shows, and engage in more Foto Fun.

✔ **Saved Games:** Ever saved a game of Chess, FreeCell, or any of Vista's many other games? Those saved games live in here, waiting for your boss to leave. You may spot saved games from other game manufacturers, as well.

✔ **Searches:** Any searches you save appear here. (You can also find your saved searches by clicking the word Search in the Navigation Pane.) I cover searches and how to save them in Chapter 6.

✔ **Videos:** Videos downloaded from camcorders and the Internet should stay here. It's the first place some video programs like Vista's Movie Maker (Chapter 16) look for them.

Keep these folder facts in mind when shuffling files in Vista:

✔ You can ignore folders and dump all your files onto the Windows Vista desktop. But that's like tossing everything into the back seat of the car and pawing around to find your tissue box a month later. Organized stuff is much easier to find.

✔ If you're eager to create a folder or two (and it's pretty easy), page ahead to this chapter's "Creating a New Folder" section.

✔ Computer folders use a *tree metaphor* as they branch out from one main folder (a disk drive) to smaller folders (see Figure 4-3), to more folders stuffed inside those folders.

✔ Folders used to be called *directories* and *subdirectories.* But some people were getting used to that, so the industry switched to the term *folders.*

Figure 4-3:
Windows' folders use a treelike structure, with main folders branching out to smaller folders.

Peering into Your Drives and Folders

Knowing all this folder stuff not only impresses computer store employees, but also helps you find the files you want. (See the preceding section for a lowdown on which folder holds what.) Put on your hard hat, go spelunking among your computer's drives and folders, and use this section as your guide.

Seeing the files on a disk drive

Like everything else in Windows Vista, disk drives are represented by buttons, or icons. Computer also shows information stored in other areas, such as MP3 players, digital cameras, or scanners. (I explain these icons in the section "Browsing Your Computer's File Cabinets," earlier in this chapter.)

Opening these icons usually lets you access their contents and move files back and forth, just as with any other folders in Windows Vista.

When you double-click an icon in Computer, Vista guesses what you want to do with that icon and takes action. Double-click on a hard drive, for example, and Vista promptly opens the drive to show you the folders packed inside.

Double-click your CD drive after inserting a music CD, by contrast, and Vista doesn't always open it to show the files. Instead, it usually loads Media Player and begins playing the music. To change Vista's guesswork as to how Vista treats an inserted CD, DVD, or USB drive, right-click that inserted item's icon and open AutoPlay. Vista lists everything it can do with that drive, and asks you to plot the course.

Adjusting the AutoPlay settings comes in particularly handy for USB thumbdrives. If your thumbdrive carries a few songs, Vista wants to call up Media Center to play them, slowing your access to your thumbdrive's other files.

- ✔ When in doubt as to what you can do with an icon in Computer, right-click on it. Windows Vista presents a menu of all the things you can do to that object. (You can choose Open, for example, to see the files on a CD that Vista wants to play in Media Player.)

- ✔ If you click an icon for a CD, DVD, or floppy drive when no disk is in the drive, Windows Vista stops you, gently suggesting that you insert a disk before proceeding further.

- ✔ Spot an icon under the heading Network Location? That's a little doorway for peering into other computers linked to your computer — if there are any. You find more network stuff in Chapter 14.

What's all this path stuff?

A *path* is merely the file's address, similar to your own. When mailed to your house, for example, a letter travels to your country, state, city, street, and finally, hopefully, your apartment or house number. A computer path does the same thing. It starts with the letter of the disk drive and ends with the file's name. In between, the path lists all the folders the computer must travel through to reach the file.

For example, look at the Music folder in Figure 4-3. For Windows Vista to find a file stored there, it starts from the computer's C: hard drive, travels through the Users folder, and then goes through the Andy folder. From there, it goes into the Andy folder's Music folder.

Take a deep breath. Exhale slowly. Now add in the computer's ugly grammar: In a path, a disk drive letter is referred to as **C:** The disk drive letter and colon make up the first part of the path. All the other folders are inside the big C: folder, so

they're listed after the C: part. Windows separates these nested folders with something called a *backslash,* or \ The file's name — *Rivers of Babylon,* for example — comes last.

Put it all together, and you get `C:\Users\ Andy\Music\Rivers of Babylon.` That's your computer's official path to the Rivers of Babylon file in Andy's Music folder.

This stuff can be tricky, so here it is again: The letter for the drive comes first, followed by a colon and a backslash. Then come the names of all the folders leading to the file, separated by backslashes. Last comes the name of the file itself.

Windows Vista automatically puts together the path for you when you click folders. Thankfully. But whenever you click the Browse button to look for a file, you're navigating through folders and traversing along the path leading to the file.

Seeing what's inside folders

Because folders are really little storage compartments, Windows Vista uses a picture of a little folder to represent a place for storing files.

To see what's inside a folder, either in Computer or on Vista's desktop, just double-click that folder's picture. A new window pops up, showing that folder's contents. Spot another folder inside that folder? Double-click that one to see what's inside. Keep clicking until you find what you want or reach a dead end.

Reached a dead end? If you mistakenly end up in the wrong folder, back your way out as if you're browsing the Web. Click the Back arrow at the window's top-left corner. (It's the same arrow that appears in the margin.) That closes the wrong folder and shows you the folder you just left. If you keep clicking the Back arrow, you end up right where you started.

The Address Bar provides another quick way to jump to different places in your PC. As you move from folder to folder, the folder's Address Bar — that little word-filled box at the folder's top — constantly keeps track of your trek. For example, Figure 4-4 shows the Address Bar as you peruse a folder in your Music folder. Notice the little arrows between each word, like between Andy and Music?

Figure 4-4:
The little
arrows
between
folder names
provide
jumping off
places to
other folders.

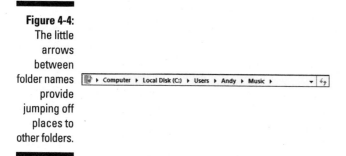

Those little arrows provide quick shortcuts to other folders and windows. Try clicking any of the arrows; menus appear, listing the places you can jump to from that point. For example, click the arrow after Computer, shown in Figure 4-5, to jump quickly to your CD drive.

Figure 4-5:
Here, a click
on the little
arrow after
Computer
lets you jump
to any place
that appears
in the
Computer
folder.

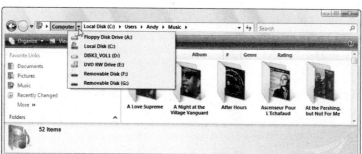

Here are some more tips for finding your way in and out of folders:

✔ Sometimes, a folder contains too many files or folders to fit in the window. To see more files, click that window's scroll bars. What's a scroll bar? Time to whip out your field guide, Chapter 3.

✔ While burrowing deeply into folders, the Forward arrow provides yet another quick way to jump immediately to any folder you've plowed through: Click the little downward-pointing arrow (shown in the margin) next to the Forward arrow in the window's top-left corner. A menu drops down, listing the folders you've plowed through on your journey. Click any name to jump quickly to that folder.

✔ Can't find a particular file or folder? Instead of aimlessly rummaging through folders, check out the Start button's Search command, which I describe in Chapter 6. Windows can automatically find your lost files and folders.

✔ When faced with a long list of alphabetically sorted files, click anywhere on the list. Then quickly type the first letter or two of the file's name. Windows immediately jumps up or down the list to the first name beginning with those letters.

Creating a New Folder

To store new information in a file cabinet, you grab a manila folder, scrawl a name across the top, and start stuffing it with information. To store new information in Windows Vista — a new batch of letters to the hospital's billing department, for example — you create a new folder, think up a name for the new folder, and start stuffing it with files.

To create a new folder quickly, click Organize from the folder's toolbar buttons and choose New Folder when the little menu drops down. If you don't spot a toolbar, here's a quick and foolproof method:

1. **Right-click inside your folder and choose New.**

   The all-powerful right-click shoots a menu out the side.

2. **Select Folder.**

   Choose Folder, as shown in Figure 4-6, and a new folder appears in the folder, waiting for you to type a new name.

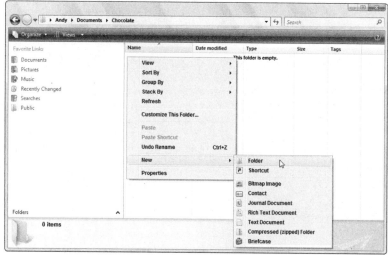

Figure 4-6:
Right-click
where you
want a new
folder to
appear,
choose
New, and
select
Folder from
the menu.

3. **Type a new name for the folder.**

   A newly created folder bears the boring name of New Folder. When you begin typing, Windows Vista quickly erases the old name and fills in your new name. Done? Save the new name by either pressing Enter or clicking somewhere away from the name you've just typed.

   If you mess up the name and want to try again, right-click on the folder, choose Rename, and start over.

   ✔ Certain symbols are banned from folder (and file) names. The "Using legal folder names and filenames" sidebar spells out the details, but you never have trouble when using plain old letters and numbers for names.

   ✔ Shrewd observers noticed that in Figure 4-6 Windows offers to create many more things than just a folder when you click the New button. Right-click inside a folder anytime you want to create a new shortcut or other common items.

   ✔ Confused observers may remark that their right-click menu looks different than the one shown in Figure 4-6. There's nothing wrong; installed programs often add their own items to the right-click list, making the list look different on different PCs.

Using legal folder names and filenames

Windows is pretty picky about what you can and can't name a file or folder. If you stick to plain old letters and numbers, you're fine. But don't try to stick any of the following characters in there:

: / \ * | < > ? "

If you try to use any of those characters, Windows Vista bounces an error message to the screen, and you have to try again. Here are some illegal filenames:

```
1/2 of my Homework
JOB:2
ONE<TWO
He's no "Gentleman"
```

These names are legal:

```
Half of my Term Paper
JOB=2
Two is Bigger than One
A #@$%) Scoundrel
```

Renaming a File or Folder

Sick of a file or folder's name? Then change it. Just right-click on the offending icon and choose Rename from the menu that pops up.

Windows highlights the file's old name, which disappears as you begin typing the new one. Press Enter or click the desktop when you're through, and you're off.

Or you can click the file or folder's name to select it, wait a second, and click the file's name again to change it. Some people click the name and press F2; Windows automatically lets you rename the file or folder.

✔ When you rename a file, only its name changes. The contents are still the same, it's still the same size, and it's still in the same place.

✔ To rename large groups of files simultaneously, select them all, right-click on the first one, and choose Rename. Type in the new name and press Enter; Windows Vista renames that file. However, it also renames all your *other* selected files to the new name, adding a number as it goes: cat, cat (2), cat (3), cat (4), and so on.

✔ Renaming some folders confuses Windows, especially if those folders contain programs. And please don't rename these folders: Documents, Pictures, or Music.

✔ Windows won't let you rename a file or folder if one of your programs currently uses it. Sometimes closing the program fixes the problem, if you know which one is hanging onto that file or folder. One surefire cure is to restart your PC to release that program's clutches and try again to rename it.

Selecting Bunches of Files or Folders

Although selecting a file, folder, or other object may seem particularly boring, it swings the doors wide open for further action: deleting, renaming, moving, copying, and doing other goodies discussed in the rest of this chapter.

To select a single item, just click it. To select several files and folders, hold down the Ctrl key when you click the names or icons. Each name or icon stays highlighted when you click the next one.

To gather several files or folders sitting next to each other in a list, click the first one. Then hold down the Shift key as you click the last one. Those two items are highlighted, along with every file and folder sitting between them.

Windows Vista lets you *lasso* files and folders as well. Point slightly above the first file or folder you want; then, while holding down the mouse button, point at the last file or folder. The mouse creates a colored lasso to surround your files. Let go of the mouse button, and the lasso disappears, leaving all the surrounded files highlighted.

- ✔ You can drag and drop armfuls of files in the same way that you drag a single file.

- ✔ You can also simultaneously cut or copy and paste these armfuls into new locations using any of the methods described in the "Copying or Moving Files and Folders" section, later in this chapter.

- ✔ You can delete these armfuls of goods, too, with a press of the Del key.

- ✔ To quickly select all the files in a folder, choose Select All from the folder's Edit menu. (No menu? Then press Ctrl+A.) Here's another nifty trick: To grab all but a few files, press Ctrl+A and, while still holding down Ctrl, click the ones you don't want.

Getting Rid of a File or Folder

Sooner or later, you'll want to delete a file that's not important anymore — yesterday's lottery picks, for example, or a particularly embarrassing digital photo. To delete a file or folder, right-click on its name. Then choose Delete from the pop-up menu. This surprisingly simple trick works for files, folders, shortcuts, and just about anything else in Windows.

To delete in a hurry, click the offending object and press the Delete key. Dragging and dropping a file or folder to the Recycle Bin does the same thing.

The Delete option deletes entire folders, including any files or folders stuffed inside those folders. Make sure that you select the correct folder before you choose Delete.

✔ After you choose Delete, Windows tosses a box in your face, asking whether you're *sure.* If you're sure, click Yes. If you're tired of Windows' cautious questioning, right-click on the Recycle Bin, choose Properties, and remove the check mark next to Display Delete Confirmation Dialog. Windows now deletes any highlighted items whenever you — or an inadvertent brush of your shirt cuff — press the Delete key.

✔ Be extra sure that you know what you're doing when deleting any file that has pictures of little gears in its icon. These files are usually sensitive hidden files, and the computer wants you to leave them alone. (Other than that, they're not particularly exciting, despite the action-oriented gears.)

Freecell

✔ Icons with little arrows in their corner (like the one in the margin) are *shortcuts* — push buttons that merely load files. (I cover shortcuts in Chapter 5.) Deleting shortcuts deletes only a *button* that loads a file or program. The file or program itself remains undamaged and still lives inside your computer.

✔ As soon as you find out how to delete files, trot off to Chapter 2, which explains several ways to *un*delete them. (***Hint for the desperate:*** Open the Recycle Bin, right-click your file's name, and choose Restore.)

Don't bother reading this hidden technical stuff

You're not the only one creating files on your computer. Programs often store their own information in a *data file.* They may need to store information about the way the computer is set up, for example. To keep people from confusing the files for trash and deleting them, Windows hides them.

You can view the names of these hidden files and folders, however, if you want to play voyeur:

1. **Open any folder, click the Organize button, and choose Folder and Search Options.**

   The Folder Options dialog box appears.

2. **Select the View tab from along the dialog box's top, find the Hidden Files and Folders line in the Advanced Settings section, and click the Show Hidden Files and Folders button.**

3. **Click the OK button.**

The formerly hidden files appear alongside the other filenames. Be sure not to delete them, however: The programs that created them will gag, possibly damaging them or Windows itself. In fact, please click the View tab's Restore Defaults button to hide that stuff again, and click Apply to return the settings to normal.

Copying or Moving Files and Folders

To copy or move files to different folders on your hard drive, it's sometimes easiest to use your mouse to *drag* them there. For example, here's how to move a file to a different folder on your desktop. In this case, I'm moving the Traveler file from the House folder to the Morocco folder.

1. **Aim the mouse pointer at the file or folder you want to move.**

   In this case, point at the Traveler file.

2. **While holding down the right mouse button, move the mouse until it points at the destination folder.**

   As you see in Figure 4-7, the Traveler file is being dragged from the House folder to the Morocco folder. (I describe how to make windows sit neatly next to each other in Chapter 3.)

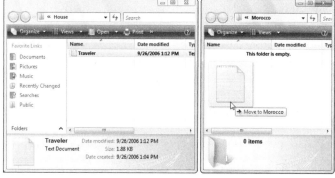

Figure 4-7: To move a file or folder from one window to another, drag it there.

Moving the mouse drags the file along with it, and Vista explains that you're moving the file, shown in Figure 4-7. (Be sure to hold down the right mouse button the entire time.)

Always drag icons while holding down the *right* mouse button. Windows Vista is then gracious enough to give you a menu of options when you position the icon, and you can choose to copy, move, or create a short-cut. If you hold down the *left* mouse button, Windows Vista sometimes doesn't know whether you want to copy or move.

3. **Release the mouse button and choose Copy Here, Move Here, or Create Shortcuts Here from the pop-up menu.**

Moving a file or folder by dragging it is pretty easy, actually. The hard part is placing both the file and its destination on-screen, especially when one folder is buried deep within your computer.

When dragging and dropping takes too much work, Windows offers a few other ways to copy or move files. Depending on your screen's current layout, some of the following on-screen tools may work more easily:

- **Right-click menus:** Right-click on a file or folder and choose Cut or Copy, depending on whether you want to move or copy it. Then right-click on your destination folder and choose Paste. It's simple, it always works, and you needn't place the item and its destination on-screen simultaneously.

- **Menu bar commands:** Click your file and then press Alt to reveal the folder's hidden menus. Click Edit from the menu and choose Copy to Folder or Move to Folder. A new window appears, listing all your computer's drives. Click through the drive and folders to reach the destination folder, and Windows carries out the Copy or Move command. A bit cumbersome, this method works if you know the exact location of the destination folder.

- **Navigation Pane's Folder view:** Described in the Navigation Pane section of Chapter 3, the Folder button displays a list of your folders along the bottom of the Navigation Pane. That lets you drag a file into a folder inside the Navigation Pane, sparing you the hassle of opening a destination folder.

After you install a program on your computer, don't ever move that program's folder. Programs wedge themselves into Windows. Moving the program may break it, and you'll have to reinstall it. Feel free to move the program's shortcut, though, if it has one.

Seeing More Information about Files and Folders

Whenever you create a file or folder, Windows Vista scrawls a bunch of secret hidden information on it: the date you created it, its size, and even more trivial stuff. Sometimes it even lets you add your own secret information: lyrics and reviews for your music files and folders, or thumbnail pictures for any of your folders.

You can safely ignore most of the information. Other times, tweaking that information is the only way to solve a problem.

To see what Windows Vista is calling your files and folders behind your back, right-click on the item and choose Properties from the pop-up menu.

Choosing Properties on a Jimi Hendrix song, for example, brings up bunches of details, as shown in Figure 4-8. Here's what each tab means:

- ✔ **General:** This first tab (shown on the left of Figure 4-8) shows the file's *type* (an MP3 file of the song "Hey Joe"), its *size* (3.27 MB), the program that *opens* it (in this case, Windows Media Player), and the file's *location*.

  Does the wrong program open your file? Right-click the file, choose Properties, and click the Change button on the General tab. There, you can choose your preferred program from a list.

- ✔ **Security:** On this tab, you control *permissions:* who can access the file, and what they can do with it — details that only become a chore when Vista won't let your friend (or even you) open the file. If this problem develops, copy the folder to your Public folder, which I cover in Chapter 14. That folder provides a haven where everybody can access the file.

- ✔ **Details:** True to its name, this tab reveals minute details about a file. On digital photos, for example, this tab lists EXIF (Exchangeable Image File Format) data: the camera model, F-stop, aperture, focal length, and other items photographers love. On songs, this tab displays the song's *ID3 tag* (*ID*entify MP*3*): the artist, album title, year, track number, genre, length, and similar information. (I cover ID3 Tags in Chapter 15.)

- ✔ **Previous Versions:** An obsessive collector, Vista constantly saves previous versions of your files. Made some terrible changes to today's spreadsheet? Take a deep breath, head here, and grab *yesterday's* copy of the spreadsheet. Vista's Previous Versions feature works in tandem with Windows XP's trusty System Restore. I cover both of these lifesavers in Chapter 17.

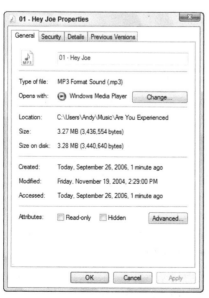

Figure 4-8: A file's Properties page shows which program automatically opens it, the file's size, and other details.

Normally, all these details remain hidden unless you right-click a file and choose Properties. But a folder can display the details of *all* your files simultaneously, handy for quick searches. To choose which details appear — the word count in your Microsoft Word documents, for example — right-click any word listed at the top of a column, as shown in Figure 4-9. (Click More, at the list's bottom, to see dozens more details, including word count.)

✔ To change the way a folder displays your files, click the arrow by the Views button on the toolbar (shown in the margin.) A menu appears, listing the seven ways a folder can display your files: Extra Large Icons, Large Icons, Medium Icons, Small Icons, List, Details, and Tiles. Try them all to see which view you prefer. (Vista remembers which views you prefer for different folders.)

✔ If you can't remember what a folder's toolbar buttons do, rest your mouse pointer over a button. Windows Vista displays a helpful box summing up the button's mission.

✔ Although some of the additional file information is handy, it can consume a lot of space, limiting the number of files you can see in the window. Displaying only the filename is often a better idea. Then, if you want to see more information about a file or folder, try the following tip.

✔ Folders usually display files sorted alphabetically. To sort them differently, right-click a blank spot inside the folder and choose Sort By. A pop-up menu lets you choose to sort items by size, name, type, and other details. Click More at the bottom of that pop-up menu's list to be astounded by the 250 ways you can sort files.

✔ When the excitement of the Sort By menu wears off, try clicking the words at the top of each sorted column. Click Size, for example, to quickly place the largest files at the list's top. Click Date Modified to quickly sort by the date of their last change, instead.

Flipping a file's secret switches

Windows Vista gives each file special switches called *attributes*. The computer looks at the way those switches are set before it fiddles with the file. To view a file's attributes, right-click on the file and choose Properties. Here's what you'll probably find at the window's bottom:

✔ **Read Only:** Choosing this attribute allows the file to be read, but not deleted or changed in any way.

✔ **Hidden:** Setting this attribute makes the file invisible during normal operations.

By clicking the Advanced button, Windows Vista presents more switches:

✔ **File Is Ready for Archiving:** Some backup programs look at this one to see whether they've backed up that file. When backed up, this attribute changes to reflect its new status.

✔ **Index This File For Faster Searching:** Normally set to On, this setting tells Windows to let its Indexing Service take note of the file and its contents for faster searching.

✔ **Compress Contents to Save Disk Space:** Available on most modern computers, this setting lets Windows Vista squish the file to save space. Be careful, though, as it sometimes makes the files load more slowly.

✔ **Encrypt Contents to Secure Data:** This switch brings up a much-too-complicated way to password-protect your file. Ignore it.

The Properties box makes it easy — perhaps too easy — to change these attributes. In most cases, you should leave them alone. I just mention them here so that you'll know what computer nerds mean when they tell cranky people, "Boy, somebody must have set your attribute wrong when you got out of bed this morning."

Writing to CDs and DVDs

Most computers today can write information to a CD and DVD using a flameless approach known as *burning*. To see whether you're stuck with an older drive that can't burn the discs, remove any discs from inside the drive; then open Computer from the Start menu and look at the icon for your CD or DVD drive. You want to see the letters *RW* in the drive icon's name.

If the drive says DVD/CD-RW, like the one in the margin, it can play *and* write to CDs and play but *not* write to DVDs. (I explain how to play DVDs in Chapter 15.)

If your drive says DVD-RW Drive, like the one in the margin, you've hit the jackpot: Your drive can both read and write to CDs *and* DVDs.

Vista is the first version of Windows that knows how to write to DVDs, something Windows XP couldn't do without the help of a third-party program.

If your PC has two CD or DVD burners, tell Vista which drive you want to handle the burning chore: Right-click the drive, choose Properties, and click the Recording tab. Then choose your favorite drive in the top box.

Buying the right kind of blank CDs and DVDs for burning

Stores sell two types of CDs: CD-R (short for CD-Recordable) and CD-RW (short for CD-ReWritable). Here's the difference:

- ✔ **CD-R:** Most people buy CD-R discs because they're very cheap, and they work fine for storing music or files. You can write to them until they fill up; then you can't write to them anymore. But that's no problem, because most people don't want to erase their CDs and start over. They want to stash their burned CD for a backup.

- ✔ **CD-RW:** Techies sometimes buy CD-RW discs for making temporary backups of data. You can write information to them, just like CD-Rs. But when a CD-RW disc fills up, you can erase it and start over with a clean slate — something not possible with a CD-R. However, CD-RWs cost more money, so most people stick with the cheaper and faster CD-Rs.

DVDs come in both R and RW formats, just like CDs, so the preceding R and RW rules apply to them, as well. Beyond that, it's chaos: The manufacturers fought over which storage format to use, confusing things for everybody. To buy the right blank DVD, check your DVD burner to see what formats it uses: DVD-R, DVD-RW, DVD+R, DVD+RW, and/or DVD-RAM. (Most new DVD burners support *all* of the first four formats, making your choice much easier.)

- ✔ The disc's "x" speed refers to the speed at which it can accept information. Your drive can write information onto a 40x CD five times faster than onto an 8x CD. Buy CDs with as fast an x rating as your burner can handle.

- ✔ You'll often find your CD or DVD burner's format and speed listings printed directly on the drive's face. If the information isn't there, check the receipt for your computer. If you still have no clue, buy reasonably fast discs. Slow burners can still write to speedy discs, but not as quickly as faster burners.

- ✔ Blank CDs are cheap; borrow one from a neighbor's kid to see whether it works in your drive. If it works fine, buy some of the same type. Blank DVDs, by contrast, are more expensive. Most neighbors' kids won't let you have one. Ask the store whether you can return them if your DVD drive doesn't like them.

✔ For some odd reason, Compact Discs and Digital Video Discs are spelled as "discs," not "disks." Be prepared for the agape mouths of shocked proofreaders.

✔ Although Windows Vista can handle simple CD-burning tasks, it's extra-ordinarily awkward at *copying* music CDs. Most people give up quickly and buy third-party CD burning software from Roxio or Nero. I explain how Windows Vista creates music CDs in Chapter 15.

✔ It's currently illegal to make duplicates of movie DVDs in the United States — even to make a backup copy in case your kids scratch up your new Disney DVD. Vista certainly can't do it, but some programs on Web sites from other countries can. (Don't ask me where to get them, as I don't know.)

Copying files from or to a CD or DVD

CDs and DVDs once hailed from the school of simplicity: You simply slid them into your CD player or DVD player. But as soon as those discs graduated to PCs, the problems intensified. When you create a CD or DVD, you need to tell your PC *what* you're copying, and *where* you intend to play it: Music for a CD player? Movies for a DVD player? Or simply files for your computer? If you choose the wrong answer, the disc won't work.

Here are the Disc Creation rules:

✔ **Music:** To create a CD that plays music in your CD player or car stereo, flip ahead to Chapter 15. You need to fire up Vista's Media Player program.

✔ **Movies and photo slide shows:** To create a DVD with movies or slide shows that play on a DVD player, jump to Chapter 16. You want Vista's new DVD Maker program.

But if you just want to copy *files* to a CD or DVD, perhaps to save as a backup or give to a friend, stick around.

Follow these steps to write files to a new, blank CD or DVD. (If you're writing files to a CD or DVD that you've written to before, jump ahead to Step 4.)

Note: If your PC has a third-party disc-burning program, that program may automatically take charge as soon as you insert the disc, bypassing these steps completely. If you want Vista or a different program to burn the disc instead, close the third-party program. Then right-click the drive's icon and choose Open AutoPlay. There, you can tell how Vista to react to an inserted blank disc.

1. **Insert the blank disc into your disc burner and choose Burn Files to Disc.**

   Vista reacts slightly differently depending on whether you've inserted a CD or DVD, shown in Figure 4-10.

Figure 4-10:
Inserting a
blank CD
(left) or DVD
(right) brings
up one of
these boxes;
choose Burn
Files to Disc
to copy files
to the disc.

CD: Vista offers two options:

- **Burn an audio CD:** Choosing this option fetches Media Player to create an audio CD that plays music in most CD players. (I describe how to do this task in Chapter 15.)

- **Burn Files to Disc:** Choose this option to copy files to the CD.

DVD: Vista offers three options:

- **Burn a DVD Data Disc:** Choosing this option fetches Media Player (Chapter 15), letting you select music files from your library and copy them to a DVD for backup. (If your DVD player supports MP3 or WMA files, it *might* be able to play the music.)

- **Burn Files to a Disc:** Choose this option to copy files to the DVD.

- **Burn a DVD Video Disc:** Choosing this option starts Vista's DVD Maker program to create a movie or photo slide show, chores I cover in Chapter 16.

2. **Enter a name for the disc and click Next.**

   After you insert the disc and choose Burn Files to a Disc in Step 1, Vista displays a Burn a Disc dialog box and asks you to create a title for the disc.

   Unfortunately, Vista limits your CD or DVD's title to 16 characters. Instead of typing **Family Picnic atop Orizaba in 2006**, stick to the facts: **Orizaba, 2006**. Or, just click Next to use Vista's default name for the disc: the current date.

Curious folks will spot the Show Formatting Options option in the Burn a Disc box. If you succumb to the clicking urge, you'll see that Vista offers two choices for storing information on your disc: Live File System or Mastered. Stick with Live File System except under two conditions: You're using CD-RW or DVD-RW discs or you're worried about compatibility with older PCs and Apple computers. Under those conditions, choose Mastered instead of Vista's usual Live File System format.

Armed with the disc's name, Vista prepares the disc for incoming files, leaving you with the disc's empty window on-screen, waiting for incoming files.

3. **Tell Vista which files to write to disc.**

   Now that your disc is ready to accept the files, tell Vista what information to send its way. You can do this any of several ways:

   - Right-click the item you want to copy, be it a single file, folder, or selected files and folders. When the pop-up menu appears, choose Send To and select your disc burner from the menu.

   - Drag and drop files and/or folders into the disc burner's open window, or on top of the burner's icon in Computer.

   - Choose the Burn button from the toolbar of any folder in your Music folder. This button copies all of that folder's music (or the music files you've selected) to the disc as *files,* readable by some newer car and home stereos that can read WMA or MP3 files.

   - Choose the Burn button from the toolbar of any folder in your Picture folder. This copies all that folder's pictures (or the pictures you've highlighted) to the disc for backup or giving to others.

   - Choose the Burn button from the toolbar of any folder in your Documents folder. This copies all that folder's files to the disc.

   - Tell your current program to save the information to the disc rather than your hard drive.

   No matter which method you choose, Vista dutifully looks over the information and copies it to the disc you inserted in the first step.

4. **Close your disc burning session by ejecting the disc.**

   When you're through copying files to the disc, tell Vista you're finished by closing the Computer window: Double-click the little red X in the window's upper-right corner.

   Then push your drive's Eject button (or right-click the drive's icon in Computer and choose Eject), and Vista closes the session, adding a finishing touch to the disc that lets it be read in other PCs.

Duplicating a CD or DVD

Windows Vista doesn't have a command to duplicate a CD or DVD. It can't even make a copy of a music CD. (That's why so many people buy CD burning programs.)

But it can copy all of a CD or DVD's files to a blank disc using this two-step process:

1. **Copy the files and folders from the CD or DVD to a folder on your PC.**

2. **Copy those same files and folders back to a blank CD or DVD.**

That gives you a duplicate CD or DVD, handy when you need a second copy of an essential backup disc.

You can try this process on a music CD or DVD movie, but it doesn't work. (I tried.) It only works when duplicating a disc containing programs or data files.

You can keep writing more and more files to the same disc until Windows complains that the disc is full. Then you need to close your current disc, explained in Step 4, insert another blank disc, and start over at Step 1.

If you try to copy a large batch of files to a disc — more than will fit — Windows Vista complains immediately. Copy fewer files at a time, perhaps spacing them out over two discs.

Most programs let you save files directly to disc. Choose Save from the File menu and select your CD burner. Put a disc (preferably one that's not already filled) into your disc drive to start the process.

Working with Floppy Disks and Memory Cards

Digital camera owners eventually become acquainted with *memory cards* — those little plastic squares that replaced those awkward rolls of film. Vista can read digital photos directly from the camera, once you find its cable and plug it into your PC. But Vista can also grab photos straight off the memory card, a method praised by those who've lost their camera's special cables.

The secret is a *memory card reader:* a little slot-filled box that stays plugged into your PC. Slide your memory card into the slot, and your PC can read the card's files, just like reading files from any other folder.

Most office supply and electronics stores sell memory card readers that accept most popular memory card formats: Compact Flash, SecureDigital, Mini-Secure Digital, Memory Sticks, and others.

The beauty of card readers is that there's nothing new to figure out: Windows Vista treats your inserted card or floppy just like an ordinary folder. Insert your card, and a folder appears on your screen to show your digital camera photos. The same "drag and drop" and "cut and paste" rules covered earlier in this chapter still apply, letting you move the pictures or other files off the card and into a folder in your Pictures folder.

✔ First, the warning: Formatting a card or disk wipes out all its information. Never format a card or disk unless you don't care about the information it currently holds.

✔ Now, the procedure: If Windows complains that a newly inserted card or floppy isn't formatted, right-click on its drive and choose Format. (This problem happens most often with damaged cards or floppies.) Sometimes formatting also helps one gadget use a card designed for a different gadget — your digital camera may be able to use your MP3 player's card, for example.

✔ Floppy drives, those disk readers from days gone by, still appear on a few older PCs. They work just like memory cards or CDs: Insert the floppy disk into the floppy drive and double-click the floppy drive's icon in Computer to start playing with its files.

✔ Press the F5 key whenever you stick in a different floppy disk and want to see what files are stored on it. Windows Vista then updates the screen to show that *new* disk's files, not the files from the first one. (You only have to do this step when working with floppy disks.)

Part II
Working with Programs and Files

The 5th Wave   By Rich Tennant

UBER-USER DWAYNE GRANTZ CHALKS UP BEFORE PUTTING WINDOWS VISTA THROUGH ITS PACES.

In this part . . .

The first part of the book explains how to manipulate Vista by poking and prodding its sensitive parts with the mouse.

This part of the book finally lets you get some work done. For example, here's where you find out how to run programs, open existing files, create and save your own files, and print your work when you're through. A primer details Windows' essentials: Copying information from one window or program and pasting it into another.

And when some of your files wander (it's unavoidable), Chapter 6 explains how to unleash Windows' new robotic search hounds to track them down and bring them within reach.

Chapter 5

Playing with Programs and Documents

. . . .

. . . .

*I*n Windows, *programs* are your tools: They let you add numbers, arrange words, and shoot spaceships. *Documents,* by contrast, are the things you create with programs: tax forms, heartfelt apologies, and high scores.

This chapter starts with the basics of opening programs, creating shortcuts, and cutting and pasting information between documents. Along the way, it throws in a few tricks — how to add things like © to your documents, for example. Finally, it ends with a tour of Windows Vista's free programs, showing how to write a letter, create an appointment book, or take notes that you spice up with special characters and symbols.

Starting a Program

Clicking the Start button presents the Start menu, the launching pad for your programs. The Start menu is strangely intuitive. For example, if it notices you've been making lots of DVDs, the Start menu automatically moves Windows DVD Maker program's icon to its front page for easy access, as shown in Figure 5-1.

Don't see your favorite program on the Start menu's front page? Click All
Programs near the bottom of the Start menu. The Start menu covers up its
previously displayed icons with an even *larger* list of programs and category-
stuffed folders. Still don't spot your program? Click some of the folders to
unveil even *more* programs stuffed inside.

Figure 5-1:
Click the
Start button
and then
click the
program
you want
to open.

When you spot your program, click its name. The program opens onto the
desktop, ready for work.

If your program doesn't seem to be living on the Start menu, Windows Vista
offers plenty of other ways to open a program, including the following:

- Open the Documents folder from the Start menu and double-click the file
  you want to work on. The correct program automatically opens, with
  that file in tow.

- Double-click a *shortcut* to the program. Shortcuts, which often sit on
  your desktop, are handy, disposable push buttons for launching files and
  folders. (I explain more about shortcuts in this chapter's "Taking the
  Lazy Way with a Shortcut" section.)

✔ If you spot the program's icon on the Windows' Quick Launch toolbar —
a small, handy strip of icons that resides next to the Start button — click
it. The program leaps into action. (I cover the Quick Launch toolbar,
including how to add and remove it, in Chapter 2.)

✔ Right-click on your desktop, choose New, and select the type of document
you want to create. Windows Vista loads the right program for the job.

✔ Type the program's name in the Search box at the bottom of the Start
menu and press Enter.

Windows offers other ways to open a program, but these methods usually get
the job done. I cover the Start menu more extensively in Chapter 2.

On its front page, the Start menu places *shortcuts* — push buttons — for
your most-used programs. Those shortcuts constantly change to reflect the
programs you use the most. Don't want the boss to know you play FreeCell?
Right-click on FreeCell's icon and choose Remove from This List. The shortcut disappears, yet FreeCell's "real" icon remains in its normal spot in the
Start menu's Games folder (in the All Programs folder).

Opening a Document

Like Tupperware, Windows Vista is a big fan of standardization. All Windows
programs load their documents — often called *files* — exactly the same way:

1. **Click the word File on any program's *menu bar*, that row of staid
   words along the program's top.**

   No menu bar? Press Alt to reveal it.

2. **When the File menu drops down, click Open.**

   Windows gives you a sense of déjà vu with the Open box, shown in
   Figure 5-2: It looks (and works) just like your Documents folder, which
   I cover in Chapter 4.

   There's one big difference, however: This time, your folder displays only
   files that your program knows how to open — it filters out all the others.

3. **See the list of documents inside the Open dialog box in Figure 5-2?
   Point at your desired document, click the mouse, and click the Open
   button.**

   The program opens the file and displays it on the screen.

When programmers fight over file types

When not fighting over fast food, programmers fight over *formats* — ways to pack information into a file. To accommodate the format wars, some programs have a special feature that lets you open files stored in several different types of formats.

For example, look at the drop-down list box in the bottom-right corner of Figure 5-2. It currently lists Text Documents (*.txt) format, the format used by Notepad. So, the Open box displays only files stored in Notepad. To see files stored in *other* formats, click in that box and choose a different format. The Open box quickly updates its list to show files from that new format, instead.

And how can you see a list of *all* your folder's files in that menu, regardless of their content? Choose All Files from the drop-down list box. You'll see all your files, but your program probably won't be able to open all of them and will choke if it tries.

Notepad lists digital photos in its All Files menu, for example. But if you try to open a photo, Notepad dutifully displays the photo as obscure coding symbols. (If you ever mistakenly open a photo in a program and *don't* see the photo, don't try to save what you've opened. If the program is like Notepad, it will ruin it. Simply turn tail and exit immediately to find a program that will oblige your request.)

Opening a file works this way in *any* Windows program, whether written by Microsoft, its corporate partners, or the teenager down the street.

- ✔ To speed things up, double-click a desired file's name; that opens it immediately, automatically closing the Open box.

- ✔ If your file isn't listed by name, start browsing by clicking the buttons shown along the left side of Figure 5-2. Click the Documents folder, for example, to see files stored in that folder. Click Recently Changed to see files you've saved recently; if you spot the one you want, pluck it from the list with a double-click.

- ✔ Puny humans store things in the garage, but computers store their files in neatly labeled compartments called *folders*. (Double-click a folder to see what's stored inside.) If browsing folders gives you trouble, Chapter 4's folders section offers a refresher.

- ✔ Whenever you open a file and change it, even by accidentally pressing the spacebar, Windows Vista assumes that you've changed the file for the better. If you try to close the file, Windows Vista cautiously asks whether you want to save your changes. If you changed the file with masterful wit, click Yes. If you made a mess or opened the wrong file, click No or Cancel.

- ✔ Confused about any icons or commands along the Open box's top or left side? Rest your mouse pointer over the icons, and a little box announces their occupations.

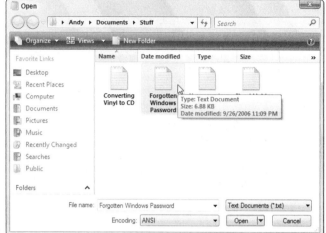

Figure 5-2:
Double-click
the filename
you want
to open.

Saving a Document

Saving means to send the work you've just created to a disk or hard drive for safekeeping. Unless you specifically save your work, your computer thinks that you've just been fiddling around for the past four hours. You must specifically tell the computer to save your work before it will safely store it.

Thanks to Microsoft's snapping leather whips, the same Save command appears in all Windows Vista programs, no matter what programmer wrote them. Click File from the top menu, choose Save, and save your document in your Documents folder or to your desktop for easy retrieval later.

What's the difference between Save and Save As?

Huh? Save as *what?* A chemical compound? Naw, the Save As command just gives you a chance to save your work with a different name and in a different location.

Suppose that you open the *Ode to Tina* file in your Documents folder and change a few sentences. You want to save your new changes, but you don't want to lose the original words, either. Preserve *both* versions by selecting *Save As* and typing the new name, *Tentative Additions to Odes to Tina*.

When you're saving something for the *first* time, the Save and Save As commands are identical: Both make you choose a fresh name and location for your work.

If you're saving something for the first time, Windows Vista asks you to think up a name for your document. Type something descriptive using only letters, numbers, and spaces between the words. (If you try to use one of the illegal characters I describe in Chapter 4, the Windows Police step in, politely requesting that you use a different name.)

- ✔ Choose descriptive filenames for your work. Windows Vista gives you 255 characters to work with, so a file named *June Report on Squeegee Sales* is easier to locate than one named *Stuff*.

- ✔ You can save files to any folder, CD, or even a memory card. But files are much easier to find down the road when they stay in the Documents folder. (Feel free to save a *second* copy onto your CD as a backup.)

- ✔ Most programs can save files directly to a CD. Choose Save from the File menu and choose your CD burner. Put a CD (preferably one that's not already filled) into your CD-writing drive to start the process.

- ✔ If you're working on something important (and most things are), choose the program's Save command every few minutes. Or use the Ctrl+S keyboard shortcut (while holding down the Ctrl key, press the S key). Programs make you choose a name and location for a file when you *first* save it; subsequent saves are much speedier.

Choosing Which Program Opens a File

Most of the time, Windows Vista automatically knows which program should open which file. Double-click any file, and Windows tells the correct program to jump in and let you view its contents. But when Windows Vista gets confused, the problem lands in *your* lap.

The next two sections explain what to do when the wrong program opens your file or, even worse, *no* program offers to do the job.

If somebody says something about "file associations," feel free to browse the technical sidebar section, which explains that awful subject.

The wrong program loads my file!

Double-clicking a document usually brings up the correct program, usually the same program you used to create that document. But sometimes the wrong program keeps jumping in, hijacking one of your documents. (Different brands of media players constantly fight over the right to play your music or videos, for example.)

The awkward world of file associations

Every Windows program slaps a secret code known as a *file extension* onto the name of every file it creates. The file extension works like a cattle brand: When you double-click the file, Windows Vista eyeballs the extension and automatically summons the proper program to open the file. Notepad, for example, tacks on the three-letter extension .txt to every file it creates. So the .txt extension is associated with Notepad.

Windows Vista normally doesn't display these extensions, isolating users from Windows' inner mechanisms for safety reasons. If somebody accidentally changes or removes an extension, Windows won't know how to open that file.

If you're curious as to what an extension looks like, sneak a peek by following these steps:

1. **Click the Organize button from inside any folder and choose Folder and Search Options from the drop-down menu.**

The Folder Options dialog box appears.

2. **Click the View tab and then click the Hide Extensions for Known File Types box to remove the check mark.**

3. **Click the OK button.**

The files all reveal their extensions.

Notice that if you open two different files with the same extension, these files open in the same program. Now that you've peeked, hide the extensions again by repeating the steps, but putting a check mark back in the Hide Extensions for Known File Types box.

The moral? Don't *ever* change a file's extension unless you know exactly what you're doing; Windows Vista will forget what program to use for opening the file, leaving you holding an empty bag.

When the wrong program suddenly begins opening your document, here's how to make the *right* program open it instead:

1. **Right-click your problematic file and select Open With from the pop-up menu.**

   As shown in Figure 5-3, Windows names a few programs you've used to open that file in the past.

   Don't see the Open With option on the menu? Then choose Open. Vista jumps straight to the Open With window shown in Figure 5-4, described in the next section.

2. **Click Choose Default Program and select the program you want to open the file.**

   The Open With window, shown in Figure 5-4, lists many more programs. If you spot your favorite program, you *could* double-click it to open your file immediately. But that wouldn't prevent the same problem from recurring. The *next* step tackles that challenge.

Figure 5-3:
Click the
program you
want to
open the file.

If Windows doesn't list your favorite program anywhere on its list, you
have to look for it. Choose Default Programs, click the Browse button, and
navigate to the folder containing the program you want. (*Hint:* Hover
your mouse pointer over the folders to see some of the files and programs inside.)

**3. Click the Always Use the Selected Program to Open This Kind of File
check box and click OK.**

That box makes Windows return top-billing status to your selected program. For example, choosing Paint Shop Pro (and checking the Always
box) tells Windows to summon Paint Shop Pro every time you double-
click that type of file.

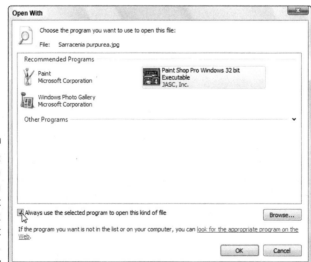

Figure 5-4:
Choose the
program
you want
and click
the box at
the bottom.

✔ Sometimes you'll want to alternate between two programs when working on the same document. To do so, right-click on the document, choose Open With, and select the program you need at that time.

✔ Sometimes you can't make your favorite program open a particular file because it simply doesn't know how. For example, Windows Media Player can usually play videos, *except* when they're stored in QuickTime, a format used by Microsoft's competition. Your only solution is to install QuickTime (www.apple.com/quicktime) and use it to open that particular video.

✔ Can't find *any* program to open your file? Then you're primed for the very next section.

No program will open my file!

It's frustrating when several programs fight to open your file. But it's even worse when *no program* ponies up to the task. Double-clicking your file merely summons the cryptic error message shown in Figure 5-5.

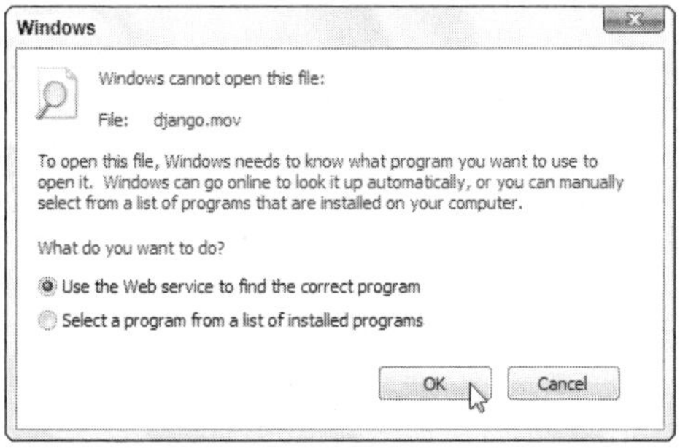

Figure 5-5:
Sometimes
Windows
refuses to
open a file.

> **Windows**
>
> Windows cannot open this file:
>
> File: django.mov
>
> To open this file, Windows needs to know what program you want to use to open it. Windows can go online to look it up automatically, or you can manually select from a list of programs that are installed on your computer.
>
> What do you want to do?
>
> ⦿ Use the Web service to find the correct program
> ○ Select a program from a list of installed programs
>
> [OK]   [Cancel]

If you already know the program needed to open your file, choose the second option: Select a Program from a List of Installed Programs. That summons the familiar window from Figure 5-4, letting you choose your program and click OK to open the file.

But if you have no idea which program should open your mystery file, choose the Use the Web Service to Find the Correct Program option and click OK. Windows dashes off to the Internet in search of the right program. If you're lucky, Internet Explorer displays a Microsoft Web site. There, Microsoft identifies your file, describes its contents, and suggests a Web site for downloading a capable program. Visit the Web site Microsoft suggests, download and install the program (after scanning it with a virus-checking program described in Chapter 10), and you've solved the problem.

Sometimes Microsoft routes you directly to a Web site, shown in Figure 5-6, where you can download a program that opens the file.

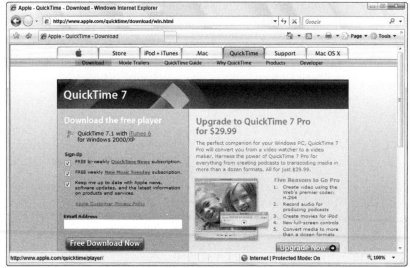

Figure 5-6:
Windows sometimes helps you find a program for opening an orphaned file.

✔ In Figure 5-6, Microsoft identified a *QuickTime video* file. (Microsoft's rival, Apple, created that format to store movies, but Windows Media Player won't open it.) Luckily, Microsoft sends you to Apple's QuickTime Web site, where you can download and install Apple's QuickTime Movie Viewer program.

✔ When you visit a Web site to download a suggested program like the QuickTime and RealPlayer movie players, you often find *two* versions: Free and Professional (expensive). The free version often works fine, so try it first.

✔ If you can't find *any* program that lets you open your file, you're simply stuck. You must contact the people who gave you that file and ask them what program you need to open it. Then, unfortunately, you'll probably have to buy that program.

Taking the Lazy Way with a Shortcut

Some items are buried *way* too deeply inside of your computer. If you're tired of meandering through the woods to find your favorite program, folder, disk drive, document, or even a Web site, create a *shortcut* — an icon push button that takes you directly to the object of your desires.

Freecell

Because a shortcut is a mere push button that launches something else, you can move, delete, and copy shortcuts without harming the original. They're safe, convenient, and easy to create. And they're easy to tell apart from the original, because they have a little arrow lodged in their bottom-left corner, such as the FreeCell shortcut shown in the margin.

Follow these instructions to create shortcuts to these popular Windows doodads:

- **Folders or Documents:** Right-click on the folder or document, choose Send To, and select the Desktop (Create Shortcut) option. When the shortcut appears on your desktop, drag and drop it to a handy corner.

- **Web sites:** See the little icon in front of the Web site's address in Internet Explorer's Address Bar? Drag and drop that little icon to your desktop — or anyplace else. (It helps to drag one of Internet Explorer's window edges inward so that you can see part of your desktop.) You can also add Web sites to Internet Explorer's handy list of Favorites, which I describe in Chapter 8.

- **Anything on your Start menu:** Right-click on the Start menu icon and choose Copy. Then right-click where you want the shortcut to appear and choose Paste Shortcut.

- **Nearly anything:** Drag and drop the object to a new place while holding down your right mouse button. When you let go of the mouse button, choose Create Shortcuts Here, and the shortcut appears.

- **Control Panel:** Found a particularly helpful setting in Control Panel, Windows Vista's built-in switch box? Drag the helpful icon onto your desktop, the Navigation Pane along a folder's side, or any other handy spot. The icon turns into a shortcut for easy access.

- **Disk drives:** Open Computer from the Start menu, right-click on the drive you want, and choose Create Shortcut. Windows immediately places a shortcut to that drive on your desktop.

Here are some more tips for shortcuts:

- For quick CD burning, put a shortcut to your CD burner on your desktop. Burning files to CD becomes as simple as dragging and dropping them onto the CD burner's new shortcut. (Insert a blank disc into the CD burner's tray, confirm the settings, and begin burning.)

- Feel free to move shortcuts from place to place but *don't* move the items they launch. If you do, the shortcut won't be able to find the item, causing Windows to panic, searching (usually vainly) for the moved goods.

- Want to see what program a shortcut will launch? Right-click on the shortcut, and click Open File Location (if available). The shortcut quickly takes you to its leader.

The Absolutely Essential Guide to Cutting, Copying, and Pasting

Windows Vista took a tip from the kindergartners and made *cut and paste* an integral part of life. You can electronically *cut* or *copy* and then *paste* just about anything somewhere else with little fuss and even less mess.

Windows programs are designed to work together and share information, making it fairly easy to put a scanned map onto your party invitation fliers. You can move files by cutting or copying them from one place and pasting them into another. And you can easily cut and paste paragraphs to different locations within a program.

The beauty of Windows Vista is that, with all those windows on-screen at the same time, you can easily grab bits and pieces from any of them and paste all the parts into a brand new window.

Don't overlook copying and pasting for the small stuff. Copying a name and address from your Contacts program is much quicker than typing it into your letter by hand. Or, when somebody e-mails you a Web address, copy and paste it directly into Internet Explorer's Address Bar. It's easy to copy most items displayed on Web sites, too (much to the dismay of many professional photographers).

The quick 'n' dirty guide to cut 'n' paste

In compliance with the Don't Bore Me with Details Department, here's a quick guide to the three basic steps used for cutting, copying, and pasting:

1. **Select the item to cut or copy: a few words, a file, a Web address, or any other item.**

2. **Right-click on your selection and choose Cut or Copy from the menu, depending on your needs.**

   Use *Cut* when you want to *move* something. Use *Copy* when you want to duplicate something, leaving the original intact.

   Keyboard shortcut: Hold down Ctrl and press X to cut or C to copy.

3. **Right-click on the item's destination and choose Paste.**

   You can right-click inside a document, folder, or nearly any other place.

   Keyboard shortcut: Hold down Ctrl and press V to paste.

The next three sections explain each of these three steps in more detail.

Selecting things to cut or copy

Before you can shuttle pieces of information to new places, you have to tell Windows Vista exactly what you want to grab. The easiest way to tell it is to *select* the information with a mouse. In most cases, selecting involves one swift trick with the mouse, which then highlights whatever you've selected.

✔ **To select text in a document, Web site, or spreadsheet:** Put the mouse arrow or cursor at the beginning of the information you want and hold down the mouse button. Then move the mouse to the end of the information and release the button. That's it! That selects all the stuff lying between where you clicked and released, as shown in Figure 5-7.

Be careful after you highlight a bunch of text. If you accidentally press the letter *k,* for example, the program replaces your highlighted text with the letter *k.* To reverse that calamity, choose Undo from the program's Edit menu (or press Ctrl+Z, which is the keyboard shortcut for Undo).

✔ **To select any files or folders:** Simply click a file or folder to select it. To select *several* items, try these tricks:

- **If all the files are in a row:** Click the first item in the bunch, hold down the Shift key, and then select the last item. Windows highlights the first and last items, as well as everything in between.

- **If the files *aren't* in a row:** Hold down the Ctrl key while clicking each file or folder you want to select.

Figure 5-7: Windows highlights the selected text, changing its color for easy visibility.

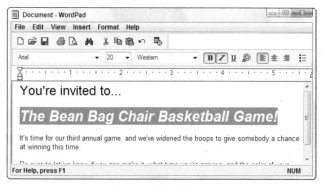

Selecting individual letters, words, paragraphs, and more

When dealing with words in Windows Vista, these shortcuts help you quickly select information:

✔ To select an individual *letter or character,* click in front of the character. Then while holding down the Shift key, press your → key. Keep holding down these two keys to keep selecting text in a line.

✔ To select a single *word,* point at it with the mouse and double-click. The word changes color, meaning it's highlighted. (In most word processors, you can hold down the button on its second click, and then by moving the mouse around, you can quickly highlight additional text word by word.)

✔ To select a single *line* of text, click next to it in the left margin. Keep holding down the mouse button and move the mouse up or down to highlight additional text line by line. You can also keep selecting additional lines by holding down the Shift key and pressing the ↓ key or the ↑ key.

✔ To select a *paragraph,* double-click next to it in the left margin. Keep holding down the mouse button on the second click and move the mouse to highlight additional text paragraph by paragraph.

✔ To select an entire *document,* hold down Ctrl and press A. (Or choose Select All from the Edit menu.)

Now that you've selected the item, the next section explains how to cut or copy it.

✔ After you've selected something, cut it or copy it *immediately.* If you absentmindedly click the mouse someplace else, your highlighted text or file reverts to its boring self, and you're forced to start over.

✔ To delete any selected item, be it a file, paragraph, or picture, press the Delete key.

Cutting or copying your selected goods

After you select some information (which I describe in the preceding section, in case you just arrived), you're ready to start playing with it. You can cut it or copy it. (Or just press Delete to delete it.)

This bears repeating. After selecting something, right-click on it. When the menu pops up, choose Cut or Copy, depending on your needs, as shown in Figure 5-8. Then right-click your destination and choose Paste.

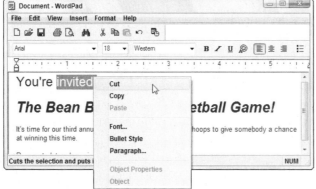

Figure 5-8:
Right-click
on your
selection
and choose
Cut to move
it into
another
window.

The Cut and Copy options differ drastically. How do you know which one to choose?

- ✔ **Choose Cut to move information.** *Cutting* wipes the selected information off the screen, but you haven't lost anything: Windows stores the cut information in a hidden Windows Vista storage tank called the *Clipboard,* waiting for you to paste it.

  Feel free to cut and paste entire files to different folders. When you cut a file from a folder, the icon dims until you paste it. (Making the icon disappear would be too scary.) Changed your mind in mid-cut? Press Esc to cancel the cut, and the icon reverts to normal.

- ✔ **Choose Copy to make a copy of the information.** Compared with cutting, *copying* information is quite anticlimactic. Whereas cutting removes the item from view, copying the selected item leaves it in the window, seemingly untouched. Copied information also goes to the Clipboard until you paste it.

To copy a picture of your entire Windows Vista desktop (the *whole screen*) to the Clipboard, press the Print Screen key, which is sometimes labeled PrtScrn or something similar. (And, no, the Print Screen key doesn't send anything to your printer.) You can then paste the picture into Windows Vista's Paint program and print it from there.

Pasting information to another place

After you cut or copy information to Windows Vista's Clipboard, it's ready for travel. You can *paste* that information nearly anyplace else.

Undoing what you've just done

Windows Vista offers a zillion different ways for you to do the same thing. Here are four ways to access the Undo option, which unspills your spilled milk:

✔ Hold down the Ctrl key and press the Z key. The last mistake you made is reversed, sparing you from further shame. (Pressing a program's Undo button, if you can find one, does the same thing.)

✔ Hold down the Alt key and press the Backspace key. Vista goes back and retrieves what you deleted.

✔ Click Edit and then click Undo from the menu that falls down. The last command

you made is undone, saving you from any damage.

✔ Press and release the Alt key, press the letter E (from Edit), and then press the letter U (from Undo). Your last bungle is unbungled, reversing any grievous penalties.

Don't bother learning all four methods. For example, if you can remember the Ctrl+Z key combination, you can forget about the others. Best yet, just write Ctrl+Z on the cover of the book. (The publisher's marketing people wouldn't let me put it there — or my picture, but that's another story.)

Pasting is relatively straightforward:

1. **Open the destination window and move the mouse pointer or cursor to the spot where you want the stuff to appear.**

2. **Right-click the mouse and choose Paste from the pop-up menu.**

   Presto! The item you just cut or copied immediately leaps into its new spot.

Or, if you want to paste a file onto the desktop, right-click on the desktop and choose Paste. The cut or copied file appears where you've right-clicked.

✔ The Paste command inserts a *copy* of the information that's sitting on the Clipboard. The information stays on the Clipboard, so you can keep pasting the same thing into other places if you want.

✔ Some programs have toolbars along their tops, offering one-click access to Cut, Copy, and Paste, as shown in Figure 5-9.

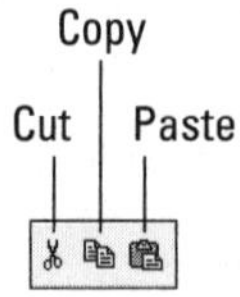

Figure 5-9:
Cut, Copy, and Paste buttons.

Copy

Cut | Paste

Windows Vista's Free Programs!

Windows Vista, the fanciest Windows version yet, comes with oodles of free programs, such as Media Player and Mail. These freebies make customers happy and make the European Antitrade Commission flap their long black robes.

I cover the larger free programs in other chapters. (Media Player, for example, gets its due in Chapter 15; Mail lives in Chapter 9.) This chapter merely focuses on Windows Vista's most useful freebies: its WordPad word processor, the Calendar scheduling program, and Character Map.

Writing letters with WordPad

WordPad is nowhere near as fancy as some of the more expensive word processors on the market. It can't create tables or multiple columns, like the ones in newspapers or newsletters, nor can you double-space your reports. Forget the spell checker, too.

WordPad is great for quick letters, simple reports, and other basic stuff. You can change the fonts, too. And because all Windows users have WordPad on their computers, most computer owners can read anything you create in WordPad.

 To give WordPad a whirl, choose All Programs from the Start menu, choose Accessories, and click WordPad.

 If you've just ditched your typewriter for Windows, remember this: On an electric typewriter, you have to press the Return key at the end of each line, or else you start typing off the edge of the paper. Computers avoid that. They automatically drop down a line and continue the sentence. (Tech Hipsters call this phenomenon *word wrap.*)

- ✔ To change fonts in WordPad, select the words you'd like to change (or select the entire document by choosing Select All from the Edit menu). Then choose Font from the Format menu. Click the name of the font you want; the Sample box offers a preview. Click the OK button, and WordPad displays your changes.

- ✔ Quickly insert the current day, date, or time into your document by choosing Date and Time from the Insert menu. Choose the style of date or time you want, and WordPad inserts it into your document.

Keeping appointments with Calendar

Vista tosses in a new program not found in Windows XP: Windows Calendar. Just like it sounds, Windows Calendar is a full-fledged scheduling program that replaces hastily scribbled sticky notes on the refrigerator. Fire it up by clicking the Start menu, choosing All Programs, and selecting Windows Calendar.

Shown in Figure 5-10, Calendar presents a monthly calendar on the left side, your day's appointments in the middle, and the highlighted appointment's details on the right.

To add an appointment, click a day on the calendar, click the time of the appointment, type a description, and start filling out the additional details on the right.

The beauty of Calendar is the way it lets you share appointments through e-mail or by publishing them to a Web site where friends and relatives can automatically *subscribe* to them, meaning Calendar will download and display them automatically.

The downside of Calendar is that you have no excuse for being late anymore.

- ✔ For a quick way to add dates for holidays, sporting events, TV shows, moon phases, and similar items, visit iCalShare (`www.icalshare.com`). The Web site lets people publish and share calendars.

- ✔ Windows Calendar lets you share calendars with people using Microsoft's Outlook program, Apple's iCal program, and Google's online calendar (`www.google.com/calendar`). For a real downer, you may be able to share your calendar from work, as well — ask your office network guru.

- ✔ To share your own calendar with friends, click your calendar's name from the Calendars section shown in Figure 5-10. Then choose Send Via E-mail from the Share menu. Calendar will e-mail your calendar to your friend, where it will appear on your friend's calendar program.

- ✔ Calendar lets you assign different colors to your friends' calendars so that you can easily tell which appointment belongs to which person. To remove somebody's appointments from your calendar, click their calendar's name and press Delete: All their appointments disappear.

Add an appointment

Delete selected   View today's appointments
appointment

Change to week or month view

Add a task

Subscribe to other calendars

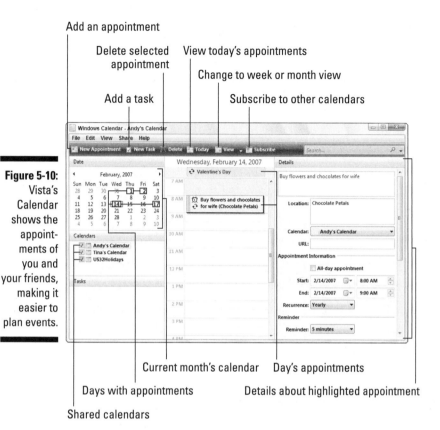

Figure 5-10:
Vista's
Calendar
shows the
appoint-
ments of
you and
your friends,
making it
easier to
plan events.

Current month's calendar   Day's appointments

Days with appointments   Details about highlighted appointment

Shared calendars

Finding symbols like © with Character Map

Character Map lets you insert common symbols and foreign characters into your current document, giving your documents that extra *coup de grâce*. The handy little program displays a box like the one shown in Figure 5-11, listing every available character and symbol.

For example, follow these steps to insert the copyright character — © — somewhere in your work:

1. **Click the Start menu, choose All Programs, select Accessories, choose System Tools, and select Character Map.**

   Make sure that your current font — the name for the style of your letters — appears in the Font box.

Figure 5-11:
Character
Map finds
symbols and
foreign
characters
to place in
your work.

If the font you're using in your document isn't showing, click the Font box's down arrow and then scroll down and click your font when it appears in the drop-down list.

2. **Scan the Character Map box until you see the symbol you're after; then pounce on that character with a double-click.**

The symbol appears in the Characters to Copy box.

3. **Right-click in the document where you want the symbol to appear and choose Paste.**

The symbol appears, conveniently using the same font as your document.

- If you use foreign words a lot, place a shortcut to Character Map on your desktop, ready for quick consultation. Right-click on Character Map from the Start menu and choose Copy. Right-click on your desktop and choose Paste Shortcut. *¡Que conveniencia!*

- Find yourself constantly typing the same foreign character or symbol? Then memorize its shortcut key sequence, the little numbers shown in Character Map's bottom-right corner. See how Figure 5-11 says `Keystroke Alt+0169`? That's the shortcut for the copyright symbol. To paste © into any document any time, hold down Alt and type **0169** using your keyboard's numeric keypad. The copyright symbol appears as you release the Alt key. (Make sure that your Num Lock key is turned on.)

- Table 5-1 lists the shortcut keys for some commonly used symbols.

Table 5-1	Handy Codes for Handy Characters
To Insert This . . .	*. . . Press This*
©	Alt+0169
®	Alt+0174
° (as in 75°)	Alt+0176
™	Alt+0153
£	Alt+0163
¢	Alt+0162

Chapter 6

Briefly Lost, but Quickly Found

In This Chapter

▶ Finding lost windows and files

▶ Finding lost programs, e-mails, songs, and documents

▶ Finding other computers on a network

▶ Finding information on the Internet

▶ Saving common searches

▶ Fine-tuning Windows' searches

Sooner or later, Windows Vista gives you that head-scratching feeling. "Golly," you say, as you tug on your mouse cord, "that stuff was *right there* a second ago. Where did it go?" When Windows Vista starts playing hide-and-seek with your information, this chapter tells you where to search and how to make it stop playing foolish games.

Finding Lost Windows on the Desktop

Windows Vista works more like a spike memo holder than an actual desktop. Every time you open a new window, you toss another piece of information onto the spike. The window on top is easy to spot, but how do you reach the windows lying beneath it? If you can see any part of a buried window's edge or corner, a well-placed click will fetch it, bringing it to the top.

 When your window is completely buried, look at the desktop's taskbar, that strip along your monitor's bottom edge. (If the taskbar's missing, retrieve it with a press of the Windows key, shown in the margin.) Click your missing window's name on the taskbar to dredge it back to the top. (See Chapter 2 for details about the taskbar.)

Still missing? Try Vista's fancy new Flip 3D view by holding down the Windows key and pressing Tab. Shown in Figure 6-1, Vista does a magician's shuffle with your windows, letting you see them hanging in the air. While holding down the Windows key, keep pressing Tab (or rolling your mouse's scroll wheel) until your lost window rises to the front of the pack. Let go of the Windows key to place that window at the top of your desktop.

If your older PC can't handle Vista's 3D View (or if your newer PC's graphics card isn't up to snuff), hold down Alt and press Tab for the two-dimensional substitute that works the same or perhaps better. While holding down Alt, keep pressing Tab until Vista highlights your window; let go of Alt to place your newfound window atop your desktop.

If you're convinced a window is open but still can't find it, spread all your windows across the desktop: Right-click the taskbar along the desktop's bottom and choose Show Windows Side By Side from the menu. It's a last resort, but perhaps you'll spot your missing window in the lineup.

Figure 6-1:
Hold down the Windows key and press Tab repeatedly to cycle through your windows; release the Windows key to drop the top window onto the desktop.

Locating a Missing Program, E-mail, Song, Document, or Other File

Finding information on the Internet rarely takes more than a few minutes, even though you're searching through millions of PCs worldwide. But try to find a document on your own PC, and you may spend days — if it even turns up at all.

To solve the search problem, Vista took a tip from Internet search engines like Google and created an index of your PC's main files. To find your missing file, open the Start menu and click in the Search box along the Start menu's bottom.

Start typing the first few letters of a word, name, or phrase that appears somewhere inside the file you're looking for. As soon as you begin typing, Vista's Start menu begins listing matches. With each letter you type, Vista whittles down the list. After you type enough letters, your lost document floats alone to the top of the list, ready to be opened with a double-click.

For example, typing the first few letters of **Thelonious** into the Start menu's Search box shown in Figure 6-2 brought up every Thelonious Monk song on my PC.

Figure 6-2:
Type a few words from your document, e-mail, or music file, and Vista locates the files, placing the closest matches at the top.

When the Search box comes up empty

Sooner or later, your trusty Search box won't strike gold. When you're faced with an empty list, these tips may help you mine that precious nugget from the veins of riches hidden in your PC:

✔ **Check for typos.** Windows Vista can't tell that "recieve" means you *really* want to find "receive." A typo will kill the search, every time.

✔ **Try the Big Search.** The Start menu's Search box offers simplicity and speed. If it's not coming up with the goods, however, switch to the Start menu's Search command. It brings up a new search window stuffed with so many options that it's slow and awkward. Covered in the "Commanding Vista's Big Search" section, the Search window may be worth a try in an emergency.

✔ **Add places to Vista's index.** Windows Vista normally finds everything in your User account folder, which includes your Documents, Pictures, and Music folders, as well as your e-mail and downloaded Web sites. But if you're storing files elsewhere — perhaps on an external hard drive or a tiny flash drive pushed into your PC's USB port — Vista won't find them unless you tell it about them, a chore covered in this chapter's "Fine-tuning Vista's Searches" section.

✔ **Rebuild the index.** People constantly move files in and out of their PCs. Vista's index tries to keep up, but eventually, the index may lose track of what's what. To start anew, tell Vista to rebuild the index, another chore covered in this chapter's "Fine-tuning Vista's Searches" section. Although Vista rebuilds the index in the background as you work, the process takes several hours. For best results, rebuild your index in the evening and let your PC run all night.

When you spot your file, click its name on the Start menu to open it. Or right-click its name and choose Open File Location from the pop-up menu to see the folder where your file's been hiding away.

✔ Vista's index includes every file in your Documents, Pictures, Music, and Videos folders, which makes storing your files in those folders more important than ever. (Vista doesn't let you search through files stored in accounts of *other* people who may be using your PC.)

✔ The index also includes any files strewn across your desktop, recently deleted files languishing in your Recycle Bin, people you've entered as contacts, and all your e-mail in Windows Mail. (Vista also indexes any files you're sharing in your Public folder — the folder that other PCs can access from a network.)

✔ If you're searching for a common word and Vista turns up too many files, limit your search by typing a short phrase: **Thelonious Monk played Tuesday night**. The more letters of a phrase you type, the better your chances of pinpointing a particular file.

✔ When searching for files, begin typing with the *first* letter of a word or phrase: **t** for Thelonious, for example. If you type **onious**, Vista won't find Thelonious, even though Thelonious contains that string of letters.

✔ The Search Box ignores capital letters. It considers **Bee** and **bee** to be the same insect.

✔ If Vista finds more matches than it can stuff into the small Start menu, shown in Figure 6-2, click the words See All Results directly above the Search box. That brings up the Advanced Search feature, which I cover later in this chapter's "Commanding Vista's Big Search" section.

✔ Want to route your search to the Internet rather than your PC? After typing your word or phrase, click the words Search the Internet, shown directly above the Search box in Figure 6-2. Vista sends your search to the search engine you've chosen in Internet Explorer. (Chapter 8 explains how to assign your search engine of choice to Internet Explorer.)

Finding a Missing File in a Folder

The Start menu's Search box probes Vista's entire index, making sure that it's looked everywhere. But that's overkill when you're poking around inside a single folder, looking randomly for a missing file. To solve the "sea of filenames in a folder" problem, Vista placed a Search box in every folder's upper-right corner. That Search box limits your search to files within that *particular* folder.

To find a missing file within a specific folder, click inside that folder's Search box and begin typing a word or short phrase from your missing file. As you begin typing letters and words, Vista begins filtering out files that don't contain that word or phrase. It keeps narrowing down the candidates until the folder displays only a few files, including, hopefully, your runaway file.

When a folder's Search box locates too many possible matches, bring in some other helping hands: the headings above each column. (For best results, choose Details from the folder's Views button, which lines up your file names in one column, shown in Figure 6-3.) The first column, Name, lists the name of each file; the adjacent columns list specific details about each file.

See the column headers, such as Name, Date Modified, and Type, atop each column? Click any of those headers to sort your files by that term. Here's how to sort by some of the column headers in your Documents folder:

✔ **Name.** Know the first letter of your file's name? Then click here to sort your files alphabetically. You can then pluck your file from the list. Click Name again to reverse the sort order.

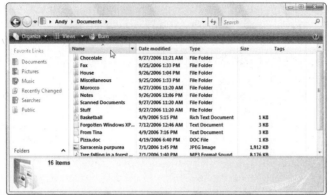

Figure 6-3:
Viewing
files in
Details view
lets you sort
your files
by name,
making
them easier
to find.

✔ **Date Modified.** When you remember the approximate date you last changed a document, click the Date Modified header. That places your newest files atop the list, making them easy to locate. (Clicking Date Modified again reverses the order, a handy way to weed out old files you may no longer need.)

✔ **Type.** This header sorts files by their contents: All your photos group together, for example, as do all your Word documents. It's a handy way to find a few stray photos swimming in a sea of text files.

✔ **Authors.** Microsoft Word and some other programs tack your name onto your work. A click on this label alphabetically sorts the files by their creators' names.

✔ **Tags.** Vista often lets you assign tags to your documents, a task I describe later in this chapter. Adding the tags "Moldy Cheese Photos" to that pungent photo session lets you retrieve those pictures by either typing their tags or sorting a folder's files by their tags.

Whether you're viewing your files as thumbnails, icons, or filenames, the column headers always provide a handy way to sort your files quickly.

Folders usually display about five columns of details, but you can add more columns. In fact, you can sort files by their word count, song length, photo size, creation date, and dozens of other details. To see a list of available detail columns, right-click an existing label along a column's top. When the drop-down menu appears, select More to see the Choose Details dialog box. Click to put check marks next to the new detail columns you'd like to see and then click OK.

Deep sort

A folder's Details view (seen in Figure 6-3) arranges your files into a single column, with oodles of detail columns flowing off to the right. You can sort a folder's contents by clicking the word atop any column: Name, Date Modified, Author, and so on. But Vista's sort features go much deeper, as you'll notice when clicking the little downward pointing arrow to the right of each column's name.

Click the little arrow by the words "Date Modified," for example, and a calendar drops down. Click a date, and the folder quickly displays files modified on that particular date, filtering out all the rest. Beneath the calendar, check boxes also let you view files created Today, Yesterday, Last Week, Earlier This Month, Earlier This Year, or simply "A Long Time Ago."

Similarly, click the arrow next to the Authors column head, and a drop-down menu lists the authors of every document in the folder. Click the check boxes next to the author names you'd like to see, and Vista immediately filters out files created by other people, leaving only the matches.

These hidden filters can be dangerous, however, because you can easily forget that you've turned them on. If you spot a check mark next to any column header, you've left a filter turned on, and the folder is hiding some of its files. To turn off the filter and see *all* that folder's files, click the check mark next to the column header and examine the drop-down menu. Click any checked boxes on that drop-down menu; that removes their check marks and removes the filter.

Sorting, Grouping, and Stacking Files

Sorting your folders by their name, date, or type, described in the previous sections, provides enough organization for most people. To please the meticulous, Vista also lets you organize your files two other ways: *grouping* and *stacking*. What's the difference?

Stacking works much like organizing stray papers into piles on your office desk. You might pile them up by the date you created them, for example, tossing today's work in one big pile, and last week's work in another. Or you might want to put all your unpaid bills in one pile, and the bank statements in another.

Vista does something similar if you choose to stack your files by Date Modified, shown in Figure 6-4, as it tosses your current work in one pile, and last month's work in another. Or, stack your files by Type to separate your spreadsheets from your letters.

Vista's Grouping function also clumps similar items together. But instead of stacking the files into tall piles, Vista spreads them out flat, keeping related items next to each other. Grouping items by Date Modified, shown in Figure 6-5, groups your files by date, but places a label by each group: Last Week, Earlier this Month, Earlier this Year, and others.

To stack or group your files, right-click a blank spot inside the folder and choose either Stack By or Group By from the pop-up menu. Be sure to click a *blank* part inside the folder, which can be difficult in a crowded folder. To "unstack" or "ungroup," follow the same steps, but choose None from the Stack By or Group By menu.

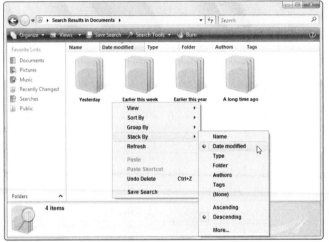

Figure 6-4: Right-click a blank part of a folder and choose Stack By to organize your work into neatly sorted piles.

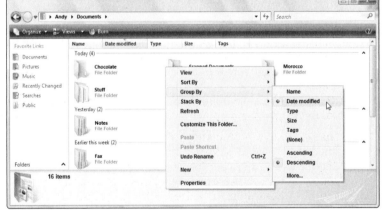

Figure 6-5: Right-click a blank part of a folder and choose Group By to organize your work into groups of similar files.

You can also stack and group by pressing Alt, clicking the View menu, and selecting Group By or Stack By.

There's no right or wrong time to choose Sort, Group, or Stack. It's up to your own preference, and the files you're dealing with at the time. Think of Vista as a card shuffler, able to quickly stack all your Costa Rica vacation photos into one stack. To see your photos, click the stack.

Finding Lost Photos

Windows Vista indexes your e-mail down to the last word, but it can't tell the difference between your Yosemite photos and your photo shoot at Dog Beach. When it comes to photos, the ID work lies in your hands, and these four tips make the chore as easy as possible:

- ✔ **Tag your photos.** When you connect your camera to your PC, described in Chapter 16, Vista graciously offers to copy your photos to your PC. While copying, Vista also asks you to "Tag these pictures." That's your big chance to type in a *tag* — a computer term for a descriptive word or short phrase. Tags give Vista something to index, making the photos easier to retrieve later.

- ✔ **Store shooting sessions in separate folders.** Vista's photo importing program, covered in Chapter 16, automatically creates a new folder to store each session, named after the current date and the tag you choose. But if you're using some other program to dump photos, be sure to create a new folder for each session. Then name the folder with a short description of your session: Sushi Dinner, Parboiling Potatoes, or Truffle Hunt.

- ✔ **Sort by date.** Have you stumbled onto a massive folder that's a huge mishmash of digital photos? Here's a quick sorting trick: Repeatedly click View from the folder's top menu until the photos morph into identifiable thumbnails. Then right-click a blank part of the folder, choose Sort By, and select either Date Modified or Date Taken. Sorting the photos by date usually lines them up in the order you snapped them, turning chaos into organization.

- ✔ **Rename your photos.** Instead of leaving your Belize vacation photos named DSCM1045, DSCM1046, and so on, give them meaningful names: Select all the files in your folder by holding down Ctrl and pressing A. Then right-click the first picture, choose Rename, and type **Belize**. Windows names them as Belize, Belize (2), Belize (3), and so on.

Following those four simple rules helps keep your photo collection from becoming a jumble of files.

Be *sure* to back up your digital photos to a portable hard drive, CDs, DVDs, or another backup method I describe in Chapter 12. If they're not backed up, you'll lose your family history when your PC's hard drive eventually crashes.

Finding Other Computers on a Network

A *network* is simply a group of connected PCs that can share things, such as your Internet connection, files, or a printer. Most people use a network every day without knowing it: Every time you check your e-mail, your PC connects to another PC to grab your waiting messages.

Much of the time, you don't need to care about the other PCs on your network. But when you want to find a connected PC, perhaps to grab the files from the PC in your family room, Vista is happy to help.

To find a PC on your network, choose Network from the Start menu. Vista lists every PC that's connected to your own PC. To browse files on any of those PCs, just double-click their names, as shown in Figure 6-6.

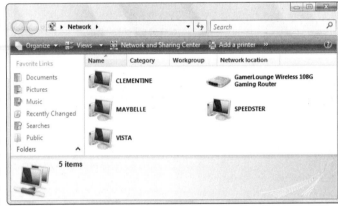

Figure 6-6:
To find computers connected to your PC through a network, click the Start menu and choose Network.

I explain how to create your own network in Chapter 14.

Finding Information on the Internet

When Vista comes up short while digging for information within your PC, tell it to search the Internet instead. Although you could fire up Internet Explorer, you can save a step by using the Start menu's Search box. Click in the Search box, type your words, and click Search the Internet above the Search box.

Vista sends your query to the search engine normally used by Internet Explorer's Search box, covered in Chapter 8.

Saving Your Searches

When you find yourself repeatedly searching for the same pieces of information, save yourself time by *saving* your search. Once you save your search, Vista keeps it current, automatically adding any newly created items that fit your search.

Click your saved search's name, and it opens like any other folder, but with the contents of your search already inside. For an example, click the word Searches, found on the Navigation Pane of every folder. Inside, Vista displays some saved searches that let you find files you've changed recently.

 To save any search, perhaps one you've made from the Start menu's Search box, click the Save Search button (shown in the margin) along the top of the Search window. Type a name for your saved search and click Save.

Your saved search joins those already waiting in the Navigation Pane's Searches area. Tired of seeing an old Search on the list? Right-click its name and choose Delete. (That deletes only the search, not the files listed inside.)

Commanding Vista's Big Search

The Start menu's Search box performs remarkably well for most searches. It's simple, and it almost always delivers the goods promptly. So, how does the Start menu's Search *box* differ from the Start menu's Search *command* that's affixed to the right column?

Well, the Search command works best when the Search box leaves you with too many search results. For example, a search for "ice cream" on your PC may turn up recipes, photographs, Web sites, e-mails, and zillions of other matches.

To narrow down those results, click the Start menu's Search command to bring up the Search folder. The Search folder sports a standard-issue Search box at the top-right corner, as well as a strip of little buttons along the top: All, E-Mail, Document, Picture, Music and Other. Each button works as a filter, letting you narrow the scope of your search.

Type your search into the Search box — **ice cream**, for example — to see every file mentioning "ice cream." Then click the top buttons to narrow your results. Click the E-mail button, for example, to weed out every file but your e-mail mentioning "ice cream." Or click Picture to see pictures you've labeled with the word "ice cream."

Vista's Search command is overkill unless you're dealing with large amounts of information. But when you're stuck with a hard drive full of similar information, the Search command may be the tool you need to begin mining it.

Fine-Tuning Vista's Searches

Vista's Search feature has two dirty secrets. First, Vista doesn't index *every* file on your PC. Although that keeps your searches fast, it also means you may not be able to retrieve a particular file.

Second, Vista's index deteriorates with age, just like a rusty car. This section explains how to solve both problems.

Adding places to Vista's index

Vista indexes the files it thinks you need: everything in your Documents, Pictures, and Music folders, your e-mail, your Contacts, and more. But many people store important files elsewhere, out of the index's reach. Perhaps you've plugged an external hard drive into your PC. Or maybe you store some important files on a networked PC in the other room.

Follow these steps to add those places to the index's usual stomping grounds. (You must own an Administrator account, which I describe in Chapter 13, to add different folders to the index.)

1. **Open the Start menu and choose Control Panel.**

   The Control Panel, Vista's bundle of switches and options described in Chapter 11, appears in a window.

2. **Open the Indexing Options window.**

   On some PCs, you may have to click the System and Maintenance icon first. The Indexing Options window appears, listing the number of indexed files, and the folders it indexes.

3. **Click the Modify button.**

   The Indexed Locations window appears, shown in Figure 6-7, letting you pick and choose which areas of your hard drive should be indexed.

   Note: Only Administrators may see or change indexed locations. If you hold a less mighty account, you must click a Show All Locations button and enter an Administrator account holder's password to see the locations shown at the top of Figure 6-7.

4. Select the areas you want to index and then click OK.

Vista refers to external hard drives and thumbdrives as "removable disks." So, to make Vista index a particular folder on your F drive, click the little downward-pointing arrow next to the F drive's name, shown in Figure 6-7. The folder names tumble beneath the drive's name.

To add a single folder to the index, click the box next to its name. To add the entire drive's contents, click the box next to the drive's name.

When you click OK, Vista adds that location to the index, a process that may take from minutes to hours depending on the number of files.

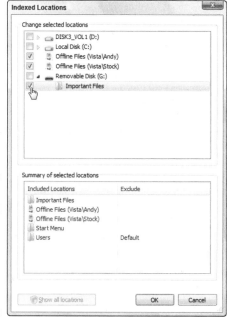

Figure 6-7:
Click to put
a check
mark next to
the areas
you want to
add to the
index.

Rebuilding the index

When Vista's Search feature slows down considerably or doesn't seem to find files you *know* are in the pile, try Vista to rebuild the index from scratch.

Vista's kind enough to re-create its index in the background while you keep working, but to avoid slowing down your PC for several hours, consider sending the rebuild command in the evening. That way, Vista can toil while you sleep, ensuring that you'll have a complete index the next morning.

Follow these steps to rebuild your index:

1. **Open the Start menu and click the Control Panel.**

   The Control Panel appears in a window.

2. **Open the Indexing Options icon.**

   Don't spot it? Click the System and Maintenance icon to reveal the Indexing Options icon.

3. **Click the Advanced button and then click the Rebuild button.**

   Vista warns you, just as I do, that rebuilding the index takes a *long* time.

4. **Click OK.**

   Vista begins indexing anew, waiting until it's finished with the new index before it deletes the old one.

Chapter 7

Printing Your Work

. . . .

. . . .

*O*ccasionally you'll want to slip something away from your PC's whirling electrons and onto something more permanent: A piece of paper.

This chapter tackles that job by explaining all you need to know about printing. Here, you find out how to make that troublesome document fit on a piece of paper without hanging off the edge. I also cover the mysterious *print queue,* a little-known area that lets you cancel documents mistakenly sent to the printer — before they waste all your paper. In addition, when you're ready to spiff up your work with some new fonts, you discover how to install them and view them on the screen, before they're even printed.

Printing Your Masterpiece

Windows Vista shuttles your work off to the printer in any of a half-dozen different ways. Chances are, you'll be using these methods most often:

  ✔ Choose Print from your program's File menu.

  ✔ Right-click your document icon and choose Print.

  ✔ Click the Print button on a program's toolbar.

  ✔ Drag and drop a document's icon onto your printer's icon.

If a dialog box appears, click the OK button; Windows Vista immediately begins sending your pages to the printer. Take a minute or so to refresh your coffee. If the printer is turned on (and still has paper and ink), Windows handles everything automatically. If your coffee cup is still full, keep on working or playing FreeCell. Windows prints your work in the background.

If the printed pages don't look quite right — perhaps the information doesn't fit on the paper correctly or it looks faded — then you need to fiddle around with the print settings or perhaps change the paper quality, as described in the next sections.

- ✔ If you stumble upon a particularly helpful page in the Windows Help system, right-click inside the topic or page and choose Print. (Or, click the page's Print icon, if you spot one.) Windows prints a copy for you to tape to your wall or save in this book.

- ✔ For quick 'n' easy access to your printer, right-click your printer's icon and choose Create Shortcut. Click Yes to confirm, and Windows Vista puts a shortcut to your printer on your desktop. To print things, just drag and drop their icons onto your printer's new shortcut. (You can find your printer's icon by opening the Control Panel from the Start menu and choosing Printer in the Hardware and Sound area.)

- ✔ To print a bunch of documents quickly, select *all* their icons. Then right-click the selected icons and choose Print. Windows Vista quickly shuttles all of them to the printer where they emerge on paper, one after the other.

- ✔ Still haven't installed a printer? Flip to Chapter 11, where I explain how to plug one in and make Windows Vista embrace it.

Peeking at your printed page *before* it hits paper

For many, printing requires a leap of faith: You choose Print from the menu and close your eyes while the thing prints. If you're blessed, the page looks fine. But if you're cursed, you've wasted another sheet of paper.

The Print Preview option, found on nearly every program's File menu, foretells your printing fate *before* the words hit paper. Print Preview compares your current work with your program's page settings and then displays a detailed picture of the printed page. That preview makes it easy to spot off-kilter margins, dangling sentences, and other printing fouls.

Different programs use slightly different Print Preview screens, with some offering more insight than others. But almost any program's Print Preview screen lets you know whether everything will fit onto the page correctly.

If the preview looks fine, choose Print at the window's top to send the work to the printer. If something looks wrong, however, click Close to return to your work and make any necessary adjustments.

Adjusting how your work fits on the page

In theory, Windows *always* displays your work as if it were printed on paper. Microsoft's marketing department calls it *What You See Is What You Get,* forever disgraced with the awful acronym WYSIWYG and its awkward pronunciation: "wizzy-wig." If what you see on-screen *isn't* what you want to see on paper, a trip to the program's Page Setup dialog box, shown in Figure 7-1, usually sets things straight.

Page Setup, found on nearly any program's File menu, offers several ways to flow your work across a printed page (and subsequently your screen). Page Setup dialog boxes differ among programs and print models, but the following list describes the options that you'll find most often and the settings that usually work best.

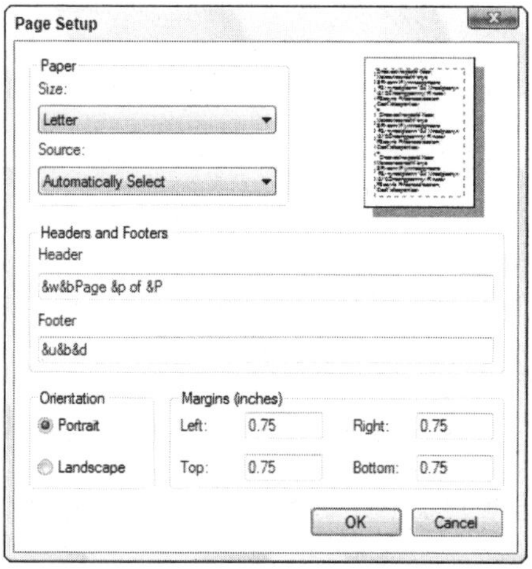

Figure 7-1: Choose Page Setup from a program's File menu to adjust the way your work fits onto a piece of paper.

- ✔ **Size:** Lets your program know what size of paper you're currently using. Leave this option set to Letter to print on standard, 8.5-x-11-inch sheets of paper. Change this setting if you're using legal size paper (8.5 x 14), envelopes, or other paper sizes. (The nearby sidebar, "Printing envelopes without fuss," contains more information about printing envelopes.)

- ✔ **Source:** Choose Automatically Select or Sheet Feeder unless you're using a fancy printer that accepts paper from more than one printer tray. People with two or more printer trays can select the tray containing the correct paper size. Some printers offer Manual Paper Feed, making the printer wait until you slide in that single sheet of paper.

Printing envelopes without fuss

Although clicking the word Envelopes in a program's Page Setup area is fairly easy, printing addresses in the correct spot on the envelope is extraordinarily difficult. Some printer models want you to insert envelopes upside down, while others prefer right side up. Your best bet is to run several tests, placing the envelope into your printer's tray in different ways until you finally stumble on the magic method. (Or you can pull out your printer's manual, if you still have it, and pore over the "proper envelope insertion" pictures.)

After you've figured out the correct method for your printer, tape a successfully printed envelope above your printer and add an arrow pointing to the correct way to insert it.

When you eventually give up on printing envelopes, try using Avery's mailing labels. Buy your preferred size of Avery labels and then download the free Avery Wizard from Avery's Web site (`www.avery.com/us/software/index.jsp`). Compatible with Microsoft Word, the wizard places little boxes on your screen that precisely match the size of your particular Avery labels. Type the addresses into the little boxes, insert the label sheet into your printer, and Word prints everything onto the little stickers. You don't even need to lick them.

Or do like I did: Buy a little rubber stamp with your return address. It's much faster than stickers or printers.

✔ **Header/Footer:** Type secret codes in these boxes to customize what the printer places along the top and bottom of your pages: page numbers, titles, and dates, for example, as well as their spacing. For example, notice the letters *&u&b&p* in the Footer box of Figure 7-1? That means to print the Web page's address along the bottom left side and the current date along the bottom right. (The tip that follows explains how to locate and decipher your particular program's secret codes.)

Unfortunately, programs don't all use the same secret codes for their header and footer. If you spot a little question mark in the Page Setup dialog box's top-right corner, click it; then click inside the Header or Footer box for clues. No little question mark? Then press F1 and search for **page setup** in the program's Help menu.

✔ **Orientation:** Leave this option set to Portrait to print normal pages that read vertically like a letter. Choose Landscape only when you want to print sideways, a great way to print wide spreadsheets. (If you choose Landscape, the printer automatically prints the page that way; you don't need to slide the paper sideways into the printer.)

✔ **Margins:** Feel free to reduce the margins to fit everything on a single sheet of paper. You may need to change them for homework requirements, as well.

✔ **Printer:** If you have more than one printer installed on your computer or network, click this button to choose which one to print your work. Click here to change that printer's settings as well, a job discussed in the next section.

When you're finished adjusting settings, click the OK button to save your changes. (Click the Print Preview button, if it's offered, to make sure that everything looks right.)

To find the Page Setup box in some programs (including Internet Explorer), click the little arrow next to the program's Printer icon and choose Page Setup from the menu that drops down.

Adjusting your printer's settings

When you choose Print from a program's File menu, Windows offers one last chance to spruce up your printed page. The Print dialog box, shown in Figure 7-2, lets you route your work to any printer installed on your computer or network. While there, you can adjust the printer's settings, choose your paper quality, and select the pages you'd like to print.

Figure 7-2:
The Print dialog box lets you choose your printer and adjust its settings.

You're likely to find these settings waiting in the dialog box:

TIP

- **Select Printer:** Ignore this option if you have only one printer because Windows chooses it automatically. If your computer has access to more than one printer, click the one that should receive the job.

  The printer you may see called Microsoft XPS Document Writer sends your work to a specially formatted file, usually to be printed or distributed professionally. Chances are, you'll never use it.

- **Page Range:** Select All to print your entire document. To print just a few of its pages, select the Pages option button and enter the page numbers you want to print. For example, enter **1-4, 6** to leave out page 5 of a 6-page document. If you've highlighted a paragraph, choose Selection to print that particular paragraph — a great way to print the important part of a Web page and leave out the rest.

- **Number of Copies:** Most people leave this set to 1 copy, unless everybody in the boardroom wants their own copy. You can only choose Collate if your printer offers that option. (Most don't, leaving you to sort the pages yourself.)

- **Preferences:** Click this button to see a dialog box like the one in Figure 7-3, where you can choose options specific to your own printer model. The Preferences dialog box typically lets you select different grades of paper, choose between color or black and white, set the printing quality, and make last-minute corrections to the page layout.

Figure 7-3:
The Printing Preferences dialog box lets you change settings specific to your printer, including the paper type and printing quality.

Canceling a print job

Just realized you sent the wrong 26-page document to the printer? So you panic and flip the printer's off switch. Unfortunately, most printers automatically pick up where they left off when you turn them back on.

To purge your mistake from your printer's memory, double-click your Printer's icon (which sometimes sits near the Taskbar's clock) to reveal the *print queue,* shown in Figure 7-4. Right-click your mistaken document and choose Cancel to end the job. When you turn your printer back on, it won't keep printing that same darn document.

- ✔ If you can't find your printer's icon, try choosing Control Panel from the Start menu and choose the Printers icon.

- ✔ The print queue, also known as the print spooler, lists every document waiting patiently to reach your printer. Feel free to change their printing order by dragging and dropping them up or down the list. (You can't move anything in front of the currently printing document, though.)

- ✔ If your printer runs out of paper during a job and stubbornly halts, add more paper. Then to start things flowing again, open the Print Queue, right-click your document, and choose Restart. (Some printers let you push their Online button to begin printing again.)

- ✔ You can send items to the printer even when you're working in the coffee shop with your laptop. When you connect the laptop to your office printer, the print queue notices and begins sending your files. (Beware: When they're in the print queue, documents are formatted for your specific printer model. If you subsequently connect your laptop to a *different* printer model, the print queue's waiting documents won't print correctly.)

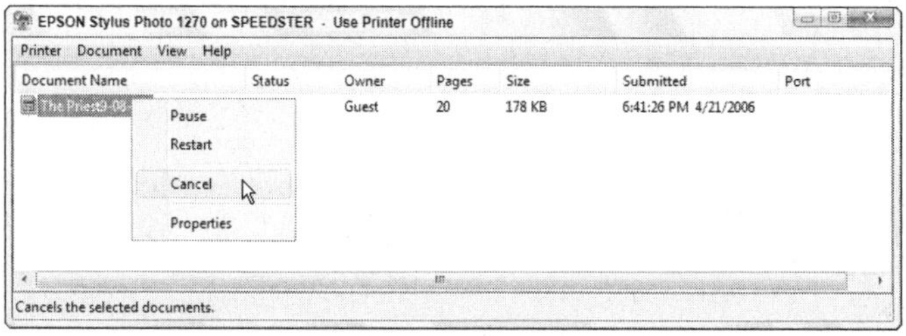

Figure 7-4:
Use the print queue to cancel a print job.

Printing a Web page

Although information-chocked Web pages look awfully tempting, *printing* those Web pages is rarely satisfying because they look so awful on paper. When sent to the printer, Web pages often run off the page's right side, consume zillions of additional pages, or are much too small to read.

To make matters worse, all those colorful advertisements can suck your printer's color cartridges dry fairly quickly. Only four things make for successfully printed Web pages, and I rank them in order of success:

 ✔ **Use the Web page's built-in Print option.** Some, but not all, Web sites offer a tiny menu option called Print This Page, Text Version, Printer-Friendly Version, or something similar. That option tells the Web site to strip out its garbage and reformat the page so that it fits onto a sheet of paper. This option is the most reliable way to print a Web page.

 ✔ **Choose Print Preview from your browser's File or Print menu.** After 15 years, some Web page designers noticed that people want to print their pages, so, they tweaked the settings, making their pages *automatically* reformat themselves when printed. You may have stumbled onto one of those sites.

 ✔ **Copy the portion you want and paste into WordPad.** Try selecting the desired text from the Web page, copying it, and pasting it into WordPad or another word processor. Delete any unwanted remnants, adjust the margins, and print the portion you want. Chapter 5 explains how to select, copy, and paste.

 ✔ **Copy the entire page and paste it into a word processor.** Although it's lots of work, it's an option. Choose Select All from Internet Explorer's Edit menu. Then choose Copy (which is also on the Edit menu) or press Ctrl+C. Next, open Microsoft Word or another full-featured word processor and paste it inside a new document. By hacking away at the unwanted portions, you can sometimes end up with something printable.

These tips may also come in handy for moving a Web page from screen to paper:

 ✔ The only surefire way to print a Web page is if the Web page's designer was thoughtful enough to build in a print option. If you spot an E-Mail option but no Print option, e-mail the page to yourself. You'll probably have better success printing it as an e-mail message.

 ✔ To print just a few paragraphs of a Web page, use the mouse to select the portion you're after. (I cover selecting in Chapter 5.) Choose Print from Internet Explorer's File menu to open the Print dialog box, shown in Figure 7-2, and then click the word Selection in the Page Range box.

✔ If a Web page's table or photo insists on vanishing off the paper's right edge, try printing the page in Landscape mode rather than Portrait. See the "Adjusting how your work fits on the page" section, earlier in this chapter, for details on Landscape mode.

Installing new fonts

Fonts change the appearance of letters, adding a different *mood* to your document. Windows Vista comes with several dozen different fonts, and you can view them all fairly easily.

To see all your currently installed fonts, open the Control Panel from the Start menu, click Classic View, and double-click the Fonts icon (shown in the margin). Windows Vista lists all your fonts by name. Double-click any font — the Impact font icon, for example — and Windows Vista shows how that font looks on the printed page, as shown in Figure 7-5. (Click the Print button to send a sample to your printer.)

Printing your Address Book

Although backing up Windows Mail is important, it's downright handy to print a list of your contacts — or at least print contact information for the people you'll be meeting that day. Here's how to turn a piece of paper into a personalized, on-the-fly address book:

1. Open your Contacts folder and select the people to print.

Click your username atop your Start menu's top-right corner and then open your Contacts folder. Press Ctrl+A to highlight *all* your contacts or hold down Ctrl and click the names you want to print.

2. Click the folder's Print button, select your printer, if necessary, and choose your Print Style.

The Print Style section offers three ways to print your contact sheet:

✔ **Memo:** Print *everything* about the contact.

✔ **Business Card:** Print standard business card items for each person, including name, phone, address, company, and e-mail address.

✔ **Phone List:** Print each contact's name and phone numbers (cell, fax, home, business).

3. Click Print.

Windows Mail prints a neatly formatted list according to your specifications. If you've never printed your contacts before, try each of the three printing options to see their look. It's worth three sheets of paper.

Figure 7-5:
Double-click
any font's
name to see
what it
would look
like on
paper.

If you're not happy with your current font selection, you can buy or download new ones and install them on your computer. Most fonts sold at stores come with installation programs that spare you the messy details in Windows Vista's font installer. But if your new font didn't come with an installation package, here's how to install it:

1. **Place your new font in your Documents folder.**

Many downloaded fonts arrive inside a *compressed* folder, also called a *zipped* folder. (Zipped folders have a little zipper on their icon, shown in the margin.) If your font arrived this way, right-click its icon, choose Extract All, and let the wizard extract its contents to a folder inside your Documents folder.

If you'll be installing a lot of fonts, create a new folder called Fonts inside your Documents folder and use it as a dumping ground for newly extracted font folders.

2. **Right-click the downloaded font and choose Install.**

The downloaded font's icon looks like one of the two shown in the margin. When you choose Install, Vista adds the font to your Control Panel's Fonts area, where it's available to all your programs.

✔ To delete any unwanted fonts, right-click their names in the Control Panel's Fonts area and choose Delete.

✔ Please don't delete any fonts that came with Windows Vista. Just delete fonts *you've* installed. Deleting some of Windows Vista's built-in fonts will remove letters from your menus, making Windows Vista even *more* difficult to use.

> ✔ If you can't resist downloading free fonts from the Internet, remember that Windows Vista can handle TrueType fonts, OpenType fonts, and PostScript fonts. And if you *really* get into fonts, you'll want to buy a font management program sold at most office supply stores. Finally, always scan downloaded fonts with your virus checker.

Troubleshooting your printer

If you can't print your document, are you *sure* that the printer is turned on, plugged into the wall, full of paper, and connected securely to your computer with a cable?

Choosing the right paper for your printer

If you've strolled the aisles at an office-supply store lately, you've noticed a bewildering array of paper choices. Sometimes the paper's packaging lists its application: Premium Inkjet Paper, for example, for high-quality memos. Here's a list of the paper types to keep on hand for different jobs. Before printing, be sure to click the Printer's Preferences area to select the grade of paper you're using for that job.

✔ **Junk:** Keep some cheap or scrap paper around for testing the printer, printing quick drafts, leaving notes to spouses, and printing other on-the-fly jobs. Botched print jobs work great here; just use the paper's other side. (Be sure you insert the paper in the right direction.)

✔ **Letter quality:** Bearing the words Premium or Bright White, this paper works fine for letters, memos, and other things designed for showing to others.

✔ **Photos:** You can print photos on any type of paper, but they look good only on actual Photo-Quality paper — the expensive stuff.

Slide the paper carefully into your printer tray so that the picture prints on the glossy, shiny side. Some photo paper uses a little cardboard sheet beneath it, which helps glide the paper smoothly through the printer.

✔ **Labels:** They've never sent me a T-shirt, but I still say that Avery's Wizard program (www.avery.com) makes it easy to print Avery labels and cards. The wizard teams up with Microsoft Word to mesh perfectly with Avery's preformatted mailing labels, greeting cards, business cards, CD labels, and many others.

✔ **Transparencies:** For powerful PowerPoint presentations, buy special transparent plastic sheets designed to be used with your type of printer.

Before plunking down your money, make sure that your paper is designed specifically for your printer type, be it laser or inkjet. Laser printers heat the pages, and some paper can't take the heat.

If so, then try plugging the printer into different outlets, turning it on, and seeing whether its power light comes on. If the light stays off, your printer's power supply is probably blown.

Printers are almost always cheaper to replace than repair. But if you've grown fond of your printer, grab an estimate from a repair shop before discarding it.

If the printer's power light beams brightly, check these things before giving up:

- ✔ Make sure that a sheet of paper hasn't jammed itself inside the printer somewhere. (A steady pull usually extricates jammed paper; sometimes opening and closing the lid starts things moving again.)

- ✔ Does your inkjet printer still have ink in its cartridges? Does your laser printer have toner? Try printing a test page: Click the Start menu, open the Control Panel, and choose Printers. Right-click your printer's icon, choose Properties, and click the Print Test Page button to see whether the computer and printer can talk to each other.

- ✔ Try updating the printer's *driver,* the little program that helps it talk with Windows Vista. Visit the printer manufacturer's Web site, download the newest driver for your particular printer model, and run its installation program.

Finally, here are a couple of tips to help you protect your printer and cartridges:

- ✔ Turn off your printer when you're not using it. Inkjet printers, especially, should be turned off when they're not in use. The heat tends to dry the cartridges, shortening their life.

- ✔ Don't unplug your inkjet printer to turn it off. Always use the on/off switch. The switch ensures that the cartridges slide back to their home positions, keeping them from drying out or clogging.

Part III
Getting Things Done on the Internet

The 5th Wave   By Rich Tennant

"Honey—remember that pool party last summer where you showed everyone how to do the limbo in just a sombrero and a dish towel? Well, look at what the MSN Daily Video Download is."

In this part . . .

The Internet used to be clean, quiet, and helpful, just like a new library. You could find detailed information about nearly anything, read newspapers and magazines around the world, listen to music in the media section, or quietly browse the card catalogs.

Today, this wonderful global library has been bombarded with noisy people who toss ads in front of what you're trying to read. Some won't even let you close that book you inadvertently opened — the book keeps opening back up to the wrong page. Pickpockets and thieves stalk the halls.

This part of the book helps you turn the Internet back into that quiet, helpful library it once was. It shows how to stop pop-up ads, browser hijackers, and spyware. It explains how to send and receive e-mail so that you can keep in touch with friends.

Finally, it shows you how to stay safe using Windows Vista's new User Account Protection, firewall, security center, cookie manager, and other tricks to help bring back the Internet you love.

Chapter 8

Cruising the Web

Some people consider an Internet connection to be optional, but Windows Vista prefers mandatory, thank you very much. Even when being installed, Windows Vista starts reaching for the Internet, eager for any hint of a connection. After checking in with the Internet, for example, Windows Vista kindly nudges your computer's clock to the correct time. Some motives are less pure: Windows Vista checks with Microsoft to make sure that you're not installing a pirated copy.

This chapter explains how to connect with the Internet, visit Web sites, and find all the good stuff online. For ways to keep out the bad stuff, be sure to visit Chapter 10 for a quick primer on safe computing. The Internet's full of bad neighborhoods, and that chapter explains how to avoid viruses, spyware, hijackers, and other Internet parasites.

Once your computer's wearing its appropriate helmet and kneepads, however, hop onto the Internet and enjoy the ride.

What Is the Internet?

Today, most people take the Internet for granted, much like a telephone line. Instead of marveling at the Internet's internal gearing, they've grown accustomed to this new land called *cyberspace,* and its healthy stock of attractions:

- **Library:** The Internet is stuffed with educational material: classic books, hourly news updates, foreign language dictionaries, specialized encyclopedias, and more. Visit RefDesk (`www.refdesk.com`) for a detailed list of some of the Internet's best free reference materials.

- **Store:** Although the Internet seemed like a novelty ten years ago, today the Internet revolves around making money. You can purchase nearly anything available in stores (and some things *not* sold in stores) on the Internet and ship it to your thatch hut. Amazon (`www.amazon.com`) even lets you listen to song snippets and read reviews before putting that John Coltrane CD on your credit card.

- **Communicator:** Some people treat the Internet as a private postal service for sending messages to friends, coworkers, and even strangers around the world. Unfortunately, unwelcome marketers do the same, filling everybody's inboxes with increasingly desperate, unsolicited sales pitches known as *spam*. (I cover Windows Mail, Vista's e-mail program, in Chapter 9.)

- **Time waster:** When sitting in a waiting room, everybody naturally reaches for the magazine table. The Internet, too, offers zillions of ways to waste time. Jumping from one Web site to another is much like flipping pages in a magazine, but each flip often reveals a completely different, yet oddly related, magazine, brimming with fascinating information. Or at least it seems so at the time.

- **Entertainment:** The Internet brings not only a movie's show times into your home, but also its trailers, cast lists, reviews, and celebrity gossip. If you're tired of movies that week, browse for online games, research exotic travel destinations, or look up sporting statistics.

Simply put, the Internet is a 24-hour international library that's stocked with something for everyone.

- Just as a television channel surfer flips from channel to channel, a Web surfer moves from page to page, sampling the vast and esoteric piles of information.

- Almost every government but China loves the Internet. In the United States, the FBI shares pictures of its ten most wanted criminals (`www.fbi.gov`), and the Internal Revenue Service (`www.irs.ustreas.gov`) lets Internet users make free copies of tax forms 24 hours a day. Protesting a parking ticket? Your city's Web site probably hands you the right number faster than the phone book.

- Universities and scientists love the network, too, because they can file grant forms more quickly than ever. Worried about the goo coagulating in the crevices of your bromeliads? The Internet's famed botanical site (`www.botany.net`) enables researchers to study everything from Australian acacias to zoosporic fungi.

✔ Nearly all computer companies support their products on the Internet. Visitors can swap messages with technicians and other users about their latest computing woes. You may be able to download a fix or uncover the magic sequence of keystrokes that solves a problem.

What's an ISP, and Why Do I Need One?

Everybody needs four things to connect to the Web: a computer, Web browser software, a modem, and an Internet service provider (ISP).

You already have the computer, and Vista comes with a Web browser called Internet Explorer. Most PCs include a built-in modem. (If yours doesn't, you'll find out when you first try to set up your ISP, as I describe in the next section.)

That means most people need to find only an ISP. Although television signals come wafting through the air to your TV set for free, you must pay an ISP for the privilege of surfing the Web. Specifically, you pay the ISP for a password and account name. When your computer's modem connects to your ISP's computers, Internet Explorer automatically enters your password and account name, and you're ready to surf the Web.

Don't know which ISP to choose? First, different ISPs serve different areas. Ask your friends, neighbors, or local librarians how they connect, and whether they recommend their ISP. Call several ISPs for a rate quote and then compare rates. Most bill on a monthly basis; if you're not happy, you can always switch.

✔ Although a few ISPs charge for each minute you're connected, most charge a flat monthly fee between $15 and $50 for unlimited service. Make sure that you know your rate before hopping aboard, or you may be surprised at the month's end.

✔ Most free ISPs went out of business when the bottom fell out of the Internet market. At the time of this writing, you can still find limited Internet access for free from Juno (www.juno.com) and NetZero (www.netzero.com), but you have to peek around the ads to see the screen.

✔ ISPs let you connect to the Internet in a variety of ways. The slowest ISPs use a dialup modem and an ordinary phone line. Faster still are *broadband* connections: special DSL or ISDN lines provided by some phone companies, and the even faster cable modems, supplied by your cable company. When shopping for speedy ISPs, your geographic location usually determines your options, unfortunately.

> ✔ Some ISPs let their tech-savvy customers create their *own* Web pages for other Internet members to visit. Show the world pictures of your kids and cats, share your favorite recipes, talk about your favorite car waxes, or swap tips on constructing fishing flies or prom gowns.

Setting Up Internet Explorer the First Time

Windows Vista constantly looks for a working Internet connection in your PC. If it finds one, either through a network or wireless hotspot, you're set: Vista passes the news along to Internet Explorer, and your PC can connect to the Internet immediately. If Vista can't find the Internet, though — a frequent occurrence with dialup modems — the job's up to you.

To guide you smoothly through the turmoil of setting up an Internet connection, Vista passes you a questionnaire, quizzing you about the details. After a bit of interrogation, Vista helps connect your computer to your ISP so that you can Web surf like the best of them.

Setting up a wired or wireless network? Vista should automatically find the network's Internet connection and share it with every PC on your network. If not, see Chapter 14 for troubleshooting details.

To transfer your existing Internet account settings to or from another computer, use Windows Vista's Easy Transfer program, covered in Chapter 19. The program copies one PC's Internet settings into the other PC, sparing you the bother of following these steps.

Here's what you need to get started:

> ✔ **Your username, password, and access phone number.** If you don't have an ISP yet, the wizard finds you one, so grab a pencil and paper. (The wizard's ISP suggestions are a tad pricey, however.)

> ✔ **A plugged-in modem.** Most new computers come with a modem lodged in their innards. To see whether one's inside of yours, look for telephone jacks on the back of your computer, near where all the other cables protrude. Then connect a standard phone cable between that jack (the computer's jack says *Line,* not *Phone*) and the phone jack in your wall.

Whenever your Internet connection gives you log-on problems, head here and run through the following steps. The wizard walks you through your current settings, letting you make changes. Summon the wizard by following these steps:

1. **Click the Start button and choose Connect To.**

   The Connect To button fetches a list of every way your PC currently knows how to connect with the Internet. But when Vista can't find a way for your PC to connect, it comes up with an empty list.

   Instead, Vista may complain that it can't find any wireless networks in range of your PC. If so, ignore its whines and move to Step 2.

    If Vista did find a *wireless* network, by chance, you're in luck. You can hop aboard the signal by double-clicking the network's name. (I cover wireless networks in Chapter 14.)

2. **Choose Set Up a Connection or Network.**

   Scour the window's fine print for this option. When clicked, depending on your PC's model and setup, Vista may display any or all of these options:

   • **Connect to the Internet:** Vista makes yet another valiant effort to sniff out an Internet signal. Broadband users should click here, for example, to let Vista find and automatically set up their Internet connection.

   • **Set Up a Wireless Router or Access Point:** Head here to set up a private wireless Internet connection for your home or office, a task I cover in Chapter 14.

   • **Manually Connect to a Wireless Network:** If a wireless network demands a name and password, head here to enter them. You click here mostly when connecting to paid wireless networks at airports or coffee shops.

   • **Set Up a Wireless Ad Hoc (Computer-to-Computer) network:** Very rarely used, this option lets you connect two or more PCs for exchanging files and other information.

   • **Set Up a Dial-Up Connection:** This one lets you tell Vista what to do with that phone line you've plugged into your PC's phone jack.

   • **Connect to a Workplace:** This setting lets you connect securely to your office — if your office network supports this sophisticated type of connection. You'll need the settings and instructions from your office's computer department.

   • **Connect to a Bluetooth Personal Area Network (PAN):** If your PC has Bluetooth — a short-range form of wireless that replaces cables — click here to set up the connection. You head here to connect with Bluetooth cell phones, for example.

3. **Choose Set Up a Dial-Up Connection.**

   Because you're not choosing wireless or broadband, dialup is your only Internet connection option. To speed things along, Vista passes you a questionnaire, seen in Figure 8-1, ready for you to enter your dialup ISP's information.

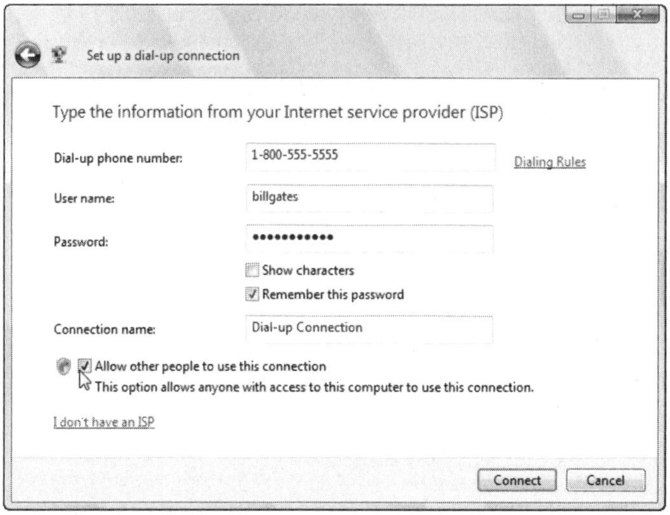

Figure 8-1:
Enter your
ISP's dial-up
phone
number,
your
username,
and your
password.

4. **Enter your dialup ISP's information.**

   Here's where you enter your three all-important pieces of information: Your ISP's dialup number, your username, and your password, as described in the following list.

   - **Dial-up Phone Number:** Enter the phone number your ISP gave you, complete with the area code.

   - **User-Name:** This isn't necessarily your own name, but the username your ISP assigned to you when giving you the account. (It's often the first part of your e-mail address, as well.)

   - **Password:** Type your password here. To make sure that you're entering your password correctly, check the box called Show Characters. Then uncheck the box when you've entered the password without typos.

     Be sure to check Remember This Password. That keeps you from reentering your name and password each time you want to dial the Internet. (*Don't* check that box if you don't want your roommate or others to be able to dial your connection.)

   - **Connection Name:** Vista simply names your connection Dial-Up Connection. Change it to something more descriptive if you're juggling dialup accounts from several ISPs.

   - **Allow Other People to Use This Connection:** Check this option to let people with other user accounts on your PC log on with this connection.

Clicking the words I Don't Have an ISP brings up a window where you can sign up with Microsoft's own ISP or with one of Microsoft's partners.

Click the words Dialing Rules, next to the phone number. There, you can enter key details like your country, area code, and whether you need to dial a number to reach an outside line. Windows remembers this information, making sure that it dials a 1 if you're dialing outside your area code, for example. Laptoppers should visit Dialing Rules for every city they visit.

5. Click the Connect button.

If you're lucky, your PC connects to the Internet (but doesn't offer any clues that you've connected). Load Internet Explorer from the Start menu, and see if it lets you visit Web sites.

If Internet Explorer still can't visit the Internet, move to Step 6.

6. Click the Start menu and choose Connect To.

Your newly created dialup connection will be waiting, shown in Figure 8-2.

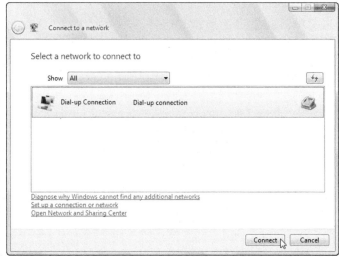

Figure 8-2:
Click your newly created dialup listing and click Connect to dial the Internet.

7. Click the Dial-Up Internet connection and click Connect.

Vista tosses one more screen in your face, shown in Figure 8-3. This gives you a chance to type in your password, for example, if you didn't check Remember This Password in Step 4. It's also where you can tweak your connection settings, handy for temporarily changing the phone number, for example.

Figure 8-3:
Change the
phone
number, if
necessary,
and then
click Dial to
dial the
Internet.

8. **Click Dial to dial the Internet and connect to your ISP.**

You're done. Windows Vista automatically leaps into action, uses your settings to call your Internet provider, and lets you know when it's connected.

Then it's time to load Internet Explorer from the Start menu and start browsing. In the future, though, just load Internet Explorer when you want to browse. Your PC automatically dials the Internet using the connections you've created here.

Always plugging its own products, Microsoft drops you off at one of its own Web pages (Windows Live), and you're ready to browse. Need a place to go for a quick test? Log on to www.andyrathbone.com and see what happens.

Don't be afraid to bug your ISP for help. The best ISPs come with technical support lines. A member of the support staff can talk you through the installation process.

Internet Explorer doesn't automatically hang up when you're done browsing. To make your PC hang up the phone when you close Internet Explorer, choose Internet Options from the program's Tools menu and click the Connections tab. Click the Settings button and then the Advanced button. Finally, put a check mark by the words Disconnect When Connection May No Longer Be Needed and click OK.

But I want to see some pop-ups!

Early versions of Internet Explorer had no way to stop pop-up advertisements from exploding across your screen. Internet Explorer now offers a pop-up ad blocker that stops 90 percent of them. To make sure that it's turned on, choose Pop-up Blocker from Internet Explorer's Tools menu and make sure that no check mark appears in the Turn Off Pop-up Blocker box.

If you *want* to see pop-ups on certain sites, that same menu lets you choose Pop-up Blocker Settings. Add the Web site address, and Internet Explorer allows that site's pop-ups to pop unblocked.

If a site tries to send a pop-up ad or message, Internet Explorer places a strip along its top edge saying, `A pop-up was blocked. To see this pop-up or additional options, click here.` Click the strip to do any one of these three things: temporarily allow that pop-up to appear, always allow pop-ups from that particular site, or change the pop-up blocker's settings.

Finally, to stop the informational strip from making that obnoxious pop noise when it stops a pop-up, choose Pop-up Blocker from Internet Explorer's Tools menu, choose Pop-up Blocker Settings, and remove the check mark from the Play a Sound When a Pop-Up Is Blocked box.

Navigating the Web with Microsoft Internet Explorer

Your Web browser is your Internet surfboard — your transportation between the Internet's thousands of Web sites. Internet Explorer comes free with Windows Vista, so many people use it out of convenience. Other people prefer browsers published by other software companies, such as Mozilla's Firefox (`www.getfirefox.com`).

Simply put, you're not forced to stick with Internet Explorer. Feel free to try other browsers, as they all do pretty much the same thing: take you from one Web site to another.

Moving from Web page to Web page

All browsers work basically the same way. Every Web page comes with a specific address, just like houses do. Internet Explorer lets you move between pages in three different ways:

✔ By pointing and clicking a button or link that automatically whisks you
away to another page

✔ By typing a complicated string of code words (the Web address) into the
Address box of the Web browser and pressing Enter

✔ By clicking the navigation buttons on the browser's toolbar, which is
usually at the top of the screen

Clicking links

The first way is the easiest. Look for *links* — highlighted words or pictures on
a page — and click them. See how the mouse pointer turned into a hand
(shown in the margin) as it pointed at the word *Books* in Figure 8-4? Click that
word to see more information about my books. Many words on this page are
links, as well; the mouse pointer becomes a hand when near them, and the
words become underlined. Click any linked word to see pages dealing with
that link's particular subject.

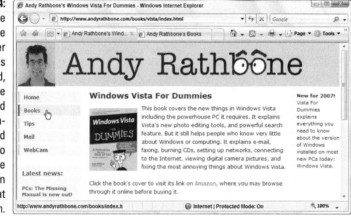

Figure 8-4:
When the
mouse
pointer
becomes
a hand,
click the
underlined
or high-
lighted word
or picture to
see more
information
about that
item.

Web page designers get mighty creative these days, and without the little
hand pointer, it's often hard to tell where to point and click. Some buttons
look like standard elevator buttons; others look like fuzzy dice or tiny vegetables. But when you click a button, the browser takes you to the page relating
to that button. Clicking the fuzzy dice may bring up a betting-odds sheet for
local casinos, for example, and vegetables may bring information about the
local farmers market.

Typing Web addresses in the Address box

The second method is the most difficult. If a friend gives you a napkin with a cool Web page's address written on it, you need to type the Web site's address into your browser's Address box yourself. You'll do fine, as long as you don't misspell anything. See the Web site address for my Web site along the top of Figure 8-4? I typed www.andyrathbone.com into the Address box. When I pressed Enter, Internet Explorer scooted me to my Web page. (You don't need to type the http:// part, thank goodness.)

Using Internet Explorer's toolbar

Finally, you can maneuver through the Internet by clicking various buttons on Internet Explorer's toolbar, which sits at the top of the screen. Table 8-1 offers a handy reference of the important navigation buttons.

Hover your mouse pointer over a confusing Internet Explorer button to see its purpose in life.

Table 8-1	Navigating with Internet Explorer's Buttons	
This Button . . .	*Is Called This . . .*	*And It Does This . . .*
⬅	Back	Pointed and clicked yourself into a dead end? Click the Back button to head for the last Web page you visited. If you click the Back button enough times, you wind up back at your home page, where you began.
➡	Forward	After you click the Back button, you can click Forward to revisit a page, too.
☆	Favorites Center	Clicking the Favorites button along the top reveals the Favorites Center, a list of links leading to your favorite Web sites.
✚	Add to Favorites	Click this yellow plus sign to add your currently viewed Web page to your Favorites list.
🏠 ▾	Home	If you get stuck as you explore the Internet, click the Home button along the top to move back into familiar territory.

(continued)

Table 8-1 *(continued)*

This Button . . .	Is Called This . . .	And It Does This . . .
	RSS Feed	When this orange button lights up, you know the site offers Real Simple Syndication, a quick way to read the site's headlines without actually visiting.
	Print	Click here to print the Web site as you see it. (Click the tiny arrow to its right for printing options, including seeing a preview.)
Page ▼	Page	These options relate to the current page: Enlarging its text size, for example, or saving it as a file.
Tools ▼	Tools	This button opens a menu full of Internet Explorer tweaks, letting you make adjustments to the pop-up blocker and phishing filter, among others.

Making Internet Explorer open to your favorite site

Your Web browser automatically displays a Web site when you first log on. That Web site is called your *home page,* and you can tell Internet Explorer to use any site you want for your home page by following these steps:

1. **Visit your favorite Web site.**

   Choose any Web page you like. I use Google News (`news.google.com`) so Internet Explorer always opens with the hour's current headlines.

2. **Choose the tiny arrow to the right of the Home icon and choose Add or Change Home Page.**

   The new, security-conscious Internet Explorer asks whether you'd like to use that Web page as your only home page.

3. **Click Use This Webpage As Your Only Home Page and click Yes.**

   When you click Yes, seen in Figure 8-5, Internet Explorer always opens to the page you're currently viewing.

   Clicking No sticks with your current home page, which starts out as Microsoft's Windows Live site.

Figure 8-5:
Click Use
This
Webpage
As Your Only
Home Page,
and Internet
Explorer
always
opens to
that page.

After Internet Explorer remembers your chosen home page, you can move around the Internet, searching for topics in Google (www.google.com) or other search engines, simply pointing and clicking different links.

✔ A home page of a Web site is its "cover," like the cover of a magazine. Whenever you jump to a Web site, you usually jump to the site's home page, and start browsing from there.

✔ If your home page is suddenly hijacked to a different site and these instructions don't fix it, then it's probably been hijacked by evil forces. Read the spyware section in Chapter 10.

✔ Internet Explorer lets you choose several pages as home pages, loading each one simultaneously and placing a tab atop each page for switching between them. To add home pages to your collection, choose Add This Webpage to Your Home Page Tabs in Step 3 of the preceding list (Figure 8-5).

Revisit favorite places

Sooner or later, you'll stumble across a Web page that's indescribably delicious. To make sure that you can find it again later, add it to Internet Explorer's built-in list of favorite pages by following these steps:

1. **Click the Add to Favorites icon (shown in the margin) on Internet Explorer's toolbar.**

   A little menu drops down.

2. **Click Add to Favorites from the drop-down menu and click the Add button.**

Internet Explorer's secret history of your Web visits

Internet Explorer keeps a record of every Web site you visit. Although Internet Explorer's History list provides a handy record of your computing activities, it's a spy's dream.

To keep tabs on what Internet Explorer is recording, click your Favorites button and click the History icon on the drop-down menu. Internet Explorer lists every Web site you've visited in the past 20 days. Feel free to sort the entries by clicking the little arrow to the right of the word History. You can sort them by date, alphabetically, most visited, or by the order you've visited on that particular day — a handy way to jump back to that site you found interesting this morning.

To delete a single entry from the history, right-click it and choose Delete from the menu. To delete the entire list, exit the Favorites area. Then choose Internet Options from Internet Explorer's Tools menu and click the Delete button in the Browsing History section. A menu appears, letting you delete your History and other items.

To turn off the History, click the Settings button instead of the Delete button. Then in the History section, change the Days To Keep Pages in History option to 0.

A box appears, offering to name the Web page by its title — the words that appear on the tab at the page's top. Feel free to shorten the title so that it fits better on the narrow Favorites menu.

When you're happy with the name, click the Add button to add the page to your Favorites list.

 Whenever you want to return to that page, click Internet Explorer's Favorites button. When the Favorites menu drops down, click your favorite site's name.

 Librarian-types like to organize their menu of favorite links: Right-click the Add Favorites button and choose Organize Favorites. That lets them create folders for storing similar and group-related links in single folders.

Don't see your favorites on the drop-down menu when you click the Favorites button? Click the word Favorites at the menu's top to switch to them. (You may be looking at the History, covered in the sidebar, or the RSS feeds, which list a site's headline.)

Finding things on the Internet

Just as finding a book in a library without a card catalog is nearly impossible, finding a Web site on the Internet without a good index is nearly impossible, too. Luckily, Internet Explorer lets you access an index — known as a search engine — through the Search box in its top-right corner.

Type a few words into the Search box about what you're seeking — **exotic orchids**, for example — and press Enter. Internet Explorer fires your search off to Windows Live, Microsoft's own Search engine. You can change that search engine to Google (www.google.com) or any other search engine you like.

In fact, you can add a variety of search engines, for example, routing most of your searches to Google, but sending searches for books and CDs to Amazon. Follow these steps to customize Internet Explorer's Search box to your liking:

1. **Click the downward-pointing arrow on the Search box's right edge.**

   A drop-down menu appears.

2. **Choose Find More Providers.**

   Internet Explorer visits Microsoft's Web site and lists a few dozen popular search engines.

3. **Click your favorite Search engine and choose Add Provider from the pop-up window.**

   When the window pops up, asking whether you want to add that Search Engine, click Add Provider.

   If you want your searches to all go to one search engine — Google, for example — also click the Make This My Default Search Provider box. That tells Internet Explorer to automatically send all your searches to that provider.

4. **Feel free to add any other search engines you like, as well.**

   Choose other search engines you'd like to add. They'll all appear on the Search box's drop-down menu, seen in Figure 8-6.

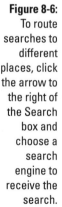

Figure 8-6: To route searches to different places, click the arrow to the right of the Search box and choose a search engine to receive the search.

✔ You can change your default search engine at any time by choosing Change Search Defaults from the bottom of the drop-down menu in Figure 8-6. A window appears, listing all your search engines; click your favorite, and Internet Explorer sends it all your searches.

✔ If Google finds Web sites in foreign languages, it often translates them into your own language for you.

✔ Sometimes Google brings up a Web site that's been updated and no longer lists what you're searching for. If that happens, click the word Cached instead of the site's name. That brings up a snapshot of the Web site as it looked when it contained what you're searching for.

✔ Click Google's I'm Feeling Lucky button, and Google displays the site most likely to contain what you're after. This option works best when searching for common information.

The Web Page Says It Needs a Weird Plug-In Thing!

Computer programmers abandoned their boring old TV sets and turned to their exciting new computers for entertainment. Now, they're trying to turn their computers back into TV sets. They're using fancy programming techniques called Java, Flash, RealPlayer, QuickTime, and other goodies to add animation and other movies to the Internet.

Programmers are also adding little software tidbits called *plug-ins* that increase your computer's capability to display these flashy items — as well as splash moving advertisements along the top of your screen. You'll know when you need a plug-in when the Web site sticks a threatening notice in your face, as shown in Figure 8-7.

Figure 8-7: A site asks to install software.

Internet Explorer Add-on Installer - Security Warning

Do you want to install this software?

Name: Adobe Flash Player 9
Publisher: **Adobe Systems Incorporated**

More options   Install   Don't Install

While files from the Internet can be useful, this file type can potentially harm your computer. Only install software from publishers you trust. What's the risk?

What's the problem? If your computer says it needs a plug-in or its latest version, click the button that takes you to its download area — *but only if you can trust it.* Although it's often difficult to tell the good programs from the evil ones, I explain in Chapter 10 how to judge a plug-in's trustworthiness. The following plug-ins are both free and safe:

- **QuickTime (www.apple.com/quicktime):** The free version of QuickTime plays many video formats that Microsoft's Media Player can't handle, including those required to view most movie trailers.

- **RealPlayer (www.real.com):** Although I find this software offensive, sometimes it's the only way to see or view some things on the Internet. Be sure to download the *free* version, no matter now much the Real folks try to hide it behind the pay version on its Web site.

- **Adobe Flash/Shockwave (www.adobe.com):** Although this free download plays most of the elaborate moving advertisements on Web sites, it also lets you watch funny cartoons and animations.

- **Adobe Acrobat Reader (www.adobe.com):** Another popular freebie, Acrobat Reader lets you view documents as if they're printed on paper. (Sometimes it doesn't let you copy parts of them, though, or read them with your word processor.)

Beware of sites that try to slip in other programs when you download the plug-in. For example, Macromedia Flash Player sometimes tries to sneak in a copy of Yahoo!'s toolbar along with the plug-in. Examine the check boxes carefully and uncheck any that you don't want, need, or trust before you click the Install or Download button. If it's too late, I describe how to remove unwanted add-ons in this chapter's Troubleshooting section.

Saving Information from the Internet

The Internet places a full-service library inside your house, with no long checkout lines. And just as every library comes with a copy machine, Internet Explorer provides several ways for you to save interesting tidbits of information for your personal use. (Check your country's copyright laws for specifics.)

The following sections explain how to copy something from the Internet onto your computer, whether it's an entire Web page, a single picture, a sound or movie, or a program.

I explain how to print a Web page (or information it contains) in Chapter 7.

Saving a Web page

Hankering for a handy Fahrenheit/Centigrade conversion chart? Need that Sushi Identification Chart for dinner? Want to save the itinerary for next month's trip to Russia? When you find a Web page with indispensable information, sometimes you can't resist saving a copy onto your computer for further viewing, perusal, or even printing at a later date.

When you save a Web page, you're saving the page as it *currently exists* on your screen. To see any subsequent changes, you must revisit the actual site.

Saving your currently viewed Web page is easy:

1. **Choose Save As from Internet Explorer's Page menu.**

   When the Save Webpage box appears, Internet Explorer enters the Web page's name in the File Name box, as shown in Figure 8-8, and fills out the Encoding box automatically.

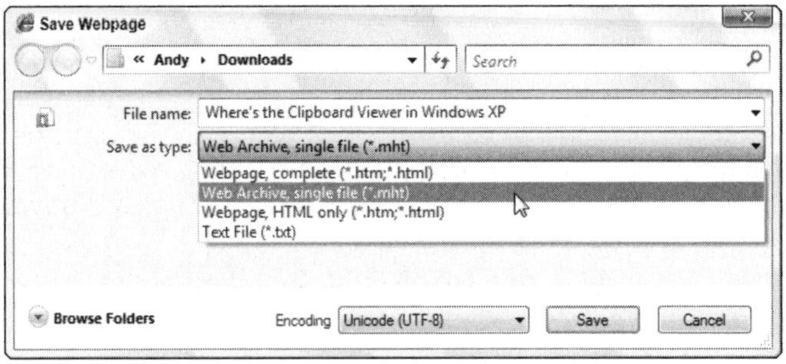

Figure 8-8:
Internet
Explorer
offers four
different
formats for
saving a
Web page.

Save Webpage			
« Andy ▸ Downloads		Search	
File name:	Where's the Clipboard Viewer in Windows XP		
Save as type:	Web Archive, single file (*.mht)		
	Webpage, complete (*.htm;*.html)		
	Web Archive, single file (*.mht)		
	Webpage, HTML only (*.htm;*.html)		
	Text File (*.txt)		
Browse Folders	Encoding	Unicode (UTF-8)	Save Cancel

2. **Use the Browse Folders drop-down list to choose where you want to save the file.**

   Internet Explorer normally saves the Web page in your Downloads folder, accessible with a click on your username that sits atop the Start menu's right corner. To save the Web page in a different folder, perhaps Documents, click the Browse Folders drop-down list.

3. **Choose how you want to save the page in the Save As Type box.**

   Internet Explorer offers *four* different ways to save the Web page:

   • **Webpage, Complete (*.htm;*.html):** Fast, handy, but a tad awkward, this option tells Internet Explorer to divide the Web page into two parts: a folder containing the page's pictures and graphics, and an adjacent link that tells the computer to display that folder's contents.

- **Web Archive, Single File (*.mht):** A much tidier option, this choice also saves an exact copy of the Web page. However, everything's packaged neatly into a single file named after the Web page. Unfortunately, only Internet Explorer can open this type of file, ruling out people who use other Web browsing programs.

- **Web Page, HTML Only (*.htm;*.html):** This option saves the page's text and layout but strips away the images. It's handy for stripping pictures and advertisements from tables, charts, and other formatted chunks of text.

- **Text File (*.txt):** This option scrapes all the text off the page and dumps it into a Notepad file, without taking many pains to preserve the formatting. It's handy for saving simple lists but not much else.

4. Click the Save button when you're done.

To revisit your saved Web page, open your Downloads folder and click the saved file. Internet Explorer leaps back to life and displays the page.

Saving text

To save just a little of the text, select the text you want to grab, right-click it, and choose Copy. Open your word processor and paste the text into a new document and save it in your Documents folder with a descriptive name.

To save *all* the text from a Web site, it's easiest to save the entire Web page, as described in the previous section.

Saving a picture

As you browse through Web pages and spot a picture that's too good to pass up, save it to your PC: Right-click the picture and search the horribly overcrowded menu for the words Save Picture As, shown in Figure 8-9.

The Save Picture window appears, letting you choose a new filename for the picture or stick with the filename used by the Web page. Click Save, and your pilfered picture appears in your Pictures folder.

The right-click menu shown in Figure 8-9 offers other handy options, as well, letting you choose to print or e-mail the picture or even set it as your desktop's background.

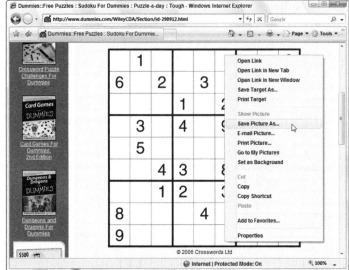

Figure 8-9:
Right-click
the coveted
picture and
choose
Save
Picture As
from the
pop-up
menu.

Remember the little picture by your name on Windows Vista's Welcome screen? Feel free to use any picture from the Internet. Right-click the new picture and save it to your Pictures folder. Then use the Control Panel (see Chapter 11) to transform that picture into your new user account picture.

Downloading a program or file

Sometimes downloading is as easy as clicking a Web site's Click to Download Now button. The Web site asks where to save your file, and you choose your Documents or Downloads folder for easy retrieval. The file arrives in a few seconds (if you have a cable modem) or a few minutes to hours (if you have a dialup modem).

But sometimes downloading takes a few extra steps:

1. **Right-click the link pointing to your desired file and choose Save Target As.**

   For example, to download Cory Doctorow's science fiction novel, *Someone Comes to Town, Someone Leaves Town,* from his Web site, right-click its link (the words "plain text file," in this case). Then choose Save Target As from the pop-up menu, similar to the menu shown earlier in Figure 8-9.

   When you try to download a *program,* Windows asks whether you want to Save the File or Run It from Its Current Location. Choose Save the File.

Saving a sound or movie you've played

Some downright mean Web sites don't let you save movies or sounds you've just played in Media Player. But friendly sites let you choose Save Media As from Media Player's File menu to save the show to your hard drive. (Press Alt to see the hidden File menu.) But if that option's grayed out or Media Player doesn't automatically fill in the format, you're not allowed to save what you've just watched or heard.

This trick doesn't work for all media (especially for Internet radio stations), and it doesn't always work on different media players like QuickTime or RealPlayer. But it's sometimes worth a try.

2. **Navigate to your Downloads folder, if necessary, and click the Save button.**

   Vista normally offers to save the file in your Downloads folder, saving you the trouble of navigating to it. (You can see Downloads listed in the folder's Address Bar in Figure 8-10.) But if you prefer to download it to a different folder, navigate to that folder and click the Save button.

Figure 8-10:
Navigate to your Downloads folder and click the Save button.

Windows Vista begins copying the file from the Web site to your hard drive. Windows Vista tells you when it finishes downloading, and you can click the Open Folder button to open your Downloads folder and see your downloaded file.

✔ Before running any downloaded programs, screen savers, themes, or other items, be sure to scan them with your antivirus program. Windows Vista doesn't come with one built-in, leaving it up to you to purchase one.

✔ Many downloaded programs come packaged in a tidy folder with a zipper on it, known as a *Zip file*. Windows Vista treats them like normal folders; just double-click them to open them. (The files are actually compressed inside that folder to save download time, if you care about the engineering involved.)

It Doesn't Work!

If something doesn't work, don't feel bad. The Internet's been around for a while, but this whole Web thing is relatively new and complicated. It's not supposed to work smoothly yet, and it isn't something you can figure out overnight. This section explores common problems and possible solutions.

The person holding the Administrator account — usually the computer's owner — is the only one who is authorized to make some of the changes you read about in this section. If a mean message pops up, waving its finger and mumbling about Administrator restrictions, you're locked out. Better find the computer's owner to proceed.

Here are some general tips that you may want to try before you explore the following sections:

✔ When a Web site gives you problems, try emptying Internet Explorer's wastebasket. Choose Internet Options from its Tools menu and click the Delete button. Look for the Temporary Internet Files section and click its Delete button. Twiddle your thumbs until it finishes, then click the Close button, revisit the problematic site, and try again.

✔ If your connection settings seem askew, try setting up your Internet connection again. Described in this chapter's "Setting Up Internet Explorer the First Time" section, the steps guide you through your current settings, letting you change things that look suspicious.

✔ If you can't connect to the Internet at all, your best bet is to call your ISP's tech support number and ask for help. (Be sure to call your Internet service provider, not Microsoft.)

✔ If a page doesn't seem to display correctly, look for Internet Explorer's warning strip along the page's top. Click the strip and tell Internet Explorer *not* to block what it's trying to block.

Removing Unneeded Plug-ins

Lots of Web sites install little programs inside Internet Explorer to help you navigate the Web or play with some Web sites. Not all of those little programs are well behaved. To help you pry off the leeches, Internet Explorer lets you see a list of all the currently installed little programs, called *add-ons*.

To see what's hanging onto your copy of Internet Explorer, click the program's Tools button and choose Manage Add-ons. Then select Enable or Disable Add-ons. (Don't click Find More Add-ons, as that just takes you to Microsoft's online shopping center.)

Internet Explorer's Manage Add-ons window appears, shown in Figure 8-11, letting you see add-ons currently loaded, add-ons currently running without your permission, and add-ons that have run in the past.

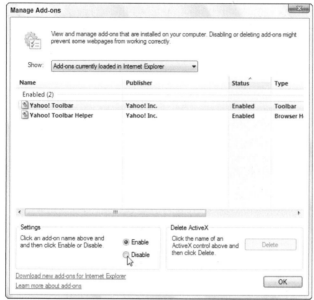

Figure 8-11:
Click a suspicious add-on and choose Disable in the Settings area.

Most add-ons listed in the Manage Add-ons window are fine. (The ones from Microsoft are generally harmless.) But if you spot an add-on that you don't recognize, or that you think is causing problems, look up its name in Google (www.google.com) to see what people say about it. If you find one that seems bad, click its name and click the Disable button.

If disabling the add-on keeps something from working correctly, return to the screen, click the add-on's name, and click the Enable button.

Managing add-ons turns into a game of trial and error, but it's a handy way to disable a rogue add-on installed by a nasty Web site.

The Pages Won't All Fit on My Screen

Some people (with good eyesight) can afford huge monitors that pack lots of information onto the screen. Other folks have smaller monitors that simply don't have the real estate to display everything. So, how does a Web site reshape itself to fit every screen? It can't.

Some try by fitting squarely onto smaller monitors but leaving white space along the edges of larger monitors. Others try to guess a monitor's size and resize themselves to fit. Others simply fall off your screen's right edge.

The best way to fight back is to experiment with your *screen resolution* — the amount of information your screen can display. Although I describe the process in Chapter 11, here are the quick-and-dirty steps:

1. **Right-click a blank part of your desktop and choose Personalize.**

2. **Click the Display Settings icon.**

3. **Slide the Resolution bar to adjust your Screen Resolution.**

   Sliding the bar to the *right* packs more information onto the screen but makes everything smaller. Sliding to the *left* makes everything larger but sometimes leaves parts of the screen hanging off the edge.

Although the resolution setting of 800 x 600 pixels works well for average to small monitors, many sites now pack their information into a resolution of 1024 x 768 pixels.

Internet Explorer Now Fills My Entire Screen!

Internet Explorer normally lives safely within its own menu-filled window. But occasionally it swells up to fill the entire screen, neatly trimming away both your menus and the desktop's taskbar. Full-screen mode looks great for movies, but the sparcity of menus leaves you with no way to switch to a different program.

To switch out of full-screen mode, press F11. That toggles full-screen mode, putting your menus back within reach. Press F11 again to watch the movie.

Pressing the Windows key brings back the Start menu and taskbar, handy for running a quick program and then returning to Internet Explorer.

Chapter 9

Sending and Receiving E-mail

*I*nternet Explorer turns the Internet into a multimedia magazine, but Windows Mail turns it into your personalized post office, where you never need to fumble for a stamp. A Windows Vista freebie, Windows Mail lets you send letters and files to anybody in the world who has an e-mail account. (And that's just about anybody, these days.)

Quite the bargain for a freebie, Windows Mail automatically sorts your incoming mail and stuffs it into the correct folder, juggles several e-mail accounts simultaneously, and adds some security to your e-mail as well.

If you've used Outlook Express, Windows XP's bundled e-mail program, you'll feel right at home with Windows Mail. Both programs are basically the same, with almost identical menus. Windows Mail can import all your old Outlook Express accounts, contacts, and e-mail. If you upgrade to Vista on your Windows XP computer, Windows Mail is even smart enough to import your information automatically.

Using Windows Mail

The Windows Mail screen, shown in Figure 9-1, splits your e-mail into two columns: The Folders side, along the left, automatically stores and sorts your e-mail. The work screen, along the right, lets you see and tinker with your e-mail.

Figure 9-1:
On the left,
Windows
Mail dis-
plays your
folders; the
selected
folder's
contents
spill out to
the top
right, and
the preview
of the high-
lighted mail
appears
in the
bottom right.

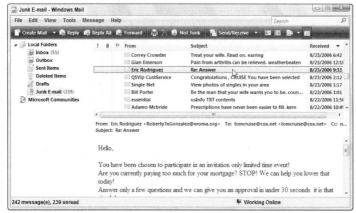

The folders in Windows Mail work much like traditional in baskets and out baskets for sorting memos. Click any folder's name to peek inside, and you're in for a pleasant surprise. Unlike your own office, Windows Mail automatically sorts your information into the following folders:

- ✔ **Inbox:** When you connect to the Internet, Windows Mail grabs any waiting e-mail and places it in your Inbox folder. On PCs with a broadband Internet connection, Windows Mail checks for new mail every 30 minutes — or whenever you click the Send/Receive button on the toolbar.

  Reduce your 30-minute wait by choosing Options from the Tools menu, clicking the General tab, and changing the number of minutes in the Check for New Messages Every X Minutes box.

- ✔ **Outbox:** When you send or reply to a message, Windows Mail immediately tries to connect to the Internet and send it. If you're already connected, Windows Mail immediately fires it off to its recipient.

- ✔ **Sent Items:** *Every* piece of e-mail you've sent lingers in here, leaving a permanent record. (To kill the particularly embarrassing ones, right-click them and choose Delete.)

- ✔ **Deleted Items:** The Deleted Items folder serves as Windows Mail's Recycle Bin, letting you retrieve accidental deletions. To delete something permanently from the Deleted Items folder, right-click it and choose Delete from the pop-up menu.

To keep deleted mail from cluttering your Deleted Items folder, choose Options from the Tools menu, click the Advanced tab, and click the Maintenance button. From there, select the Empty Messages from the 'Deleted Items' Folder on Exit check box.

✔ **Drafts:** When you're midway through writing an e-mail and want to finish it later, choose Save from your e-mail's File menu. The letter moves to your Drafts folder until you're ready to revive it.

✔ **Junk E-mail:** Windows Mail sniffs out potential junk mail and drops suspects into this folder.

To see the contents of any folder, click it. That folder's contents spill out to the top right. Click any mail, and its contents appear in the Preview Pane beneath.

Want to transfer all your e-mail from your old computer to a new one? I explain that chore in Chapter 19.

Exactly what do I need to send and receive e-mail?

To send e-mail to a friend or foe with Windows Mail, you need three things:

✔ **An e-mail account:** The next section describes how to set up Windows Mail to work with your e-mail account. Most ISPs (Internet service providers, covered in Chapter 8) give you a free e-mail address along with your Internet access.

✔ **Your friend's or foe's e-mail address:** Locate your friends' e-mail addresses by simply asking them. An address consists of a *username* (which occasionally resembles the user's real name), followed by the @ sign, followed by the name of your friend's ISP. The e-mail address of an America Online user with the username of Jeff9435 would be jeff9435@aol.com. (Unlike your local post office, e-mail doesn't tolerate any spelling errors. Precision is a must.)

✔ **Your message:** Here's where the fun finally starts: typing your letter. After you type the person's e-mail address and your message, hit the Send button. Windows Mail routes your message in the right direction.

You'll find people's e-mail addresses on business cards, Web sites, and even return addresses: Whenever you reply to e-mail, Windows Mail automatically adds that person's e-mail address to your list of contacts.

If you misspell part of an e-mail address, your sent message bounces back to your own Inbox, with a confusing *undeliverable* message attached. Check the spelling of the address and try again. If it bounces again, humble yourself: Pick up the phone and ask the person whether you have the right address.

Setting Up Your E-Mail Account

In order to send or receive e-mail in Windows Mail, you need these three things, all available from your ISP: your username, your password, and a working Internet connection. (You've already used these things if you successfully set up your Internet account, as described in Chapter 8.)

Most people set up more than one e-mail address, as well as the free account from their ISP. Whether you're setting up your 1st or your 40th e-mail account, follow these six steps:

1. **Set up your Internet account and open Windows Mail.**

   You need to set up your Internet account *first,* as described in Chapter 8, or your e-mail won't have any way to reach the Internet.

    To call up Windows Mail for the first time, open the Start menu and click the Windows Mail icon (shown in the margin). If you don't see this icon, choose All Programs and then click Windows Mail. Windows Mail hops onto the screen, ready to be set up to send and receive your e-mail, as shown in Figure 9-2.

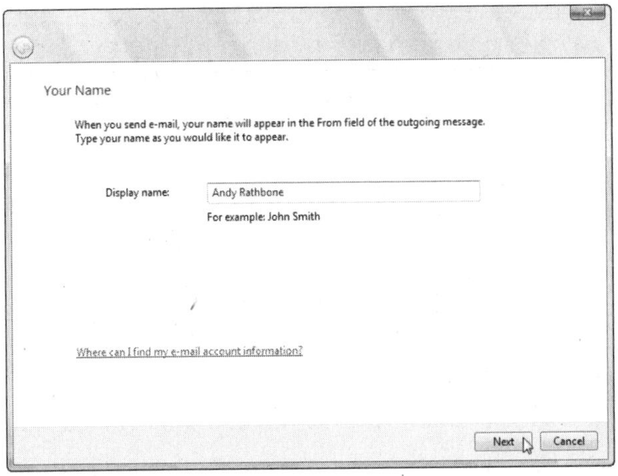

Figure 9-2:
When
loaded for
the first
time,
Windows
Mail offers
to set up
your e-mail
account.

Your Name

When you send e-mail, your name will appear in the From field of the outgoing message.
Type your name as you would like it to appear.

Display name: Andy Rathbone

For example: John Smith

Where can I find my e-mail account information?

Next   Cancel

If the screen in Figure 9-2 doesn't appear automatically, open Windows Mail and choose Accounts from the Tools menu. Click the Add button, choose E-mail Account, and click Next to bring up the window in Figure 9-2, ready to add an e-mail account.

2. **Type your name and click Next.**

This name appears in the From box of all your e-mail, so most people simply type their own name, as shown in Figure 9-2. Names like *DragonSlayer* may come back to haunt you.

3. Type your e-mail address and click Next.

Your e-mail address is your username, the @ sign, and your ISP, all information that your ISP must provide you with. For example, if your username is *jeff4265* and your ISP's name is *charternet.com,* then type **jeff4265@charternet.com** into the E-Mail Address box.

4. Choose your server type and the names for your incoming and outgoing mail servers and click Next.

Here, you need to know what *type* of e-mail account the service uses. It's a weird word like POP3 or IMAP. (If it uses HTTP, Windows Mail can't work with it, which leaves out Hotmail users.) Most ISPs send you these handy settings and instructions through the post office. If you've lost them, visit your ISP's Web site or call your ISP's tech support folks and ask them for their mail server's *name* and *type*. Table 9-1 lists the information required by some common e-mail services.

Google's Gmail, AOL, and Yahoo! all require you to click the box marked Outgoing Server Requires Authentication on this page.

Table 9-1	E-Mail Settings for Popular ISPs		
Service	*E-Mail Type*	*Incoming Mail Server*	*Outgoing Mail Server*
Google Gmail (See the related sidebar for additional settings that Gmail accounts need.)	POP3	pop.gmail. com	smtp.gmail. com
America Online (AOL) (See the related sidebar for additional settings that AOL accounts need.)	IMAP	imap.aol. com	smtp.aol.com
Yahoo! (Only paid Yahoo! e-mail accounts can receive mail through Windows Mail.)	POP3	pop.mail. yahoo	smtp.mail. yahoo

5. Type your account name and password and click Next.

For your account name, enter the part of your e-mail address before the @ sign. Then type that account's password. Check the Remember Password box to fetch your mail automatically in the background.

Check the Secure Password Authentication box *only* if your Internet provider requests it. (Yahoo! does, for example.)

6. **Click Finish.**

That's it. Windows Mail should immediately fetch any waiting e-mail and let you begin sending e-mail.

- ✔ If the settings don't work or don't look right, they're easy to change. Choose Accounts from the Tools menu and double-click the name of the account that needs tweaking. Those steps also let you change the way Windows Mail lists your account's name, perhaps changing the obtuse *pop.mail.yahoo* to plain old *Yahoo,* for example.

- ✔ If your ISP lets you sign up for additional e-mail accounts for family members, feel free to create a second, "disposable" e-mail account for yourself. Use that e-mail address when signing up for online offers or filling out temporary forms. When that account becomes plagued with spam, simply delete it and create a new one.

- ✔ Be sure to make your favorite e-mail account your *default* account — the one listed as the return address on every mail you send. To set your default account, choose Accounts from the Tools menu, click your most-often used account, and click the Set as Default button.

- ✔ Back up these settings to avoid the hassle of ever filling them out again: Choose Tools, select Accounts, and click your account's name. Then click the Export button to save your account information as an IAF (Internet Account File), a format that works with most other mail programs. To import those settings back into mail — or into your laptop's mail program — choose Tools, select Accounts, and choose Import.

Finishing up your AOL account in Windows Mail

Even after finishing Steps 1 to 6 to set up your AOL account in Windows Mail, your account won't work correctly until you jump through the following hoops:

1. **Choose Accounts from Windows Mail's Tools menu to see your e-mail account (or accounts).**

2. **Select the AOL account you created, choose Properties, and click the Servers tab.**

3. **Click the My Server Requires Authentication box and click Apply.**

4. **Click the Advanced tab.**

5. **In the Outgoing Mail (SMTP) box, change the number to 587 and click Apply.**

6. **Click the IMAP tab and click to remove the check from the Store Special Folders on IMAP Server box.**

7. **Click Apply, click OK, and click Close.**

If a message asks you to download folders from the mail server, click Yes.

Finishing up your Gmail account in Windows Mail

After you set up your Gmail account, you need to jump through a few extra hoops before it works with Windows Mail:

1. **Choose Accounts from Windows Mail's Tools menu to see your e-mail account (or accounts).**

2. **Select the Gmail account you created, choose Properties, and click the Servers tab.**

3. **Click the My Server Requires Authentication box and click Apply.**

4. **Click the Advanced tab.**

5. **Check the box next to This Server Requires a Secure Connection (SSL) under Outgoing Mail (SMTP).**

   The Incoming Mail port changes to 995.

6. **Enter 465 in the Outgoing mail (SMTP) field.**

7. **Click Apply, click OK, and click Close.**

Composing and Sending an E-Mail

Ready to send your first e-mail? After you've set up Windows Mail with your e-mail account, follow these steps to compose your letter and drop it in the electronic mailbox, sending it through virtual space to the recipient's computer:

1. **Open Windows Mail and click the Create Mail icon from the program's menu.**

   If you don't see a Create Mail icon along the top (it looks like the one in the margin), click the File menu, select New, and choose Mail Message.

   A New Message window appears, as shown in Figure 9-3.

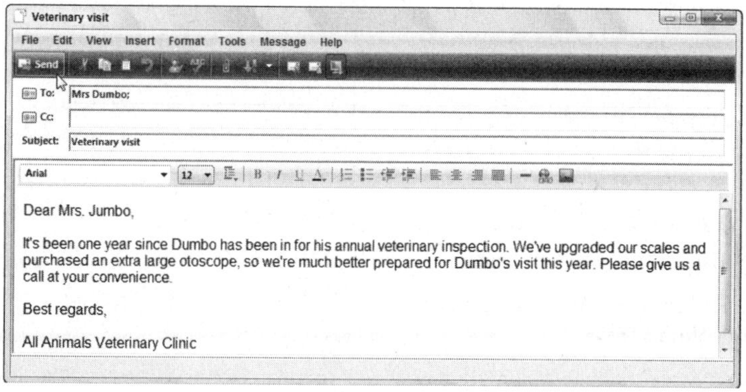

Figure 9-3: Click the Create Mail button, and a window appears for you to compose and send e-mail.

If you've set up more than one account, as described in the previous section, Windows Mail automatically addresses the mail with your *default* account — usually the first e-mail account you create in Windows Mail. To send your mail from one of your other e-mail accounts, should you have one, click the downward-pointing arrow in the From box — the box currently listing your e-mail address — and select the other account.

To send a quick e-mail to somebody in your Contacts folder, right-click his or her name, choose Action, and select Send E-mail. Windows Mail opens an e-mail already addressed to that person, saving you a step.

2. Type your friend's e-mail address into the To box.

Type the person's e-mail address into the To box. Or, click the To button next to where you type an address: A window appears, listing the names of people listed in your Contacts folder. Click your friend's name, click the To button, and click OK.

Sending or forwarding a message to several people? Preserve their privacy by clicking the Bcc button (shown in the margin) instead of the To button. That still sends them the same message but hides their e-mail addresses from each other, preserving their privacy. (If your Bcc button is missing, reveal it by clicking an e-mail's View menu and choosing All Headers.)

To let *everybody* see each other's e-mail addresses, select their names and click the Cc button, shown in the margin. (Unless the recipients all know each other, this is considered bad etiquette.)

3. Fill in the Subject box.

Although optional, the Subject line lets your friends know why you're bugging them. That makes it easier for your friends to sort their mail.

4. Type your message into the large box at the bottom of the window.

Type whatever you want and for as long as you want. There's very little limit on the size of a text file.

5. To attach a file to your message, drag and drop the file onto the message or click the paper clip icon, navigate to the file, and double-click the file's name to attach it.

Most ISPs balk at sending files larger than about 5MB, however, which rules out most MP3 files and some digital photos. I explain an easy way to send nearly any photo in Chapter 16.

6. Click the Send button in the box's top-left corner.

Whoosh! Windows Mail dials your modem, if necessary, and whisks your message through the Internet to your friend's mailbox. Depending on the speed of the Internet connection, mail arrives anywhere within 15 seconds to a few days, with a few minutes being the average.

No Send button? Then click File in the New Message window and choose Send Message.

✔ Some people like the row of buttons along the top of Windows Mail, as shown in Figure 9-3. If your buttons are missing, and you want 'em back, right-click a blank part of the Windows Mail menu — an inch to the right of the word Help will do the trick. Choose Toolbar, and the buttons appear. To get rid of 'em and stick with the menus, right-click in the same place and choose Toolbar again to toggle them off.

✔ If the buttons are too small, make them larger: Right-click any part of the toolbar, choose Customize, and choose Large Icons from the Icon Options drop-down menu. Click Close, and your icons double in size.

✔ Are you a lousy speller? Then before you send the message, click the Spelling button (shown in the margin) from the icons along the top. Or choose Spelling from the Tools menu. Or press your F7 key. Or grab a dictionary off the shelf. (Pressing F7 is quicker.)

Reading a Received E-Mail

If you keep Windows Mail running while you're connected to the Internet, you'll know when a new letter arrives. Your computer makes a little hiccup to herald its arrival. You'll also spot a tiny envelope icon in your desktop's bottom-right corner, right next to the clock.

To check for any new mail when Windows Mail isn't running, load the program from the Start menu. When it loads, click the Send/Receive button (or click the Tools menu, choose Send and Receive, and then choose Send and Receive All). Windows Mail logs onto the Internet, sends any outgoing mail you have sitting around, and grabs any incoming mail to place in your Inbox.

Follow these steps to read the letters in your Inbox and either respond or file them away into one of the program's many folders:

1. Open Windows Mail and look at your Inbox.

Depending on how Windows Mail is set up, you can do this step several different ways. If you see an opening screen announcing that you have unread mail in your Inbox, click the words Unread Mail to start reading. Or, if you see folders along the left side of Windows Mail, click the word Inbox.

Either way, Windows Mail shows you the messages in your Inbox, and they look something like Figure 9-4. Each subject is listed, one by one, with the newest one at the top.

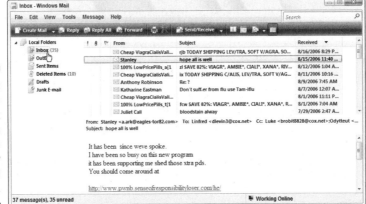

Figure 9-4:
Click the word Inbox in Windows Mail to see your newly received messages.

Want your newest e-mails to appear at the list's *bottom?* Then click the word Received at the top of the Received column. Windows Mail resorts everything but now places your newest message at the bottom. (You can also sort mail by subject or the sender's name by clicking the Subject or From column headers, too.)

2. Click any message's subject to read it.

Click any message, and Windows Mail spills that message's contents into the screen's bottom portion, as shown in Figure 9-5, ready for you to read. Or, to see the entire message in its own window, double-click it.

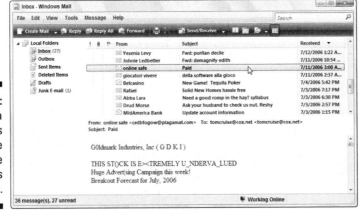

Figure 9-5:
Click a message's subject line to see the message's contents.

3. **From here, Windows Mail leaves you with several options, each described in the following list:**

   • **You can do nothing.** The message simply sets up camp in your Inbox folder until you delete it.

   • **You can respond to the message.** Click the Reply button along the top of Windows Mail (or choose Reply to Sender from the Message menu), and a new window appears, ready for you to type your response. The window is just like the one that appears when you first compose a message but with a handy difference: This window is preaddressed with the recipient's name and the subject. Also, the original message usually appears at the bottom of your reply for reference.

   • **You can file the message.** Right-click the message and choose either Move to Folder or Copy to Folder and then select the desired folder from the menu and click OK. Or simply drag and drop the message to the desired folder along the left side of your screen. (Don't see the folders there? Click the Folder List button, shown in the margin.)

   • **You can print the message.** Click the Print button along the menu's top, and Windows Mail shoots your message to the printer to make a paper copy.

   • **You can delete the message.** Click the Delete button to toss the message into your Deleted Items folder. Your deleted messages sit inside the folder until you right-click the Deleted Items folder and choose Empty 'Deleted Items' Folder. For automatic deletion, choose Tools, select Options, click the Advanced tab, click Maintenance, and choose Empty Messages from the Deleted Items folder on Exit.

These tips help you wring the most work out of Windows Mail:

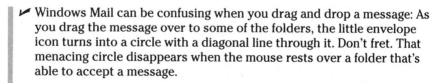 Windows Mail can be confusing when you drag and drop a message: As you drag the message over to some of the folders, the little envelope icon turns into a circle with a diagonal line through it. Don't fret. That menacing circle disappears when the mouse rests over a folder that's able to accept a message.

✔ To organize your incoming messages, right-click your Inbox and choose New Folder to create another folder inside. Create as many folders as you need to categorize your spam offers.

✔ Some people's e-mails contain not only words but a file, which computer folk refer to as an *attachment*. Attachments cause enough problems to warrant their own section, which appears next.

✔ If you ever receive e-mail from a bank, eBay, or other money-oriented Web site, think twice before visiting. A criminal industry called *phishing* sends e-mails that try to trick you into entering your name and password. That gives your coveted information to the evil folk, who promptly steal your money. Windows Mail sends you a warning when it spots suspicious phishing e-mails; I write more about phishing in Chapter 10.

✔ When you see a little red *X* in place of a picture or photo on your e-mail, that means Windows Mail is blocking it. To view the image, click the blue message Windows Mail places atop that e-mail. To keep Windows Mail from blocking images, choose Options from the Tools menu, click the Security tab, and remove the check mark from the Block Images and Other External Content in HTML E-Mail box.

Sending and Receiving an Attachment

Like a little photograph slipped into the envelope of a thank-you note, an *attachment* is a file that piggybacks onto an e-mail message.

Windows Mail lets you send files any of several ways. Start by composing a new message, as described earlier in this chapter. But before clicking the Send button, drag and drop your file inside the message. Windows Mail tacks on the file, listing its name in the new "Attach" line beneath the mail's subject line, shown in Figure 9-6.

Figure 9-6: Attached files appear listed in the Attach line of an e-mail.

> **Help!**
>
> File Edit View Insert Format Tools Message Help
>
> Send
>
> To: Guruji Jois;
> Cc:
> Bcc:
> Subject: Help!
> Attach: pretzel pose.JPG (1.75 MB)
>
> Arial   12   B I U A   ...
>
> Hello Mr. Jois,
>
> Forgive any spelling errors, because I find myself in no position to type. Rather, it's because of my position that I'm writing now. I fell backwards and to the right during my daily yoga practice this morning, and now find myself stuck like conjoined pretzels. I've enclosed a photo for your reference. Can you recommend a method to extricate myself? Thanks for your help, and I hope to hear from you quickly.

You can also right-click a file, choose Send To from the pop-up menu, and select Mail Recipient. Windows Mail opens a new e-mail for you with that file attached, waiting for you to choose a recipient.

Added a file you want to remove? Right-click its name and choose Remove.

You can e-mail just about any file, the only exception being size: E-mails larger than about 5MB tend to stick in the Internet's pipes rather than fly off to their recipient. To check a file's size, right-click its name or icon and choose Properties: The file's size appears among the fine print on the General tab.

Because digital files often surpass the 5MB limit, especially when you try to attach more than one, Windows Mail helps out by shrinking the photos — a process I cover in Chapter 16. The photos still fit on your recipient's screen nicely, but they consume much less file space.

E-mail makes it easy to send files to friends around the world. They're so easy to send, in fact, that virus writers quickly picked up on the trend, creating viruses that spread themselves by mailing a copy of themselves to everybody in the recipient's address book.

That brings me to the following warnings:

- If a friend sends you an attached file unexpectedly, *don't open it.* E-mail your friend and ask whether he or she *really* sent it. That attachment may be sent by a virus without your friend knowing about it. To be safe, drag received attachments onto your desktop and scan them with your antivirus program before opening. Don't open them directly from the e-mail itself.

- To prevent you from opening a virus, Windows Mail refuses to let you open almost *any* attached file. If Windows Mail won't let you open a file you're expecting from a friend, turn off that protection: Choose Options from the Tools menu, click the Security tab, and remove the check mark from the Do Not Allow Attachments to Be Saved or Opened That Could Potentially Be a Virus check box.

Finding Lost Mail

Eventually, an important a e-mail will disappear into a pile of folders and file names. Vista offers you three ways to retrieve it.

If you know which folder it's lurking in, click that folder's name. Then click in Windows Mail's Search box in the upper-right corner. Type the sender's name, or perhaps a few words from the e-mail, and press Enter.

Don't know the folder? Try the Start menu's Search box. The Start menu's Search box, which I cover in Chapter 6, constantly indexes your e-mail — and the Start menu's Search box works like a mini-Google to find it.

But when the Search boxes let you down, try Windows Mail's built-in search. It provides a meticulous search through all your folders when you follow these steps:

1. **Choose Find from the Edit menu and select Message.**

2. **In the Find Message dialog box that appears, shown in Figure 9-7, search for messages containing certain items.**

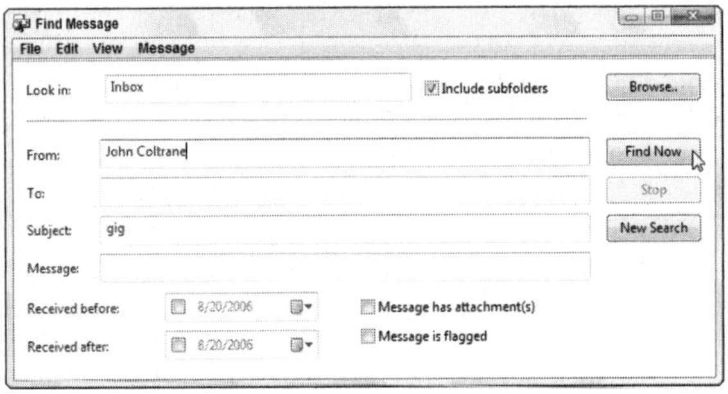

Figure 9-7: Search for messages from John Coltrane mentioning "gig."

Here are your options:

- **Look in:** Normally, Search scours only your Inbox. To search *all* your mail folders, click Browse to choose Local Folders, click OK and then put a check mark in Include Subfolders. Then the Search looks in every folder: your Inbox, Outbox, Sent Items, Deleted Items, Drafts, and even your Junk E-mail folder. Or, to limit the search to a single folder, click Browse and click that folder's name.

- **From:** Looking for mail from a specific person? Type that person's name to see every message that person has sent you.

- **To:** To see messages you've sent to a particular person, type that person's name.

- **Subject:** Type a word that appeared in an e-mail's subject line to locate it.

- **Message:** Type any word that you *know* appears in the message.

- **Received before/after:** These two boxes let you isolate your search to a certain day or group of days.

- **Message has Attachment(s):** To retrieve any and all messages with attachments, click in this box.

- **Message is Flagged:** To retrieve any and all messages that you've *flagged* to catch your attention later — an option available in a message's Message menu — click in this box.

Usually filling out one box catches your message. Try entering just a few letters of a person's e-mail address or a single word that appeared in the message. If a search turns up too many items, keep adding more and more search terms to limit the number of matches.

3. **Click Find Now when you're done filling out the boxes.**

   Vista rummages through your folders, listing any e-mails that fit your search.

Managing Your Contacts

Just as every desk needs a business card holder, Windows Mail needs an address book to store everybody's contact information. Vista dumps Windows XP's old Address Book program in favor of a Contacts folder (shown in Figure 9-8).

Figure 9-8:
Vista's
Contacts
folder keeps
track of
everybody
you contact.

To see your Contacts folder, open the Start menu, click your username at the top-right corner, and open the Contacts folder. Or, from within Windows Mail, click the Contacts button in the toolbar.

You can beef up your list of contacts several ways:

✔ **Let Windows Mail do it automatically.** When you respond to an e-mail, Windows Mail automatically tosses that person's name and e-mail address into your Contacts folder. If Windows Mail ever stops doing that, fix it: Choose Options from the Tools menu, click the Send tab, and select the Automatically Put People I Reply to in my Contacts List check box.

Keeping Windows Mail secure, but convenient

Windows Mail automatically turns on many security measures. To see what security switches it has flipped (and to turn them off if they annoy you), choose Options from Windows Mail's Tools menu and click the Security tab. Then examine these three sections, making changes as needed:

Virus Protection: Although some of these measures protect you from viruses, they do that by filtering out nearly *every* attached file. Here's the rundown:

✔ **Internet Explorer Security Zone:** Ignore this area. But if you've deliberately set *restricted* security zones in Internet Explorer, as explained in Chapter 10, head there for more information.

✔ **Warn Me When Other Applications Try to Send Mail as Me:** Leave this option on because it's an inoffensive way to keep worms and viruses from spreading.

✔ **Do Not Allow Attachments to Be Saved or Opened That Could Potentially Be a Virus:** Because nearly *any* file can contain a virus these days, this setting effectively stops you from opening most attachments. Uncheck this box to open your attachments again.

Download Images: Windows Mail hides any pictures that are embedded in your e-mail. You can see them by clicking the little blue strip above the message, or you can remove this check mark to avoid that inconvenience.

Secure Mail: This area is much too complicated to worry about. Ignore it.

✔ **Import an Old Address Book.** To import an Address Book file from another computer, open your Contacts folder and choose Import from the toolbar. (This step assumes that you've already used your old Address Book's Export command to create a file you can import in any of these formats: CSV, LDIF, vCard or, if from Outlook Express, Windows Address Book File.)

✔ **Add Contacts Manually.** When somebody hands you a business card, you must enter the information by hand. From inside Windows Mail, choose New from the File menu and choose Contact. Simply add the person's name and e-mail address, or create a detailed dossier by filling out every box on every tab. Click OK when you're through.

These other tasks come in handy when you find yourself staring into your Contacts folder:

✔ To send a quick message to a contact in your Contacts folder, right-click that person's name, choose Action, and choose Send E-mail. Vista calls up a handy, preaddressed New Message window, ready for you to type your message and click Send.

  ✔ I explain how to turn your Contacts folder into a handy printed address book in Chapter 7.

  ✔ To back up your Contacts folder, just copy the entire folder to a CD. To back up just a few contacts, select them, choose Export from the Contact folder's toolbar, and export them as either CSV (Comma Separated Values) or vCards (folder of .vcf files).

  ✔ You can copy contacts to your iPod's Contacts list, as well. After you've connected your iPod, export your Contacts folder's most essential people in the vCards format, as described in the preceding bullet. When Vista asks you to select the folder for VCF export, choose the Contacts folder on your iPod. (Vista lists your iPod as a hard drive.)

Reducing Your Spam

Unfortunately, you can't get rid of spam completely. Believe it or not, some people still buy things from spammers, making the junk e-mails profitable enough for spammers to continue. Scowl at any neighbors who confide that they've bought a spammer's merchandise.

Luckily, Vista's wised up a bit when it comes to recognizing spam. In fact, when Windows Mail spots an e-mail that smells suspiciously like spam, it sends you a message, seen in Figure 9-9, and deposits the suspect into your Junk E-mail folder.

If you spot mail in the Junk E-mail folder that's *not* junk, click the good piece of mail and click the Not Junk button on the toolbar. Windows Mail quickly whisks that piece of mail back into your Inbox.

Figure 9-9:
Windows
Mail's spam
filter auto-
matically
moves spam
to your
Junk E-mail
folder.

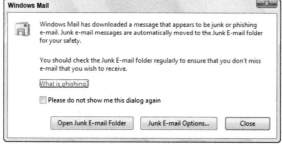

But although you can't completely stop spam, you can weed out much of it by following these rules:

- ✔ Give your e-mail address only to close friends, relatives, and trusted business contacts. Don't give it to strangers or post it on Web sites.

- ✔ Create a second, *disposable* e-mail account to use when signing up for online offers, filling out online forms, or carrying out any short-term correspondence. As I describe in this chapter's "Setting Up Your E-Mail Account" section, delete that address once it's plagued with spam, and create a new one.

- ✔ Never post your real e-mail address in an Internet's chat forum, newsgroup, or other public conversation area. And never respond to a spammer, even if it's to click the unsubscribe link. That merely adds you to the spammer's list of confirmed e-mail addresses.

- ✔ See whether your ISP offers built-in spam filtering. The filters work so well that many spammers now try to evade the filters by using nonsensical words. If they do make it through, the nonsense in the subject gives it away as being spam.

- ✔ Although Windows Mail offers some simple filtering rules in its Tools menu, spammers figured out how to fool them long ago. They're no longer handy for filtering spam, but they work fine for routing e-mail from certain people to certain folders.

Chapter 10

Safe Computing

- -

- -

*L*ike driving a car, working with Windows is reasonably safe, as long as you steer clear of the wrong neighborhoods, obey traffic signals, and don't steer with your feet while you stick your head out the sunroof.

But in the world of Windows and the Internet, there's no easy way to recognize a bad neighborhood, spot the traffic signals, or even distinguish between your feet, the steering wheel, and the sunroof. Things that look totally innocent — a friend's e-mail or a program on the Internet — may be a virus or prank that sneakily rearranges everything on your dashboard or causes a crash.

This chapter helps you recognize the bad streets in Windows' virtual neighborhoods and explains the steps you can take to protect yourself from harm and minimize any damage.

Understanding Those Annoying Permission Messages

After 20 years of Windows development, Vista's still pretty naive. For example, when you run a program to change settings on your PC, Vista can't tell whether *you're* loading the program or a *virus* is loading it in an attempt to mess with your PC.

Turning off permissions

Turning off Vista's nagging permission screens leaves your PC much more vulnerable to the dark forces of computing. But if you find yourself grinding your teeth more than working, Administrator account holders may turn off the permission screens by following these steps:

1. **Click the Start button, choose Control Panel, and then click User Accounts and Family Safety.**

   Vista's Control Panel, which I explain in Chapter 11, lets you tweak how Windows runs on your PC.

2. **Click User Accounts and choose Turn User Account Control On or Off.**

   As you try to shut it up, Windows sends out one last gasping permission screen.

3. **Give permission to continue.**

   Click Continue or enter your password and click OK to access the System Configuration area.

4. **Click to remove the check mark from the Use User Account Control (UAC) to Help Protect Your Computer check box and click OK.**

   A window appears, saying that you must restart your computer to apply your changes. Click the window's handy Restart Now button to restart your PC. It will wake up in a much more permissive mood.

These steps leave one side-effect, however. Vista's Security Center, described in the next section, immediately begins nagging that you've turned off User Account Control.

If you change your mind, turn the Permissions screens back on by following Steps 1 through 4 but adding the check mark in Step 4.

Vista's solution? When Vista notices anybody (or anything) trying to open something that can potentially harm Windows or your PC, it flashes a message asking for permission, like the one shown in Figure 10-1.

Figure 10-1: Click Cancel if this message appears unexpectedly.

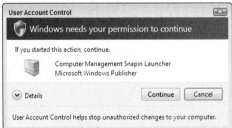

If one of these permission messages appears out of the blue, Vista may be warning you about a bit of nastiness trying to sneak in. So click Cancel to deny it permission. But if *you're* trying to do something specific with your PC and Vista puts up its guard, click Continue instead. Vista drops the boxing gloves and lets you in.

Or, if you don't hold an Administrator account, track down any Administrator account holder and ask her to type her password.

Yes, an annoyingly dimwitted security-guard robot polices Vista's front door, but it's also an extra challenge for the people who write the viruses.

Vista's permission screens are called *User Account Protection*.

Assessing Your Safety in Security Center

Take a minute to check your PC's safety with Windows Vista's Security Center. The Security Center more closely resembles a large panel of On switches than a command post. It lists Windows Vista's four main defenses, tells you whether they're activated, and provides handy "On" switches to activate any that may be turned off.

Shown in Figure 10-2, the Security Center shows whether you've turned on Windows Firewall, Microsoft's Automatic Updates feature, Malware protection against viruses and spyware, and other security settings like the ones in Internet Explorer and Vista's new User Account Control.

Figure 10-2:
The Security Center lets you turn on your computer's main defenses: Windows Firewall, Automatic Updates, and a virus checker.

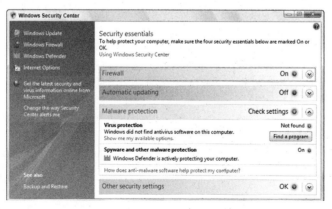

The computer tested in Figure 10-2 passes the firewall test, as it's listed as On. But the Security Center cautions that Windows isn't updating automatically, nor is it protected from maladies like viruses and spyware.

All these defenses should be up and running for maximum safety, because each protects you against different things.

To make sure that your computer's big cannons are loaded and pointing in the right direction, open the Security Center and ogle the settings:

1. **Open the Start menu's Control Panel, choose Security, and then choose Security Center.**

   The Security Center, shown earlier in Figure 10-2, hops into action and displays your computer's current security status in these four categories:

   If the Security Center says that *it's* been disabled, click Turn on Security Center.

   • **Firewall:** Windows Vista's updated, more powerful firewall monitors every connection arriving at your PC. When the firewall notices an unrequested connection trying to enter, it blocks it, stopping potential intruders.

   • **Automatic Updating:** When turned on, Windows Update automatically checks in with Microsoft through the Internet, downloads any new safety patches, and installs them, all for free, and all without any effort on your part.

   • **Malware protection:** Vista's Malware protection contains two parts: Virus protection and Spyware protection. Vista lacks a virus checker, so you must buy your own online or at a computer or office-supply store and pay subscription fees to keep it up-to-date.

     Vista does include a spyware remover, however, called Windows Defender.

   • **Other Security Settings:** This category covers security settings for both Internet Explorer and Vista's User Account Control, otherwise known as "those nagging permission screens," covered in this chapter's first section.

2. **Click the Turn On Now or Restore Settings buttons to fix any potential security problems.**

   Whenever the Security Center notices that one of Vista's defenses is turned off, it alerts you by placing a red shield icon (shown in the margin) near your taskbar's clock.

   Click any item with a red shield icon or that says Check Settings to reveal the Turn On Now or Restore Settings buttons.

By following the two preceding steps, your computer will be much safer than under any other version of Microsoft Windows.

The Security Center's four sections let you flip only an On switch. For more advanced fiddling, look for their names atop the Security Center's leftmost pane. A click on a name takes you to that area's settings menu, where you can change how it works, or even turn it off. (Each option— Windows Update, Windows Firewall, Windows Defender, and Internet Options — receives its own section later in this chapter.)

Changing the firewall settings

Just about everybody has dropped a fork to pick up the phone, only to hear a recorded sales pitch. Telemarketers run programs that sequentially dial phone numbers until somebody answers. Computer hackers run similar programs that automatically try to break into every computer that's currently connected to the Internet.

Broadband Internet users are especially vulnerable because their computers are constantly connected to the Internet. That increases the chances that hackers will locate them and try to exploit any available vulnerability.

That's where Windows Firewall comes in. The firewall sits between your computer and the Internet, acting as an intelligent doorman. If something tries to connect and you or one of your programs didn't request it, the firewall stops the connection.

Occasionally, however, you'll *want* another computer to interact with your computer over the Internet. You may be playing a multiplayer game, for example, or using a file-sharing program. To stop the firewall from blocking those programs, add their names to the firewall's Exceptions list by following these steps:

1. **Choose Control Panel from the Start menu, click Security, and choose Security Center (shown in the margin).**

2. **Click the words Windows Firewall from the window's left side and choose Change Settings.**

   Click Continue or enter an Administrator account's password if Vista's permissions screen nags you.

3. **Click the Exceptions tab.**

   Shown in Figure 10-3, Windows Firewall lists every program currently allowed to communicate through its firewall. (Windows Vista adds some of its programs automatically, so don't be surprised to see them already listed.)

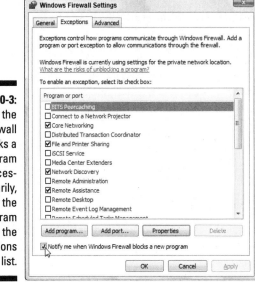

Figure 10-3:
If the
firewall
blocks a
program
unneces-
sarily,
add the
program
to the
Exceptions
list.

Make sure that a check mark appears in the Notify Me When Windows Firewall Blocks a New Program box, shown in Figure 10-3. When a program doesn't work correctly, that message lets you know that the firewall may be the culprit.

4. Click the Add Program button, select the program (or click Browse to locate the program), and click OK.

Almost all programs live in the Program Files folder on your C drive; the program's name bears the same icon you see on its Start menu entry.

The firewall adds your selected program to its Exceptions list and begins allowing other computers to connect to it.

- Don't add programs to the Exceptions list unless you're *sure* the firewall is the problem. Each time you add a program to the list, you're leaving your computer slightly more vulnerable.

- If a program requires you to open a port on the firewall, choose Add Port instead of Add Program in Step 4. Type the required port's name and number and then choose whether it's a TCP (Transmission Control Protocol) or UDP (User Datagram Protocol) port. Click OK to finish.

- If you think you've messed up the firewall's settings, it's easy to revert to its original settings. Click the Advanced tab in Step 3 and click the Restore Defaults button. Click the Yes button and then click OK, and the firewall removes *every* change you've made, letting you start from scratch.

Changing Windows Update settings

Whenever somebody figures out a way to break into Windows, Microsoft releases yet another patch to keep Windows users safe. Unfortunately, the bad folks find holes in Windows as quickly as Microsoft can patch them. The result? Microsoft ends up releasing a constant stream of patches.

In fact, the flow became so strong that many users couldn't keep up. Microsoft's solution is to make Windows Update work *automatically:* Whenever you go online, whether to check e-mail or browse the Web, your computer automatically visits Microsoft's Windows Update site and downloads any new patches in the background.

When your computer's through downloading the new patches, it installs them at 3 a.m. to avoid disturbing your work. Occasionally, you're prompted to restart your computer the next morning to make the patches start working; other times, you don't even notice the action taking place.

Vista's Security Center, covered earlier in this chapter, explains how to make sure that Windows Update is up and running. But if you want to adjust its settings, perhaps not installing new patches until you've had a chance to review them, follow these steps:

1. **Click the Start button, choose All Programs, and choose Windows Update.**

   The Windows Update window appears.

2. **Choose Change Settings from the leftmost pane.**

   Windows Update's settings page appears, shown in Figure 10-4.

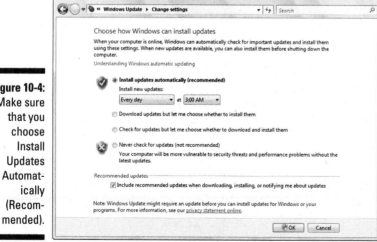

Figure 10-4: Make sure that you choose Install Updates Automatically (Recommended).

3. Make your changes and then click OK.

Chances are, you won't need to make any changes. But night owls might want to change the 3 a.m. automatic installation time.

Some experienced computer users select the option Download Updates but Let Me Choose Whether to Install Them. That option gives them a chance to ogle the incoming patches before installing them.

Avoiding viruses

When it comes to viruses, *everything* is suspect. Viruses travel not only in e-mail and programs, but also in screen savers, themes, toolbars, and other Windows add-ons. Because Vista doesn't include a built-in virus program, follow these rules to reduce your risk of infection:

- ✔ When shopping for an antivirus program, look for one that runs automatically in the background. If you don't yet have an antivirus program, open the Control Panel's Security area, choose Security Center, and click the Malware Protection section's Find a Program button for free trial offers.

- ✔ Tell your antivirus program to scan everything you download, as well as anything that arrives through e-mail or a messaging program.

- ✔ Only open attachments that you're expecting. If you receive something unexpected from a friend, don't open it. Instead, e-mail or phone that person to see whether he or she *really* sent you something.

- ✔ Don't run two virus checkers simultaneously because they often quarrel. If you want to test a different program, first uninstall your existing one from the Control Panel's Programs area. It's then safe to install another virus checker that you want to try.

- ✔ Simply buying a virus checker isn't enough; you must also pay an annual fee to keep your virus checker smart enough to recognize the latest viruses. Without the most up-to-date virus definitions, virus checkers detect only older viruses, not the new ones sprouting daily on the Internet. (The newest viruses always spread most quickly, causing the most damage.)

If you think you have a virus and you don't have an antivirus program, unplug your PC's network or telephone cable before heading to the store and buying an antivirus program. Install and run the antivirus program *before* reconnecting your computer to the Internet. That stops your computer from infecting others before you're able disinfect it.

McAfee offers a free virus-removal tool that removes more than 50 common viruses. Downloadable from `http://vil.nai.com/vil/stinger/`, it's a handy tool for times of need.

Staying Safe on the Internet

The Internet is not a safe place. Some people design Web sites specifically to exploit Windows' latest vulnerabilities — the ones Microsoft hasn't yet had time to patch. This section explains some of Internet Explorer's safety features, as well as other safe travel tips when navigating the Internet.

Setting Internet Explorer's security zones

Chances are, you won't need to fiddle with Internet Explorer's security zones. They come preset to offer the most protection with the least amount of effort. But if you're curious about Internet Explorer's zones, choose Internet Options from the program's Tools menu, and click the Security tab. Think you've messed up the preset security settings? Click the Reset All Zones to Default Level button.

Internet Explorer offers four security zones, each offering different levels of protection. When you add different Web sites to different zones, Internet Explorer treats the sites differently, placing restrictions on some and lifting restrictions for others. Here's the rundown:

✔ **Internet:** Unless you play with Internet Explorer's zones, Internet Explorer treats every Web site as if it were in this zone. This zone offers medium-high security, which works very well for most needs.

✔ **Local Intranet:** This zone is intended for Web sites running on an internal network. (Home users rarely have to deal with intranets because they're mostly found in corporations and large businesses.) Because internal Web sites are created in-house and self-contained, this zone removes some restrictions, letting you do more things.

✔ **Trusted Sites:** Putting sites in here means you trust them *completely.* (I don't trust any Web site completely.)

✔ **Restricted Sites:** If you don't trust a site at all, place it in here. Internet Explorer lets you visit it but not download from it or use any of its *plug-ins* — small downloadable programs adding extra graphics, animation, and similar enhancements. I used to place a few sites in here to strip their pop-up ads, but Internet Explorer's built-in pop-up blocker now eliminates the need.

Windows Mail respects the settings you've used for these zones. Normally, Windows Mail treats all incoming e-mail as if it were a Web site in the Restricted zone. (Many e-mails now come formatted as Web pages.) To change the zone that Windows Mail uses, choose Options from its Tools menu and choose the Security tab.

Avoiding evil add-ons and hijackers

Microsoft designed Internet Explorer to let programmers add extra features through *add-ons*. By installing an add-on program — toolbars, stock tickers, and program launchers, for example — users can wring a little more work out of Internet Explorer. Similarly, many sites use *ActiveX* — a fancy word for little programs that add animation, sound, video, and other flashy tricks to a Web site.

Unfortunately, dastardly programmers began creating add-ons and ActiveX programs that *harm* users. Some add-ons spy on your activities, bombard your screen with additional ads, redirect your home page to another site, or make your modem dial long-distance numbers to porn sites. Worst yet, some renegade add-ons install themselves as soon as you visit a Web site — without asking your permission.

Windows Vista packs several guns to combat these troublemakers. First, if a site tries to sneak a program onto your computer, Internet Explorer quickly blocks it, sending a warning (shown in Figure 10-5) across the top of Internet Explorer's screen. Clicking the warning reveals your options, shown in Figure 10-6.

Figure 10-5:
Internet
Explorer
blocks a
program.

Figure 10-6:
The warning
strip
shows your
options.

Unfortunately, Internet Explorer can't tell the good downloads from the bad, leaving the burden of proof to you. But if you see a message like the one shown in Figure 10-5 and you *haven't* requested a download, chances are the site's trying to harm you: Don't download the program or install the ActiveX control.

If a bad add-on creeps in somehow, you're not completely out of luck. Internet Explorer's Add-on Manager lets you disable it. To see all the add-on programs installed in Internet Explorer (and remove any that you know are bad), follow these steps:

1. **Choose Manage Add-ons from Internet Explorer's Tools menu and then choose Enable or Disable Add-ons from the pop-up menu.**

   Don't mistakenly choose Find More Add-ons. That takes you to Microsoft's store, which tries to sell you bushels of overpriced add-ons.

   The Manage Add-ons window appears, as shown in Figure 10-7, letting you see all currently or previously loaded add-ons, as well as add-ons running without permission. It also lets you see downloaded ActiveX controls, which often cause the most trouble.

Figure 10-7: Internet Explorer's Manage Add-ons window lets you see all installed add-ons and disable the ones you don't like.

2. **Click the Add-on that gives you trouble and choose Disable.**

   Click the Show drop-down list at the top of the Manage Add-ons Window to see the four types of add-ons. Choose another of these types to see add-ons listed for that category. If you spot the name of an unwanted toolbar or other bad program, here's your chance to purge it.

3. **Repeat the process for each unwanted add-on and then click the OK button.**

   You probably need to restart Internet Explorer for the change to take effect.

Not all add-ons are bad. Many good ones let you play movies, hear sounds, or view special content on a Web site. Don't delete an add-on simply because it's listed in the Add-on Manager.

✔ On the rare instance that disabling an add-on prevents a page from loading, click that add-on's name in Step 2 of the preceding steps and click the Enable button to return it to working order.

✔ Internet Explorer's Add-on Manager disables add-ons fairly easily, but if you spot a particularly evil one, remove it completely by clicking the Delete ActiveX button instead of the Disable button.

✔ How the heck do you tell the good add-ons from the bad? Unfortunately, there's no sure way of telling, although the name listed under Publisher provides one clue. The best way is to avoid being hijacked in the first place, mainly by not installing things Internet Explorer has tried to block.

✔ Make sure that Internet Explorer's pop-up blocker runs by choosing Pop-up Blocker from the Tools menu. If you see Turn Off Pop-up Blocker in the pop-up menu, you're all set. If you see Turn On Pop-up Blocker, click the command to turn it back on.

Avoiding phishing scams

Eventually, you'll receive an e-mail from your bank, eBay, PayPal, or a similar Web site announcing a problem with your account. Invariably, the e-mail offers a handy link to click, saying that you must enter your username and password to set things in order.

Don't do it, no matter how realistic the e-mail and Web site may appear. You're seeing an ugly industry called *phishing:* Fraudsters send millions of these messages worldwide, hoping to convince a few frightened souls into typing their precious account name and password.

How do you tell the real e-mails from the fake ones? It's easy, actually, because *all* these e-mails are fake. Finance-related sites never, ever e-mail you a link for you to click on and enter your password. If you're suspicious, visit the company's *real* Web site — by typing the Web address by hand. Then look for their security area and forward them the e-mail, asking whether it's legitimate. Chances are, it's not.

Vista employs four safeguards to thwart phishing scams:

- Windows Mail warns you with a message, shown in Figure 10-8, when it spots a suspicious e-mail in your Inbox. Then Windows Mail routes the e-mail to the Junk E-mail folder. Feel free to delete the e-mail, should you spot it in that folder.

- When you first run Internet Explorer, the program offers to turn on its Phishing Filter. Take Internet Explorer up on its offer. Unlike many of Vista's safety features, the Phishing Filter provides a very non-obtrusive safety net.

- Internet Explorer examines every Web page for suspicious signals. If a site seems suspicious, Internet Explorer's Address Bar — the normally white area that lists the Web site's address — turns yellow. Internet Explorer sends a pop-up warning that you're viewing a suspected phishing site.

- Internet Explorer compares a Web site's address with a list of known phishing sites. If it finds a match, the Phishing Filter keeps you from entering, shown in Figure 10-9. Should you ever spot that screen, close the Web page.

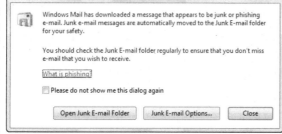

Figure 10-8:
Windows
Mail warns
you when it
detects an
incoming
phishing
e-mail.

Figure 10-9:
Internet
Explorer
warns you
when you
visit a
known
phishing
site.

So, why can't the authorities simply arrest those people responsible? Because Internet thieves are notoriously difficult to track down and prosecute. The reach of the Internet lets them work from any place in the world.

- ✔ If you've already entered your name and password into a phishing site, take action immediately: Visit the *real* Web site and change your password. Change your username, too, if possible. Then contact the bank or company and ask it for help. It may be able to stop the thieves before they wrap their electronic fingers around your funds.

- ✔ You can warn Microsoft if you spot a site that smells suspiciously like phish. Choose Phishing Filter from Internet Explorer's Tools menu and choose Report This Website. Internet Explorer takes you to Microsoft's Phishing Filter Web site. Telling Microsoft of suspected phishing sites helps them warn other visitors.

- ✔ Curious about what phishing e-mails look like? Drop by www. antiphishing.org and browse through its archive of thousands of phishing e-mails.

Avoiding and removing spyware and parasites with Windows Defender

Spyware and *parasites* are programs that latch onto Internet Explorer without your knowledge. The sneakiest programs may try to change your home page, dial toll numbers with your modem, or spy on your Web activity, sneaking your surfing habits back to the spyware program's publisher.

Most spyware programs freely admit to being spies — usually on the 43rd page of the 44-page agreement you're supposed to read before installing the program.

Nobody wants these ugly programs, of course, so they do tricky things to keep you from removing them. That's where Vista's new Windows Defender program comes in. It stops some spyware from installing itself automatically, and pries off spyware that's already latched onto your PC. Best yet, Windows Update keeps Windows Defender up-to-date to recognize and destroy the latest strains of spyware.

To make sure that Windows Defender is running automatically on your PC, visit Windows Security Center, described in this chapter's "Assessing Your Safety in Security Center" section. When running automatically, Windows Defender scans your PC each evening and alerts you to any newfound spyware.

To make Windows Defender scan your PC immediately, a potential solution when your PC's acting strange, click the Start menu, choose All Programs, and launch Windows Defender. Click the Scan button and wait for it to finish.

Several other antispyware programs can also scan your computer for spyware, carefully snipping out any pieces that they find. Some programs are free in the hopes that you'll buy the more full-featured version later. Ad-Aware (www.lavasoftusa.com) and Spybot Search & Destroy (www.safernetworking.org) are two of the most popular programs.

Don't be afraid to run more than one spyware scanner on your PC. Each does its own scan, killing off any spyware it finds.

Using parental controls

A feature much-welcomed by parents and much-booed by their children, Vista's Parental Controls offer several new ways to police how people can access the computer, as well as the Internet. In fact, people who share their PCs with roommates may welcome the Parental Controls, as well.

The Parental Controls let you dictate what a person can and can't do on the Internet. They also keep tabs on how the person's using the PC, sending you reports on exactly when they're using the PC, what Web sites they're visiting, and what programs they're using.

To set Parental Controls, you must own an Administrator account. (I explain how to create the two types of accounts in Chapter 13.) If everybody shares one PC, make sure that the kids have Standard accounts. If your children have their own PCs, create an Administrator account on their PCs for yourself and change their accounts to Standard.

To set up Vista's Parental Controls, follow these steps:

1. **Open the Control Panel from the Start menu and choose Parental Controls in the User Accounts and Family Safety section.**

   If Vista's built-in policeman says, "A program needs your permission to continue," feel free to click the Continue button.

2. **Click the User account you want to restrict.**

   Vista only lets you add Parental Controls to one User account at a time, a process that caused considerable grief for Mr. and Mrs. Brady.

   When you choose a User account, the Parental Controls screen appears, shown in Figure 10-10. The next steps take you through each section of the controls.

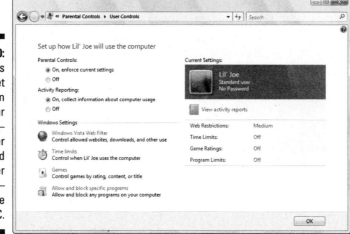

Figure 10-10:
Vista lets
you set
controls on
how your
children —
or any other
Standard
User
account —
may use
the PC.

3. Turn the Parental Controls on or off.

The Parental Controls area first presents two switches, letting you turn monitoring on or off:

- **Parental Controls:** This toggle switch simply turns on or off any restrictions you've set. It's a handy way to turn on the restrictions when your suspicions are aroused or turn them off when they're not needed.

- **Activity Reporting:** This switch toggles Vista's activity reporting. That tells the PC to spy on your children's habits, telling you exactly when they've logged on and off, what programs they've used or tried to use, and what Web sites they've visited or tried to visit.

4. Set the Windows Vista Web Filter to determine what parts of the Web your child may visit.

The Web Filter lets you choose the parts of the Internet your child may view. To block some Web sites, click Edit the Allow and Block List. There, you can punish your child by keeping her off of MySpace.com for one week, for example. For ultimate control, block *every* Web site by clicking the Only Allow Websites Which Are on the Allow List box, and then adding a few safe sites to the allowed list.

The Block Web Content Automatically area comes set to Medium, meaning Internet Explorer blocks sites containing mature content, pornography, drugs, hate speech, and weapons. Switch it to High to block everything not specifically designed for children. Or switch it to Custom and pick and choose specific categories you'd like blocked from your child's view.

Encrypting your PC with BitLocker

Vista's new BitLocker program scrambles the contents of your PC's hard drive. Then it automatically unscrambles it whenever you enter your User account's password. Why bother? To keep your information safe from thieves. If they steal your PC or even its hard drive, they won't be able to access your data, and its stash of passwords, credit-card numbers, and other personal information.

Unfortunately, BitLocker provides more protection than most people need. It's difficult to set up, and if you ever lose your password, you've lost all your data, as well. BitLocker also requires your PC to be set up in a special way, with an extra *partition* — a separate storage area — on your hard drive. For full protection, it requires a PC with a special chip, something not found on many PCs today.

If you're interested in BitLocker, take your PC to your office's information technology person and ask them for help and advice on setting it up. It's not as simple as merely throwing a switch.

Be aware, however, that Web filters aren't 100 percent accurate, and some unwanted sites will always slip through the cracks.

5. **Choose whether to allow file downloads and then click OK.**

   The final box at this page's bottom lets you stop your child from downloading files, an easy way to keep them from downloading and installing programs without your knowledge. However, checking this box may also keep them from downloading files needed for schoolwork.

   Clicking OK returns you to the Parental Controls opening screen, shown in Figure 10-10.

6. **Add restrictions on time limits, games, and specific programs and then set activity reports, clicking OK after each.**

   This huge category lets you block specific things on your PC rather than the Internet:

   - **Time limits:** This option brings up a grid, letting you click on the hours when your child should be restricted from using the PC. Here's where you can make the PC off-limits after bed time, for example.

   - **Games:** You may allow or ban all games here, restrict access to games with certain ratings (ratings appear on most software boxes), and block or allow specific games.

   - **Allow and Block Specific Programs:** Here's where you can keep the kids out of your checkbook program, as well as particular games. You can block all programs, only allowing access to a few. Or, you can allow access to all but a few programs.

- **Activity Reports:** This setting lists the activity of every User account on your PC. You can view lists of everybody's visited Web sites, downloaded files, log on and off times, played games, newly added contacts, Web Cam usage, accessed songs and videos, and much, much more. A handy summary on the first page sorts this vast amount of information into "Top Ten" lists for easy viewing.

7. Click OK to exit Parental Controls.

To see what your child's been up to, return to Parental Controls and choose View Activity Reports.

Part IV
Customizing and Upgrading Windows Vista

The 5th Wave   By Rich Tennant

"Ms. Gretsky, tell the employees they can have internet games on their computers again."

In this part . . .

*W*hen your life changes, you want Windows Vista to change with it, and that's where this part of the book comes in. Here's where you discover Windows Vista's reorganized Control Panel, which lets you change nearly everything but your computer's disposition.

Chapter 12 describes easy click-through tune-ups you can perform to keep your computer in top shape, backed up, and running smoothly. If you're sharing your computer with others, you discover how to dish out user accounts to each of them, with *you* deciding who can do what.

This part also walks you through Vista's new Parental Controls, which let you automatically control what your kids can and *can't* do when sitting down at the keyboard.

Finally, when you're ready to buy that second (or third, fourth, or fifth) computer, a chapter walks you through linking them all to create a home network, where they can all share the same Internet connection, printer, and files.

Chapter 11

Customizing Windows Vista with the Control Panel

*A*nybody who's seen a science-fiction movie knows that robots come with secret control panels, the best of which include an emergency Off switch. Windows Vista's Control Panel lives in plain sight, thankfully, living one click away on the Start menu.

Inside the Control Panel, you'll find hundreds of switches and options that let you customize Windows' look, feel, and vibe. This chapter explains the switches and sliders you'll want to tweak, and it steers you away from the ones to avoid.

I also list shortcuts that whisk you directly to the right Control Panel setting, bypassing the long, twisting corridors of menus.

One word of caution, however: Some of the Control Panel's settings can be changed only by the person holding the almighty Administrator account — usually the computer's owner. If Vista refuses to open the Control Panel's hatch, call over the PC's owner for help.

Finding the Right Switch in the Control Panel

Flip open the Start menu's Control Panel, and you can while away an entire work week opening icons and flipping switches to fine-tune Vista. Part of the attraction comes from the Control Panel's magnitude: It houses more than *50* icons in the Classic View, and some icons summon menus with more than two dozen settings and tasks.

To save you from searching aimlessly for the right switch, the Control Panel lumps similar items together in its Category View, shown in Figure 11-1.

Below each category's name live shortcuts for that category's most popular offerings. The Security category icon in Figure 11-1, for example, offers short-cuts to check for the latest security updates, as well as evaluate your PC's current security status.

Windows XP veterans already familiar with the Control Panel's icons can switch to the Control Panel's Classic View, instead. (The mouse points to that option in Figure 11-1.) The Classic View drops the categories facade and presents *all* of Vista's icons, as shown in Figure 11-2.

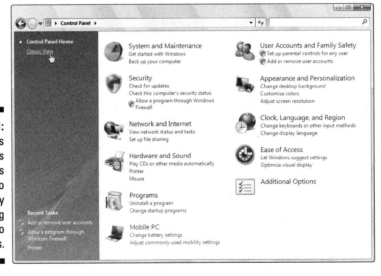

Figure 11-1: Windows Vista makes settings easier to find by grouping them into categories.

Figure 11-2: Designed for experienced PC owners, Windows Vista's Classic View displays *all* the Control Panel's icons.

Don't think something's astray if your Control Panel differs from the one in Figure 11-2. Different programs, accessories, and computer models often add their own icons to the Control Panel. Different versions of Vista, which I describe in Chapter 1, also leave out some of the icons seen here.

Rest your mouse pointer over any confusing icon or category in the Control Panel, and Windows Vista thoughtfully explains its meaning in life.

The Control Panel gathers all of Vista's main switches into one well-stocked panel, but it's certainly not the only way to change Vista's settings. You can almost always jump to these same settings by right-clicking the item you want to change — be it your desktop, Start menu, or a folder — and choosing Properties from the pop-up menu.

The rest of this chapter lists the Control Panel's Categories shown in Figure 11-1, the reasons you'd ever want to visit them, and the shortcuts for jumping straight to the setting you need.

System and Maintenance

Like a '67 Mustang, Windows Vista needs occasional maintenance. In fact, a little bit of maintenance can make Windows Vista run so much more smoothly that I devote the best of Chapter 12 to that subject.

That chapter explains how to speed up Windows, free up hard drive space, back up your data, and create a safety net called System Restore.

Like most Control Panel categories, the System and Maintenance section is jam-packed with options. To find things more easily, double-click the Control Panel's menu bar to make it fill the screen. Also, if necessary, scroll down the window to see the entries hiding below view along the menu's bottom.

User Accounts and Family Safety

I explain in Chapter 13 how to create separate accounts for other people to use your computer. That lets them use your PC, but limits the amount of damage they can do to Windows and your files.

Here's a refresher if you don't want to flip ahead to that chapter: Choose Control Panel from the Start menu. Then, in the User Accounts And Family Safety section, click Add Or Remove User Accounts.

That opens the Manage Accounts area, where you can also create accounts and change existing ones, including their name, password, or Start menu picture.

The Control Panel's User Accounts And Family Safety category also includes a link to the Security section, where you can place Parental Controls on what your kids do with the PC. I explain Parental Controls in Chapter 10.

Security

The Control Panel's Security category contains a full brigade of soldiers. I've written field manuals for them all in Chapter 10: Windows Firewall, Windows Update, Windows Defender, and Vista's new Parental Controls.

Changing Windows' Appearance (Appearance and Personalization)

One of the most popular categories, the Appearance and Personalization area lets you change Vista's look and feel in a wide variety of ways. Open the category to see the following six icons:

✔ **Personalization:** For many people, this icon is pay dirt. Choose this to splash a new picture or digital photo across your desktop, choose which screen saver kicks in when you're away from your PC, change the colors of Vista's window frames, and change your monitor's *screen resolution* — a nifty way to pack more information onto your screen.

✔ **Taskbar and Start menu:** Ready to add your own photo to that boring picture atop your Start menu? Want to customize the taskbar living along your desktop's bottom edge? I cover both these things in Chapter 2's Start menu and taskbar sections, but those same settings are available here, as well.

✔ **Ease of Access Center:** Designed to help people with special needs, these settings make Windows more navigable by the blind, deaf, and people with other physical challenges. Because the Control Panel offers Ease of Access as its own category, I describe it in its own section later in this chapter.

✔ **Folder Options:** Used mainly by experienced users, this area lets you add subtle tweaks to how folders look and behave.

✔ **Fonts:** Here's where you install new fonts to spruce up your printed work. I cover fonts where they belong, in the printing chapter (Chapter 7).

✔ **Windows Sidebar Properties:** This area lets you add gadgets to Vista's *Sidebar,* that thick strip along the desktop's right edge. I explain the Sidebar and its gadgets in Chapter 2, but here's the trick: Add gadgets by right-clicking a blank part of the Sidebar and choosing Add Gadgets.

In the next few sections, I explain the tasks in this category that you'll reach for most often.

Changing the desktop background

A *background,* also known as wallpaper, is simply the picture covering your desktop. To change it, follow these steps:

Right-clicking your desktop, choosing Personalize, and selecting Desktop Background jumps you quickly to Step 3.

1. **Click the Start menu, choose Control Panel, and find the Appearance and Personalization category.**

   Its icon appears in the margin.

2. **Choose Change Desktop Background from the Personalization section.**

   The window shown in Figure 11-3 appears.

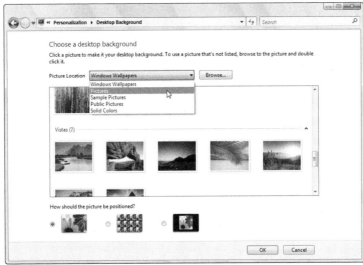

Figure 11-3: Click the drop-down menu to find more pictures to splash across your desktop as the background.

3. **Click on a new picture for the background.**

   Be sure to click the drop-down menu, shown in Figure 11-3, to see all the available photos, textures, paintings, and light auras that Vista offers. To rummage through folders not listed, click Browse. Feel free to search your own Pictures folder for potential backgrounds.

   Background files can be stored as BMP, GIF, JPG, JPEG, DIB, or PNG files. That means you can use nearly any photo or art found on the Internet or from a digital camera.

   When you click a new picture, Windows Vista immediately places it across your desktop. If you're pleased, jump to Step 5.

4. **Decide whether to stretch, tile, or center the picture.**

   Not every picture fits perfectly across a monitor. Small pictures, for example, need to be either stretched to fit the space or spread across the screen in rows like tiles on a floor. When tiling and stretching still looks odd, try centering the image and leaving blank space around its edges.

From left to right, the three large buttons along the bottom of Figure 11-3 let you stretch, tile, or center your photo.

5. **Click OK to save your currently displayed background.**

Did you happen to spot an eye-catching picture while Web surfing with Internet Explorer? Right-click that Web site's picture and choose Set As Background. Sneaky Windows copies the picture and splashes it across your desktop as a new background.

Choosing a screen saver

In the dinosaur days of computing, computer monitors suffered from *burn-in:* permanent damage when an oft-used program burned its image onto the screen. To prevent this burn-in, people installed a screen saver to jump in with a blank screen or moving lines. Today's monitors no longer suffer from burn-in problems, but people still use screen savers because they look cool.

Windows comes with several built-in screen savers. To try one out, follow these steps:

Right-clicking your desktop, choosing Personalize, and choosing Screen Saver jumps you quickly to Step 3.

1. **Open the Control Panel from the Start menu and select the Appearance and Personalization category.**

   The Appearance and Personalization category opens to show its offerings.

2. **Choose Change Screen Saver from the Personalization area.**

   The Screen Saver Settings dialog box appears.

3. **Click the downward-pointing arrow in the Screen Saver box and select a screen saver.**

   After choosing a screen saver, click the Preview button for an audition. View as many candidates as you like before making a decision.

   Be sure to click the Settings button, as most screen savers offer options, letting you specify the speed of a photo slide show, for example, and the direction the photos should travel across the screen.

4. **If desired, add security by selecting the On Resume, Display Logon Screen check box.**

   This safeguard keeps people from sneaking into your computer while you're fetching coffee. It makes Windows ask for a password after waking up from screen-saver mode. (I cover passwords in Chapter 13.)

5. **When you're done setting up your screen saver, click OK.**

If you *really* want to extend your monitor's life (and save electricity), don't bother with screen savers. Instead, click Change Power Settings in Step 3. The resulting Select a Power Plan window lets you choose the Power Saver plan, which tells Windows Vista to turn off your monitor when you haven't used it for 20 minutes or so. (Tailor any plan to match your work habits by clicking Change Plan Settings.)

Changing the computer's theme

Themes are simply collections of settings: You can save your chosen screen saver and desktop background, for example, as one theme, letting you switch easily between them.

If you haven't created any themes on your own, then you won't find much in here. Windows Vista comes with *very* few prebuilt themes to slip on. To try one on, right-click your desktop, choose Personalize, and choose Theme. The Theme Settings dialog box appears, shown in Figure 11-4.

Figure 11-4: Choose a pre-configured theme to change how Windows looks and sounds.

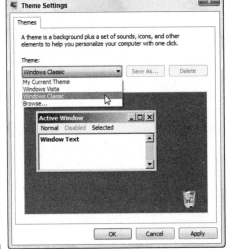

Windows Vista lists its token bundled themes (and an option to browse for your own); click any of them to see a preview in the Sample window shown in Figure 11-4:

- ✔ **My Current Theme:** If you've somehow messed up Windows Vista's appearance settings — but haven't yet saved them — choose this command to revert to your last saved theme.

- ✔ **Windows Vista:** This setting reverts to the "stock" Windows Vista theme, the one it wore when first installed.

- ✔ **Windows Classic:** Retro users choose this setting to bring back the lean, mean, and lightening-fast look of the venerable Windows 98.

- ✔ **Browse:** Click here to grab a Theme you've saved in a specific folder. (Vista normally saves Themes in the Program Files folder.)

Choose any of the themes, and Windows Vista automatically slips into the new clothes. To preview a listed theme's look, click its name and watch the Sample window.

Instead of choosing from Vista's pre-assembled themes, feel free to make your own by changing Vista's background, colors, the screen saver, and other details. Then save your Theme by clicking Save As, shown in Figure 11-4, and naming your Theme.

- ✔ Vista's basic tools for creating themes wear thin after awhile. If you're really into creating Windows themes (called *skinning* by aficionados), pick up a third-party program like WindowBlinds (www.windowblinds.net). You can download Themes created by WindowBlinds aficionados at WinCustomize (www.wincustomize.com).

- ✔ Before you begin downloading themes from the Web or e-mail attachments, be sure that you're using an updated antivirus program. Viruses sometimes masquerade as themes.

- ✔ To change themes quickly, right-click your desktop and choose Personalize. When the Control Panel's Personalization area appears, select Theme and choose your new theme.

Changing the screen resolution

One of Vista's many change-it-once-and-forget-about-it options, screen resolution determines how many things Vista can cram onto your monitor at one time. Changing the resolution either shrinks windows to pack more of 'em on-screen, or it enlarges everything at the expense of desktop real estate.

Doubling your workspace with a second monitor

Blessed with an extra monitor, perhaps a leftover from a deceased PC? Connect it to your PC, place it aside your first monitor, and you've doubled your Windows desktop: Vista stretches your workspace across both monitors. That lets you view the online encyclopedia in one monitor while writing your term paper in the other.

To perform these video gymnastics, your PC needs a video card with two *ports*, and those ports must match your monitor's *connectors* — technical topics all covered in my book *Upgrading and Fixing PCs For Dummies*, published by Wiley Publishing, Inc.

To find your most comfortable resolution — or if a program or game mutters something about changing your *screen resolution* or *video mode* — follow these steps:

1. **Choose Control Panel from the Start menu and choose the Appearance and Personalization category.**

   The Appearance and Personalization area lists the main ways you can change Vista's appearance.

2. **In the Personalization area, choose Adjust Screen Resolution.**

   The Display Settings dialog box appears, as shown in Figure 11-5.

Figure 11-5: Depending on the screen resolution, Windows can squeeze different amounts of information onto your monitor.

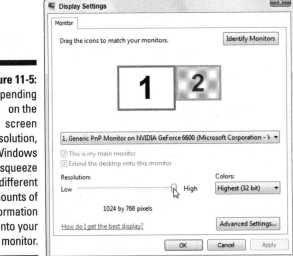

3. **Change the number of colors your monitor displays, if desired.**

   Vista lets you select several settings from the Colors drop-down menu.

   To fully experience the rain forest in your digital camera photos, make sure that Windows Vista displays the highest number of colors as possible. Highest, or 32-bit mode, paints your photos with up to 16 million glorious colors. Medium (16-bit mode) displays only up to 65,000 colors, which makes a surprisingly large difference.

4. **To change the screen resolution, use your mouse to drag the little bar in the Resolution area.**

   Watch the little preview screen change as you move the mouse. The more you slide the bar to the right, the larger your monitor grows. Unfortunately, the more information Vista can pack onto your monitor, the smaller that information appears.

   There's no right or wrong choice here, but here's a word of advice: Most Web sites won't fit onto your screen well at 640 by 480 pixels. A setting of 800 by 600 is better, and 1,024 by 768, Vista's favorite, will accommodate just about any Web size you visit.

5. **View your changes by clicking the Apply button.**

   When Windows Vista switches to a new resolution, it gives you 15 seconds to click a button approving the change. If the new resolution leaves your monitor blacked out, you won't see the on-screen button. After a few seconds, Windows notices that you didn't click the approval button and reverts to your original resolution.

6. **Click OK when you're done tweaking the display.**

   After you've chosen the highest color setting and a comfortable screen resolution, you'll probably never return here. Unless you plug a second monitor into your PC, of course, which I describe in the sidebar.

Changing Network and Internet Connections

Vista normally reaches out and touches other PCs and the Internet automatically. Plug an Internet connection into your PC, and Vista quickly starts slurping information from the Web. Plug in another PC, and Vista tries to create a network.

But when Vista can't handle the job by itself, turn to the Control Panel's Network and Internet category: Choose Control Panel from the Start menu and choose the Network and Internet category.

I devote Chapter 14 completely to networking; the Internet gets its due in Chapter 8.

Setting the Date, Time, Language, and Regional Options

Microsoft designed this area mostly for laptoppers who frequently travel to different time zones and locations. Otherwise, you touch this information only once — when first setting up your computer. Windows Vista subsequently remembers the time and date, even when your PC's turned off.

 To drop by here, choose Control Panel from the Start menu and click the Clock, Language, and Region category. Two sections appear, Date and Time, and Regional and Language Options. Those sections let you perform these tasks:

- ✔ **Date and Time:** This area is fairly self explanatory. (Clicking your taskbar's clock and choosing Date and Time Settings lets you visit here, as well.)

- ✔ **Regional and Language Options:** Traveling in Italy? Click this task, and choose Italian from the Current Format menu. Windows switches to that country's currency symbols and date format. While you're there, click the Location tab and choose Italy — or whatever country you're currently visiting.

  Bilinguals also visit this area when working on documents that require characters from different languages. (Foreign characters occasionally require installing another font, which I cover in Chapter 7.)

Hardware and Sound

 Vista packs oodles of icons into its Hardware and Sound category, shown in Figure 11-6. It's a virtual warehouse of switches that control your PC's *hardware:* its mouse, speakers, keyboard, printer, telephone, scanner, digital camera, game controllers, and, for you graphic artists out there, a digital pen.

You won't spend much time in here, especially coming in through the Control Panel's doors. Most settings appear elsewhere, where a mouse-click will bring you directly to the setting you need.

Whether you arrive at these pages through the Control Panel or a shortcut, this section explains the most popular reasons for visiting here.

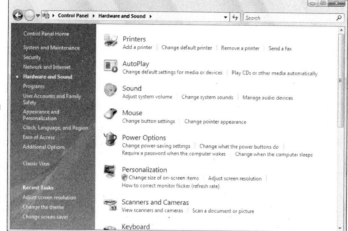

Figure 11-6: Vista's Hardware and Sound category brims with settings.

Adjusting Vista's volume and sounds

The Sound area lets you adjust your PC's volume, as well as connect seven speakers and a subwoofer to your PC, a feature much loved by World of Warcraft enthusiasts.

To turn down your PC's volume knob, shown in Figure 11-7, click the little speaker by your clock and slide down the volume. No speaker on your taskbar? Restore it by right-clicking the taskbar's clock, choosing Properties, and adding a check mark to the Volume check box.

To mute your PC, click the little speaker icon in Figure 11-7. Clicking that icon again removes the gag.

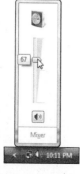

Figure 11-7: Click the speaker and move the sliding control to adjust your PC's volume.

Vista one-ups Windows XP by letting you set different volumes for different programs. You can quietly detonate explosives in MineSweeper, allowing Windows Mail to loudly announce any new messages. To juggle volume levels between programs, follow these steps.

Double-clicking the little speaker icon next to your clock jumps you ahead to Step 3.

1. **Choose Control Panel from the Start menu and choose Hardware and Sound.**

   The Control Panel's Hardware and Sound area (shown in Figure 11-6) displays its tools.

2. **Find the Sound icon and then click Adjust System Volume.**

   Vista's Volume Mixer box appears, show in Figure 11-8, listing each noisemaker on your PC.

3. **Slide any program's control up or down to muzzle it or raise it above the din.**

   Close the Volume Mixer box by clicking the little red X in its corner.

Figure 11-8:
Turn down one program's volume without affecting the others.

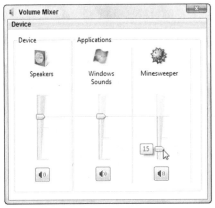

Installing or setting up speakers

Most PCs come with only two speakers. Some PCs today come with four, and PCs that double as home theaters or gaming rigs sometimes have up to eight. To accommodate the variety of setups, Vista includes a speaker setup area, complete with a speaker test.

If you're installing new speakers, or you're not sure your old ones are working, follow these steps to introduce them properly to Vista.

Right-click your taskbar's Speaker icon and choose Playback Devices to jump to Step 2.

1. **Click the Start button, choose Control Panel, and select the Hardware and Sound category.**

   The familiar Hardware and Sound category from Figure 11-6 appears.

2. **In the Sound area, choose Manage Audio Devices.**

   The Sound dialog box appears, open to the Playback tab, which lists your speakers.

3. **Click your speaker or speaker's icon, and click Configure.**

   The Speaker Setup dialog box appears, shown in Figure 11-9.

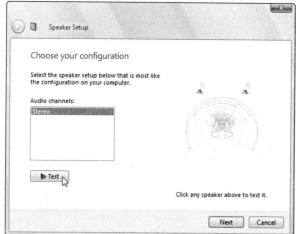

Figure 11-9:
Click Test to hear your speakers.

4. **Click the Test button, adjust your speaker's settings, and click Next.**

   Vista walks you through selecting your number of speakers and their placement and then plays each one in turn so that you can hear whether they're in the correct locations.

5. **Adjust any other sound devices and then click OK when you're done.**

While visiting, feel free to check your microphone volume by clicking the Recording tab in Step 2, as well as tabs for any other gadgetry you can afford.

Adding a printer

Quarrelling printer manufacturers couldn't agree on how printers should be installed. As a result, you install your printer in one of two ways:

- ✔ Some printer manufacturers say simply to plug in your printer, usually by pushing its connector into a little rectangular USB port. Flip your PC's On switch, and Windows Vista automatically recognizes and embraces your new printer. Add any needed ink cartridges, toner, or paper, and you're done.

- ✔ Other manufacturers took an uglier approach, saying you must install their bundled software *before* plugging in your printer. And if you don't install the software first, the printer may not work correctly.

The only way to know how your printer should be installed is to check the printer's manual. (Sometimes this information appears on a colorful, one-page Installation Cheat Sheet packed in the printer's box.)

If your printer didn't come with installation software, install the cartridges, add paper to the tray, and follow these instructions to put it to work:

1. **With Vista up and running, plug your printer into your PC and turn on the printer.**

   If your printer's rectangular connector slides into a rectangular hole or *port* on your PC, you have a *USB printer,* the type used by most printers today. Vista may send a message saying that your printer is installed successfully, but follow the next two steps to test it.

   If your printer's evil-looking, pronged connector pushes into a long oval connector full of holes, it plugs into your PC's *printer port.* (That connector is called *LPT1:* in computer language.)

2. **Choose Control Panel from Vista's Start menu.**

   The Control Panel displays its categories of settings.

3. **Open the Hardware and Sound category and choose Printers.**

   The Printers window appears, listing icons for any currently attached printers. If you spot your USB printer listed by its model name, right-click its icon, choose Properties, and click the Print Test Page button. If it prints correctly, you're finished. Congratulations. If your printer's name doesn't appear, though, move to Step 4.

   Vista lists a printer named Microsoft XPS Document Writer that's not really a printer. Choosing to print to that printer creates a special file much like Adobe's PDF files, which require a special program to view and print. Vista can view or print XPS files; Windows XP, by contrast, first requires you to download and install Microsoft's XPS Viewer (www.microsoft.com/downloads).

4. **Click the Add a Printer button from the Printers window's top menu.**

   When the Choose a Local or Network Printer window appears, choose Add a Local Printer. (If you're installing a printer on a network, see Chapter 14 for the lowdown.)

5. **Choose how you've connected the printer to your PC and click Next.**

   Choose LPT1 (the oblong connector). If you're using a USB printer, click Cancel, install the printer's software, and start over. No software? You need to download it from the printer manufacturer's Web site.

6. **Choose your printer's port and click Next.**

   When Vista asks which printer port to use, choose LPT1: (Printer Port).

7. **Click your printer's manufacturer and model names when you see them listed and click Next.**

   The Add Printer dialog box lists the names of printer manufacturers on the left; choose yours from the list. The right side of the box lists that manufacturer's printer models. (Vista knows how to talk to hundreds of different printer models.)

   Windows Vista may ask you to stick the appropriate set-up CD into a drive. Stuck? Click the Windows Update button; Vista connects to the Internet to find software for that printer.

   After a moment, you see the new printer listed. If Vista offers to print a test page, take it up on the offer.

That's it. If you're like most people, your printer will work like a charm. If it doesn't, I've stuffed some tips and fix-it tricks in Chapter 7's printing section.

 If you have two or more printers attached to your computer, right-click the icon of your most oft-used printer and select Set As Default Printer from the menu. Windows Vista then prints to that printer automatically, unless you tell it otherwise.

✔ To remove a printer you no longer use, right-click its name and then choose Delete from the menu. That printer's name no longer appears as an option when you try to print from a program. If Vista asks to uninstall the printer's drivers and software, click Yes — unless you think you may install that printer again sometime.

✔ You can change printer options from within many programs. Choose File in a program's menu bar and then choose Print Setup or choose Print. From there, you can often access the same box of printer options as you find in the Control Panel. That area also lets you change things such as paper sizes, fonts, and types of graphics.

✔ To share a printer quickly over a network, right-click its icon and choose Sharing. Select the Share This Printer option and click OK. That printer shows up as an installation option for all the computers on your network.

✔ If your printer's software confuses you, try clicking the Help buttons in its dialog boxes. Many buttons are customized for your particular printer model, and they offer advice not found in Windows Vista.

Installing or adjusting other items

The Control Panel's Hardware and Sound area lists items tethered to most PCs: the mouse, keyboard, scanner, digital camera, game controllers, and perhaps a telephone. Click the name of any item to adjust its settings.

The rest of this section explains how to tweak the most common lazy gadgets into behaving.

To reach any of the following areas, choose Control Panel from the Start menu and choose Hardware and Sound. Click the area's name to see and change its settings.

Mouse

You'll find lots of settings inside here for standard-issue, two-button mice, but most are frivolous: Dressing up your mouse pointer's arrow, for example.

Southpaws should click here to swap their mouse buttons. Click the Switch Primary and Secondary Buttons box. (The change takes place immediately, even before you click Apply.)

People with slow fingers should fine tune their double-click speed. Test your current speed by double-clicking the test folder. If it opens, your settings are fine. If it doesn't open, though, slow down your mouse's double-click speed with the sliding control.

Owners of mice with extra buttons or wireless connections often hide extra settings in here, as well.

Scanners and Cameras

Click here to see your currently installed (and turned on) scanners and/or cameras. Or, to install *new* scanners or cameras, just plug them in and turn them on. Windows Vista almost always recognizes and greets them by name. On the rare occasion Windows doesn't recognize your model, though, take these extra steps:

1. **Open Control Panel from the Start menu and choose Hardware and Sound.**

2. **Click the Scanners and Cameras icon.**

   The Scanners and Cameras window appears, listing all the attached scanners and cameras Vista currently recognizes.

3. **Choose the Add Device button and click Next.**

   Windows brings up its Scanner and Camera Installation wizard.

4. **Choose the manufacturer and model, and click Next.**

   Click the manufacturer's name on the window's left side and choose the model on the right.

5. **Type a name for your scanner or camera, click Next, and click Finish.**

   Type a name for the device (or keep the suggested name), click Next, and then click Finish. If you've turned on your camera or scanner and plugged in its cable correctly, Windows should recognize it and place an icon for it in both your Computer area and your Control Panel's Scanners and Cameras area.

Unfortunately, the installation of older cameras and scanners doesn't always work this easily. If Windows doesn't automatically accept your gear, fall back on the scanner or camera's bundled software. The scanner or camera should still work — you just won't be able to use Windows Vista's built-in software tools to grab its images.

Chapter 16 explains how to grab photos from a digital camera, and that chapter's same tips apply to scanners: Vista treats digital cameras and scanners the same way.

Keyboard

If your keyboard is not working or not plugged in, your computer usually tells you as soon as you turn it on. If you see your computer's startled Keyboard Error message — and Windows can't find the keyboard, either — it's time to buy a new one. When you plug in the new one, Windows Vista and your computer should find it automatically.

If your new keyboard comes with extra buttons along the top for things like "Internet," "Email" or "Volume," you need to install the keyboard's bundled software to make those buttons work. (Wireless keyboards almost always require their own software, as well.)

Enter this area mainly for minor keyboard adjustments like how fast the keys rrrrrrrepeat when you hold them down.

Phone and Modem Options

You'll rarely use these phone and modem options unless you're a traveling laptop owner who constantly encounters different area codes. If you fit that description, click this area's Set Up Dialing Rules option and then add your new location and area code.

Windows thankfully saves all your previously entered area codes. Should you revisit the same place, reselect that location from the list to spare yourself from re-entering the information.

Game Controllers

Windows Vista almost always recognizes a newly plugged-in *game controller* (a fancy word for joystick, gamepad, flight yoke, rudder control, and similar gaming gear). Click the Game Controllers area to make any necessary sensitivity adjustments.

Adding new hardware

When you plug something into your PC's USB port, like iPods, cameras, or scanners, Vista almost always recognizes it and leaves it ready for action. But if Vista *doesn't* recognize something, call in the Add Hardware Wizard. Here's the process:

1. **Choose Control Panel from the Start menu and choose the Classic View.**

   Shown back in Figure 11-2, the Classic View shows *all* your icons — it's a hidden route to the Add Hardware icon.

2. **Double-click the Add Hardware icon, click Continue (if prompted), and then click Next to let the wizard search for and install the hardware automatically.**

   The Add Hardware Wizard introduces Windows Vista to whatever part you've plugged into your computer — if Vista recognizes one.

   Here's where the path branches off:

   • **If Windows Vista locates your new part,** click the newly installed part's name from the Windows Vista list, click Finish, and follow the rest of the wizard's instructions.

   • **If the wizard *doesn't* find your new part,** click Next and follow the instructions. If you get lucky, rejoice — and click the device's name for Windows to install it.

But if Windows can't locate your newly installed part automatically, you need to contact the part's manufacturer and ask for a Windows Vista *driver* — a piece of software that lets Vista understand the new part. (Drivers are often downloadable from the manufacturer's Web site.) Some drivers come bundled with installation software to minimize installation chores. I cover driver-hunting in Chapter 12.

Adding or Removing Programs

Whether you've picked up a new program or you want to purge an old one, the Control Panel's Programs category handles the job fairly well. One of its categories, Programs and Features, lists your currently installed programs, shown in Figure 11-10. You click the one you want to discard or tweak.

The next two sections describe how to remove or change existing programs, and how to install new ones.

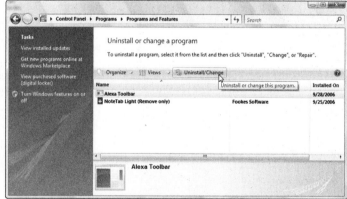

Figure 11-10: The Uninstall or Change a Program window removes any of your currently installed programs.

Removing or changing programs

To remove or change settings on a troublesome program, follow these steps:

1. **Choose the Control Panel from the Start menu and choose Programs and Features from the Programs area.**

   The Uninstall or Change a Program window appears, as shown in Figure 11-10, listing your currently installed programs, their publisher, size, and the date you installed the program.

2. **Click the unloved program and then click its Uninstall, Change, or Repair button.**

   The Uninstall button always appears on the menu bar. Other buttons, called Change, and Repair appear only for some programs. If you spot the Repair or Change button, click it: Vista tries to repair the program or change some of its components. It sometimes fixes malfunctioning programs, but you often need its original CD handy.

3. **When Windows asks whether you're *sure*, click Yes.**

   Windows Vista summons the program's built-in uninstall program — if it has one — or simply yanks the program off your computer's hard drive, sometimes rebooting your PC in the process.

   Be careful, though. After you delete a program, it's gone for good unless you kept its installation CD. Unlike other deleted items, deleted programs don't linger inside your Recycle Bin.

When a program doesn't have an installation program . . .

Sometimes programs — especially small ones downloaded from the Internet — don't come with an installation program. If you've downloaded one of these low-budget creations to your computer, create a new folder for it and move the downloaded file inside. (Be sure to scan any downloaded file with your antivirus program.) Then try double-clicking the program's file. (It's usually the file with the fanciest icon.) One of two things may happen:

✔ **The program may simply start running.** That means you're done — the program doesn't need to be installed. (Drag and drop its program icon to your Start button to add it to the Start button.) If you need to uninstall the program, just right-click it and choose Delete. These types of programs rarely appear on your Uninstall or Change a Program list.

✔ **The program may start installing itself.** That means you're also done. The program's installation program takes over, sparing you any more trouble. To uninstall the program, use the Control Panel's Uninstall or Change a Program option.

But if the program comes in a *zipped* folder — the folder icon bears a little zipper — you have an extra step. Right-click the zipped folder, choose Extract All, and then click Extract. Windows automatically *unzips* the folder's contents and places them into a new folder, usually named after the program. From there, you can either run the program directly or, if it has an installation program, run the installation program. I describe zipped folders in Chapter 4.

Always use the Control Panel's Uninstall or Change a Program window to uninstall unwanted programs. Simply deleting their folders won't do the trick. In fact, doing so often confuses your computer into sending bothersome error messages.

Adding new programs

Chances are, you'll never have to use this option. Today, most programs install themselves automatically as soon as you slide their CD into the drive. If you're not sure whether a program has installed, click the Start button and poke around in your All Programs menu. If it's listed there, the program has installed.

But if a program doesn't automatically leap into your computer, here are some tips that can help:

- ✔ You need an Administrator account to install programs. (Most computer owners automatically have an Administrator account.) That keeps the kids, with their Limited or Guest accounts, from installing programs and messing up the computer. I explain User accounts in Chapter 13.

- ✔ Downloaded a program? Vista usually saves them in your Downloads folder, accessible by clicking your username on the Start menu. Double-click the downloaded program's name to install it.

- ✔ Many eager, newly installed programs want to add a desktop shortcut, Start menu shortcut, *and* a Quick Launch toolbar shortcut. Say "no" to all but the Start menu. All those extra shortcuts clutter your computer, making programs difficult to find. You can safely delete these shortcuts if any program adds them by right-clicking the shortcut and choosing Delete.

- ✔ It's always a good idea to create a restore point before installing a new program. (I describe creating restore points in Chapter 12.) If your newly installed program goes haywire, use System Restore to return your computer to the peaceful state of mind it enjoyed before you installed the troublemaker.

Add/remove parts of Windows Vista

Just as you can install and uninstall programs, you can remove parts of Windows Vista that you don't need. You can remove the games, for example, to keep employees from playing them at the office.

Choosing the default program

Microsoft lets computer vendors replace Internet Explorer, Media Player, Outlook Express, and Windows Messenger with different programs from other companies. Your new computer may come with the Firefox Web browser, for example, instead of Microsoft's Internet Explorer. Some PCs may come with both browsers installed.

When more than one program can handle a task — opening a Web link, for example — Vista needs to know which program it should summon.

That's where Vista's program defaults area comes in. To choose your default programs, choose Control Panel from the Start button, choose Programs, select Default Programs, and choose Set Your Default Programs.

The Set Your Default Programs window lists programs along the right edge. Click the program you use the most and then choose Set This Program As Default. Repeat for any other listed programs that you prefer over Vista's bundled programs and then click OK.

To see what parts of itself Windows Vista has left off your computer or to remove unwanted components that Windows Vista *has* installed, follow these steps:

1. **Click the Start menu, choose Control Panel, and click the Programs icon.**

2. **In the Programs and Features area, choose Turn Windows Features On or Off and click Continue (if prompted).**

   Windows brings up a window listing all its features. The features with check marks by their names are already installed. No check mark? Then that feature's not installed. If you see a box that's filled — neither empty nor checked — then double-click the component to see what's installed and what's left out.

3. **To add a component, click in its empty check box. To remove an installed component like Windows' Games, click its check box to uncheck its box.**

4. **Click the OK button.**

   Windows Vista adds or removes the program. (You may need to insert your Windows Vista DVD during the process.)

Modifying Vista for the Physically Challenged

 Nearly everybody finds Windows Vista to be challenging, but some people face special physical challenges, as well. To assist them, the Control Panel's Ease of Access area makes Windows easier to use for people with a wide variety of physical limitations.

Follow these steps to modify Vista's settings:

1. **Choose Control Panel from the Start menu, choose Ease of Access, and choose Ease of Access Center.**

   The Make Your Computer Easier to Use window appears, as shown in Figure 11-11. Vista's ethereal voice kicks in, explaining how to change Vista's programs.

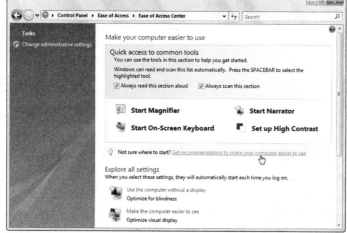

Figure 11-11:
The Ease of Access area contains a wide variety of ways to help users with physical limitations.

2. **Choose Get Recommendations to Make Your Computer Easier to Use.**

   Look for the task called, **Get Recommendations to Make Your Computer Easier to Use** (shown with the mouse pointing to it in Figure 11-11). That makes Vista give you a quick interview so that it can gauge what adjustments you may need. When it's through, Vista automatically makes its changes, and you're done.

   If you're not happy with Vista's changes, move to Step 3.

3. **Make your changes manually.**

   The Ease of Access Center window offers these toggle switches to make the keyboard, sound, display, and mouse easier to control:

   - **Start Magnifier:** Designed for the visiually impaired, this option magnifies the mouse pointer's exact location.

   - **Start Narrator:** Vista's awful built-in narrator reads on-screen text for people who can't view it clearly.

   - **Start On-Screen Keyboard:** This setting places a clickable keyboard along the screen's bottom, letting you type by pointing and clicking.

   - **Set up High Contrast:** This setting eliminates most screen colors, but helps vision-impaired people view the screen and cursor more clearly.

Choose any of these options to turn on the feature immediately. Close the feature's window if the feature makes matters worse.

If you're still not happy, proceed to Step 4.

4. **Choose a specific setting in the Explore All Available Settings area.**

Here's where Vista gets down to the nitty gritty, letting you optimize Vista specifically for the following things:

- Blindness or impaired vision

- Using an alternative input device rather than a mouse or keyboard

- Adjusting the keyboard and mouse sensitivity to compensate for limited movements

- Turning on visual alerts instead of Vista's sound notifications

- Making it easier to focus on reading and typing tasks

Some centers that assist physically challenged people may offer software or assistance for helping you make these changes.

Options for Laptops (Mobile PC)

 The Mobile PC area, shown only on laptops, lets you adjust the things dear to the heart of laptop owners: adjusting the screen's brightness, changing the sound volume, saving battery power, checking wireless network signals, and setting up external displays or projectors. I cover most of these settings in Chapter 22.

Additional Options

 Vista normally leaves this catch-all area empty, but you may find controls for other programs and hardware you add to your PC.

Chapter 12

Keeping Windows from Breaking

- -

In This Chapter

▶ Creating your own restore point

▶ Backing up your computer

▶ Freeing up hard drive space

▶ Making your computer run faster

▶ Tracking down and installing a new driver

▶ Cleaning your mouse, keyboard, and monitor

- -

*I*f something in Windows is already broken, hop ahead to Chapter 17 for the fix. But if your computer seems to be running reasonably well, stay right here. This chapter explains how to keep it running that way for the longest time possible.

This chapter is a checklist of sorts, with each section explaining a fairly simple and necessary task to keep Windows running at its best. There's no need to call in a techie because much of this upkeep takes place using either Windows' built-in maintenance tools or standard household cleaners. For example, you run Vista's built-in Disk Cleanup program to free up space on a crowded hard drive.

This chapter also helps you fix the annoying and ubiquitous "bad driver" problem by explaining how to put a fresh driver behind the wheel.

Finally, you discover a quick way to clean your mouse — a necessary but oft-overlooked task that keeps the pointer on target. (Feel free to grab the vacuum cleaner and suck all the cookie crumbs out of your keyboard during the same cleaning spree.)

In addition to the checklist this chapter offers, make sure that Vista's Windows Update and Windows Defender programs are running on auto-pilot, as I describe in Chapter 10. They both go a long way to keep your computer running safely and securely.

Creating a Restore Point

When your computer's ailing, System Restore (which I cover in Chapter 17) provides a magical way to go back in time to when your computer was feeling better. Although System Restore creates restore points automatically, feel free to create your own. A restore point lets you return to a spot when you *know* your PC was working.

1. **Click the Start menu's All Programs menu, click Accessories, click System Tools, and click System Restore.**

   The System Restore window appears.

2. **Choose Open System Protection and click the Create button.**

   Found near the bottom of the System Restore window, the Open System Protection option fetches the System Protection page.

3. **Click Create, type a name for your new Restore Point and then click Create to save the Restore Point.**

   Windows Vista creates a restore point with that name, leaving you with a bunch of open windows to close.

By creating your own restore points on good days, you'll know immediately which ones to use on bad days. I describe how to resuscitate your computer with System Restore in Chapter 17.

Tuning Up Windows Vista with Built-In Maintenance Tools

Vista contains a slew of tools for keeping Vista running smoothly. Several run automatically, limiting your work to checking their On switches. Others help you prepare for global warming by backing up your PC's files. To check them out, click the Start menu, choose Control Panel, and select the System and Maintenance category.

You'll need these tools most often:

- **Backup and Restore Center:** Windows Vista comes with an awkward backup program. But it's free, leaving you no excuse not to back up your files. All hard drives eventually die, and you've stored lots of memories on yours.

- **System:** Technical support people thrive in here. The System area lists your version of Vista, your PC's horsepower and networking status, and a scorecard rating of what Vista thinks of your PC's performance.

✔ **Windows Update:** This tool lets Microsoft automatically siphon security fixes into your PC through the Internet, usually a good thing. Here's where you can turn Windows Update back on, if necessary.

✔ **Power Options:** Not sure whether your PC or laptop is sleeping, hibernating, or just plain turned off? Chapter 2 explains the difference, and this section lets you decide your PC's degree of lethargy when you press its Off button. (Or, for you laptop owners, when you close its lid.)

✔ **Administrative Tools:** One gem lives here: Freeing up space on your hard drive by deleting your PC's garbage.

I describe these tasks more fully in this chapter's next five sections.

Backing up your computer

Your hard drive will eventually die, unfortunately, and it will take everything with it: years of digital photos, songs, letters, financial records, scanned items, and anything else you've created or stored on your PC.

That's why you must back up your files on a regular basis. That backup copy lets you pick up the pieces gracefully when your hard drive suddenly walks off the stage.

Windows Vista's solution, its bundled Backup program, offers a rare combination: It's basic *and* awkward to use. But if you have more time than money, here's how to make Windows Vista's built-in Backup program back up your important files. If you prefer something a little easier to use, ask your computer retailer to recommend a third-party backup program.

Before you can use Windows Vista's Backup program, you need three things:

✔ **A CD burner, DVD burner, or external hard drive:** Windows' free Backup program can write to CDs and DVDs — if you're willing to sit there and feed those discs to your PC. But for dependable, automatic backups, nothing beats an external hard drive. Buy one that simply plugs into your computer's FireWire or USB 2.0 port; Vista recognizes it on the spot.

✔ **An Administrator account:** You must be logged on to the computer with an Administrator account. I explain passwords and User accounts in Chapter 13.

✔ **Windows Vista's Backup program:** The Backup program comes for free in every version of Windows Vista. Unfortunately, the Backup program doesn't run *automatically* in Windows Home Basic — you must remember to run it every evening. (That's one of the reasons that version costs less than the Home Premium and Ultimate versions of Vista.)

Should I back up files and folders or my entire PC?

Vista's Backup and Restore Center offers two ways to back up your PC. Each takes an entirely different approach to stashing away your PC's contents.

✔ **File and Folder Backup:** The option chosen by most people — and the only option available for owners of Vista's Home and Premium versions — this lets you choose the files and folders you want backed up. Vista saves them all as one jumbo file, letting you break it up across several CDs or DVDs, if needed. When disaster strikes, this option lets you restore any or all of your backed-up files and folders.

✔ **CompletePC Backup:** Only available with Vista's Ultimate and Business versions, this creates an "image" of your entire PC and then packs it into a jumbo file, just like the File and Folder Backup method. The difference, however, is that CompletePC Backup won't let you restore just a few files and folders from its stash. It only lets you restore your *entire* PC, which overwrites any files you've created since making the backup.

The CompletePC Backup comes in handy mostly with new PCs, or PCs you've laboriously set up just the way you want it. That CompletePC backup then provides a safe base to return to in case of catastrophe. For most people, though, File and Folder Backup provides the most versatile backup.

When you take care of those three things, follow these steps to make your computer back up your work automatically each month (good), week (better), or night (best):

1. **Open Vista's Backup and Restore Center.**

   Click the Start button, choose Control Panel, select the System and Maintenance category, and click Backup and Restore Center.

   Do you want to change the way you've previously told Vista to back up your PC? When the Backup and Restore Center window appears, choose Change Settings and then choose Change Backup Settings from the next window.

2. **Choose Backup Files.**

   If you're using Vista's Ultimate or Business version, the Backup and Restore Center offers two slightly different ways to back up your PC, both described in the sidebar. But you want to click the Backup Files button.

   The thoughtful program asks where you want to save the files.

3. **Choose where to save your backup and click Next.**

   Vista lets you save your backup nearly anywhere: CDs, DVDs, USB drives, portable hard drives, or even a drive on a *networked* computer (see Chapter 14).

Although your choice depends on the amount of information you're backing up, the best solution is a *portable hard drive:* A hard drive in a box that plugs into one of your PC's USB or FireWire ports, allowing for unattended backups.

If you can't afford a portable hard drive, then CDs or DVDs are the next best thing.

If you try to save to a networked drive on another PC, Vista will ask for an Administrator account's username and password on the other PC.

If Vista asks which disks you want to include in the backup, choose Local Disk (C:) (System).

4. **Choose the types of files you want to back up and click Next.**

   Although Windows asks what types of files you want to back up, shown in Figure 12-1, it's already selected *every* type of file on the list. If you have a very good reason for not backing up some of them, remove the check marks next to those files.

   If you don't remove any check marks, Vista backs up all the files in every User account on the PC.

   What Vista doesn't back up, though, are programs. But because you've saved their installation discs, you can simply reinstall them as necessary.

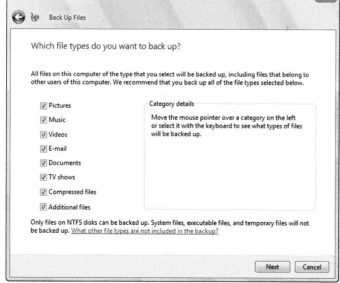

Figure 12-1: Choose what file types you want to back up.

Vista saves every file and folder in each user's user account folder. To be precise, that's the C:\Users folder, including all the folders inside it.

5. **Choose how often to back up, and click the Save Settings and Start Backup button.**

   Choose between Daily, Weekly, or Monthly backups, as shown in Figure 12-2, and then choose the day and time for the Backup program to kick in. You can choose a time when you'll already be working on your PC, but the backup will slow down your PC.

   For the most convenient backups, choose a daily backup taking place in the wee hours of the morning. If you turn off your PC at night, choose a daytime schedule.

   When you click the Save Settings and Start Backup button, Vista immediately starts its backup — even if one's not scheduled yet. That's because the ever-vigilant Vista wants to make sure that it grabs everything right now — before something goes wrong.

6. **Restore a few files to test your backup.**

   Now it's time to make sure that everything worked. Repeat the first step, but choose Restore Files. Follow Vista's menus until you can browse the list of backed-up files. Restore a test file to make sure that it's copied back to its original place.

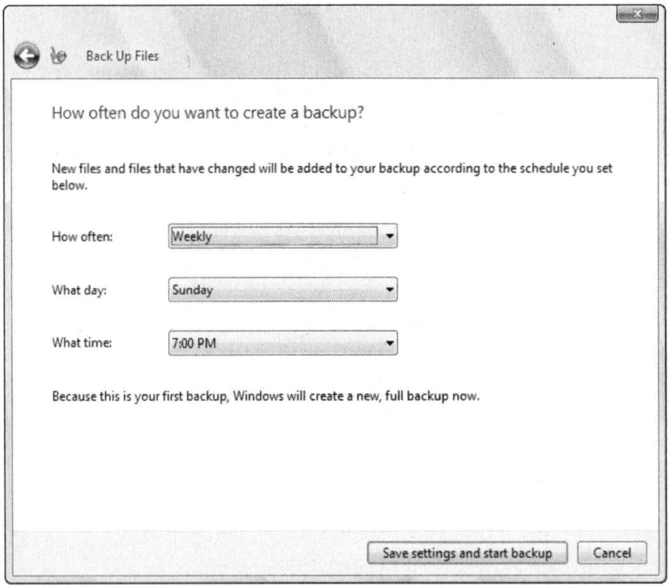

Back Up Files

How often do you want to create a backup?

New files and files that have changed will be added to your backup according to the schedule you set below.

How often: Weekly

What day: Sunday

What time: 7:00 PM

Because this is your first backup, Windows will create a new, full backup now.

Save settings and start backup   Cancel

Figure 12-2: Choose the frequency, day, and time of your automatic backups.

Speeding up your PC by toning down the visual effects

As it frantically crunches numbers in the background, Windows Vista tries to project a navel-gazing image of inner peace. Its menus and windows open and close with a fade; aesthetically pleasing shadows surround each menu and the mouse pointer. If your video card possesses enough oomph, Vista even makes the window borders translucent, allowing part of the desktop to glow from behind.

All these extra visual decisions require extra calculations on Windows's part, however, slowing it down a bit. To change Windows' attitude from peaceful to performance, head for the

Control Panel's System and Maintenance category, choose System, and click Advanced System Settings. When the System Properties box opens to the Advanced tab, click the Settings button in the Performance area.

For fastest action, choose Adjust for Best Performance. Windows quickly strips away all the visuals and reverts to Classic mode — a faster way of working that mimics earlier, no-frills Windows versions. To return to a prettier, but slower, Windows, choose Let Windows Choose What's Best for My Computer.

The Backup program in Windows Vista Basic version can't run automatically. If you own the Basic version, it's up to you to remember to run the Backup program at least once a week.

✔ For your computer to back up automatically each night, you must leave it *turned on* during the scheduled backup time. I leave mine turned on 24 hours a day, as most PCs consume less power than a light bulb. (Please turn off your computer's monitor, though.)

✔ Vista saves your backup in a folder named Vista in the location you choose in Step 3. Don't change the backup's location. Vista may not be able to find it again when you choose to restore it.

✔ After making its first backup, Vista only starts backing up files that have changed since your last backup. Don't be surprised if subsequent backups are faster or don't require as many CDs or DVDs. Eventually, Vista tells you it's time for another complete backup, which will take longer.

Finding technical information about your computer

 If you ever need to look under Windows Vista's hood, heaven forbid, open the Control Panel's System and Maintenance section and choose System. Shown in Figure 12-3, the System window offers an easily digestible technical briefing about your PC's viscera:

- ✔ **Windows edition:** Vista comes in way-too-many versions to remember. To jog your memory, Vista lists the version that's running on your PC.

- ✔ **System:** Here, Vista rates your PC's strength — its *Windows Experience Index* — on a scale of 1 (frail) to 5 (robust). Your PC's type of *CPU* (Central Processing Unit) also appears here, as well as its amount of memory.

- ✔ **Computer name, domain, and workgroup settings:** This section identifies your computer's name and *workgroup,* a term used when connecting to other computers in a network.

- ✔ **Windows Activation:** To keep people from buying one copy of Windows Vista and installing it on several PCs, Microsoft requires Windows Vista to be *activated,* a process that chains it to a single PC.

The pane along the left also lists some more advanced tasks you may find handy during those panic-stricken times when something's going wrong with your PC. Here's the rundown:

- ✔ **Device Manager:** This option lists all the parts inside your computer, but not in a friendly manner. Parts with exclamation points next to them aren't happy. Double-click them and choose Troubleshoot to diagnose their problem.

- ✔ **Remote Settings:** Rarely used, this complicated setup lets other people control your PC through the Internet, hopefully to fix things. If you can find one of these helpful people, let them walk you through this procedure over the phone, or through an instant messaging program.

- ✔ **System Protection:** This option lets you create restore points (described in this chapter's first section), as well as let a restore point take your PC back to another point in time — hopefully when it was in a better mood.

- ✔ **Advanced System Settings:** Professional techies spend lots of time in here. Everybody else ignores it.

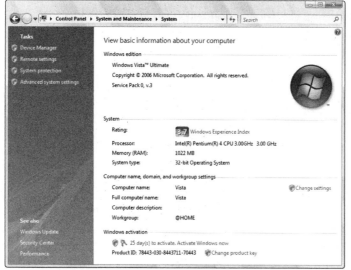

Figure 12-3:
Clicking the
System icon
brings up
technical
information
about
your PC.

Most of the stuff listed in Vista's System area is fairly complicated, so don't mess with it unless you're sure of what you're doing or a technical support person tells you to change a specific setting. If you want a taste of it, check out the sidebar on adjusting Vista's visual effects.

Freeing up space on your hard drive

Vista grabs more space on your hard drive than any other version of Windows. If programs begin whining about running out of room on your hard drive, this solution grants you a short reprieve:

1. **Click the Start button and choose the Control Panel's System and Maintenance category. Then choose Free Up Disk Space from the Administrative Tools section.**

   Vista asks whether it should clean your files, or every user's files.

2. **Choose Files from All Users on This Computer.**

   This step empties the Recycle Bin and cleans up trash from every user account on your PC.

If your PC asks you which drive you want to clean, choose the first one listed, the C: drive, and click OK.

3. **Check all the items and then click OK.**

Vista presents the Disk Cleanup window, shown in Figure 12-4. Check all the check boxes and then click OK. As you check a box, the Description section explains what's being deleted.

4. **Click Delete Files when Windows Vista asks whether you're sure.**

Windows Vista then proceeds to empty your Recycle Bin, destroy leftovers from old Web sites, and remove other hard drive clutter.

Figure 12-4:
Make sure that all the check boxes are checked.

For a shortcut to Disk Cleanup, click the Start menu and type **disk cleanup** in the Search box.

Empowering your power button

Normally, a press of a PC's power button turns off your PC, whether Vista's ready or not. That's why you should always turn off Vista with its *own* Off button, found by clicking the Start menu, clicking the little arrow by the lock icon, and choosing Shut Down. That gives Vista time to prepare for the event.

To avoid jolting Vista with an unexpected shutdown, consider reprogramming your laptop or PC's power button so that it doesn't turn off your PC at all. Instead, it puts your PC to sleep, Vista's new power-saving mode.

To change your power button's mission, choose Start, choose the Control Panel, and select the System and Maintenance category. Choose Power Options, and the Power Options window appears.

From the left side panel, click Choose What the Power Buttons Do. There, you can tell your PC's Power and Sleep buttons to either Sleep, Hibernate, Shut Down your PC, or do nothing, which prevents people from turning off your PC. (I describe the difference between Sleep and Hibernate in Chapter 2.)

For extra security, click Require a Password so that anybody waking up your PC will need your password to see your information.

For quick access to this area, type **Power Options** into the Start menu's Search box. Laptop owners will see an additional option letting them change how their laptop reacts when they close its lid.

Setting up devices that don't work (fiddling with drivers)

Windows comes with an arsenal of *drivers* — software that lets Windows communicate with the gadgets you plug into your PC. Normally, Vista automatically recognizes your new part, and it works. Other times, Vista heads to the Internet and fetches some instructions before finishing the job.

But occasionally, you'll install something that's either too new for Windows Vista to know about or too old for it to remember. Or perhaps something attached to your PC no longer works right, and Vista's Welcome Center grumbles about needing a "new driver."

In these cases, it's up to you to track down and install a Windows Vista driver for that part. The best drivers come with an installation program that automatically places the software in the right place. The worst drivers leave all the grunt work up to you.

If Windows Vista doesn't automatically recognize and install your newly attached piece of hardware — even after you restart your PC — follow these steps to locate and install a new driver:

1. **Visit the part manufacturer's Web site and download the latest Windows Vista driver.**

   You often find the manufacturer's Web site stamped somewhere on the part's box. If you can't find it, try searching for the part manufacturer's name on Google (www.google.com) and locate its Web site.

   Look in the Web site's Support or Customer Service area. There, you usually need to enter your part, its model number, and your computer's operating system (Windows Vista) before the Web site coughs up the driver.

   No Windows Vista driver listed? Try downloading a Windows XP or Windows 2000 driver instead because they sometimes work just as well. (Be sure to scan *any* downloaded file with a virus checker.)

2. **Run the driver's installation program.**

   Sometimes clicking your downloaded file makes its installation program jump into action, installing the driver for you. If so, you're through. If not, head to Step 3.

    If the downloaded file has a little zipper on the icon, right-click it and choose Extract All to *unzip* its contents into a new folder. (Vista names that new folder after the file you've unzipped, making it easy to relocate.)

3. **Choose Hardware and Sound from the Start menu's Control Panel and select Device Manager.**

   The Device Manager appears, listing an inventory of every part inside or attached to your computer.

4. **Click anywhere inside the Device Manager, click Action, and then choose Add Legacy Hardware.**

   The Add Hardware Wizard guides you through the steps of installing your new hardware and, if necessary, installing your new driver.

   ✔ Avoid problems by keeping your drivers up-to-date. Even the ones packaged with newly bought parts are usually old. Visit the manufacturer's Web site and download the latest driver. Chances are, it fixes problems earlier users had with the first set of drivers.

   ✔ Problems with the new driver? Click the Start menu, choose Control Panel, and open the System and Maintenance category. Choose Device Manager and double-click the part name — *Keyboards,* for example — on the window's left side. Vista reveals the make and model of your part. Double-click the part's name and click the Driver tab on the Properties box. Breathe steadily. Finally, click the Roll Back Driver button. Windows Vista ditches the newly installed driver and returns to the previous driver.

Cleaning Your Computer

Even the best housekeeper or janitor draws the line at cleaning a computer. This chore's up to you, and you'll know when it's necessary. You don't need to turn off your computer for any of this — *except* if you need to remove your keyboard for cleaning.

Cleaning your mouse

If your mouse pointer jumps around on-screen or doesn't move at all, your mouse is probably clogged with desktop gunk. Follow these steps to degunkify it:

1. **Turn the mouse upside down and clean off any dirt stuck to the bottom.**

   Your mouse must lie flat on its pad to work correctly.

2. **Inspect the bottom of your mouse.**

   If your mouse has a little ball on the bottom, proceed to Step 3.

   If your mouse has a little light on the bottom, proceed to Step 4.

3. **Cleaning a mouse that has a ball.**

   Twist off the mouse's little round cover and remove the ball. Wipe off any crud from the ball and blow dust out of the hole. A little air blower, sold at office and computer stores, works well here. (It also blows off the dust layers clogging your computer's air vents.)

   Pull out any stray hairs, dust, and roller goo. A cotton swab moistened with alcohol cleans the most persistent goo from the little rollers. (The rollers should be smooth and shiny.) Dirty rollers cause the most mouse problems.

   Replace the cleaned ball into the cleaned hole and reinsert the clean little round cover.

4. **Cleaning an optical mouse.**

   An *optical mouse* replaces the old-fashioned rubber ball with a tiny laser. With no moving parts, optical mice rarely need cleaning. But if yours is acting up, remove any stray hairs clinging to the bottom around the light.

   Also, make sure that the mouse rests on a textured surface that's not shiny. If your desktop is glass or shiny (polished wood grain, for example), put your mouse on a mouse pad for best traction.

If your newly cleaned mouse still has problems, it may be time for a new one. But before shelling out the cash, check these things:

- ✔ Wireless mice go through batteries fairly quickly. If your mouse doesn't have a connecting cord, it's wireless. Check its battery and make sure that it's within range of its receiving unit. (The receiving unit plugs into your PC, perhaps in the back.)

- ✔ Check your mouse's settings: Click Start, choose Control Panel, and choose Mouse in the Hardware and Sound category. Look through the settings to see whether something's obviously wrong.

Cleaning your monitor

Don't spray glass cleaner directly onto your monitor because it drips down into the monitor's guts, frightening the circuits. Instead, spray the glass cleaner onto a soft rag and wipe the screen. Don't use paper because it can scratch the glass.

For cleaning flat panel monitors, use a soft, lint-free cloth, and a mix of half water and half vinegar. Feel free to clean your monitor's front panels, too, if you're feeling especially hygienic.

Cleaning your keyboard

Keyboards are usually too wide to shake over a wastebasket. The best way to clean them is to shut down Windows, turn off your computer, and unplug the keyboard from the computer. (If your keyboard has a rectangular plug that pushes into a USB port, you don't need to turn off your PC.)

Take the keyboard outdoors and shake it vigorously to remove the debris. If the keyboard's grimy, spray some household cleaning solution onto a rag and wipe off any goo from around the keyboard's edges and its keycaps.

Plug it back in, turn on your computer, and your computer looks almost new.

Chapter 13

Sharing One Computer with Several People

*V*ista's brimming with flashy new graphics, a souped-up search feature, a free calendar program, and even a three-dimensional chess game. But Microsoft's betting that something else will pry open people's wallets: Vista's enhanced security. Security's *everywhere* in Vista, which contains more warning signs than an electric fence.

One big part of security is the way Vista allows several people to share one computer, without letting anybody peek into anybody else's files.

The secret? Windows Vista grants each user his or her own *user account,* which neatly separates that person from other users. When people log on using their own user account, the computer looks tailor-made for them: It displays their personalized desktop background, menu choices, programs, and files — and it forbids them from seeing items belonging to other users.

This chapter explains how to set up a separate user account for everybody in the house, including the computer's owner, family members or roommates, and even occasional visitors who ask to check their e-mail.

Understanding User Accounts

Windows Vista wants you to set up a *user account* for everybody who uses your PC. A user account works like a cocktail-party name tag that helps Windows recognize who's sitting at the keyboard. Windows Vista offers three types of user accounts: Administrator, Standard, and Guest. To begin playing with the PC, people click their account's name when Windows Vista first loads, as shown in Figure 13-1.

Who cares? Well, Windows Vista gives each type of account permission to do different things on the computer. If the computer were a huge apartment building, the Administrator account would belong to the manager, each tenant would have a Standard account, and Guest accounts would belong to visitors trying to use the bathroom in the lobby. Here's how the different accounts translate into computer lingo:

- **Administrator:** The administrator controls the entire computer, deciding who gets to use it and what each user can do on it. On a computer running Windows Vista, the owner usually holds the almighty Administrator account. He or she then sets up accounts for each household member and decides what they can and can't do with the PC.

- **Standard:** Standard accounts can use most of the computer, but they can't make any big changes to it. They can't install programs, for example, but they can still run them. (Windows XP referred to Standard accounts as Limited accounts.)

- **Guest:** Guests can use the computer, but the computer doesn't recognize them by name. Guest accounts function much like Standard accounts, but with no privacy: Anybody can log on with the Guest account, and the desktop will look the way the last guest left it.

Giving yourself a Standard account

Whenever an evil piece of software slips into your computer — and you're logged in as an Administrator — that software controls all the powers you do. That's dangerous because Administrator accounts can delete just about anything. That's why Microsoft suggests creating *two* accounts for yourself: An Administrator account and a Standard account. Then, log on with your Standard account for everyday computing.

That way, Vista treats you just like any other Standard user: When the computer is about to do something potentially harmful, Vista asks you to type the password of an Administrator account. Type your Administrator account's password, and Vista lets you proceed. But if Vista unexpectedly asks for permission to do something odd, you know something may be suspect.

This second account is inconvenient, no doubt about it. But so is reaching for a key whenever you enter your front door. Taking an extra step is the price of extra security.

Figure 13-1:
Windows
Vista lets
users log
on under
their own
accounts.

Here are some ways accounts are typically assigned when you're sharing the same computer under one roof:

- ✔ In a family, the parents usually hold Administrator accounts, the kids usually have Standard accounts, and the babysitter logs on using the Guest account.

- ✔ In a dorm or shared apartment, the computer's owner holds the Administrator account, and the roommates have either Standard or Guest accounts, depending on their trustworthiness level (and perhaps how clean they've left the kitchen that week).

To keep others from logging on under your user account, you must protect it with a password. (I describe how to choose a password for your account in this chapter's "Setting Up Passwords and Security" section.)

When you created new accounts in Windows XP, they were always made Administrator accounts — unless you clicked the Limited button. Vista reverses that to add a layer of security. When you create a new account, it's automatically granted *Standard* account status. To create an Administrator account in Vista, you must specifically click the Administrator Account button.

Setting Up or Changing User Accounts

Being second-class citizens, Standard account holders lack much power. They can run programs and change their account's picture, for example, or even change their password. But the administrators hold the *real* power: They can create or delete any user account, effectively wiping a person off the computer. (That's why you should never upset a computer's administrator.)

If you're an administrator, create a Standard user account for everybody who's sharing your computer. That account gives them enough control over the computer to keep them from bugging you all the time, yet it keeps them from accidentally deleting your important files or messing up your computer.

Follow these steps to add another user account to your PC or change an existing account:

1. **Click the Start menu, choose Control Panel, and choose Add or Remove User Accounts from the User Accounts and Family Safety area.**

   A window pops up, as shown in Figure 13-2.

Figure 13-2: Use the Manage Accounts area to create or change user accounts.

2. **Create a new account, if desired.**

   If you click Create a New Account, shown in Figure 13-2, Windows lets you choose between creating a Standard or Administrator account. Choose Standard User unless you have an important reason to create another Administrator account. Type a name for the new account and click Create Account to finish — you're finished.

   To tweak the settings of an existing account, move to Step 3.

3. **Click the account you want to change.**

   Click either the account's name or photo. Vista displays a page with that user account's photo and lets you tweak the account's settings in any of these ways:

   - **Change the Account Name:** Here's your chance to correct a misspelled name on an account. Or, feel free to jazz up your account name, changing Jane to Crystal Powers.

   - **Create/Change a Password:** Every account should have a password to keep out other users. Here's your chance to add one or change the existing one.

   - **Remove the Password:** You shouldn't use this option, but it's here, just in case.

   - **Change the Picture:** Any account holder can change his own picture, so you needn't bother with this one — unless, of course, you somehow know more about computers than your kid.

   - **Set Up Parental Controls:** A mainstay of both spies and parents, Parental Controls lets you restrict an account holder's activities. You can see what programs and Web sites an account holder has accessed, listed by time and date. This setting creates a *lot* of information, so I give Parental Controls full coverage in Chapter 10.

   - **Change the Account Type:** Head here to promote a Standard user of high moral character to an Administrator account or bump a naughty administrator down to Standard.

   - **Delete the Account:** Don't choose this setting hastily, as deleting somebody's account also deletes all their files. Even System Restore can't retrieve the files of a deleted account holder.

   - **Manage Another Account:** Save your current crop of changes and begin tweaking somebody else's account.

4. **When you're through, close the window by clicking the red X in its top, right corner.**

   Any changes made to a user's account take place immediately.

Switching Quickly between Users

Windows Vista enables an entire family, roommates, or a small office to share a single computer. Best yet, the computer keeps track of everybody's programs while different people use the computer. Mom can be playing chess and then let Jerry log on to check his e-mail. When Mom logs back on a few minutes later, her chess game is right where she left it, pondering the sacrifice of her bishop.

The big problem with Standard accounts

Standard account holders have no problem accessing their own files. But they can't do anything that affects other users — delete a program, for example, change one of the computer's settings, or even adjust the computer's clock. If they try, Vista freezes the screen, demanding an Administrator's password. That's when the administrator must walk over to type it in.

While some people appreciate the extra security, others feel like a slave to their PC. You have several ways to make Vista less demanding. Unfortunately, none of these options is a winner:

✔ **Upgrade everybody to Administrator accounts:** The upgrades allow *any* user to type a password and override the security screens. Beware, though: This option also lets any user do *anything* on your PC, including delete your entire user account and your personal files.

✔ **Turn off User Account Protection:** Flip this switch, described in Chapter 10, and Vista stops caring: It no longer displays permission screens, disabling Vista's attempts to keep your PC secure.

✔ **Live with it:** You could just put up with Vista's new nag screens as the price of a secure computer in today's world. Juggle your own security and convenience levels and then make your own decision.

If you've turned off User Account Protection and want to turn it back on, head for the Control Panel's User Accounts and Family Safety category, choose User Accounts, and then choose Turn User Account Control On or Off.

Known as *Fast User Switching,* switching between users works fairly easily. While holding down the Windows key (it's usually between your keyboard's Ctrl and Alt keys), press the letter L. Wham! The Switch User button appears, letting you hand over the reins to the other person — or any other account holder.

When that person finishes, he can log off normally: Click the little arrow next to the Start button's lock icon (shown in the margin) and choose Log Off from the pop-up menu. Then you can log back on and see your desktop, just as you left it.

✔ With all this user switching, you may forget whose account you're actually using. To check, open the Start menu. The current account holder's name and picture appear at the menu's top right corner. Also, Vista's opening screen lists the words "logged on" beneath the picture of every user who's currently logged on.

✔ Don't restart the PC while another person's still logged on in the background, or that person will lose any work they haven't saved. (Vista warns you before restarting the PC, giving you a chance to ask the other person to save their work.)

✔ You can also switch users by clicking the Start button and clicking the little arrow by the Start menu's Lock sign (shown earlier in the margin). When the menu appears, click Switch User instead of Log Off.

✔ If you need to change a security setting while your child's logged on, you don't need to switch to your Administrator account. Just sit down at the PC and begin changing the setting: Like your child, you'll see a message asking for an Administrator's password. Type your Administrator password, and Vista lets you change the setting, just as if you'd logged on under your own account.

✔ Fast User Switching slows down older computers that lack gobs of memory. If your computer runs slowly with more than one person logged on, avoid Fast User Switching. Log on one person at a time, then log off when you're done to give somebody else some keyboard time.

Changing a User Account's Picture

Okay, now the important stuff: changing the dorky picture Windows automatically assigns to your user account. For every newly created user account, Windows Vista dips into its image bag and adds a random picture of plants, fish, soccer balls, or some similarly boring image. Feel free to change the picture to something more reflective of the Real You: You can use digital camera photos, as well as any pictures or graphics found on the Internet.

To change your user account's picture, click the Start button and click your picture at the menu's top. When the User Accounts window appears, click the Change Your Picture option. Vista lets you choose from its current stock, shown in Figure 13-3.

Figure 13-3:
Windows
Vista lets
each user
choose an
account
picture.

To assign a picture that's *not* currently shown, select Browse for More Pictures, shown in Figure 13-3. A new window appears, this time showing the contents of your Pictures folder. (Your digital camera usually stores its pictures in that folder.) Click a desired picture from the folder and choose Open. Vista quickly slaps that picture atop your Start menu.

Here are a few more options:

✔ You can also grab any picture off the Internet and save it to your Pictures folder for use as your user account picture. (Right-click the Internet picture and choose Save Picture As.)

✔ Don't worry about choosing a picture that's too big or too small. Windows Vista automatically shrinks or expands the image to fit the postage-stamp-sized space.

✔ All users may change their pictures — Administrator, Standard, and Guest accounts. (Pictures are about the only thing that guests *are* allowed to change.)

Setting Up Passwords and Security

There's not much point to having a user account if you don't have a password. Without one, Charles from the next cubicle can click your account on the logon screen, giving him free reign to snoop through your files.

Administrators, especially, should have passwords. If they don't, they're automatically letting anybody wreak havoc with the PC: When a permission's screen appears, anybody can just press Enter at the password screen to gain entrance.

To create or change a password, follow these steps:

1. **Open the Start menu, choose Control Panel, and select User Accounts and Family Safety.**

   The User Accounts screen opens.

2. **Choose Change Your Windows Password.**

   People who haven't created a password should instead choose Create a Password for Your Account.

3. **Make up an easy-to-remember password and type it into the New Password box, shown in Figure 13-4, and then retype the same characters into the Confirm New Password box below it. (Retyping eliminates the chance of typos.)**

   Changing an existing password works slightly differently: The screen shows a Current Password box where you must first type your existing password. (That keeps pranksters from sneaking over and changing your password during lunch hours.)

   I offer some tips on thinking up passwords a little later in this section.

Figure 13-4:
Type a hint that helps you — and only you — remember your password should you forget it.

4. **In the Type a Password Hint box, type a clue that helps you remember your forgotten password.**

   Make sure that the clue works only for you. Don't choose "My hair color," for example. If you're at work, choose "My cat's favorite food" or "The director of my favorite movie." If you're at home, choose something only you know — and not the kids. And don't be afraid to change your password every once in a while, too. You can find out more about passwords in Chapter 2.

5. **When the User Accounts screen returns, choose Create a Password Reset Disk from along the screen's left side.**

   Vista walks you through the process of creating a Password Reset Disk from a floppy, a memory card, or a USB thumbdrive.

When you forget your password, you can insert your Password Reset Disk as a key. Windows Vista will let you in to choose a new password, and all will be joyous. (But if you lose the Password Reset Disk, you have to beg for mercy from the administrator.) Hide your Password Reset Disk in a safe place, because it lets *anybody* into your account.

Creating a Password Reset Disk won't format or destroy any information on the disk you insert. It just adds a file named userkey.psw, which Vista uses to reset your password (but nobody else's).

Here are some tips that help you create a better password:

- ✔ When creating a password, use a word or combination of letters, numbers, and symbols of at least 7 to 14 characters. Don't *ever* use your name or username. (That's the first thing that thieves try when breaking in.)

- ✔ Don't choose a common word or name. Try to think of something that wouldn't appear in a dictionary. Combine two words, for example, to make a third. No grammar teachers will chide you this time.

- ✔ On a more serious note, keep a copy of your password in a safety deposit box for your spouse or heirs to find. Or, if you'd prefer to keep your financial records and memoirs secret, take your password to the grave.

- ✔ Uppercase and lowercase letters are treated differently. *PopCorn* is a different password than *popcorn*.

Chapter 14

Connecting Two or More Computers with a Network

*B*uying that second PC brings you yet another computing problem: How can two PCs share the same Internet connection and printer? And how do you move your old files to your new PC?

The solution involves a *network*. By connecting two or more computers with a cable, Windows Vista introduces them to each other, and lets them swap information, share an Internet connection, and print with the same printer.

If your computers live too far apart to extend a cable, go *wireless*. Also known as *WiFi*, this option lets your computers chatter through the airwaves like radio stations that broadcast and take requests.

This chapter explains several ways to link a handful of computers so that they can share things. Be forewarned, however: This chapter contains some pretty advanced stuff; don't tread here unless you're running an Administrator account on your computer and you don't mind doing a little head-scratching as you wade from conceptualization to actualization to, "Hey, it works!"

Understanding a Network's Parts

A *network* is two or more computers that have been connected so that they can share things. Although computer networks range from pleasingly simple to agonizingly complicated, they all have three things in common:

- ✔ **A network adapter:** Every computer on your network needs its own network adapter. Adapters come in two main forms. A *wired* network adapter is a special jack where you plug in a cable to connect one computer with the other computers. A *wireless* network adapter translates your computer's information into radio signals and broadcasts them to the other computers. (Feel free to mix wired and wireless adapters; they get along fine.)

- ✔ **A router:** When you connect two computers with a single cable or with wireless connections, each computer is smart enough to swap messages with the other one. But connecting three or more computers requires a traffic cop in the form of a *router.* Each computer connects to the boxlike router, which sends the right messages to the right computer.

- ✔ **Cables:** Wireless networks don't require cables. But wired networks need cables to connect the computers' network adapters to each other or to the router.

After you connect your computers to each other through cables, wirelessly,, or by using a combination of both, Windows Vista jumps in. On a good day, Vista automatically flips the right switches, letting everything communicate with each other. Most networks resemble a spider, as shown in Figure 14-1, with each computer's cable connecting to the router in the center.

A wireless network looks identical but without the cables. (The wireless router coordinates the messages' paths.) Or, you can mix wired and wireless adapters to create a network resembling Figure 14-2. Many routers come with built-in wireless access, letting your PCs connect to them with both wired and wireless adapters.

- ✔ Windows Vista divides its attention between networked computers quite well. It lets every networked computer share a single Internet connection, for example, so that everyone can surf the Internet or check their e-mail simultaneously. Everyone can share a single printer, too. If two people try to print something simultaneously, Windows stashes one person's files until the printer is free and then prints them when the printer's ready.

- ✔ Don't know whether you're already connected to a network or what other computers may be connected? Click the Start button and choose Network. Vista searches for a network and then shows the names of every computer connected to your own. To connect to another PC, double-click its name or icon. Vista then lets you browse its shared files as if you were browsing your own.

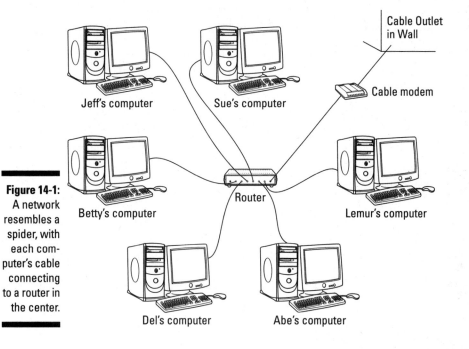

Figure 14-1:
A network resembles a spider, with each computer's cable connecting to a router in the center.

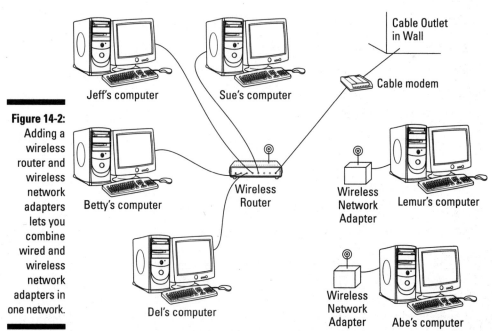

Figure 14-2:
Adding a wireless router and wireless network adapters lets you combine wired and wireless network adapters in one network.

Choosing between wired and wireless networks

Today, *wireless* (also known as *WiFi*) is the buzzword, and it's easy to see why. It's easy to string cables between computers that sit on the same desk or live in one room. But cables quickly become messy if the computers live in separate rooms. The solution comes with *wireless* network adapters, which convert the information to radio waves and broadcast the waves to other computers on the network. The wireless adapters on the other computers catch the waves and convert them back into information.

But just as radio broadcasts fade as you drive out of the city, wireless signals fade as they travel through obstacles. The more they fade, the slower the connection becomes. If your wireless signals pass through more than two walls, your computers may not be able to communicate. Wireless networks also take longer to set up because they have *a lot* more settings to tweak.

Wired connections work more quickly, efficiently, and inexpensively than wireless. But if your spouse says to remove the cables from the hallways, wireless may be your best option. Remember, you can set up adjacent computers with cables and use wireless for the rest.

To use wireless with broadband Internet access, buy a router with a built-in wireless access point.

Setting Up a Small Network

If you're trying to set up a lot of computers — more than five or ten — you probably need a more advanced book; networks are fairly easy to set up, but sharing their resources can be scary stuff, especially if the computers contain sensitive material. But if you're just trying to set up a handful of computers in your home or home office, this information may be all you need.

So without further blabbing, here's a low-carb, step-by-step list of how to set up a small and inexpensive network. The following sections show how to buy the three parts of a network — network adapters, cables (or wireless connections), and a router for moving information between each computer. I explain how to install the parts and, finally, how to make Windows Vista create a network out of your handiwork.

You find much more detailed instructions about home networking in my book *Upgrading & Fixing PCs For Dummies* (Wiley).

Buying parts for a network

Walk into the computer store, walk out with this stuff, and you're well on your way to setting up your network:

Fast Ethernet or 100BaseT cable: Buy a cable for each PC that won't be using wireless. You want *Ethernet* cable, which resembles phone cable but with slightly thicker jacks. Ethernet cable is sometimes called Ethernet RJ-45, Cat 5, or TPE (Twisted Pair Ethernet). The names usually include a number relating to the cable's speed rating: 10, 100, or 1,000. (Big numbers are faster.) When in doubt, buy Fast Ethernet or 100BaseT cable.

Some of today's newer homes come conveniently prewired with network jacks in the wall, sparing their owners the bother of buying and stringing long cables from room to room. If your computers are too far apart for cables, buy a wireless network adapter, described next.

Network adapters: Each computer on the network needs its own network adapter, and those gadgets come in many varieties. Most computers come with a built-in network adapter, sparing you the cost. Most newer laptops come with both wired *and* wireless adapters preinstalled, letting you connect either way.

If you need to buy a network adapter, keep these factors in mind:

- A wired adapter needs a 10/100 Ethernet connector. Adapters can plug into a USB port, plug inside one of your computer's unused slots, or even piggyback on your home's power or telephone lines.

- The adapter's box should say that it's *Plug and Play* and supports Windows Vista.

The easiest way to connect two computers

Sometimes you simply need to link two computers, quickly and easily, to move information from one to another (from an old computer to a new one, for example). You don't need expensive equipment, just a single cable called a *crossover cable,* which is a special breed of Ethernet cable. Be sure to emphasize *crossover* or *crossed* cable when shopping at the computer store; a regular Ethernet cable won't work. Connect the crossed cable between the two computers' network adapters, and Vista creates a quick network between the two computers. If

one computer connects to the Internet, the other computer should be able to share its Internet connection.

To connect two computers that each have wireless adapters, let Vista set them both up in ad-hoc mode, set to the same channel, using the same workgroup name, and the same type of security and password. Warning: This is complicated. (Windows Vista no longer supports connections between PCs with FireWire cable, unlike its predecessor, Windows XP.)

Router: Many of today's routers come with built-in wireless, and some even come with a built-in broadband modem. Your purchase depends on your Internet connection and network adapters:

✔ Broadband Internet users should purchase a *router* that has enough ports for each networked computer. If you need a wireless connection, perhaps for laptopping outdoors, buy a router with built-in wireless access. (Dialup Internet users can save money by purchasing a less expensive *switch* with enough ports for each computer.) Both a router and switch resemble the one shown in Figure 14-3. (A switch works just like a router, but lacks an outlet to plug in a broadband modem.)

✔ If you're using some or all wireless network adapters, make sure that your router has built-in wireless capabilities. If you're using a switch, buy a wireless access point to plug into it. (Wireless access points can usually accommodate dozens of wireless computers.)

✔ Buying the same brand of wireless router and wireless network adapter makes them easier to set up.

That's the shopping list. Drop this list onto the copy machine at the office and take it to the computer store.

Figure 14-3:
The router
(or switch)
needs a port
for every
computer's
cable, and
the router
needs a port
for your
broadband
modem.

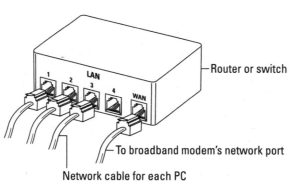

Router or switch

To broadband modem's network port

Network cable for each PC

Installing a wired network

After you've bought your network's parts, you need to plug everything into the right place. Windows Vista should automatically recognize the newly installed network adapters and embrace them gleefully.

1. **Turn off and unplug all the computers on your soon-to-be network.**

   Turn 'em all off; unplug them as well.

2. **Turn off all the computers' peripherals — printers, monitors, modems, and anything else that's attached.**

3. **Install the network adapters.**

   Plug the USB adapters into your computers' USB ports. If you're using adapter cards, remove each computer's case and push the card into the proper size of slot. (If you live in a static-prone environment, ground yourself first by touching the side of the computer's case.)

   If a card doesn't seem to fit into a slot, don't force it. Different types of cards fit into different types of slots, and you may be trying to push the wrong type of card into the wrong type of slot. See whether it fits into another slot more easily. Shameless plug: *Upgrading and Fixing PCs For Dummies* explains slots and cards in much more detail.

4. **Replace the computers' cases, if necessary, and connect each network cable between the computer's adapter and the router (or switch).**

   Unless you're using wireless adapters, you may need to route cables under carpets or around doorways. (Most routers and switches have power cords that need to be plugged into a wall outlet as well.)

5. **Broadband Internet users should plug their modem into the router's WAN port.**

   Most routers label their cable modem's port with the letters WAN (Wide Area Network). The router's other ports, labeled LAN (Local Area Network), are numbered. You can plug any PC into any of the numbered ports. (You can leave some numbered ports empty.)

   Dialup modem users can keep the modem plugged into the computer. When that computer's turned on and connected to the Internet, Windows Vista allows each networked computer to share its Internet connection.

6. **Turn on the computers and their peripherals.**

   Turn on the computers and their monitors, printers, modems, and whatever else happens to be connected to them.

7. **Select a location for your network.**

   When Windows Vista wakes up and notices the newly attached network equipment, it asks you for your network's *location:* Home, Work, or Public Location. Choose whether you're working at home or work (safe) or in public (less safe), and Vista automatically adds the proper security level to protect you.

If all goes well, Windows Vista wakes up, notices its newly installed network adapter, and automatically sets up the connection. If your computer's network adapter came with an installation CD, insert it now. (If the setup program doesn't run automatically, double-click the disc's Setup file to install the software.)

If all *doesn't* go well, you probably need a new driver for your network adapter, a task I cover in Chapter 12.

Vista does a reasonably good job of casting its networking spells on your computers. If the computers are all connected correctly and restarted, chances are they wake up in bondage with each other. If they don't, try restarting them all again.

TECHNICAL STUFF

Workgroup names and Windows XP

Like anything else in life, networks need names. A network's name is called a *workgroup,* and for some reason, Microsoft used different work-group names in different versions of Windows, and that causes problems if you have Windows XP Home PCs on your network.

Windows XP Home PCs automatically use MSHOME as their workgroup name; Windows Vista PCs use WORKGROUP as their workgroup name. The result? Put a Vista PC and a Windows XP Home PC on the same network, and they can't find or talk with each other: One PC searches in vain for other MSHOME PCs, and the other only looks for WORKGROUP PCs.

The solution is to give them both the *same* work-group name, a fairly easy task with these steps:

1. **On your Vista PC, click the Start menu, right-click Computer, and choose Properties.**

    The System screen appears, revealing basic techie information about your PC.

2. **Choose Change Settings.**

    That task lives in the section called Computer Name, Domain, and Workgroup Settings. Clicking it fetches a questionnaire.

3. **Click the Change button.**

    The Computer Name/Domain Changes dialog box appears.

4. **In the bottom box, change the Workgroup name to** MSHOME.

    That puts Vista on the same workgroup as your Windows XP PC.

    Alternatively, you can change your Windows XP PC's workgroup name to WORKGROUP by following these same five steps but click-ing the Computer Name tag in Step 2. But no matter what you call your network's work-group, make sure that every networked PC bears the *same* workgroup name.

    Tip: Be careful in this step to change each PC's *workgroup* name, not its *computer* name, as they're different things.

5. **Click OK to close the open windows and, when asked, click the Restart Now button to restart your PC.**

    Repeat these steps for your other networked PCs, making sure that the same name appears in each Workgroup box.

Keep these things in mind when setting up your network:

- ✔ Windows Vista automatically shares one folder on every networked PC: the Public folder, as well as any folders inside it. Any files you place inside that folder are available to everybody on your PC as well as anybody connected to the network. (I explain more about sharing files, folders, printers, and other items later in this chapter's "Connecting to and Sharing Files with Other PCs on Your Network" section.)

- ✔ Windows XP names its shared folder *Shared Documents.* Vista names that same folder *Public,* instead. But both do the same thing: Provide a place to share files with other people on your network.

- ✔ Click your Start menu and choose Network to see your other computers on your network.

- ✔ If your PC connects to the Internet through a dialup connection, run the Internet Connection Wizard, as described in Chapter 8. (That wizard then lets all your networked computers share that computer's Internet connection.) After that computer is set up, run the wizard on the other networked computers.

- ✔ If your PCs can't see each other, make sure that each PC uses the same Workgroup name, covered in the "Workgroup Names and Windows XP" sidebar.

Connecting Wirelessly

Setting up your own wireless home network takes two steps:

- ✔ First, set up the wireless router or wireless access point to start broadcasting and receiving information to and from your PCs.

- ✔ Second, set up Windows Vista on each PC to receive the signal and send information back, as well.

This section covers both of those daunting tasks.

Setting up a wireless router or access point

Wireless connections bring convenience, as every cell phone owner knows. But they're also more complicated to set up than wired connections. You're basically setting up a radio transmitter that broadcasts to little radios attached to your PCs. You need to worry about signal strength, finding the right signal, and even entering passwords to keep outsiders from listening in.

Wireless transmitters, known as *Wireless Access Points* (WAPs), come either built into your router or plugged into one of your router's ports. Unfortunately, different brands of wireless equipment come with different setup software, so there's no way I can provide step-by-step instructions for setting up your particular router.

However, the setup software on every model requires you to set up these three things:

- ✔ **Network name (SSID):** Enter a short, easy-to-remember name here to identify your particular wireless network. Later, when connecting to the wireless network with your computer, you'll select this same name to avoid accidentally connecting with your neighbor's wireless network.

- ✔ **Infrastructure:** Choose *Infrastructure* instead of the alternative, *Ad Hoc.*

- ✔ **Security:** This option encrypts your data as it flies through the air. Turn it on using the recommended settings.

Some routers include an installation program for changing these settings; other routers contain built-in software that you access with Windows' own Web browser.

As you enter settings for each of the three things, write them on a piece of paper: You need to enter these same three settings when setting up your PC's wireless connection, a job tackled in the next section.

Setting up Windows Vista to connect to a wireless network

After you've set up your router or wireless access point to broadcast your network, you must tell Windows Vista to receive it.

To connect to a wireless network, either your own or one in a public place, follow these steps:

1. **Turn on your wireless adapter, if necessary.**

   Many laptops turn off their wireless adapters to save power. To turn it on, open the Control Panel from the Start menu, choose Mobile PC, open the Windows Mobility Center, and click the Turn Wireless On button. Not listed? Then you need to pull out your laptop's manual, unfortunately.

2. **Choose Connect To from the Start menu.**

   Windows lists all the wireless networks it finds within range, shown in Figure 14-4. Don't be surprised to see several networks listed.

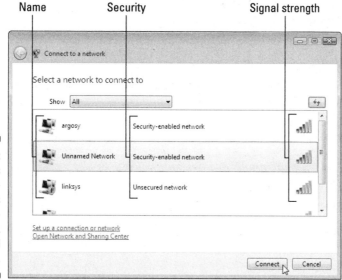

Name   Security   Signal strength

Figure 14-4:
Vista lists
each net-
work's
name, secu-
rity level,
and signal
strength.

Vista sums up each available connection three ways, all shown in Figure 14-4:

- **Name:** This is the network's name, also known as its *SSID (Service Set IDentifier)*. Because wireless networks overlap, network names let you connect to the specific network you want. Choose the SSID name you gave your wireless router when you set it up, for example, or select the name of the wireless network at the coffee shop or hotel.

- **Security:** Networks listed as *Unsecured Network* don't require a password. That means you can hop aboard and start surfing the Internet for free — even if you don't know who owns the network. However, the lack of a password means that other people can eavesdrop. Unsecured networks work fine for quick Internet access, but aren't safe for online shopping. A *Security-Enabled Network,* by contrast, is safer, as the network's password filters out all but the most dedicated snoops.

- **Signal Strength:** These little vertical bars work much like a cell phone's signal strength meter: More bars mean a stronger connection. Connecting to networks with two bars or less will be frustratingly sporadic.

If you need to revisit a previous step, click the little blue Back arrow in the window's top-left corner.

3. **Connect to the desired network by clicking its name and clicking Connect.**

   If you spot your network's name, click it and then click the Connect button.

   If you *don't* spot your network's name, head to Step 6.

4. **Choose whether you're connecting from Home, Work, or a Public Location.**

   When you connect, Vista asks you whether you're connecting from Home, Work, or a Public Location so that it can add the right layer of security. Choose Home or Work only when connecting to a wireless connection within your home or office. Choose Public Location for all others to add extra security.

   If you're connecting to an *unsecured network* — a network that doesn't require a password — you're done. Vista warns you about connecting to an unsecured network, and a click on the Connect Anyway button lets you connect.

   If you're connecting to a security-enabled network, however, Vista asks for a password, described in the next step.

5. **Enter a password, if needed, and click Connect.**

   When you try to connect to a security-enabled wireless connection, Vista sends you the window shown in Figure 14-5, asking for a password.

   Here's where you type the password you entered into your router when setting up your wireless network.

   If you're connecting to somebody else's password-protected wireless network, pull out your credit card. You need to buy some connection time from the people behind the counter.

   Don't see your wireless network's name? Then move to Step 6.

6. **Connect to an unlisted network.**

   If Vista doesn't list your wireless network's name, two culprits may be involved:

   - **Low signal strength.** Like radio stations and cell phones, wireless networks are cursed with a limited range. Wireless signals travel several hundred feet through open air, but walls, floors, and ceilings severely limit their oomph. Try moving your computer closer to the wireless router or access point. (Or just move to a different spot in the coffee shop.) Keep moving closer and clicking the Refresh button (shown in margin) until your network appears.

   - **It's hiding.** For security reasons, some wireless networks list their names as Unnamed Network. That means you must know the network's *real* name and type in that name before connecting. If you think that's your problem, move to the next step.

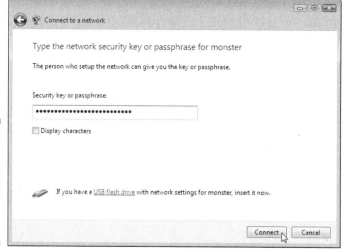

Figure 14-5: Enter the wireless network's password and click Connect.

7. **Click a wireless network listed as Unnamed Network and click Connect.**

   When asked, enter the network's name (SSID) and, if required, its password, described in Step 5. Once Vista knows the network's real name and password, Vista will connect.

Once you're connected, every user on your PC network will be able to connect to the Internet. If you're still having problems connecting, try the following tips:

- ✔ When Vista says that it can't connect to your wireless network, it offers two choices: Diagnose This Connection or Connect to a Different Network. Both messages always mean this: Move Your PC Closer to the Wireless Transmitter.

- ✔ If you can't connect to the network you want, try connecting to one of the unsecured networks, instead. Unsecured networks work fine for browsing the Internet, as long as you don't enter any passwords, credit card numbers, or other sensitive information.

- ✔ Unless you specifically tell it not to, Vista remembers the name and password of networks you've successfully connected with before, sparing you the chore of reentering all the information. Your PC will connect automatically whenever you're within range.

- ✔ Cordless phones and microwave ovens, oddly enough, interfere with wireless networks. Try to keep your cordless phone out of the same room as your wireless PC, and don't heat up that sandwich when browsing the Internet.

- ✔ If networks leave you wringing your hands, you need a book dealing more specifically with networks. Check out my other book, *Upgrading and Fixing PCs For Dummies,* by Wiley Publishing, Inc.

Connecting to and Sharing Files with Other PCs on Your Network

Even after you've set up your network, Vista *still* might not let you see your connected PCs or their files. That's right: Yet *another* security measure prevents PCs from seeing each other or sharing files on your private network. Here's how to knock some sense into Vista's security:

1. **Click the Start menu and choose Network.**

   You may see icons for all your connected PCs, shown in Figure 14-6. To connect to a PC, double-click its name. Chances are, you'll be able to see files on your Windows XP PCs, but not any other Vista PCs. To see files on Vista PCs, move to Step 2.

   Can't spot any of your networked Windows XP PCs listed? Fix the problem by reading this chapter's sidebar, "Workgroup names and Windows XP."

2. **Click the Network and Sharing Center button.**

   The Network and Sharing Center button, seen along the top of Figure 14-6, fetches the Network and Sharing Center, shown in Figure 14-7.

3. **Turn on Public Folder Sharing and click Apply.**

   Click the word Off In the Public Folder Sharing area, and the settings menu drops down, shown in Figure 14-7. To share your files, choose Turn On Sharing So Anyone with Network Access Can Open, Change, and Create Files.

   That makes your PC's Public folder fair game: Anybody on the network can open, change, or leave files in that folder. To let other people copy your Public folder's files but *not* change your copies, choose Turn On Sharing So Anyone with Network Access Can Open Files, instead.

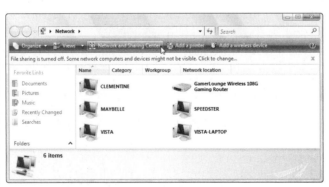

Figure 14-6: Click Network from the Start menu to see other PCs on your network.

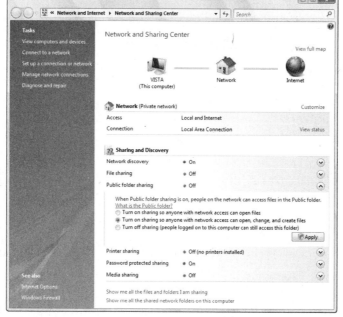

Figure 14-7:
The Network
Center
places
all your
network
settings in
one place.

4. **Turn off Password Protected Sharing and click Apply.**

   There's one last hurdle. When somebody on the network tries to see inside a Vista PC's Public folder, they must enter a name and password from an account on that *other* PC; their own name and password won't do.

   Although that makes for a *very* secure PC, it's overkill in a family environment. To remove that layer of security, click the word On in the Public Folder Sharing area, also seen in Figure 14-7. When the menu drops down, choose Turn Off Password Protected Sharing.

5. **Place files and folders you want to share with others into your PC's Public folder.**

   A handy shortcut to the Public folder lives at the bottom of every folder's Navigation pane, that strip along every folder's left edge. Drag and drop files into the Public folder to *move* them there. To *copy* them there, instead, hold down the right mouse button while dragging; drop the file and choose Copy Here from the pop-up menu. (Clicking the Public folder lets you see what's inside.)

Deleting files from a networked PC

Normally, anything you delete on your PC ends up in your Recycle Bin, giving you a last chance at retrieval. That's not true when you're working on a file in a *networked* PC's Public folder. When you delete a folder on another PC's Public folder, it's gone for good — it doesn't hop into the Recycle Bin of your PC *or* the networked PC. Beware.

If your PC still can't see other PCs, or those PCs can't see your PC or its files, check out the following tips:

- ✔ Turn off all the PCs, the router, and your broadband modem. Then turn on your broadband modem, your router, and your PCs — in that order, waiting 30 seconds between each one.

- ✔ Retrace your steps, making sure to turn on Public Folder Sharing and turn off Password Protected Sharing.

- ✔ Make sure that all your PCs have the same workgroup name, described in this chapter's sidebar, "Workgroup names and Windows XP."

Sharing a Printer on the Network

Many households or offices have several computers but only one printer. To let everybody on the network print on that printer, share it by following these steps on the Vista computer connected to the printer:

1. **Click the Start menu, choose Network, and click the Network and Sharing Center button along the top.**

   The Network and Sharing Center window appears, shown earlier in Figure 14-7.

2. **Turn on Printer Sharing and click Apply.**

   Look in the Printer Sharing category and click the Off button to reveal the menu. When the menu drops down, choose Turn On Printer Sharing and click Apply to share that printer with the network.

Now, tell your other networked PC (or PCs) about your newly shared printer by following these steps:

1. **Click the Start menu, choose Control Panel, and select Printers from the Hardware and Sound category.**

   The Printers window lists icons for any installed printers. (Ignore the Microsoft XPS Document Writer, as it's not a real printer.)

2. **Click the Add a Printer button.**

   The Add Printer window appears.

3. **Choose Add a Network, Wireless, or Bluetooth Printer and click Next.**

   Your PC glances around the network for the other PCs' shared printer. When it finds it, click its name and click Next to install it. If it doesn't find it, move to Step 4.

4. **Choose The Printer That I Want Isn't Listed and then click Browse to go to the shared printer.**

   Clicking the Browse button fetches a list of your networked PCs. Double-click the PC with the attached printer, and Vista lists the printer's name.

5. **Double-click the shared printer's icon and click Next.**

   Vista finally connects to your networked printer. You may also need to install the printer's software on your PC before it can print to the networked printer.

Can I get in trouble for looking into the wrong networked computer?

People usually *tell* you where to find files and things on your computers attached to the network. But if nobody's dropped you a hint, feel free to grab a torch and go spelunking on your own by choosing Network from the Start menu. If you're worried about getting into trouble, the rule is simple: Windows Vista rarely lets you peek into networked areas where you're not supposed to be.

In fact, Windows Vista is so security conscious that it often keeps you from seeing things that

you *should* be able to see. (That's when you call on the office administrator or the computer's owner and ask him or her for help.) If you try to peek inside a forbidden computer, you simply see an access denied message. No embarrassing sirens or harm done.

If you find yourself in a folder where you obviously don't belong — for example, the folder of employee evaluations on your supervisor's computer — quietly bring it to the administrator's attention.

Troubleshooting a Network

Setting up a network is the hardest part of networking. After the computers recognize each other (and connect to the Internet, either themselves or through the network), the network usually runs fine. But when it doesn't, here are some things to try:

- ✔ Make sure that each PC on the network has the same workgroup name. Right-click Computer from the Start menu and choose Properties. Choose Change Settings, click the Change button, and make sure that the same name appears in each PC's Workgroup box.

- ✔ Turn off every computer (using the Start menu's Shut Down option, of course). Check their cables to make sure that everything's connected. If you're not using a router, turn on the computer with the Internet connection. When it's up, running, and connected to the Internet, turn on another one. When it's connected, move to the next computer, and repeat.

- ✔ Try making Windows Vista check and repair the connection, if necessary. Choose Control Panel from the Start menu and select Network and Internet. Click Network and Sharing Center and choose Manage Network Connections from the left pane to see your connections. Right-click the one that's not working and choose Diagnose.

- ✔ Choose Help and Support from the Start menu and type **troubleshoot network** into the search box. Windows Vista offers many built-in troubleshooting tools to diagnose and repair network problems.

- ✔ On a network at home, make sure that you've set it to Private, not Public. To check, visit the Network and Sharing Center, described in the previous paragraph. Then click the word Customize next to your wireless network's name. That lets you switch from Public to Private and vice versa. If you accidentally chose Private when connected wirelessly in public, here's where you can switch back to Public to add more security.

- ✔ Click View Full Map in the Network and Sharing Center to see a map of your entire network: your Vista PCs, your router, and your Internet connection. Unfortunately, Vista leaves any Windows XP PCs *off* Vista's map. To complete your map, Microsoft offers downloadable software you can install on your Windows XP PCs to make them appear, as well.

Part V
Music, Movies, Memories (and Photos, Too)

The 5th Wave   By Rich Tennant

"This time, just for fun, let's see what you'd look like with bat ears and squash for a nose."

In this part . . .

Up until now, the book has covered the boring-but-necessary stuff: adjusting your computer so that you can get your work done. This part of the book lets you turn your computer into an entertainment center:

- ✔ Watch DVDs on your PC or laptop.
- ✔ Create greatest hits CDs for your car stereo.
- ✔ Organize a digital photo album from your digital camera.
- ✔ Edit camcorder videos into something people *want* to watch.
- ✔ Create DVDs to display your edited movies or photo slide shows.

When you're ready to play for a while, flip to this part of the book for a helping hand.

Chapter 15

Playing and Copying Music in Media Player

*W*indows Vista's Media Player 11 is a big bundle of buttons that reveals how much money you've spent on your computer. On expensive computers, Media Player rumbles like a home theater. On cheap ones, it sounds like a cell phone's ring tone.

Now on its eleventh version, Media Player sticks to the basics. It's fine for playing CDs and DVDs, organizing your music and movie files, and sending digital music to some portable MP3 players — but not iPods. If you're an iPod owner, you may want to stick with iTunes (www.apple.com/itunes).

Load up Windows Media Player from the Start menu's All Programs area. Then check out this chapter for help on using Media Player's built-in features, as well as for tips on making Media Player do the things you *really* want it to do.

The last section introduces Windows Media *Center*, a completely different program than Windows Media Player. Windows Media Center lets you watch and record TV shows on your PC — provided your PC has the right equipment.

Stocking Media Player's Library

Once you begin using Media Player, the program automatically sorts through your stash of digital music, pictures, videos, and recorded TV shows, automatically stuffing everything into its neatly organized library. But if Media Player hasn't yet stocked your library with your own files, for some reason, push it in the right direction by following these steps:

Running Media Player for the first time

The first time you open Vista's Media Player, an opening screen asks how to deal with Media Player's privacy, storage, music store, and other settings:

✔ **Express:** Designed for the impatient, this option loads Media Player with Microsoft's chosen settings in place. Media Player sets itself up as the default player for all your music and video (robbing iTunes of that job, if you currently rely on iTunes or another media player). It also starts downloading software for MTV's URGE music store. Choose Express if you're in a hurry, as you can always customize the settings later.

✔ **Custom:** Aimed at the fiddlers, this choice lets you fine-tune Media Player's behavior. A series of screens let you choose the types of music and video Media Player can play, how much of your listening habits should be sent to Microsoft, and what online store you want — if any — for buying songs. Choose this option only if you have time to wade through several minutes of boring option screens.

If you want to customize any Media Player settings — either those chosen for you in Express setup or the ones you've chosen in Custom setup — press Alt to reveal Media Player's menu, click Tools, and choose Options.

1. **Click the Library button and choose Add to Library from the drop-down menu.**

   Alternatively, you can press Alt to reveal the menu, click the File menu, and then choose Add To Library. Or, simply press F3. Windows offers enough choices to confuse everybody.

   You can load Media Player by clicking its icon in the Quick Launch toolbar near your Start button.

2. **Tell Media Player where to search for your files.**

   Make sure that My Personal Folders is selected, as shown in Figure 15-1. That tells Media Player to search your Music folder, as well as your PC's Public *folder* — the folder accessible to everybody on your PC and network (if you've set one up as described in Chapter 14).

   To add music from Music folders belonging to *other* account holders on the PC or network, choose My Folders and Those of Others That I Can Access. (Then tell those people to *share* their music by choosing Media Sharing from Media Player's Library menu and then choosing Share My Media.)

   To add music from even more folders or drives — perhaps a folder on a networked PC or flash drive — click the Advanced Options button, click Add, and navigate to the folder or drive you want to add.

TIP

3. Click the OK button to start searching.

A box appears, showing Media Player's progress as it stocks its library. When it finishes, Media Player displays your music, organized by any criteria you choose: artist, album (shown in Figure 15-2), genre, release year, song length, or rating.

Figure 15-1:
Choose My Personal Folders to add your own music; choose the other option to also add music from other people's accounts on the PC.

Figure 15-2:
Click Album from the left menu to see pictures of your albums on the right.

What are a song's tags?

Inside every music file lives a small form called a *tag* that contains the song's title, artist, album, and similar information. When deciding how to sort, display, and categorize your music, Windows Media Player reads those tags — *not* the songs' filenames. Most portable music players, including the iPod, also rely on tags, so it's important to keep them filled out properly.

It's so important, in fact, that Media Player visits the Internet, grabs song information, and automatically fills in the tags when it adds files to its library.

Many people don't bother filling out their songs' tags; other people update them meticulously. If your tags are filled out the way you prefer, stop Media Player from messing with them. Click the Library button's downward-pointing arrow, choose More Options, and remove the check box from Retrieve Additional Information from the Internet on the Library tab. If your tags are a mess, leave that box checked so that Media Player will clean up the tags for you.

To edit a song's tag manually in Media Player, right-click the song's name in the library and choose Advanced Tag Editor.

After you add your first batch of tunes to Media Player, the program continues to stock its library in the following ways:

- **Monitoring your folders:** Vista constantly *monitors* your Music, Pictures, and Videos folders, automatically updating Media Player's library whenever you add or remove files. (You can change what folders Vista monitors by following the three preceding steps.)

- **Adding played items:** Anytime you play a music file on your PC or the Internet, Vista adds the song or its Internet location to its library so that you can find it to play again later. Unless told to, Vista *doesn't* add played items that live on networked PCs, USB thumbdrives, or memory cards.

- **Ripped music from CD:** When you insert a music CD into your CD drive, Vista offers to *rip* it. That's computereze for copying the CD's music to your PC, a task described in this chapter's "Copying CDs to Your PC" section. Any ripped music automatically appears in your Media Library. (Media Player won't copy DVD movies to your library, unfortunately.)

- **Downloaded music and video from online stores:** Media Player lets you shop from URGE (Microsoft's partner store with MTV Networks) and several other stores. When you buy a song, Media Player automatically stocks its library with your latest purchase.

Feel free to repeat the steps in this section to search for files whenever you want; Media Player ignores the ones it has already cataloged and adds any new ones.

Media Player offers zillions of options when creating its library. To see or change them, click the little arrow beneath the Library button and choose More Options. There, you can make Media Player automatically update your songs' tags (explained in the sidebar), correct any misspelled song names, and perform other maintenance chores while stocking its library.

Browsing Media Player's Libraries

When first loaded, Media Player displays your music library, appropriately enough. But Media Player actually holds several libraries, designed to showcase not only your music, but photographs, video, and recorded TV shows.

To toggle between your different libraries, click the Library button on Media Player's taskbar, shown in Figure 15-3, and choose either Music, Pictures, Video, Recorded TV, or Other. Media Player immediately begins showing items in that particular category:

Figure 15-3: Click Library and choose the type of media you want to browse.

✔ **Music:** All your digital music appears here. Media Player recognizes most major music formats, including MP3, WMA, and WAV. (It *doesn't* recognize AAC files, sold by iTunes.)

✔ **Pictures:** Media Player can play back photos in a slide show, but your Pictures folder, described in Chapter 16, handles that task much better.

- ✔ **Video:** Look here for video you've saved from a camcorder or digital camera or downloaded from the Internet. Media Library recognizes AVI, MPG, WMV, ASF, and a few other formats.

- ✔ **Recorded TV:** Owners of Vista Home Premium or Vista Ultimate will see recorded TV shows listed here — if your PC has the equipment needed to record them.

- ✔ **Other:** Your playlists appear here, as well as automatically created playlists for your recently added files.

Media Player's left pane lets you display your files in different ways. Click Artist, for example, to see the music arranged alphabetically by artists' first names.

Similarly, clicking Genre separates items into different types of music. Instead of just showing a name to click — blues, for example — Media Player arranges your music into piles of covers, just as if you'd sorted your albums or CDs on your living room floor.

To play anything in Media Player, right-click it and choose Play. Or, to play all your music from one artist or genre, right-click the pile and choose Play All.

Understanding Media Player's Controls

Media Player offers the same basic controls when playing any type of file, be it a song, video, CD, DVD, or photo slide show. Figure 15-4 shows Media Player open to its Now Playing page as it plays an album. The labels explain each button's function. Or, rest your mouse pointer over an especially mysterious button, and Media Player displays a pop-up explanation.

The buttons along the bottom work like those found on any tape or CD player, letting you play, stop, rewind, fast-forward, and mute the current song or movie. Click the large square blue buttons along the player's top to perform these common tasks:

- ✔ **Now Playing:** Click here to view information about what you're currently hearing.

- ✔ **Library:** Media Player organizes your music, movies, and playlists here. To play anything listed in the library, double-click its name. To switch between libraries, click the little button directly below the big blue Back arrow button in the top-left corner.

- ✔ **Rip:** Copy a CD or some of its files to your hard drive. Customize how to copy the CD by clicking the Tools menu and choosing Options. (I cover ripping CDs in the "Copying CDs to Your PC" section.)

✔ **Burn:** Copy music from your hard drive to a CD or DVD. (See the "Creating, Saving, and Editing Playlists" section for more information.)

  ✔ **Sync:** Copy your current Now Playing list or other files to your portable music player, a task I cover in this chapter's "Copying Songs to Your Portable Player" section.

  ✔ **URGE:** New to Media Player 11, this task takes you to Microsoft's music-vending partner, MTV Network's URGE, for buying songs and movies online. I cover buying songs in this chapter's "Buying Music and Movies from Online Stores" section.

I describe each task in different sections throughout this chapter.

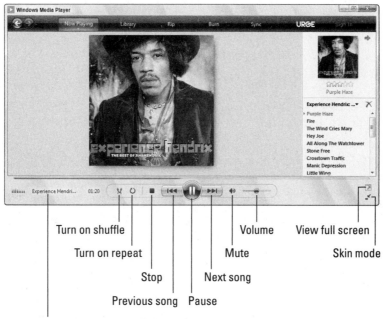

Figure 15-4:
The window's bottom buttons work much like the buttons on a VCR or CD player.

Turn on shuffle

Turn on repeat

Stop

Previous song   Pause

Volume

Mute

Next song

View full screen

Skin mode

Album, title, and time played (scrolling)

Playing CDs

As long as you insert the CD in the CD drive correctly (usually label-side up), playing a music CD is one of Media Player's easiest tasks. The biggest stumbling block comes with the pop-up form, shown in Figure 15-5, that appears when you insert the CD.

Eager to please, Windows Vista begs to know how to handle your newly inserted CD. Should it *play* the CD with Media Player? *Rip* (copy) its music onto your hard drive? Play it in *Media Center* — another Vista program described later in this chapter? *Open it* in Computer and display its files and folders?

Here's the big problem with the form: The fine print reads, "Always do this for audio CDs." No matter what option you choose, Vista will automatically make that choice the next time you insert a CD.

Figure 15-5:
When you insert a CD, Windows Vista asks you what to do with it.

To keep Vista from doing that, click to remove the check mark from that box. *Then* make your choice.

If you're not interested in anything but playing CDs, however, then leave the box checked and choose Play Audio CD using Windows Media Player. Then Vista will automatically play any music CD you insert into your PC's drive.

- ✔ Too flustered for quick decisions? Pressing the Esc key kicks the question box off your screen (until the next time you insert a CD, that is).

- ✔ When inserting a music CD, don't choose the Open Folder to View Files option. That brings up a pointless list of numbered files named Track. Windows Vista won't let you copy songs to your PC that way; you must click Media Player's Rip button, instead.

- ✔ If Vista mistakenly displays the CD's files instead of playing the darn thing, choose Default Programs from the Start menu. Choose Change AutoPlay Settings and change the Audio CD drop-down menu to Play Audio CD Using Windows Media Player. Or, to see Vista's query in Figure 15-5 whenever you insert a CD, choose Ask Me Every Time.

- ✔ Press F7 to mute Media Player's sound and pick up that phone call.

Turn off Media Player's copy protection, quickly

Many of Media Player's options and settings are simply cosmetic. But be sure to turn off the copy protection to avoid serious problems later. Press Alt to reveal the menu. Then click the Tools menu, choose Options, and click the Rip Music tab.

Then remove the check mark from the box called Copy Protect Music. That prevents Microsoft from adding *Digital Rights Management,* a fancy term meaning that you won't be able to play your copied music on other computers or some portable music players.

Although protecting the artists' rights is important, make sure that you protect your *own* rights to CDs you've purchased.

While you're there, switch to MP3 instead of Windows Media Audio in the Format drop-down menu. That makes sure that your ripped songs will play on the widest variety of portable music players, including the iPod.

Playing DVDs

Media Player plays DVDs as well as CDs, letting your laptop do double-duty as a portable DVD player. Grab your favorite DVD, some headphones, and watch what *you* like during that next long flight.

Although Media Player plays, burns, and copies CDs, it can't copy a DVD's movie to your hard drive, nor can it duplicate a movie DVD. (Remember the black FBI notice at the beginning of each DVD warning you that copies are illegal?)

When you insert a DVD into your DVD drive, Media Player sends you a window much like Figure 15-5 in the previous section, asking what it should do with it. To avoid that distraction, click the Always Do This for DVD Movies box and then click Play DVD Video using Windows Media Player. Media Player will play the DVD immediately, usually pausing at the opening screen.

Media Player works very much like your TV's DVD player, with the mouse acting as the remote. Click the on-screen words or buttons to make the DVD do your bidding.

To play the DVD full-screen, hold down the Alt key and press Enter. Media Player fills the screen with the movie. (Hold down Alt and press Enter to revert to normal play inside a window mode.) Move your mouse off-screen, and the movie's controls go away; jiggle the mouse to bring the controls back in view.

Yes, Media Player spies on you

Just like your bank, credit-card company, and grocery store club card, Media Player spies on you. Media Player's 6,223-word online Privacy Statement boils down to this: Media Player tells Microsoft every song, file, or movie that you play, and some people find that creepy. But if Microsoft doesn't know what you're playing, Media Player can't connect to the Internet and retrieve applicable artist information and artwork.

If you don't care that Microsoft hums along to your CDs, don't bother reading any further. If you *do* care, choose your surveillance level: Press Alt to reveal the menus, click Tools, select Options, and click the Privacy tab. Here's the rundown on the Privacy tab options that cause the biggest ruckus:

- **Display Media Information from the Internet:** If checked, Media Player tells Microsoft what CD or DVD you're playing and retrieves doodads to display on your screen: CD covers, song titles, artist names, and similar information.

- **Update Music Files by Retrieving Media Info from the Internet:** Microsoft examines your files, and if it recognizes any, it fills in the songs' tags with the correct information. (For more information on tags, see the "What are a song's tags?" sidebar.)

- **Send Unique Player ID to Content Providers:** Known in the biz as *data mining,* this option lets other corporations track how you use Media Player. To leave yourself out of their databases, leave this blank.

- **Cookies:** Like several other Windows Vista programs, Media Player tracks your activity with little files called *cookies*. I cover cookies in Chapter 8 because Internet Explorer controls Media Player's cookies.

- **Save File and URL History in the Player:** Media Player lists the names of your recently played files on its File menu for your convenience — and the possible guffaws of your coworkers or family. Remove this check mark to keep people from seeing the titles of music and video you've recently played.

Playing Videos and TV Shows

Many digital cameras can capture short videos as well as photos, so don't be surprised if Media Player places several videos in its library's Video section. Media Player also lists videos you've created in Windows Vista's Movie Maker program, which I cover in Chapter 16.

Playing videos works much like playing a digital song. First, switch to the video library by choosing Video from the Library button along Media Player's top. Double-click the video you want to see and start enjoying the action, as shown in Figure 15-6.

Media Player lets you watch videos in several sizes. Hold down Alt and press Enter to make it fill the screen, just as when watching a DVD. (Repeat those keystrokes to return to the original size.)

✔ To make the video adjust itself automatically to the size of your Media Player window, choose Video Size from the View menu and select Fit Video to Player on Resize.

✔ When downloading video from the Internet, make sure that it's stored in Windows Media format. Media Player can't play videos stored in *QuickTime* or *RealVideo.* Those two competing formats require free players available from Apple (www.apple.com/quicktime) or Real (www.real.com). Make sure that you download the *free* versions — those sites often try to sucker you into buying their pay versions.

✔ Some Web sites only *stream* their video to your computer — you can't save the video to play later. But you can try: After watching a streaming Web video, choose Save from Media Player's File menu. If that option is *grayed out,* the Web site has forbidden you from saving the video.

✔ When choosing video to watch on the Internet, your connection speed determines its quality. If you have a dialup connection, watch the video's 56K version. Broadband users can watch either the 100K or 300K version. You can't damage your computer by choosing the wrong one; the video just won't look right.

✔ Media Player can also play TV shows recorded by Windows Vista's Media Center, which I cover in this chapter's "Working with Media Center" section.

Figure 15-6: Double-click a video file's name to watch it in Media Player.

Playing Music Files (MP3s and WMAs)

Media Player plays several types of digital music files, but they all have one thing in common: When you tell Media Player to play a song or album, Media Player immediately places that item on your *Now Playing list* — a list of items queued up for playing one after the other.

If you want to play a song listed in Media Player's library (or a music file in any folder, for that matter), right-click the song's name and choose Play. Media Player begins playing it immediately, and the song appears in the Now Playing list.

- ✔ To play an entire album in Media Player's library, right-click the album from the library's Album Artist category and choose Play.

- ✔ Want to hear several files or albums, one after the other? Right-click the first one and choose Play. Right-click the next one and choose Add to Now Playing list. Repeat until you're done. Media Player queues them all up in the Now Playing list.

- ✔ No decent music in your music library? Then start copying your favorite CDs to your PC — a process called *ripping,* which I explain in this chapter's "Copying CDs to Your PC" section.

Playing Internet Radio Stations

Media Player no longer offers a menu to access Internet radio stations, although you can buy listening rights at some of Media Player's online stores like URGE. (I cover online stores in this chapter's "Buying Music and Movies from Online Stores" section.) If you're looking for free stations, visit these places on the Web:

- ✔ Head to Google (`www.google.com`) and search for the words Internet Radio Station to see what turns up. When you find a station broadcasting in MP3 or Windows Media Audio (WMA) format, click the Web site's Tune In or Listen Now button to load Media Player and start listening.

- ✔ I like the stations at SomaFM (`www.somafm.com`), particularly Secret Agent, Drone Zone, and Space Station Soma.

- ✔ Download and install a copy of Winamp (`www.winamp.com`), an MP3 player that lets you listen to the thousands of free radio stations available through Shoutcast (`www.shoutcast.com`). It's an incredible resource.

Creating, Saving, and Editing Playlists

A *playlist* is simply a list of songs (and/or videos) that play in a certain order. So what? Well, the beauty of a playlist comes with what you can *do* with it. Save a playlist of your favorite songs, for example, and they're always available for play back with a single click.

You can create specially themed playlists to liven up long-distance drives, parties, special dinners, workouts, and other events.

To create a playlist, follow these steps:

1. **Click the drop-down menu from Media Player's Library button.**

   Double-clicking a button also reveals the drop-down menu, as does clicking the little arrow beneath the button.

2. **Choose Create Playlist from the drop-down menu.**

   Media Player's New Playlist window appears along its right edge, as shown in Figure 15-7.

Figure 15-7:
Choose Songs from the left pane and then drag and drop song titles and album covers to the right-most pane.

3. **Right-click the album or song you want and choose Add To Untitled Playlist. (Or drag and drop albums and songs onto the Playlist pane along Media Player's right edge.)**

   Unfortunately, Media Player isn't intuitive enough to present you with a list of albums or songs to select. To see the songs and albums in your collection, click the Library button. If they're *still* not listed, click the Library button again and choose Music from the drop-down menu.

Finally, tell Media Player to display all your songs by choosing Songs from the left pane, as shown in Figure 15-7.

Start dragging and dropping albums or individual songs onto the right-most pane. (Right-clicking and choosing Add To Playlist sometimes speeds things up.) Media Player begins playing your playlist as soon as you add the first song.

Your song choices appear in the right pane in the order you've selected them.

4. **Fine-tune your playlist to change the order or remove songs.**

   Added something by mistake? Right-click that item from the playlist and choose Remove from List. Rearrange your playlist by dragging and drop-ping items farther up or down the list.

5. **When you're happy with your playlist, click the Save Playlist button at the list's bottom, type a name in the Playlist Name box, and press Enter.**

   Media Player lists your new playlist in the library's Playlists section, ready to be heard when you double-click it.

After you save a playlist, you can burn it to a CD with one click, as described in the next tip.

Make your own Desert Island Disc or Greatest Hits playlists; you can then burn them to a CD to play in your car or on your stereo. After you create a playlist, insert a blank CD into your CD burner and click the Burn button. Then select your previously saved playlist and click the Start Burn button.

To edit a previously created playlist, right-click it from the Playlists section of the library and choose Edit in List Pane.

Copying CDs to Your PC

Unlike older Media Player versions, Vista's Media Player can create MP3s, the industry standard for digital music. But until you tell the player that you want MP3 files, it creates *WMA* files that won't play on iPods or many other portable players.

To make Media Player create songs with the more versatile MP3 format instead of WMA, press Alt to reveal the menu, choose Tools, choose Options, and click the Rip Music tab. Choose MP3 instead of WMA from the Format pull-down menu and nudge the audio quality over a tad from 128 to 192, or even 256 for better sound.

To copy CDs to your PC's hard drive, follow these instructions:

1. **Open Media Player, insert a music CD, and click the Rip button.**

   You may need to push a button on the front of the drive before the tray ejects.

   Media Player connects to the Internet, identifies your CD, and fills in the album's name, artist, and song titles. Then the program begins copying the CD's songs to your PC and listing their titles in the Library. You're through.

   If Media Player can't find the songs' titles automatically, move ahead to Step 2.

2. **Click Find Album Info, if necessary.**

   If Media Player comes up empty-handed — a common occurrence when you're not connected to the Internet — fill in the titles yourself: Right-click the first track and choose Find Album Info. Then choose Enter Information for a CD That You Burned.

   Finally, fill in Media Player's form with the artist and song title information.

Here are some tips for ripping CDs to your computer:

- ✔ Normally Media Player copies every song on the CD. To leave Tiny Tim off your ukulele music compilation, for example, remove the check mark from Tiny Tim's name. If Media Player's already copied the song to your PC, feel free to delete it from within Media Player. Click the Library button, right-click the song sung by the offending yodeler, and choose Delete.

- ✔ Some record companies add copy protection to their CDs to keep you from copying them to your computer. If you buy a copy-protected CD, try holding down the Shift key for a few seconds just before and after pushing the CD into the CD tray. That sometimes keeps the copy-protection software from working.

- ✔ Don't work with your computer while it's ripping songs — just let it sit there and churn away. Running other programs may distract it, potentially interfering with the music.

- ✔ Media Player automatically places your ripped CDs into your Music folder. You'll also find your newly ripped music there by choosing Music from the Start menu.

Media Player's ripping quality settings

Musical CDs contain a *huge* amount of information — so much, in fact, that the Rolling Stones catalog probably wouldn't fit on your hard drive. To keep music files manageably small, ripping programs, such as Media Player, *compress* songs to about one-tenth of their normal size. Compressing the songs lessens their quality, so the big question becomes, how much quality loss is acceptable?

The answer is when you can hear the difference, a much-debated point among listeners. Many people can't tell the difference between a CD and a song ripped at 128 Kbps (kilobits per second), so Media Player defaults to that standard. Also,

ripped songs are usually played on computers or portable players — not high-fidelity stereos — so 96 Kbps files might sound fine to you.

If you'd rather sacrifice a bit more disk space for better quality, kick up the quality a notch: Press Alt to reveal the menu, choose Options from the Tools menu, and click the Rip Music tab. Slide the bar to the right (Best Quality) to rip at a higher quality. To create music files that don't lose *any* fidelity, choose Windows Media Audio Lossless from the Format drop-down list, and prepare for huge files. (So much for the entire Rolling Stone catalog. . . .)

Burning Music CDs

To create a music CD with your favorite songs, create a playlist containing the CD's songs, listed in the order you want to play them; then burn the playlist to a CD. I explain how to do that in this chapter's "Creating, Saving, and Editing Playlists" section.

But what if you want to duplicate a CD, perhaps to create a disposable copy of your favorite CD to play in your car? No sense scratching up your original. You'll want to make copies of CDs for your kids, too, before they create pizzas out of them.

Unfortunately, neither Media Player nor Windows Vista offers a Duplicate CD option. Instead, you must jump through the following five hoops to create a new CD with the same songs as the original CD:

1. **Rip (copy) the music to your hard drive.**

2. **Insert a blank CD into your writable CD drive.**

3. **Click the Library button and choose Album to see your saved CDs.**

4. **Right-click the album in your library and choose Add to Burn List.**

Or, right-click the playlist containing the music you want to burn to the CD and choose Add to Burn List.

5. **Click the Start Burn button.**

Now, for the fine print. Media Player compresses your songs as it saves them on your hard drive, throwing out some audio quality in the process. Burning them back to CD won't replace that lost quality. If you want *true* duplicates of your CDs, buy CD burning software from your local office supply or computer store.

Copying Songs to Your Portable Player

Media Player 11 doesn't work with the majority of portable music players, including the bestselling iPod. And it's clearly optimized for transferring WMA files — not the MP3 files used by most portable players. Many people don't bother using Media Player, instead opting for the transfer software that came with their portable player. But if you're willing to give Media Player a go, follow these steps.

1. **Connect your player to your computer.**

This step usually involves connecting a USB cord between your device and your computer. The cord's small end pushes into a hole on your player; the large end fits into a rectangular-shaped port in the front or back of your PC.

The plugs only fit one way — the right way — on each end.

2. **Start Media Player.**

Several things may happen at this point, depending on your particular music player and the way its manufacturer set it up. (Try looking for some of these options on your player's setup menus.)

If Media Player recognizes your player, a Sync List pane appears along Media Player's right edge.

If your player is set up to *Sync Automatically*, Media Player dutifully copies all the music (and video, if your player supports it) from Media Player's library to your player. It's a fairly quick process for a few hundred songs, but if your player holds thousands, you may be twiddling your thumbs for several minutes.

If your player is set up to *Sync Manually*, click Finish. You need to tell Media Player what music to copy, covered in the next step.

If your player does nothing, or Media Player's library holds more music than will fit on your player, you're forced to Step 3.

3. **Choose what music to stuff onto your player.**

   You can choose what music goes to your player in a couple of ways:

   - **Shuffle Music:** Found on the Sync List pane, this quick and easy option tells Media Player to copy a random mix of songs to the Sync List. It's great for an on-the-fly refresher, but you give up control over exactly what music will live on your player.

   - **Playlist:** Create a *playlist* — a list of music — that you want to appear on your player. Already created a playlist or two that you like? Right-click them and choose Add to Sync List, and Media Player will toss those songs onto the Sync List that's aimed at your player.

4. **Click the Start Sync button.**

   Once you've chosen the music to transfer — and it's all sitting in the Sync List pane along the player's right side — copy it all to your player by clicking the Start Sync button at the bottom of Media Player's right pane.

   Media Player sends your music to your player, taking anywhere from several seconds to a few minutes.

✔ If Media Player can't seem to find your portable player, click the Sync button along Media Player's top and choose Refresh Devices. That tells Media Player to take another look before giving up.

✔ To change how Media Player sends files to your particular media player, press Alt to reveal the menus. Then choose Options from the Tools menu and click the Devices tab. Double-click your player's name to see its current options. Some players offer zillions of options; others only offer a few.

✔ Some players may require *firmware upgrades* — special pieces of software — before they'll work with Media Player 11. Downloadable from the manufacturer's Web site, firmware upgrades run on your PC like any software installation program. But instead of installing software on your PC, they install software onto your portable player to bring it up to date.

Buying Music and Movies from Online Stores

Media Player 11's biggest new feature could be the online partnership with URGE, run by MTV Networks. There, you can pay to download songs and movies or listen to a customized radio station. To start shopping, follow these steps:

1. **Click the word URGE in the player's upper-right corner.**

   URGE asks you to click to approve its 2,046-word licensing agreement before downloading its software to your PC. After a few minutes, URGE's Web site appears in Media Player, shown in Figure 15-8. (You may have to click the URGE button again to see the store.)

2. **Type the artist or song you want into the Search box.**

   Media Player's Search box, found in its upper-right corner, normally searches through your PC's own stash of music. But when you're connected to URGE, Media Player searches both your songs *and* those on URGE, listing the results on-screen.

   Oddly enough, URGE lists songs matching your search even if they're not for sale. The entire Beatles catalog is listed, for example, but every song is grayed out, with no price next to the name. (That's because The Beatles don't sell their music online.)

Figure 15-8:
Click URGE
to begin
shopping for
music from
MTV
Network's
digital music
store.

3. **Listen to the first 30 seconds of any song.**

Double-click an album cover, for example, to hear a snippet of the first song; double-click a song title itself to hear the song.

URGE also sells playlists — ordered lists of songs chosen by theme, genre, TV shows, decade, city, celebrity picks, and other criteria.

4. **Buy the song, album, or playlist.**

Here's where you can choose between URGE's purchase plans.

- **Subscription:** Here, you fork over a monthly fee to URGE, and the company lets you download all the songs you want. Sound sweet? Unfortunately, when you stop paying the fee, your songs stop playing, both in your player and your PC. Also, some players don't support the subscription plan's required copy protection. Subscriptions currently cost $14.95 per month, $9.95 if you don't copy songs to a portable player.

- **Ala carte:** Some songs cost 99 cents, others cost $3 or more, and some are available only if you purchase the entire album. (And unlike CDs you buy at the store, you can't resell or trade-in digital music.)

To sign up for an URGE account, click the Sign In button in Media Player's top-right corner.

Be sure to read the fine print before typing your credit-card number. URGE doesn't offer songs from every artist or record label, and it's not compatible with most portable music players.

The wrong player keeps opening my files!

You'd never hear Microsoft say it, but Media Player isn't the only Windows program for playing songs or viewing movies. In fact, you need QuickTime (www.quicktime.com) to view lots of Internet videos stored in Apple's competing QuickTime movie format. Many Internet sounds and videos come stored in Real's (www.real.com) competing RealAudio or RealVideo format, which Media Player can't handle, either.

And some people use Winamp (www.winamp.com) for playing their music, videos, and a wide variety of Internet radio stations. With all the competing formats available, many people install several different media players — one for each format. Unfortunately, these multiple installations lead to bickering among each player because they all fight to become your default player.

Vista attempts to settle these arguments with its new Default Programs area. To choose the player that should open each format, click the Start button, choose Default Programs, and click Set Your Default Programs. A window appears where you can choose which program plays your CDs, DVDs, pictures, video, audio, and other media.

Note: When you're browsing the online store, Media Player displays screens sent from URGE's Web site (www.urge.com). Unlike Windows programs, Web sites change frequently. The steps shown here may change slightly as URGE updates its Web site.

Working with Media Center

Media Center began life as a special version of Windows designed to be viewed on a TV screen and manipulated with a remote control. In fact, its large menus and simple controls seem out of place in Windows Vista. Because Media Center doubles many of Media Player's efforts, you'll probably find Media Player's familiar controls more convenient.

But if you want to give Media Center a whirl, using it to watch and record TV shows, keep in mind that all this fun comes with a few stipulations:

- ✔ **Vista Home Premium or Ultimate:** Neither Vista Home Basic nor Vista's Business versions include the Media Center.

- ✔ **TV Tuner:** Your PC doesn't need a TV set to view or record TV shows. No, your PC needs its own built-in *TV tuner:* special circuitry that lets you view TV on a monitor and change channels. Big bonus points go to TV tuners that come with remote controls, but Media Center also works with a mouse or keyboard.

- ✔ **TV signal:** Like a TV set, a PC's TV tuner can extract channels only from a TV signal. You can connect the cable that plugs into your TV set into your PC's TV tuner. Or, if you're desperate, you can attach a "rabbit ears" antenna to the tuner, but the picture won't look nearly as good.

- ✔ **Video with TV-Out port:** TV shows look fine on your computer monitor. But to watch those shows on a real TV, your PC's tuner needs a spot to plug in your TV set. Most tuners offer a combination of S-Video, composite, and occasionally coax connectors, the three connectors used by most TV sets.

When run on a properly equipped PC, Media Center should find everything — the tuner, the signal, and the monitor. To give the program a test run, click Start, choose All Programs, and choose Windows Media Center.

If Media Center *doesn't* find those things, you probably need a new Vista-compatible driver for your tuner card, a piece of software downloadable from the tuner manufacturer's Web site.

Pressing F8 mutes the sound in Media Center, a difficult thing to remember because Media Player mutes when you press F7.

Running Media Center for the first time

Don't start Media Center for the first time unless you have a good 15 or 20 minutes to kill. It takes that long to set things up. Media Center begins by poking and prodding your PC to look for an Internet connection and home network and then gives you a fairly lengthy interview. Microsoft wants you to approve its privacy policies, for example, which consist of wading through more than 68 pages of fine print.

Media Center asks you to type your zip code and select the provider supplying your TV signal. After downloading listings for upcoming shows, Media Center ends its interview by letting you select your type of monitor, speakers, and the way they're connected. These settings are most important for people who connect their PC to a TV set and home stereo to watch the videos.

When it finally finishes, Media Center displays a *TV Guide*-type of listing on the screen, which lets you browse shows and choose the ones to watch or record for later viewing.

Browsing Media Center's menus

For a souped-up VCR, Media Center offers a lot of options. Here are Media Center's menus, shown in Figure 15-9, and a briefer on what lies behind each one:

- **TV and Movies:** Media Center opens to this menu option, which lets you choose from several options: Record a TV show or movie, watch live or recorded TV, play a DVD, or Set Up TV — a must if you want to begin recording live TV shows. Once you've set up your TV, you can browse for movies and shows through a *TV Guide*-style menu.

- **Music:** Media Center can play your music, just like Media Player. Unlike Media Player's dizzying array of options, Media Center offers three choices. The Music Library option displays every album cover in your Music folder; click the cover of the album you want to hear. The Radio option doesn't tune in Internet stations, but FM stations that may piggyback on your TV signal.

- **Tools:** Enter here for settings that tweak everything from your TV reception to how Media Center displays your album art.

- **Pictures + Videos:** Just as you'd expect, this setting displays pictures from your Pictures folder, complete with slide shows. Videos from your Videos folder appear here, as well.

- **Tasks:** This section lets you burn CDs from your music collection and DVDs from recorded TV shows — without editing out the commercials, of course.

Figure 15-9:
Media
Center lets
you watch
and record
shows, play
your music,
and view
your videos.

To move from one menu to another, use the remote control that came with
your TV tuner. No remote? Then point your mouse where you want to go;
right-clicking also brings up menus. Your keyboard's arrow keys also work
well for menu hopping.

To return to a previous menu, use the remote's Back key, use the mouse to
click the Back arrow in the screen's upper-left corner, or press the keyboard's
Backspace key.

Getting the most out of Media Center

Because Media Center duplicates Media Player's functions, you probably
won't find yourself using it much. In fact, it comes in handy only on these particular occasions:

- ✔ **Xbox hooked up to TV:** Microsoft's game box, the Xbox 360, hooks up to
  a TV for playing games. But when hooked up to a network, the Xbox 360
  can connect to Media Center, sharing its libraries of music, photos, and
  movies.

- ✔ **PC hooked up to TV:** Few people want a large, noisy PC sitting next to
  their TV. But if your PC serves exclusively as part of your home theater,
  Media Center provides a nice command center.

- ✔ **Ease of access:** Media Center's large and simple menus won't satisfy control freaks. But if you're looking for easy-to-read menus for handling simple chores, you may prefer Media Center to Media Player.

- ✔ **TV tuner:** If your PC comes with a TV tuner, it probably came with software for recording and watching TV shows. If you find Media Center easier to use and more dependable, it's natural to switch.

Chapter 16

Fiddling with Photos and Movies

- -

In This Chapter

▶ Copying digital camera photos into your computer

▶ Viewing photos in your Pictures folder

▶ Saving digital photos to a CD

▶ E-mailing photos

▶ Printing photos

▶ Creating a slide show and copying it to a DVD

▶ Copying camcorder footage into your computer

▶ Editing your clips into a movie

▶ Adding transitions between clips

▶ Saving your completed movie to a DVD

- -

*T*his chapter introduces you to the growing relationship among Windows, digital cameras, and camcorders — both the new digital and older analog models. It explains how to move your digital photos and movies onto your computer, edit out the bad parts, display them to the family, e-mail them to distant relatives, and save them in easy-to-find locations on your computer.

One final note: After you've started creating your family album on your computer, please take steps to back it up properly, as I describe in Chapter 12. (This chapter explains how to copy them to a CD or DVD.) Your family memories can't be replaced.

Using Your Computer as a Digital Shoebox

With an eye on the digital camera boom, Microsoft's programmers have transformed Windows' built-in Pictures folder into a computerized family album. After you've dumped your digital camera photos into that folder, Windows Vista makes it easy to create on-the-fly slide shows, screen savers, and wallpaper, as well as apply a host of editing tricks.

Windows Vista doesn't recognize my camera!

Although Windows Vista usually greets cameras as soon as they're plugged into the computer, sometimes the two don't become friends immediately: Vista doesn't display its import Photos menu, or another program's menu tries to take over. If those problems occur, unplug your camera, and wait a few seconds before plugging it back in.

If that doesn't do the job, follow these steps:

1. **Click Start, choose Default Programs, and open Change AutoPlay Settings.**

2. **Scroll down to the Devices area.**

    The Devices area lives near the window's bottom.

3. **Choose your camera, choose Import Using Windows from the pull-down menu, and click Save.**

If Windows Vista *still* doesn't greet your camera when you plug it in, Windows Vista needs a translator to understand your camera's language. Unfortunately, that translator will have to be the camera's bundled software. If you no longer have the software, you can almost always download it from your camera manufacturer's Web site.

This section walks you through connecting your camera to your computer and copying the photos to the computer for viewing.

Dumping the camera's photos into your computer

Most digital cameras come with software that grabs your camera's photos and places them into your computer. But you needn't install it, nor even bother trying to figure it out, thank goodness. Windows Vista's built-in software easily fetches photos from nearly any make and model of digital camera when you follow these steps:

1. **Plug the camera's cable into your computer.**

    Most cameras come with two cables: One that plugs into your TV set for viewing, and another that plugs into your PC. You need to find the one that plugs into your PC for transferring photos.

    Plug the transfer cable's small end into your camera, and the larger end (shown in the margin) into your computer's *USB port,* a rectangular-looking hole about a half-inch long and a fourth-inch high. (Most USB ports live on the back of the computer, but newer computers offer them up front.)

2. **Turn on your camera, if it's not already turned on, and wait for Windows Vista to recognize it.**

   If you're plugging in the camera for the first time, Windows Vista sometimes heralds the camera's presence with a small pop-up window above your taskbar by the clock.

   If Windows Vista doesn't recognize your camera, make sure that the camera is set to Display mode — which lets you see the photos on its screen — rather than Shoot mode, which you use to take pictures. Also, try unplugging the cable from your PC, waiting a few seconds, and then plugging it back in.

3. **When the AutoPlay window appears, click Import Pictures Using Windows.**

   When you first plug a digital camera into Vista, the AutoPlay window appears, shown in Figure 16-1. Make sure that a check mark appears in Always Do This for This Device and click Import Pictures Using Windows. That tells Vista to automatically grab your camera's pictures whenever you connect it to your PC.

   Don't see the AutoPlay window? Try opening Computer from the Start menu and double-clicking your camera icon, shown in the margin.

Figure 16-1: Choose Import Pictures Using Windows so that Vista automatically extracts your camera's photos.

4. **Type a *tag* or name for your photos and click Import.**

   Type a descriptive word or two to describe the photos, as shown in Figure 16-2. Type the word **Cat**, for example, and Windows Vista names the incoming photos as Cat 001, Cat 002, Cat 003, and so on. Later, you can find these pictures by searching for the word **Cat**.

   Click Import to bring your camera's photos into your PC and automatically name them.

Figure 16-2:
Type a tag
or name that
describes
your photo
session.

Clicking the word Options, shown in Figure 16-2, lets you change how Vista imports your photos. It's worth a look-see, as it lets you "undo" any options you've mistakenly chosen when first importing your photos.

5. Click Erase After Importing.

If you don't delete your camera's photos after importing them into your PC, you won't have room to take more photos. Click Erase After Importing, shown in Figure 16-3, and Vista erases the camera's photos, saving you the trouble of rummaging through your camera's menus.

Figure 16-3:
Click Erase
After
Importing to
free up your
camera for
more
photos.

6. If asked, let Windows correct your picture's rotation.

When Windows notices that you've turned your camera sideways to take a picture — which usually happens when you take photos of trees or small groups of standing people — take it up on its offer to rotate your photos by clicking Yes. That keeps your photos from showing up sideways on your monitor.

Some older cameras don't tell Windows when you've turned the camera sideways for a photo, so you may not see this option.

When Windows finishes importing your photos, it displays the folder containing your new pictures.

Grabbing your camera's photos with a card reader

Windows Vista grabs photos from your camera fairly easily. But a *memory card reader* not only speeds up the job, it's your only option when you've lost your camera's transfer cable. A memory card reader is a little box with a cable that plugs into your computer's USB port — the same spot your camera does.

To dump your camera's pictures into your computer, remove the camera's memory card and slide the card into the slot in the card reader. Windows Vista notices that you've inserted the card and treats it like your camera, offering the same menus.

Or, choose Computer from the Start menu and double-click the card reader's drive letter to see all the photos. From there, you can select the photos you want and cut and paste them to a folder in your Pictures folder.

Memory card readers are cheap (less than $20), easy to set up, fast at copying images, and much more convenient. Plus, you can leave your camera turned off while dumping the vacation photos, saving battery life. When buying a card reader, make sure that it can read the type of memory cards used by your camera — as well as several other types of memory cards. (That ensures it will work with any new computer-related gadgets you might acquire around the holidays.)

Browsing your photos with Windows Photo Gallery

Your Pictures folder, located one click away on the Start menu's right side, easily earns kudos as the best place to store your digital photos. When Vista imports your digital camera's photos, it automatically stuffs them in there to take advantage of that folder's built-in viewing tools.

To peek inside any folder, double-click its icon. Inside, each folder offers the usual file-viewing tools found in every folder, plus a convenient row of buttons for displaying, editing, e-mailing, and printing your photos. (Click the View button to cycle quickly through three different thumbnail sizes.)

But when your Pictures folder grows too crowded for easy viewing, fire up Vista's new Photo Gallery Viewer: Click the Start button, choose All Programs, and click Windows Photo Gallery.

Shown in Figure 16-4, the Photo Gallery offers oodles of ways to sort quickly through thousands of photos by clicking different words, dates, and ratings listed on the Navigation Pane along the viewer's left side. Double-click any photo to see a larger view, then return to the Gallery by clicking the Backwards arrow in the top-left corner.

Clicking these words in the Navigation Pane let you sort your photos in a variety of ways:

- **All Pictures and Videos:** Click this option to see *all* your photos and videos, sorted chronologically by the year you snapped them or dumped them into your PC. Two subcategories let you view just pictures or just videos. If you spot the one you're after, double-click its icon to view it.

- **Recently Imported:** This option provides a handy way to find pictures you've *just* added to your PC.

- **Tags:** Remember the tag you assigned to your photos when importing them from your digital camera in Figure 16-2? The Navigation Pane lists those tags, ready to retrieve their matching photos with a click. Feel free to add tags on the fly: Select your photos of Uncle Frank (select several photos by holding down Ctrl as you click each one), click Add Tags from the pane along the right edge, and type **Uncle Frank** to add that name as a tag.

- **Date Taken:** This option lets you see all the photos taken in a certain year or month, or on a certain date. Click 2004, for example, hold down Ctrl, and click the tag Cat to see every photo of your cat from 2004.

- **Ratings:** Spot a photo that's a real keeper? Or perhaps a stinker? Hold down Ctrl and press **1**, **2**, **3**, **4**, or **5**, with 5 meaning it's an absolute favorite. Vista remembers that particular rating and lets you sort photos by their ratings. You can also rate a currently viewed photo by clicking any of the rating stars on the right side, as shown in Figure 16-4.

- **Folders:** Click any folder listed here to view photos stored in a particular folder. To add any folder to the list, right-click the word Folders, choose Add Folder to Gallery, and browse to the folder you'd like to add.

By mixing and matching dates, tags, and ratings, you can ferret out the particular photos you're after. The following tips also increase your chances of locating a particular photo:

- Spot a blurred or ugly photo? Right-click it and choose Delete. Weeding out the garbage makes the good ones easier to find.

- You can assign several different tags to one photo, adding a tag for each person in a group picture, for example. That makes that photo appear in searches for *any* of its tags.

- Type any photo's tag into the Pictures folder's Search box, located in its top-right corner, and Vista quickly displays photos assigned with that particular tag.

- Double-click any picture for a closer look, making it fill the window. The Photo Gallery's preview window displays the picture, offering buttons to fix, print, e-mail, open, and see information about the photo. (I describe those buttons in this chapter's "Fixing photos" section.)

✔ Want to cover your entire desktop with a photo? Right-click the picture and choose Set As Background. Windows immediately splashes that photo across your desktop.

✔ Hover your mouse pointer over any photo for a larger view, as well as information about its filename, rating, tags, date snapped, size, and dimensions.

Burn to CD or DVD

E-mail photo

Create slideshow (movie)

Print photo

Currently selected photo

Toggle Information pane

Open for editing in another program

Adjust or crop photo

Toolbar

Information pane

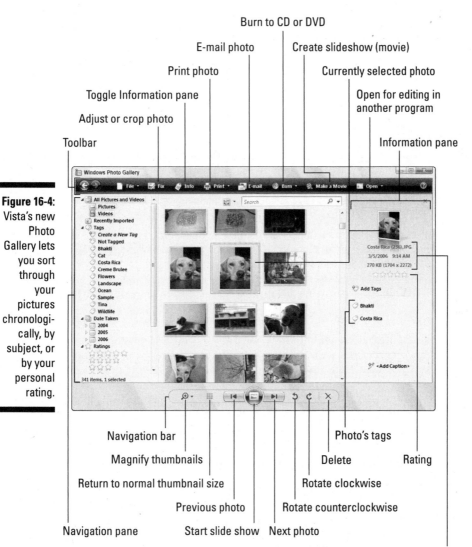

Figure 16-4:
Vista's new Photo Gallery lets you sort through your pictures chronologically, by subject, or by your personal rating.

Navigation bar

Photo's tags

Magnify thumbnails

Delete

Rating

Return to normal thumbnail size

Rotate clockwise

Previous photo

Rotate counterclockwise

Navigation pane

Start slide show

Next photo

Photo's name, date, size, and dimensions

Keeping digital photos organized

It's tempting to create a folder called New Photos in your Pictures folder and start dumping new pictures into it. But when it comes time to relocating a particular photo, that system breaks down quickly. Vista's importing tools do a fairly good job of naming each photo session after the date and the tag. These tips also help keep your pictures organized and easy to retrieve:

✔ Assign a few key tags like Home, Travel, and Holidays to photos. Searching for those tags makes it easy to see all the pictures taken at your own house, while traveling, or during holiday events.

✔ Windows assigns your chosen tag to each batch of photos you import. Spend a little time immediately afterward to assign more tags to each photo.

✔ If digital photography turns into a hobby, consider buying one of many third-party photo programs like ThumbsPlus (www.cerious.com). They provide more photo management and editing features, improving upon Windows Vista's basic tools.

Viewing a slide show

Windows XP offers a simple slide slow that displays one photo after another. In Vista's hands, the slide show turns into an extravaganza, with a whopping 15 different types of slide shows.

Start the photos flowing across the screen either of these two ways:

✔ When in your Pictures folder, click the Slide Show button (shown in the margin) from along the folder's top.

✔ While in the Photo Gallery, click the large, round Play Slide Show button (shown in the margin) from along the folder's bottom center.

Windows immediately darkens the monitor, fills the screen with the first picture, and then blends one picture into the next.

Don't see a fancy slide show? If Vista wears its drab Basic clothes, then your PC either isn't powerful enough to handle the graphics, or you're using Windows Vista Basic — Vista's least expensive version.

Click the Themes button along the slide show's bottom edge to change the pictures' presentation. The Album theme, for example, creates a scrapbook look; Classic brings back Windows XP's simple slide show; and Travel melds several different displays into one. Feel free to experiment.

The Slide Show button creates quick, on-the-fly slide shows, but if you're looking for slide shows to save to a CD or DVD and give to friends, check out this chapter's last two sections. There, I explain how to create and save slide shows with Vista's built-in Movie Maker and DVD Maker programs.

Here are more tips for successful on-the-fly slide shows:

- ✔ Before starting the slide show, rotate any "sideways" pictures, if necessary, so that they all appear right side up.

- ✔ The slide show includes all the photos in your current folder, as well as any photos living in folders inside that folder.

- ✔ Select just a few of a folder's pictures and click the Slide Show button to limit the show to just those pictures. (Hold down Ctrl while clicking pictures to select more than one.)

- ✔ You can turn any of these slide shows into screen savers. Right-click the desktop, choose Personalize, click Screensaver, and choose Photos from the Screen Saver pull-down menu. (Click the Settings button to choose your favorite type of slide show or limit displayed photos by tag, rating, and folder.)

- ✔ Feel free to add music to your slide show by playing a song in Media Player, described in Chapter 15, before starting your show. Or, if you picked up a Hawaiian CD while vacationing on the islands, insert that in your CD player to play a soundtrack during your vacation slide show.

Fixing photos

Windows Vista finally offers some photo repair tools to remove red eye from flash photos, tweak washed-out colors, and crop photos to different sizes. Oddly enough, Vista hides these repair tools inside the Windows Photo Gallery: To begin a repair job, click Start, choose All Programs, and select Windows Photo Gallery.

Select the problem photo by clicking it and then click the Fix button (shown in the margin) on the Windows Photo Gallery's toolbar. The next few sections explain how to fix your photos with the gallery's easy-to-use fix-it tools, shown in Figure 16-5.

Vista's photo fix-ups aren't permanent. If you make a mistake, click the Undo button at the screen's bottom. If you decide you've made a mistake several days later, click that problematic figure, click the Fix button, and you'll see a Revert button at the figure's bottom. Click it, and Vista can *still* revert to the original photo.

Be sure to fix your photos *before* printing them or sending them to be printed. A little bit of cropping and adjustment help make your photos look their best before you commit them to paper.

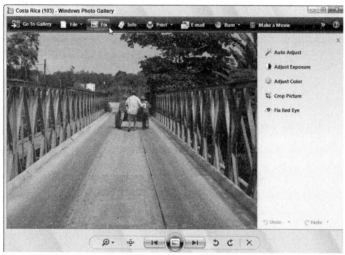

Figure 16-5: Click Windows Photo Gallery's Fix button to access the "fix-it" tools along the right side.

Adjusting exposure and color

Photographs capture the light entering the camera's lens, and that light rarely looks the same as the light beaming back at you from your computer monitor. To adjust for the difference, Windows Photo Gallery lets you adjust a photo's color, as well as correct for overexposed photos — a problem when your camera picks up too much or too little light.

Here's the quickest and easiest way to adjust a particular photo's lighting:

1. **Open the Windows Photo Gallery, click the awful photo, and click the Fix button on the toolbar.**

   The Windows Photo Gallery lives in the Start menu's All Programs area. The photo repair tools quickly appear along the window's right edge, as shown earlier in Figure 16-5.

2. **Click Auto Adjust.**

   Vista's robotic intelligence chooses the settings it thinks the photo needs. Surprisingly enough, Auto Adjust usually makes the photo look much better. If you think the photo now looks perfect, you're through. But if it looks worse or isn't quite fixed yet, move to Step 3.

3. **Click Adjust Exposure and adjust the Brightness and Contrast settings.**

   Vista's Auto Adjust tool almost always changes a photo's exposure settings slightly. The slider bars for Brightness and Contrast are normally centered, but after Auto Adjust does its work, one or both will be off-center. Slide the bars to further tweak Auto Adjust's changes. If the photo *still* doesn't look right, move to Step 4.

4. **Click Adjust Color and adjust the Tint, Color Temperature, and Saturation settings.**

   Just as before, slide the bars to the center or edge to either enhance or remove Auto Adjust's settings.

5. **Save or discard your changes.**

   If you're pleased with the outcome, save your changes by either clicking the Back To Gallery button in the top, left corner or closing the Gallery.

   But if the photo looks worse than ever, discard your changes: Keep clicking the Undo button along the bottom to remove each change, or revert to the original by clicking the little arrow next to the Undo button and choosing Undo All.

Cropping photos

You crop a photo every time you take a picture: You look through the camera's viewfinder or its color screen, aiming the camera and zooming in or pulling back until the subject appears nicely framed.

But when you go home, you may notice your quick framing wasn't as nice as you'd thought. A telephone pole protrudes from a person's head, for example, or that little tree frog disappears in the leafy background.

Cropping can solve both of those problems, letting you remove a photo's bad parts and enhance the good. These steps show how to crop a photo to make a distant object — a Costa Rican tree frog — appear closer.

1. **Open the Windows Photo Gallery, click the problem photo, and click the Fix button.**

   The Windows Photo Gallery lives in the Start menu's All Programs area.

2. **Click the Crop Picture tool and choose your Proportion.**

   The Crop Picture tool places a rectangle in your photo, shown in Figure 16-6. The rectangle shows the cropped area — everything outside the rectangle will be cropped out.

3. **Adjust the cropped area around your subject.**

   Vista places the rectangle in the center of your photo, which is rarely the best place to crop. Reposition the rectangle by pointing at it, and while holding down the mouse button, move the mouse to drag the cropping area to a new position. Then, adjust the rectangle's size by dragging the corners in and out.

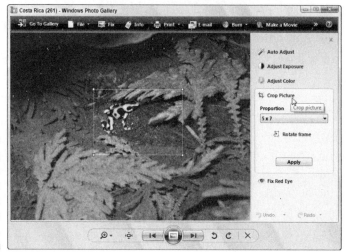

Figure 16-6:
Adjust the rectangle to fit the area you want to crop.

To crop for different paper sizes — a 5 by 7 or 4 by 6, for example — click the Proportion drop-down menu and choose a different size. Feel free to click Rotate Frame if that frames your subject better.

Don't always center your subject. For more interesting crops and shots, follow the *Rule of Thirds*. Imagine two vertical and horizontal lines dividing your photo into equal thirds, as shown in Figure 16-7. Then position the photo's subject anyplace where those lines intersect.

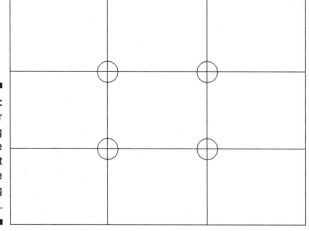

Figure 16-7:
For interesting crops, place your subject on the intersecting lines.

4. Click Apply to crop the image.

Windows Photo Gallery crops away the photo portions outside your frame, leaving a photo like the one in Figure 16-8. (Notice how the placement of the frog follows the Rule of Thirds.)

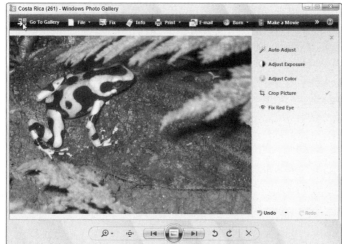

Figure 16-8:
Click Apply to crop the unwanted areas from your photo.

5. Click Undo if you're unhappy with the crop; if you're happy with it, close the program or click the Back To Gallery button.

Clicking Undo brings back the uncropped photo for you to try again. If you're happy with the crop, though, click Back To Gallery to see your photos again or close the program.

Cropping comes in handy for creating pictures for your user account photo — the photo that appears atop your Start menu. Crop out everything but your head, save the shot, and then head to the Control Panel's User Accounts area to use that head shot for your account picture. (I explain user accounts in Chapter 13.)

Removing red eye

Flash photos work so quickly that the pupil doesn't have time to contract. Instead of seeing a black pupil, the camera catches the blood-red retina in the back of the eye.

Vista's Fix Red Eye tool replaces the red with the more natural black, fixing a problem that's plagued party photographers around the world.

1. **Open the Windows Photo Gallery, click your red-eye photo, and click the Fix button.**

   The Windows Photo Gallery lives in the Start menu's All Programs area.

   Zoom in on the red eye area by clicking the magnifying glass icon on the Navigation bar along the window's bottom and sliding the bar upward. Then drag the photo with your mouse pointer until the red eye comes into view.

2. **Click Fix Red Eye, drag a rectangle around the red part of the pupil, and then release the mouse button.**

   Click just above the red portion of the pupil, hold down your mouse button, and point down and to the side to surround the red portion with a rectangle.

   Releasing the mouse button turns the red into black.

Copying digital photos to a CD or DVD

Don't lose all your digital memories because you didn't back them up. Head to the computer or office-supply store and pick up a stack of blank CDs or DVDs to match your PC's drive. (I explain how to tell what type of disc drive lives inside your PC in Chapter 4.)

Then follow these steps to copy every item in your Pictures folder to a blank CD or DVD:

1. **Open your Pictures folder from the Start menu and click the Burn button.**

   Vista asks you to insert a blank disc into your drive.

2. **Insert a blank CD or DVD into your writable disc drive.**

   DVDs can store five times as much information as a CD, so insert a DVD into your DVD burner. No DVD burner? Insert a blank CD, instead.

3. **Type a name for your backup disc and click Next.**

   Type today's date and the words Photo Backup. Vista begins backing up all your photos to your CD or DVD.

Don't have enough space on the CD or DVD to hold all your files? Unfortunately, Windows Vista isn't smart enough to tell you when to insert the second disc. Instead, it whines about not having enough room and stops in its tracks. In that case, head for Vista's much smarter Backup program (Chapter 10), which has the smarts to split your backup between several discs.

Fixing rotated pictures

In the old days, it never mattered how you tilted your camera when taking the photo; you simply turned the printed photo to view it. Most of today's computer monitors don't swivel, so Windows Vista rotates the photo for you — if you figure out how.

The trick is to right-click any photo that shows up sideways. Choose Rotate Clockwise or Rotate Counter Clockwise to turn your green cliffs into grassy meadows.

To rotate a sideways photo in Windows Photo Gallery, click the clockwise or counterclockwise Rotate icons along the picture's bottom.

E-mailing photos

Digital cameras create *huge* files, but e-mail requires *small* files. If the files are too big, they'll bounce back to your Inbox or overwhelm the recipient's e-mail account. To solve this technical conundrum, Windows Vista conveniently offers to resize your digital photos when you e-mail them. Here's how to take advantage of its kind offer:

1. **Right-click the desired photo or photos, choose Send To from the menu, and choose Mail Recipient.**

   Or, if you're looking at the photo in a folder or from within Windows Photo Gallery, click the E-mail button from the toolbar along the top.

   Windows Vista sends up a window, shown in Figure 16-9, offering to shrink your e-mailed pictures. Take it up on its offer.

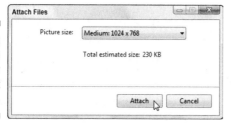

Figure 16-9:
Choose
Medium for
most
recipients.

2. **Click the Attach button.**

   Windows resizes the photos you're e-mailing, opens your default e-mail program (usually Windows Mail or Microsoft Outlook), and attaches them to a message.

3. **Fill in the recipient's e-mail address and click Send.**

   For more details about e-mail, look for my coverage of Windows Mail in Chapter 9.

4. **Click the Send button.**

   Windows Mail sends your message to the recipient with the photo or photos attached.

Printing pictures

Windows Vista's Photo Printing Wizard offers nearly as many options as the drugstore's photo counter, printing full-page glossies, wallet prints, and nearly anything in between.

The key to printing nice photos is buying nice (and expensive) photo paper and using a photo-quality printer. Ask to see printed samples before buying a printer, then buy that printer's recommended photo-quality paper.

Before printing your photos, feel free to crop and adjust their colors, as I describe earlier in this chapter's "Fixing photos" section.

Here's how to move photos from your screen to the printed page:

1. **Open Pictures from the Start menu and select the photos you'd like to print.**

   Want to print one photo? Then click it. To select more than one photo, hold down the Ctrl key as you click each one.

2. **Tell Vista to print the selected photos.**

   You can tell Vista to print your selection either of these ways:

   - Click the Print button from the folder's toolbar. You'll spot a handy Print button atop your Pictures folder, as well as in the Windows Photo Gallery.

   - Right-click the selected photos and choose Print from the pop-up menu.

   No matter which method you choose, the Print Pictures window appears, shown in Figure 16-10.

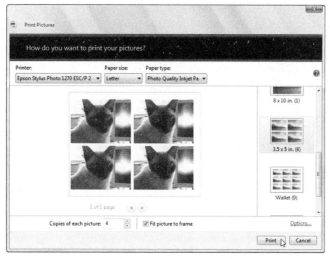

Figure 16-10:
Choose how
the photos
should
appear on
paper and
then click
the Print
button.

3. **Choose your printer, paper, and photo layout and the number of times to print each picture.**

   The Print Pictures window lets you tweak several settings. (If you don't tweak anything, Vista prints one copy of each photo across an entire sheet of 8½-by-11-inch photo paper.)

   • **Printer:** Vista lists your default printer — your only printer, if you only have one — in its top, left box. If you own a second printer you only use for photos, choose that printer from the drop-down menu.

   • **Paper size:** Vista lists different paper sizes in this drop-down menu in case you'll be printing on something besides normal 8½-by-11-inch photo paper.

   • **Layout:** Choose how Vista should arrange the photos on the paper. You can print each photo to fill an entire page, for example, print nine wallet photos, or somewhere in between. Each time you choose an option, the wizard displays a preview of the printed page, as shown in Figure 16-10.

   • **Copies of each picture:** Choose anywhere from 1 to 99 copies of each picture.

4. **Insert photo paper into your printer and click Print.**

   Follow the instructions for inserting your photo paper into your printer. It must face the correct direction and print on the correct side. Some paper requires a stiff paper backing sheet, as well.

   Click Print, and Vista shuttles your photo off to the printer.

Most photo developers print digital photos with better quality paper and ink than your own printer. And with the cost of expensive printer paper and ink cartridges, photo developers are often less expensive than printing photos yourself. Check their pricing and ask how they like their photos delivered — by CD, memory card, or over the Internet.

Creating, Editing, and Viewing Digital Movies and Slide Shows

The shelves of most camcorder owners weigh heavy with tapes filled with vacation footage, sporting events, and mud-bathing children. Windows Vista's built-in Movie Maker helps you turn that pile of tapes into complete, edited movies. Take your TV shows recorded with Vista's Media Center (Chapter 15), and edit out the commercials before sending them to a DVD.

The versatile Movie Maker considers photo slide shows to be movies, as well: Arrange your photos in the order you like, create transitions between each photo, add a musical soundtrack, and burn them to a DVD.

Vista's Movie Maker program works much like Windows XP's Movie Maker, with a few menu wording changes. The biggest improvement is that you can *finally* play back your finished movies using a standard DVD player.

Shown in Figure 16-11, Movie Maker's Tasks pane gently guides you through the three steps of creating a movie: importing your video and/or photos, editing them into a movie, and saving your creation to your PC, a DVD, CD, e-mail, or even back into your digital camera to save the edited project on tape.

Letting Movie Maker's robot build an AutoMovie

If you're not up to Movie Maker's learning curve and simply want a movie — *fast* — then let Movie Maker's AutoMovie function do it automatically. After you've imported your video footage and/or photos, choose AutoMovie from the Tools menu. Select the movie style you're after, be it clean-and-simple cuts and fades, a flashy music video, a vintage "aged" movie, or a sports flick that narrows in on your fast pans and zooms.

Movie Maker takes over from there, robotically assembling a movie from your footage and/or photos. It analyzes your work for interesting pans and zooms, and shaky and dark shots, and turns your highlights into a complete flick. Although not perfect, AutoMovie is a surprisingly quick way to turn that tall stack of videotapes into short, easily accessible movies.

Tasks pane   Collections pane   Preview window

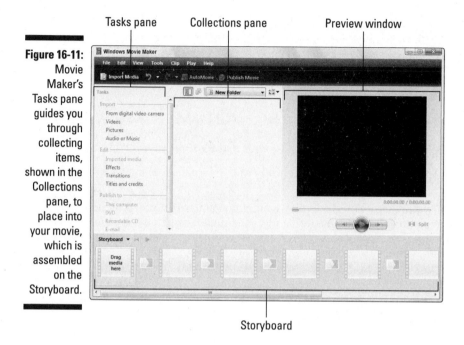

Figure 16-11:
Movie
Maker's
Tasks pane
guides you
through
collecting
items,
shown in the
Collections
pane, to
place into
your movie,
which is
assembled
on the
Storyboard.

Storyboard

The rest of this section explains the three steps involved in movie making:

1. **Import.**

   Step 1 gathers your raw materials. You'll copy a camcorder's footage onto the hard drive, watching as Movie Maker breaks each camcorder shot into a separate *clip.* Sprinkle in other videos, recorded TV shows, music files, and/or digital photos to piece together your movie.

2. **Edit.**

   This step combines your raw clips, music, and pictures into a structured movie. Drag and drop the best clips onto the Storyboard in an order that tells your movie's story. Edit each clip down to its best moments and add *transitions* between the clips — the way one clip fades into the next. Add a soundtrack, if you want, and opening/closing credits.

3. **Publish.**

   When you finish editing, Movie Maker combines your batch of clips into a complete movie, ready to be played back on your computer, saved to a DVD or CD, or saved back on your camcorder.

Creating movies requires a *lot* of free hard drive space. A 15-minute movie can consume 2.5GB. If Movie Maker complains about space, you have two choices: create smaller videos or upgrade your computer with a second hard drive.

Pressed for time? Movie Maker's AutoMovie mode, described in the sidebar, analyzes your footage and creates a quick, simple movie. AutoMovie works well as a starting point for your own movie or simply for tinkering with Movie Maker's controls.

Step 1: Import video, pictures, and music

If you've already imported footage from a digital camcorder, jump ahead to Step 4 in the steps in this section and begin there. You're several steps ahead of the pack.

But if you're importing video from a digital camcorder, you must work a little harder. Before Movie Maker can edit your digital camcorder's video, you must copy the footage onto your computer through a cable. Most digital camcorders connect to a computer's FireWire or USB 2.0 port. (FireWire ports, also known as IEEE 1394 ports, work the best.)

If your computer lacks a FireWire port, you can add one by plugging an inexpensive card inside your computer. I describe the process in *Upgrading & Fixing PCs For Dummies* (Wiley).

Still using an old *analog* rather than digital camcorder? You can still dump your movies into Windows Vista by plugging a *video capture* card inside your computer.

When importing video through FireWire (IEEE 1394), you need only connect a single cable between the camcorder and FireWire port. With that one cable, Vista grabs the sound and video, *and* controls the camera.

To copy digital video into your computer, follow these steps:

1. **Open Movie Maker, connect your digital camcorder to your computer, and (if asked) click Import Video.**

   If this is your first time plugging in the digital camcorder, Windows Vista will recognize it and offer to import its video. To catch Vista's attention, you may need to switch your camcorder to the setting where it plays back — not records — video. (Some camcorders label that setting as VCR.)

   But if you've plugged in your camcorder before, Vista immediately displays Figure 16-12. (Don't see Figure 16-12? Open Movie Maker from the Start menu's All Programs area, click File, and choose Import from Digital Video Camera.)

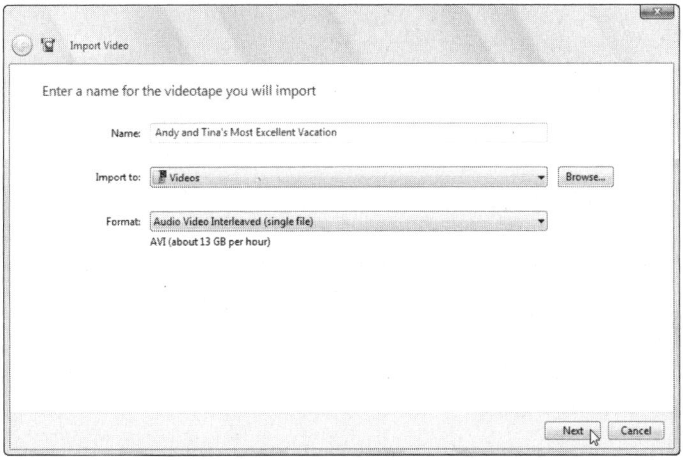

Figure 16-12:
Vista offers
to import
your video.

2. **Enter a name for your video, choose the video format, and click Next.**

    First, name your incoming video after the event you've filmed, be it a vacation, wedding, or visit to a skateboard park.

    Next, choose one of the three ways Vista offers to import the video into your Videos folder, shown in Figure 16-12:

    • **Audio Video Interleaved (single file):** The best option for people with huge hard drives, it copies the entire video as a single file without any loss in fidelity. Unfortunately, it consumes 13GB for each hour of footage.

    • **Windows Media Video (single file):** The option for people with smaller hard drives, it copies and compresses your entire video into one file consuming only 2GB per hour.

    • **Windows Media Video (one file per scene):** The option for people with teensy hard drives, this option breaks each shot into a *separate* file. That way, you can clear your hard drive quickly by deleting the bad shots, as well as the file space they consumed.

    Although the first two options save your imported video as one file, Vista still keeps track of when each shot begins and ends. When you open your video in Movie Maker, the program displays each shot separately for you to piece together.

3. **Choose whether to import the entire videotape or just portions, and click Next; click OK when it's finished importing your tape.**

    Vista offers two ways to import the video:

    • **Import the Entire Videotape to My Computer:** This option imports *all* the video on your tape. This choice works best for people who store each videotaping session on a different tape.

- **Only Parts of the Videotape to My Computer:** Choose this option for quickly importing a few portions of the tape. Vista displays a playback window with on-screen controls. Fast forward to the section you want, click the Start Video Import button, record a snippet, and then click Stop Video Import. Repeat until you've gathered any other shots you want, and then click Finish.

Let your computer work uninterrupted while it's grabbing video, because it needs lots of processing power for smooth captures. Don't work with other programs or browse the Web.

Vista saves your video in your Videos folder, available for viewing by opening the Start menu, clicking your user account's name, and opening the Videos folder.

4. **Open Movie Maker, if it's not already open.**

To summon Movie Maker, choose All Programs from the Start menu and select Windows Movie Maker.

If Windows Vista recommends that you set your screen resolution to 1024 x 768 or higher, do so now. (I explain how in Chapter 11.) That setting gives you more on-screen elbow room for editing your video.

When opened, Movie Maker shows any clips left over from your last movie editing project. To start afresh, choose New Project from the File menu. Then delete any clips left over in the Collections area by clicking anywhere inside the Collections pane, choosing Select All from the Edit menu, and pressing the Delete key. (That doesn't delete your *real* clips, as items in the Collections area are only copies.)

5. **Gather the videos, pictures, music, and sounds you want to include in your video.**

Movie Maker's Import task, the first listed on the Tasks pane along the program's left edge, lets you gather all the material you want in your video. (Don't worry about gathering too much, as you don't have to use it all.) The Import task lets you gather these items:

- **From Digital Video Camcorder:** This option launches Vista's Import Video program, which I cover in this section's first three steps.

- **Videos:** Choose this task to import video already stored on your computer.

- **Pictures:** This task lets you add digital photos to your work area, ready to be combined into a slide show or sprinkled into your movies.

- **Audio or Music:** Movie Maker lets you mix several sound sources, layering the camcorder's recorded sounds with your own voice *and* music. In fact, many movies work best if you replace the camcorder's wind-blown soundtrack with music. (I explain how to copy music from audio CDs in Chapter 15.)

At the end of this step, Movie Maker will be stocked with all the video, photos, and music you need to assemble your movie. In the next step, described in the next section, you begin combining them all into a finished work.

Step 2: Edit your movie

After you've imported the video, songs, and photos, you're ready to assemble everything into a movie, weeding out the bad shots and splicing together the good stuff. If you're not picky, you can finish in a few minutes. If you're a Kurosawa fan, you can spend days or weeks here, lining up the shots, adding transitions, and coordinating breaks with a soundtrack that holds everything together.

Don't worry that your edits will harm the original video you've saved onto your computer. You're only working with a copy, and you still have the master copy on your camcorder's tape.

As you work, feel free to play back your work at any time. Just click the Play button on the preview window.

These steps walk you through editing your movie:

1. **Familiarize yourself with the videos and pictures in your workspace.**

   Examine Movie Maker's Collections pane (the middle section, shown in Figure 16-11), which shows your imported video clips, photos, and music files. Each shot appears here as a separate clip, lined up in the order you shot them.

   Movie Maker's top-right corner shows a movie playback window. (Double-click any clip to see it play in the window.)

   Along the bottom lies the Storyboard — your workspace for linking clips in an order that tells a story, be it a vacation narrative or a science-fiction thriller.

2. **Drag and drop videos and or pictures from the Collections pane onto the Storyboard in the order you'd like them played back.**

   When you spot some clips or photos that would look good spliced together in a certain order, drag and drop them, one after another, onto the Storyboard along the bottom. Place them in the order you'd like them played back, and Movie Maker begins to look like Figure 16-13. (When you drag an item onto the Storyboard, it doesn't disappear from your clip collection; you can reuse the same video or photo as many times as you want.)

If you feel like you're done, finish the job by jumping ahead to the next section, "Step 3: Saving your edited movie or slide show." But if you'd like to trim your clips a bit, add a soundtrack, or add fades between clips, move to the next step.

3. Save your project.

Before you forget, choose Save Project from the File menu. That saves your imported clips and the edits you've placed onto the Storyboard, and gives you something to return to if you mess up in subsequent steps. You can also return to this point at any time by choosing Open Project from Movie Maker's File menu.

Save your project each time you complete something significant or time-consuming.

4. Show the Timeline view to edit your clips and add music, if desired.

Storyboard ▾

To edit your clips and add music, click the Storyboard button (shown in the margin) and choose Timeline from the drop-down menu. The Storyboard's look changes immediately, as shown in Figure 16-14. Instead of displaying clips as square blocks, Movie Maker displays the clips according to their length. The first clip on the timeline, for example, is much longer than the others and could use some trimming.

To trim the clip, click it and then click the vertical line where the clip starts. (The mouse pointer turns into a two-headed arrow, shown in Figure 16-14.) As you drag the line inward with your left mouse button pressed, keep an eye on the movie preview window; the window updates to show your current position. When you reach the point where the clip should begin, let go of the mouse button.

Figure 16-13: Drag and drop clips onto the Storyboard in the order in which they should appear in your movie.

Movie Maker quickly trims the clip to its new beginning. Similarly, sliding the line inward at a clip's end will trim the clip's end. Repeat for each clip until you've kept only the good parts.

Made a mistake and trimmed too much? Choose Undo Trim Clip from the Edit menu.

Click the little plus and minus magnifying glass buttons by the Timeline button to toggle between close-up and faraway views of your editing. Close-up views let you edit a clip to start at the crack of a baseball bat, for example.

Figure 16-14: The timeline view shows the length of your clips and lets you slide in their edges to edit them.

To add music, drag a music file onto the timeline's Audio/Music area. Windows mixes it in with the audio captured by your camcorder. (Right-click either the audio track or the music track to change its volume.) Similarly, drag any digital photos onto the timeline to incorporate them into your movie. Adjust the length of movies and photos by dragging in their borders, just as with clips.

If you're satisfied with your work, jump to the next section, "Step 3: Saving your edited movie or slide show." But if you're ready for even more fine-tuning, move to the next step.

5. **Click the Timeline button, switch back to Storyboard mode, and add transitions.**

Switch back to Storyboard mode by clicking the Timeline button and choosing Storyboard from the drop-down menu.

Transitions are how clips join together. One clip can slowly fade into another, for example. Or, an incoming clip can push an earlier clip off the side of the screen.

To add transitions, click Transitions in the Edit area of the Tasks pane. Double-click any transitions, and the preview window shows how they work. When you find one you like, drag and drop it between two adjoining clips. Click the Play button to watch the transition in the preview window, and, if you don't like it, replace the transition with a different one. (To remove a bothersome transition, right-click it and choose Remove.)

When you're satisfied with your clips, transitions, and sounds, tell Movie Maker to assemble your movie, described in the next section, "Saving your edited movie or slide show."

Movie Maker offers a huge bag of tricks. Click Titles and Credits in the Tasks pane's Edit section, for example, to type an opening title and the ending credits where you're the producer, director, cinematographer, and key grip.

Although Movie Maker provides dozens of fun transitions, they're better for slide shows than movies. Wild transitions look like somebody has been playing with effects rather than making a movie. Think about your favorite movies — how many transitions did they use? Transitions work best for slide shows.

Step 3: Save your edited movie or slide show

When you've finished editing your clips into a movie, click the Publish Movie button (shown in the margin) from Movie Maker's toolbar. The program offers to save your work as a complete movie in any of several places:

- ✔ **This Computer:** This option creates a small file suitable for playback on your PC.

- ✔ **DVD:** Click here to open Vista's DVD Maker program and burn your movie to DVD. I cover this option in this chapter's next section.

- ✔ **Recordable CD:** This option creates a small file that fits onto a CD for playback on other PCs.

- ✔ **E-mail:** It's postage-stamp sized, but your edited movie can be e-mailed to friends.

- ✔ **Digital Video Camera:** Designed for people without CDs or DVDs, this option lets you copy the edited movie back onto a blank tape in your digital camera. For large movies that won't fit onto a DVD, this is your best backup option.

After you choose an option and click Next, Windows creates your movie, choosing the appropriate file size and quality for the destination you choose. Keep these things in mind when saving your finished movie:

- ✔ Publishing movies and slide shows can take a *long* time. Windows needs to arrange all your clips, create the transitions and soundtracks, and compress everything into a single file.

- ✔ Movies saved back onto your digital camcorder receive the best size and quality because the camcorder can record the huge file on tape.

- ✔ Movies saved for e-mail and a Web site have the lowest quality; otherwise, they'd take too long for most people to download.

- ✔ If your movies are short, Windows can save a high-quality copy to a CD for playback on other PCs. But most movies won't fit onto a CD.

Saving a Movie or Slide Show to a DVD with Windows DVD Maker

Windows DVD Maker does something no earlier version of Windows could do: Create DVDs that play back on a DVD player. Before Vista, people had to buy a DVD-burning program from another company or hope that their new computer came with one pre-installed.

Note: If you want to copy or back up files to a blank DVD, don't use DVD Maker. Instead, copy the files to the DVD the same way you copy files to a CD or any folder, a process I cover in Chapter 4.

Follow these steps to create a DVD movie or slide show for playing back on a DVD player and watching on TV:

1. **Load Windows DVD Maker, if necessary.**

   Windows Movie Maker loads Windows DVD Maker automatically, leaving you at Step 3. But if you're creating a slide show or burning an already completed video, load Windows DVD Maker yourself by choosing DVD Maker from the Start menu's All Programs area.

2. **Click Add Items, add your photos or videos, and click Next.**

   Click the Add Items button and choose the movie file or photos you'd like to add to your DVD. If you're creating a slide show, here's your chance to arrange the photos' display order by dragging and dropping them in place.

3. **Customize the opening menu, if desired.**

   Spend some time here to craft your DVD's *opening menu* — the screen you watch until the last person's settled around the TV set and you can push Play. DVD Maker offers these menu options:

   - **Menu Text:** Click this button to choose the title of your movie or slide show, as well as what options should appear on the menu. Or, stick with the default options found on every DVD: Play and Scenes.

   - **Customize Menu:** Here, you can change the opening menu's font, choose a video to repeat in the background, choose music to play, and even change the shape of the *scenes menu* — that screen where you can jump quickly to different parts of your movie. Click the Preview button to make sure that it's just what you want.

   - **Slide Show:** Meant specifically for slide shows, this option lets you choose the background music, the amount of time the photos should display, and their transitions.

   - **Menu Styles:** The drop-down menu here lets you dump Movie Maker's stock background for these spruced up graphics. (I like Video Wall for movies and Photographs for slide shows.)

4. **Click Burn.**

   Then walk away from your computer for a few hours. DVD Maker's a certified slowpoke.

   When DVD Maker finishes, it spits out a DVD, ready for you to label with a magic marker and pop into your DVD player to watch on TV.

Creating and saving a slide show to DVD

Vista offers you two ways to create slide shows on a DVD, both with their pros and cons:

- **Movie Maker:** Slide shows are basically movies, so Windows Movie Maker handles them very well. The program's detailed controls take extra time and effort to master, however. But if you like hands-on projects, create a slide show by following the steps in the "Creating, Editing, and Viewing Digital Movies and Slide Shows" section.

- **DVD Maker:** When you're looking for a fast and easy slide show, Windows DVD Maker may be your ticket: Add transitions, choose background music, and burn the result to a DVD. To create a quick slide show in DVD Maker, follow the steps in the "Saving a Movie or Slide Show to a DVD with Windows DVD Maker" section.

The biggest difference between the two programs breaks down to the transitions: the way one picture flows into another. Movie Maker allows for elaborately crafted transitions, while DVD Maker uses the same transition between every photo. (DVD Maker's Random transition offers the only variety.)

Part VI
Help!

The 5th Wave   By Rich Tennant

"We should cast a circle, invoke the elements, and direct the energy. If that doesn't work, we'll read the manual."

In this part . . .

Windows Vista can do hundreds of tasks in dozens of ways, which means that several thousand things can fail at any given time.

Some problems are easy to fix — if you know how to fix them, that is. For example, one misplaced click on the desktop makes all your icons suddenly vanish. Yet, one more click in the right place puts them all back.

Other problems are far more complex, requiring teams of computer surgeons to diagnose, remedy, and bill accordingly.

This part of the book helps you separate the big problems from the little ones. You'll know whether you can fix a mistake yourself with a few clicks and a kick. You also discover how to solve one of the biggest computing problems of all: How to copy your old PC's information to your *new* PC.

Chapter 17

The Case of the Broken Window

Sometimes you just have a sense that something's wrong. The computer makes quiet grumbling noises, or Windows Vista starts running more slowly than Congress. Other times, something's obviously gone haywire. Programs freeze, menus keep shooting at you, or Windows Vista greets you with a cheery error message when you turn on your computer.

Many of the biggest-looking problems are solved by the smallest-looking solutions. This chapter may be able to point you to the right one.

Vista Keeps Asking Me for Permission!

When it came to security, Windows XP was fairly easy to figure out. If you owned an Administrator account — and most people did — Windows XP mostly stayed out of your face. Owners of the less powerful Limited and Guest accounts, however, frequently faced screens telling them that their actions were restricted to Administrator accounts.

But with Vista, even Administrator accounts get the nag screens, and often for the most innocuous actions. Vista's more secure than Windows XP, so you'll constantly brush up against Vista's barbed wire fence. As you work with your PC, Vista pokes you with a message like the one shown in Figure 17-1.

Standard account holders see a slightly different message that commands them to fetch an Administrator account holder to type in a password.

Figure 17-1:
Although
designed to
protect you,
Vista's
permission
screens
work even
better at
annoying
you.

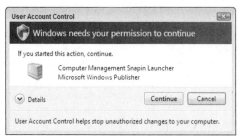

Of course, with screens like this one popping up constantly, most people will simply ignore them and click Continue — even if that means they've just allowed a piece of spyware to latch onto their PC.

When Vista sends you a permission screen, ask yourself this question:

Is Vista asking permission for something *I* did? If your answer is yes, then click Continue to give Vista permission to carry out your command. But if Vista sends you a permission screen out of the blue, when you haven't done anything, click Cancel. That keeps the nasties from invading your PC.

If you don't have time for this bothersome security layer and your PC's well protected with a firewall and an up-to-date antivirus program, you can find out how to turn off Vista's User Account Permissions by reading Chapter 10.

Restoring Calm with System Restore

When your computer is a disaster, wouldn't you love to go back in time to when Windows worked *right?* Just as with Windows XP, Windows Vista's built-in time-traveling program, System Restore, lets you turn back the clock with a few clicks.

It works like this: Every day or so, Windows takes a snapshot, known as a *restore point,* of Windows' most important settings and saves them by date. When your computer begins acting up, tell System Restore to return to a restore point created when everything worked fine.

System Restore won't erase any of your files or e-mail, but programs installed after a restore point's date may need to be reinstalled. System Restore is also reversible; you can undo your last restore point or try a different one.

To send your computer back to a restore point, when it was working much better, follow these steps:

1. **Save any open files, close any loaded programs, load System Restore, and click Next.**

   Choose Start, click All Programs, and begin weaving your way through the menus: Choose Accessories, select System Tools, and click System Restore. Click Next to move past the opening screen.

2. **Choose a Restore Point and click Next.**

   Windows XP made you guess which Restore Point to apply. Vista assumes that you're here because something happened recently, so it highlights the most recently created Restore Point for you to choose.

   If you're running these steps a second time, because Vista's recommended restore point didn't supply the magic fix, choose a Different Restore Point and click Next.

3. **Make *sure* that you've saved any open files and then click Finish.**

   Your computer grumbles a bit and then restarts, using those earlier settings that (hopefully) worked fine.

If your system is *already* working fine, feel free to create your own restore point: In Step 1, click the words, Open System Protection. When the System Properties window appears, click the Create button along the window's bottom.

Removing infected restore points

If your computer has a virus, erase all your restore points before disinfecting your computer with an antivirus program. Here's what to do:

1. **Click Start, right-click Computer, and choose Properties.**

2. **Choose System Protection from the task pane along the left.**

3. **Remove the check mark from any checked boxes in the Automatic Restore Points section.**

4. **Click Turn System Restore Off when Vista warns you that you're about to delete your restore points.**

5. **Click OK to close the window and then restart your computer.**

6. **After updating your antivirus program with the latest virus definitions, scan and disinfect your entire computer.**

7. **When the computer is disinfected, repeat Steps 1 through 3, except that in Step 3, place a check mark in the box marked Local Disk (C:) (System), and click OK.**

When you're through, create a new restore point named after the virus you just disinfected. That leaves you with a safe restore point for future use.

Name the restore point something descriptive, such as Before Letting the Babysitter Use the PC. (That way, you know which restore point to use if things go awry.)

These tips help wring the most fix-it power from System Restore:

✔ Before installing a program or any new computer toys, load System Restore and create a restore point in case the installation is a disaster. Create a restore point *after* successfully installing something, too. Returning to that restore point will keep your successful installation intact. (I describe how to create restore points in Chapter 12.)

✔ You can save quite a few restore points, depending on your hard drive's size. You'll likely have room for a dozen or more. Windows Vista deletes the oldest restore points to make room for the newer ones, so make your own Restore Points frequently.

✔ If you restore your computer to a time *before* you installed some new hardware or software, those items may not work correctly. If they're not working correctly, reinstall them. Also, as described in the "Removing infected restore points" sidebar, be sure to erase your existing restore points if your computer contracted a virus. Using an infected restore point can reinfect your computer.

Reviving Messed Up or Deleted Files

Everybody who's worked on a computer knows the agony of seeing hours of work go down the drain. You'll mistakenly delete a file by accident, for example, or change one for the better — only to realize that you've messed it up rather than improved it.

System Restore won't help here, as it memorizes your PC's settings, not your files. But Vista offers ways to not only retrieve deleted files but to dig up their earlier versions, the two tasks described in this section.

Undeleting accidentally deleted files

Vista doesn't really delete files, even if you tell it to delete them. Instead, Vista slips deleted files into your Recycle Bin (shown in the margin), which lives on your desktop. Open the Recycle Bin, and you'll find every file you've deleted in the past few weeks. Click the file you want back and click the Restore This Item button from the Recycle Bin's menu bar. The Recycle Bin places the file back in the place where you deleted it.

I cover the Recycle Bin in Chapter 2.

Retrieving previous versions of files and folders

Ever changed a file and saved it, only to realize that the original was much better? Ever wanted to start from scratch from a document you began changing last week? A new feature in some Vista versions lets you dig up documents you'd long ago given up for lost.

Vista's Business, Ultimate, and Enterprise versions now inventory your PC's nether reaches, letting you send down a grappling hook and retrieve an old version of a file you'd long ago given up as lost.

To find and retrieve an older version of an existing file, right-click the troublesome file, and choose Restore Previous Version. In the window that appears, Vista lists all the previous versions available for that particular file, as shown in Figure 17-2.

Figure 17-2: Vista tracks previous versions of your files, letting you return to older versions in case of a mishap.

Vista lists all the previous versions available, leading to the big question: Which version is the one you want? To take a quick peek at a previous version, click its name and click Open. Vista opens the file, letting you see whether you've struck paydirt.

If you're positive that the older version is better than your current version, click the Restore button. Vista warns you that restoring the old file will delete your existing file; when you approve the deletion, Vista puts the restored version in its place.

If you're not quite sure whether the older version is better, a safer alternative is to click the Copy button, instead. Vista lets you copy the previous version to a different folder, letting you manually compare the old and new files before deciding which one to save.

Retrieving a Forgotten Password

When Vista won't accept your password at the log-on screen, you're not always locked out of your own computer. Check all these things before letting loose with a scream:

- ✔ **Check your Caps Lock key.** Vista's passwords are *case-sensitive,* meaning that Vista considers "OpenSesame" and "opensesame" to be different passwords. If your keyboard's Caps Lock light is on, then press your Caps Lock key to turn off Caps Lock. Then try entering your password again.

- ✔ **Use your Password Reset Disk.** I explain how to create a Password Reset Disk in Chapter 13. When you've forgotten your password, insert that disk to use as a key. Windows Vista lets you back into your account, where you can promptly create an easier-to-remember password. (Create a Password Reset Disk now if you haven't yet.)

- ✔ **Let another user reset your password.** Anybody with an Administrator account on your PC can reset your password. Have that person choose Control Panel from the Start menu, choose User Accounts and Family Safety, and click User Accounts. There, they can choose Manage Another Account, click your account name, and choose Remove Password, letting you log in.

If none of these options work, then you're in sad shape, unfortunately. Compare the value of your password-protected data against the cost of hiring a password recovery specialist. You'll find one by searching for the words **recover password** on Google (www.google.com) or another search engine.

My Folder (Or Desktop) Doesn't Show All My Files!

When you open a folder — or even look at your desktop — you expect to see everything it contains. But when something's missing or there's nothing inside at all, check these things before panicking:

- ✔ **Check the Search box.** Whenever you type something into a folder's Search box — that little box in the folder's top-right corner — Vista begins looking for it by hiding everything that doesn't match your search. If a folder isn't showing everything it should, delete any words you see in the Search box.

- ✔ **Make sure that the desktop isn't hiding everything.** Vista tries to "clean up" the look of your PC. And since some people like an empty desktop, Vista's happy to oblige. However, it doesn't put your toys back into the closets where they belong. It just hides everything from view. To make sure that your desktop isn't hiding things, right-click an empty part of your desktop, choose View, and place a check mark by the words Show Desktop Icons.

If everything's really gone, check out the previous versions of that folder, described in this chapter's "Retrieving previous versions of files and folders" section. Vista not only tracks previous versions of files, it keeps track of a folder's past life, as well.

My Mouse Doesn't Work Right

Sometimes, the mouse doesn't work at all; other times, the mouse pointer hops across the screen like a flea. Here are a few things to look for:

- ✔ If no mouse arrow is on the screen after you start Windows, make sure that the mouse's tail is plugged snugly into the computer's USB port. (If you have an older mouse with a round PS/2 port instead of a rectangular USB port, you'll need to restart your PC to bring the mouse back to life.)

- ✔ To restart your PC when the mouse doesn't work, hold down the Ctrl, Alt, and Del buttons simultaneously. Press Tab until the tiny arrow next to the red button is surrounded by the lines and then press Enter to reveal the Restart menu. Press your up arrow to choose Restart and then press Enter to restart your PC.

✔ If the mouse arrow is on-screen but won't move, Windows may be mistaking your brand of mouse for a different brand. You can make sure that Windows Vista recognizes the correct type of mouse by following the steps on adding new hardware in Chapter 11. If you own a wireless mouse (wireless mice don't have a cord), the mouse may need new batteries.

✔ A mouse pointer can jump around on-screen when the mouse's innards become dirty. Follow the cleaning instructions I give in Chapter 12.

✔ If the mouse was working fine and now the buttons seem to be reversed, you've probably changed the right- or left-handed button configuration setting in the Control Panel. Open the Control Panel's Mouse settings area and make sure that the configuration is set up to match your needs. (I cover this in Chapter 11.)

My Double-Clicks Are Now Single Clicks!

In an effort to make things easier, Windows Vista lets people choose whether a single click or a double-click should open a file or folder.

My program is frozen!

Eventually one of your programs will freeze up solid, leaving no way to reach its normal Close command. These three steps will extricate the frozen program from your computer's memory (and the screen, as well):

1. **Hold down the Ctrl, Alt, and Delete keys simultaneously.**

   Known as the "three finger salute," this combination always catches Vista's attention, even when it's sailing o'er rough seas. In fact, if Vista doesn't respond, hold in your PC's power button to turn off your PC. After a few seconds, turn it back on to see whether Vista's in a better mood.

2. **Choose Start Task Manager.**

   Other options let you lock your PC (a security measure used when heading to the water cooler), switch users (letting somebody else log on), log off, and change a password.

3. **Click the Applications tab, if necessary, and then click the frozen program's name.**

4. **Click the End Task button, and Windows Vista whisks away the frozen program.**

   If your computer seems a bit groggy afterward, play it safe by restarting your computer from the Start menu.

But if you're not satisfied with the click method Windows Vista uses, here's how to change it:

1. **Open any folder — the Start menu's Documents folder will do.**

2. **Click the Organize button and choose Folder and Search Options.**

3. **Choose your click preference in the Click Items As Follows section.**

4. **Click OK to save your preferences.**

Don't like to follow steps? Just click the Restore Defaults button in Folder and Search Options, and Windows brings back double-clicking and other standard Windows Vista folder behaviors.

Making Older Programs Run under Windows Vista

Many programmers design their software to run on a specific version of Windows. When a new Windows version appears a few years later, some programs feel threatened by their new environment and refuse to work.

If an older game or other program refuses to run under Windows Vista, there's still hope because of Windows Vista's secret *Compatibility mode.* This mode tricks programs into thinking that they're running under their favorite older version of Windows, letting them run in comfort.

If your old program has problems with Windows Vista, follow these steps:

1. **Right-click the program's icon and choose Properties.**

2. **When the Properties dialog box appears, click the Compatibility tab.**

3. **Select the program's desired Windows version from the Compatibility mode's drop-down menu, as shown in Figure 17-3.**

   Check your program's box or look at its manual to see what version of Windows it expects.

4. **Click OK and then try running your program again to see whether it's working better.**

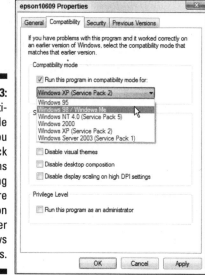

Figure 17-3:
Compati-
bility mode
lets you
trick
programs
into thinking
they're
running on
older
Windows
versions.

I Can't Find the Menus!

To keep things alarming, Vista hid the menus that users have come to depend on for the last decade. To make them reappear, press the Alt key. To make Vista glue them back atop every window where they belong, click the Organize button, choose Folder and Search Options, click the View tab, and click the Always Show Menus option. Click OK to save your changes.

My Computer Is Frozen Up Solid

Every once in a while, Windows just drops the ball and wanders off some-where to sit under a tree. You're left looking at a computer that just looks back. None of the computer's lights blink. Panicked clicks don't do anything. Pressing every key on the keyboard doesn't do anything, or worse yet, the computer starts to beep at every key press.

When nothing on-screen moves (except sometimes the mouse pointer), the computer is frozen up solid. Try the following approaches, in the following order, to correct the problem:

- **Approach 1:** Press Esc twice.

    This action rarely works but give it a shot anyway.

- **Approach 2:** Press Ctrl, Alt, and Delete simultaneously and choose Start Task Manager.

    If you're lucky, the Task Manager appears with the message that you discovered an unresponsive application. The Task Manager lists the names of currently running programs, including the one that's not responding. Click the name of the program on the Application tab that's causing the mess and then click the End Task button. You lose any unsaved work in that program, of course, but you should be used to that. (If you somehow stumbled onto the Ctrl+Alt+Delete combination by accident, press Esc to quit Task Manager and return to Windows.)

    If that still doesn't do the trick, press Ctrl+Alt+Delete again and look for the little red button in the bottom-right corner of the screen. Click the little arrow next to that button's circle, shown in the margin. Choose Shut Down from the menu that pops up. Your computer should shut down and restart, hopefully returning in a better mood.

- **Approach 3:** If the preceding approaches don't work, push the computer's reset button. If the Turn Off Computer box appears, choose Restart.

- **Approach 4:** If not even the reset button works (and some computers don't even have reset buttons anymore), turn the computer off by pushing its power button. (If that merely brings up the Turn Off the Computer menu, choose Restart, and your computer should restart.)

- **Approach 5:** If you hold in the computer's off button long enough (usually about 4 to 5 seconds), it will eventually stop resisting and turn off.

The Printer Isn't Working Right

If the printer isn't working right, start with the simplest solution first: Make sure that it's plugged into the wall and turned on. Surprisingly, this step fixes about half the problems with printers. Next, make sure that the printer cable is snugly nestled in the ports on both the printer and the computer. Then check to make sure that it has enough paper and that the paper isn't jammed in the mechanism.

Then try printing from different programs, such as WordPad and Notepad, to see whether the problem is with the printer, Windows Vista, or a particular Windows program. These tests help pinpoint the culprit.

For a quick test of a printer, click the Start button, choose the Control Panel, and select Printers from the Hardware and Sound category. Right-click your printer's icon, choose Properties, and click the Print Test Page button. If your printer sends you a nicely printed page, the problem is probably with the software, not the printer or Windows Vista.

You can find more information about printing, including troubleshooting information, in Chapter 7.

Chapter 18

Strange Messages:
What You Did Does Not Compute

*M*ost error messages in life are fairly easy to understand. A VCR's flashing clock means that you haven't set its clock yet. A car's beeping tone means that you've left your keys in the ignition. A spouse's stern glance means that you've forgotten something important.

But Windows Vista's error messages may have been written by a Senate subcommittee, if only they weren't so brief. The error messages rarely describe what you did to cause the event and, even worse, what to do about it.

In this chapter, I've collected some of Windows Vista's most common messages. Match up an error message's subject or picture with the ones here and then read your appropriate response and the chapter covering that particular problem.

Activate Windows Now

Meaning: Figure 18-1 means if you don't activate Windows, Windows will stop working in a few days.

Probable cause: Microsoft's copy-protection scheme requires every person to activate his or her Vista copy within a few weeks after installing or upgrading to Vista. Once activated, your copy of Vista is linked to your particular PC so that you can't install it onto another computer, including a laptop.

Solutions: Click the message and let Windows connect to the Internet to activate itself. No Internet connection? Then dial the activation phone number and talk to the Microsoft people personally. *Note:* If you never see this message, then your copy of Windows has already been activated by the PC's manufacturer. Don't worry about it.

Figure 18-1:
Windows
needs to be
activated.

Check Your Computer Security

Meaning: Figure 18-2 appears when your PC has security problems.

Probable cause: Your antivirus program isn't working. The message can also appear if Windows Firewall isn't turned on, Windows Defender isn't running, Windows Update isn't working, Internet Explorer's security settings are too low, or User Account Control (the perpetrator of all those permission screens) isn't turned on.

 Solutions: Click the balloon to see the exact problem. If the balloon disappears before you have a chance to click it, click the little red shield icon (shown in the margin) in the taskbar. Windows points out the problem and offers a solution, which I cover in Chapter 10.

Figure 18-2:
A security
problem
with your PC
needs
attention.

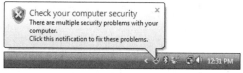

Do You Want to Get the Latest Online Content When You Search Help?

Meaning: Figure 18-3 means Vista's asking permission to connect with the Internet and search for Microsoft's databases for more helpful information.

Probable cause: Everybody sees this message when first searching for help in Vista's Help program, which I cover in Chapter 20. Click Yes, as Microsoft's databases contain much more up-to-date information than Vista's built-in Help program. Clicking No keeps the Help program off the Internet, but also freezes its content to late 2006, when Microsoft finalized the Help program.

Solutions: To make sure that Vista's Help program checks in with the Internet for up-to-date help, open Help and Support from the Start menu, click the Options menu, and choose Settings. Then turn on the check box called Include Windows Online Help and Support When You Search for Help.

Figure 18-3:
Do you want
Vista to
connect to
Microsoft's
Web site for
answers?

Do You Want to Install (Or Run) This File?

Meaning: Are you sure that this software is free from viruses, spyware, and other harmful things?

Probable cause: You've downloaded a file from the Internet, and now you're trying to run or install it.

Solutions: If you're sure the file is safe, click Install in Figure 18-4. But if this message appears unexpectedly, or you think it may not be safe, click Cancel. To be on the safe side, scan everything you download with an antivirus program. I cover safe computing in Chapter 10.

Figure 18-4:
Do you think
this
software is
safe?

Do You Want to Save Changes . . .

Meaning: Figure 18-5 means you haven't saved your work in the program you're trying to close.

Probable cause: You're trying to close an application, log off, or restart your PC before telling a program to save the work you've accomplished.

Solutions: Look in the window's title bar for the program's name — Paint, in this case. Find that program on your desktop (or click its name on the taskbar to bring it to the forefront). Then save your work (unless you don't want to save changes) by choosing Save from the File menu or clicking the program's Save icon. I cover saving files in Chapter 5.

Figure 18-5:
Do you want to save your work?

Do You Want to Turn AutoComplete On?

Meaning: Internet Explorer's AutoComplete feature, shown in Figure 18-6, guesses what you're about to type and tries to fill it in for you.

Probable cause: Every Windows user is eventually asked whether to turn on AutoComplete or leave it turned off.

Solutions: AutoComplete handily fills in some online forms with words you've used previously. Although a timesaver, AutoComplete poses a potential security problem for some people: It lets others know what words you've previously typed into forms. To see or change its settings, open Internet Explorer, click Tools, choose Internet Options, and click the Content tab.

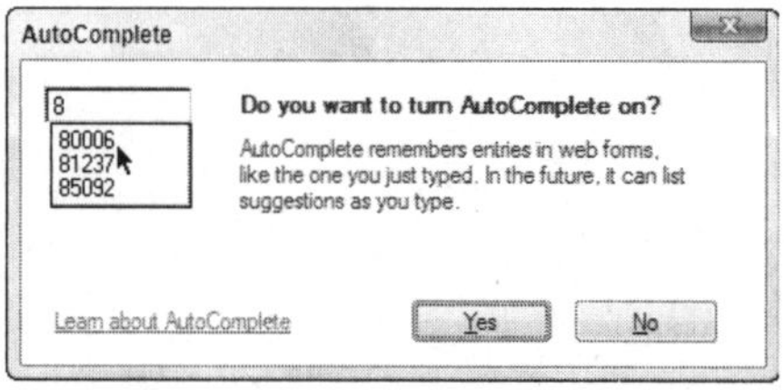

Figure 18-6:
Auto-Complete helps by filling in words as you begin to type them.

Installing Device Driver Software

Meaning: Windows recognizes a newly installed computer part and is trying to install it automatically.

Probable cause: Figure 18-7 usually appears after you plug something new into your computer's USB port.

Solutions: Relax. Windows knows what's going on and will take charge. If Windows can't find a driver, however, you need to find one on your own. I describe that tiresome process in Chapter 12.

Figure 18-7: Windows finds a new gadget.

The Publisher Could Not Be Verified

Meaning: Windows can't verify that the software you're about to install was created by its claimed publisher.

Probable cause: Microsoft's *digital signature* program works like a name tag. Windows compares the digital signatures of both the software and its claimed publisher. If they match, everything's fine. If they *don't* match, beware: The software may be trying to trick you. But most often, you'll see messages like the one shown in Figure 18-8 because the publisher simply ignored Microsoft's digital signature system, leaving Windows in the dark.

Figure 18-8: Windows doesn't recognize the software publisher.

Solutions: Many small companies skip the digital signature process because of Microsoft's testing delays or fees, leading to these messages. If this message pops up from a reputable company, you're probably still safe. But if you see it when trying to run software from a large well-known software company, don't run the software. It's probably trying to trick you.

Video Card Does Not Meet Minimum Requirements

Meaning: Figure 18-9 appears when your PC isn't powerful enough to display one of Vista's fancy graphics modes. Vista either gives up completely or switches to a lower quality display. Similar messages include This Program Can't Run Because It Requires a Newer Video Card or One that's Compatible with Direct3D, and Would You Like to Disable Desktop Composition?

Probable cause: The graphics circuitry inside your laptop or PC isn't powerful enough to display Vista's graphics-intensive displays.

Solutions: You can't do much, if anything, about a laptop. But if you upgrade your PC with a new graphics card costing between $100 and $200, you can avoid the messages, speed up your display, and see Vista's special effects.

Figure 18-9:
Your PC isn't
powerful
enough to
display
these
graphics.

Windows Cannot Open This File

Meaning: Figure 18-10 appears when Windows doesn't know which program created the file that you double-clicked.

Probable cause: Windows Vista usually sticks secret hidden codes, known as *file extensions,* onto the ends of filenames. When you double-click a Notepad text file, for example, Windows Vista spots the file's secret, hidden file extension and uses Notepad to open the file. But if Windows doesn't recognize the secret code letters, it complains with this error message.

Solutions: If *you* know what program created the mysterious file, choose Select a Program from a List of Installed Programs and choose that program from Vista's list. Then select the check box for Always Use the Selected Program to Open This Kind of File.

If you're stumped, however, choose Use the Web Service to Find the Correct Program. Windows examines the file, consults with the Internet, and offers suggestions and links for downloading the right program for the job. (I cover this problem in Chapter 5.)

Figure 18-10:
Windows doesn't know what program should open this file.

Windows

Windows cannot open this file:

File: Pandora's.Box

To open this file, Windows needs to know what program you want to use to open it. Windows can go online to look it up automatically, or you can manually select from a list of programs that are installed on your computer.

What do you want to do?

⊙ Use the Web service to find the correct program

○ Select a program from a list of installed programs

[OK]   [Cancel]

Windows Needs Your Permission to Continue

Meaning: Figure 18-11 appears when you're trying to do something that's only available to people with Administrator accounts.

Similar messages include You Need to Provide Administrator Credentials, Windows Needs Your Permission to Continue, You Don't Currently Have Permission, A Program Needs Your Permission to Use This Program.

Probable cause: The action you're trying to take may potentially damage your files or your PC or lessen your PC's security. That's not to say it *will,* but it could if used in the wrong way. The action's more like picking up a crowbar than pushing the Explode button.

Solutions: If you're sure the action is something you want to do, click Continue (if that button's available) to move on. If the message requests a password, summon an Administrator account holder to walk over to your PC and type his or her password, as I describe in Chapter 10.

Figure 18-11:
You need
an Admin-
istrator
account to
open this
program.

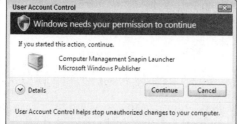

You Don't Currently Have Permission to Access This Folder

Meaning: Figure 18-12 means Vista won't let you peek inside the folder you're trying to open. (The folder's name appears in the message's title bar.)

Probable cause: The computer's owner hasn't given you permission.

Solutions: Only a person with an Administrator account — usually the computer's owner — can grant permission to open certain folders, so you need to track down that person. (If you're the administrator, you may grant access to others by copying or moving the folder or its contents into the Public folder, described in Chapter 14.)

Figure 18-12:
Find
somebody
with an
Admin-
istrator
account to
open the
folder or file.

Forbidden Fruit

You don't currently have permission to access this folder.

Click Continue to get access to this folder.

Continue   Cancel

Chapter 19

Moving from an Old Computer to a New One

*W*hen you bring home an exciting new Vista computer, it lacks the most important thing of all: your *old* computer's files. How do you copy everything from that drab old Windows XP PC to that exciting new Windows Vista PC? How do you even *find* everything you want to move? To solve the problem, Microsoft stocked Vista with a virtual moving van called Windows Easy Transfer.

Windows Easy Transfer grabs not only your old computer's data but also settings from many of your programs: your favorite Web sites, for example, and your e-mail from Outlook Express. It even grabs your e-mail settings, to save you the chore of setting up your new mail program.

Not everybody needs Windows Easy Transfer. If you're upgrading your Windows XP PC to Vista, for example, Vista automatically transfers your files and settings during Vista's installation process. You won't need the transfer program, nor this chapter.

But when you need to copy information from one PC to another, this chapter introduces the program and guides you through your mission.

Note: Windows Easy Transfer doesn't work with older Windows versions like Windows Me or Windows 98.

Preparing to Move into Your New PC

Like any other moving day, the event's success depends on your preparation. Instead of rummaging for boxes and duct tape, you must do these two things to prepare your PCs for Windows Easy Transfer:

✔ Choose the method for transferring the information between the PCs

✔ Install your *old* PC's programs onto your *new* PC

The next two sections explain each topic in more detail.

Choosing how to transfer your old information

PCs are very good at copying things, much to the concern of the entertainment industry. They're so good, in fact, that they offer a zillion different ways to copy the same thing.

For example, Windows Easy Transfer offers *four* different ways to copy your old PC's information into your new PC. Each method works at a different speed and level of difficulty. You must choose one of these four:

✔ **Windows Easy Transfer Cable:** Every PC has a USB port, so a Windows Easy Transfer cable is the fastest and simplest solution. Often sold in stores as an Easy Link, Direct Link, USB Bridge, or simply Linking USB cable, this special cable looks like a regular USB cable that's swallowed a mouse: The cable bulges in the middle, as shown in Figure 19-1. These cables cost less than $30 at most electronics stores or online.

✔ **Network:** Vista can suck your old PC's information through a network, if you've already created one between your two PCs. Creating a network requires *much* more work than plugging in an Easy Transfer cable, but I tackle the job in Chapter 14.

✔ **DVDs or CDs:** If both PCs have CD or DVD burners, you can transfer information by burning boatloads of discs. But be prepared for a *long* evening's work feeding discs to your PCs. Unless you're transferring a handful of files, this method is your slowest and most labor-intensive option.

✔ **Portable hard drive:** Costing between $100 and $200, a portable hard drive works well for transferring information from one PC to another. Most portable drives plug into both a wall outlet and your PC's USB port. (An empty iPod will work as a portable hard drive, in a pinch, if you know how to store files on it.)

When your PCs live more than a cable's reach apart, a portable hard drive is your best transfer option. Choose one that's almost as large as the hard drive inside your PC. After transferring the files, put the hard drive to work backing up your files each night, an extremely prudent task I describe in Chapter 12.

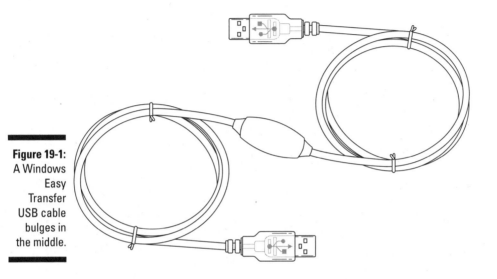

Figure 19-1:
A Windows
Easy
Transfer
USB cable
bulges in
the middle.

Installing your old PC's programs onto your new PC

Windows Vista can transfer your PC's *data* — your e-mail, digital photos, letters, and other things you've created — as well as your programs' *settings:* your e-mail account settings, for example, and your Web browser's list of favorite Web sites.

But Vista can't copy the *programs* themselves. That's right: All of your old PC's programs must be reinstalled onto your new PC. And you need to install those programs *before* running the Easy Transfer program to ensure that the programs will be ready to accept their incoming settings.

To install the old programs, dig out their installation CDs and any copy protection codes you may need to reenter. The codes are usually printed on either the CD itself, the CD's packaging, or a sticker on the program's manual. (If you purchased a program online, you may be able to retrieve the copy-protection code from the manufacturer's Web site.)

Copying Windows Easy Transfer to your old PC

Windows XP doesn't come with the Windows Easy Transfer program. That's no obstacle if your PC has a DVD drive. Just insert Windows Vista's installation DVD into your Windows XP PC's DVD drive. At the opening screen, choose Transfer Files and Settings from Another Computer, and Windows Easy Transfer hops onto the screen.

But if your decrepit Windows XP PC lacks a DVD drive, install the Windows Easy Transfer program by following these steps:

1. **Open Windows Easy Transfer on your Vista PC and click Next at the program's opening screen.**

   Click Start, choose All Programs, click Accessories, click System Tools, and click Windows Easy Transfer. If asked, click Close All to close any currently running programs.

2. **Choose Start a New Transfer.**

   Vista asks whether you're running the program on your new PC or your old one.

3. **Choose My New Computer.**

   Vista asks whether you have an Easy Transfer cable.

4. **Choose No, Show Me More Options.**

   Choose this counterintuitive option even if you *do* have a Windows Easy Transfer cable.

5. **Choose No, I Need to Install It Now.**

   Vista offers to copy the Windows Easy Transfer program to a CD, USB flash drive, external hard drive, or shared network folder.

6. **Make your choice, and Vista creates a copy of the program to run on your old PC.**

   Vista stores the program in a folder named MigWiz. To run the program on your Windows XP PC, navigate to the MigWiz folder, open it, and double-click the program's cryptic name: migwiz or migwiz.exe.

Transferring Information Between Two PCs with Windows Easy Transfer

Windows Easy Transfer works in just a few steps or a lengthy string of steps, depending on your chosen transfer method. First, you tell the program how to transfer your information, be it through a cable, network, or on discs. Second, you tell Vista what information to collect from your old PC: Everything from your own user account? From everybody's user accounts? Or perhaps just a few important files?

After dispensing with those details, the program gets to work, grabbing everything you've chosen from your Windows XP PC and stuffing it into the correct places inside your new Vista PC.

The next section describes how to make Windows Easy Transfer copy through an Easy Transfer USB cable, network, or storage area like CDs, DVDs, or a portable hard drive.

Be sure to log on with an Administrator account; Limited accounts don't have the authority to copy files. And take your time: You can always return to a previous screen by clicking the blue arrow in the window's top, left corner.

1. **Start both PCs and log on to each PC.**

    If you plan to use a USB Easy Transfer Cable, install the Easy Transfer Cable's bundled program onto your Windows XP PC now. That program lets poor ol' Windows XP understand what type of cable you're about to plug in. (Don't install the Easy Transfer Cable's bundled program on your Vista PC, as Vista already knows how to use a USB Easy Transfer Cable.)

2. **Run Windows Easy Transfer on your Windows XP PC and click Next.**

    Insert Windows Vista's installation DVD into your Windows XP PC's DVD drive. At the opening screen, choose Transfer Files and Settings from Another Computer, and the program hops onto the screen.

    If your Windows XP PC doesn't have a DVD drive, read the sidebar, "Copying Windows Easy Transfer to your old PC." It explains how to copy the program to your old PC.

3. **On your Windows XP PC, choose how to transfer files and settings to your new Vista PC.**

    The Easy Transfer program offers three options, shown in Figure 19-2:

    • **Use an Easy Transfer Cable (Recommended).** If you choose this quick 'n' easy option, connect the Easy Transfer cable between USB ports on your Windows XP PC and your Windows Vista PC. When Windows Easy Transfer opens automatically on your Windows Vista PC, jump to Step 11.

    • **Transfer Directly, Using a Network Connection.** If you choose to transfer through your PC's network, move to Step 5.

    • **Use a CD, DVD, or Other Removable Media.** If you choose this option, move to the next step.

4. **Choose how to transfer your files and settings.**

    The program offers three options:

    • **CD or DVD:** This option works if your old PC can burn CDs or DVDs *and* your new PC has a CD or DVD drive for reading them. Be prepared to spend a long evening in front of both PCs, though, copying discs and feeding them to your new PC.

- **USB Flash Drive:** Much quicker than CDs or DVDs, USB flash drives are plagued by small sizes. They work for transferring a few files, but aren't nearly large enough to hold all your old PC's information.

- **External Hard Disk or Network Location:** External hard disks (also called portable hard drives) plug into your PC's USB port to give it a big dose of storage space. They're your fastest and most reliable choice. If both PCs can connect to the same network location — a Public or Shared Documents folder on another PC — you may choose that option, as well.

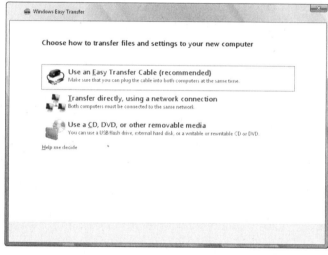

Figure 19-2:
Choose how to copy files and settings from your old PC to your new PC.

After making your choice, choose the drive letter of your CD/DVD burner, USB flash drive, external hard disk, or the path to your network location, and then create an optional password to keep your information secure. (You'll need to reenter that password on your Windows Vista PC to access the information.) Click Next and jump to Step 11.

5. **Choose how to transfer files and settings over a network.**

The program offers two options:

- **Use a Network Connection:** The most likely choice for small home networks, this option pipes the information straight from your Windows XP PC to your Windows Vista PC. If you choose this one, move to the next step, Step 6.

- **Copy to and from a Network Location:** Choose this option for more esoteric networks where your PCs can't communicate directly, but they can both access the same location on the network. If you choose this, select the network location, choose an optional password and move to Step 11.

6. **Choose whether or not you have a Windows Easy Transfer key.**

   Choose No, I Need a Key and then write down the key on a piece of paper. You'll need to enter that key later on your Vista PC. (Vista's *very* security conscious.)

7. **Move to your Windows Vista PC, run Windows Easy Transfer, and click Next.**

   Just as with Windows XP, Windows Vista lets only Administrator account holders use Windows Easy Transfer.

   Vista's Easy Transfer program asks whether you want to start a new transfer or continue one that's in progress.

8. **Choose Continue a Transfer in Progress.**

   The program asks whether the computers are connected to a network.

9. **Choose Yes, I'll Transfer Files and Settings Over the Network.**

   The program asks you to type your Easy Transfer Key.

10. **Type the key you received in Step 6, click Next, and return to your Windows XP PC.**

    Don't have the key? It's still displayed on the monitor of your Windows XP computer. Type the key, and click Next. Vista connects to your Windows XP PC.

    Then return to your Windows XP PC and move to Step 11.

11. **On your Windows XP PC, choose which accounts and information to transfer to the new Vista PC.**

    Windows Easy Transfer offers three ways to transfer your information, shown in Figure 19-3:

    - **All User Accounts, Files, and Settings:** The best and simplest option for families moving to a newer PC, this option transfers information from every user account to the new PC.

    - **Only My User Account, Files, and Settings:** This choice copies only information from your *own* user account. This option works well if you shared a PC with others, but now want to move your information to your own shiny new laptop or new PC.

    - **Advanced Options:** Tossed in for the techies, this option lets you pick and choose exactly which files and settings to move. Today's PCs contain an overwhelming amount of files and settings, so it's not for the faint of heart.

    If you're piping your information into your Windows Vista PC through an Easy Connect cable or network cable, sit down at your new Vista PC and jump to Step 16.

But if you're transferring your information in the other, more labor inten-
sive methods, move to the next step.

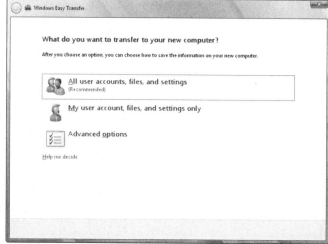

Figure 19-3:
Choose
which
information
to move
to your
new PC.

12. **Review your selected files and settings and click Transfer.**

The program lists all your selected files and settings, shown in
Figure 19-4. Note the size of your transfer, listed above the Transfer
button. Click Customize to jump back to Step 11 for further fiddling;
otherwise, click Transfer to keep the ball rolling.

Vista begins gathering your old PC's information with your chosen
method:

- **Direct Network Connection:** If you chose this method, jump to
  Step 17.

- **CDs or DVDs:** Vista leads you through burning discs on your old
  PC to insert, in order, into your new PC. As you create each disc,
  write a number (CD1, CD2, CD3, . . .) on its printed side with a
  felt pen.

- **Drive:** Insert your portable hard drive or flash drive, if necessary,
  to store your precious data.

- **Network Location:** The program begins moving the information to
  the network location for your Vista PC to grab it.

When your PC finishes stashing that last bit of information, move to the
next step to copy it all to your new PC.

13. Go to your new Vista PC, open Windows Easy Transfer, and click Next at the opening screen.

If the program complains about any open programs, choose Close All to close them. The program then asks whether it should Start a New Transfer or Continue a Transfer in Progress.

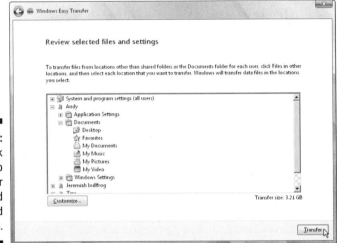

Figure 19-4:
Click
Transfer to
copy all your
selected
files and
settings.

14. Choose Continue a Transfer in Progress.

Vista asks whether you're transferring the files through a network.

15. Choose No, I've Copied Files and Settings to a CD, DVD, or other removable Media.

Vista asks where you've stored the incoming files.

16. Choose the location of the disc or drive containing the files and click Next.

Tell the program the incoming files' exact location: the letter of your CD or DVD drive, for example, the drive letter of your USB flash drive or external hard drive, or, if you've saved the information someplace on a network, the path to the network location.

Enter your password, if you password-protected the files.

When you make your choice, Vista immediately begins looking in that spot to make sure that the information's there.

If you choose CDs or DVDs, Vista leads you through inserting CDs or DVDs, in order, into your new PC.

17. Choose names for the transferred accounts and click Next.

Vista needs to know where to put the incoming user account information. The window lists the names of the incoming user accounts on the left, and the PC's existing user accounts on the right, shown in Figure 19-5. That leaves you three possible scenarios:

- **Same user account names:** If you've used the same user account names on both your old and new PCs, this step is easy: Vista automatically lines up the accounts on the two PCs so that they go to the right places.

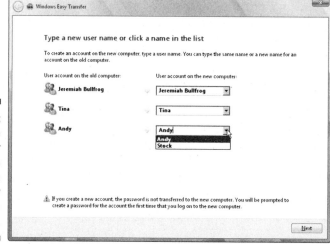

Figure 19-5:
Match the existing user account on the left with its new destination on the right.

- **Different user account names:** If some or all account names are *different* on both PCs, tell Vista which information goes into which account. Use the drop-down menus to match up the old PC's user account name with the new user account names on the new PC.

- **New user account names:** To transfer a user account's files to a brand-new account, type that new account name into the top of the adjacent drop-down menu. The Easy Transfer program creates that new account on your new Vista PC.

18. Review your selected files and, depending on your transfer option, click Next or Transfer.

Vista begins copying your chosen information into your new PC, creating new accounts as needed. Depending on the amount of information, your transfer method, and your PCs' processing power, the job can take from minutes to several hours.

The program ends by summing up all the information it moved, leaving you wondering how you'd ever get by without it.

If you transferred your information with CDs or DVDs, stash the discs in a safe place so they can serve as emergency backups. If some disaster befouls your new PC, you'll at least have your old PC's information safe.

Disposing of the Old Computer

After you've transferred everything of value from the old computer to the new, what do you do with the old computer? You're left with several options.

Many people simply pass their old computers down to the kids, much like the oldest child's clothing moves down to the next oldest child. Kids don't need powerhouse computers for typing term papers.

Others donate them to charities, although charities have grown pickier about what they'll accept. Make sure that the computer's still working well and has a monitor.

You can simply throw it in the trash. An increasing number of cities and states ban this option, however, to keep hazardous waste out of the landfills. It's illegal to throw away PCs or monitors in California, Texas, and other states, for example.

Recycle it. Dell, for example, will recycle your old Dell computer for free. Dell even recycles competitors' PCs when you buy a new Dell computer. Even if you're not buying Dell, visit the recycling page (`www.dell.com/recycling`) at Dell's Web site for lots of general recycling information. Ask your IBM dealer about its recycling plan as well.

Erasing the old computer's hard drive

A freshly donated hard drive can be a thief's delight. If it's like most hard drives, it contains passwords to Web sites, e-mail accounts, and programs; credit-card numbers; identifying information; and possibly financial records. None of this information should fall into the wrong hands.

If your hard drive contains particularly sensitive information, purchase a data destruction program, available in the Utilities section of most computer stores. These specially designed programs completely erase the hard drive and then fill it up again with random characters. (Many programs repeat that process several times to reach the required government privacy specification.)

Alternatively, take it out to the street and hit it with a sledgehammer until it's beyond repair. (Dan Gookin, author of *Word For Dummies,* shoots his old drives with a shotgun.)

Freecycle it. When your old PC is no longer loved by either you or your friends, visit the Freecycle Network (`www.freecycle.org`). The Web site lets you post goods you no longer value so that strangers can swing by and take them off your hands. A starving student may still find some value in your old PC.

Keep your old computer around for a few weeks while you use your new computer. You might remember an important file or setting on the old computer that hasn't yet been transferred over.

Chapter 20

Help on the Windows Vista Help System

In This Chapter

▶ Finding helpful hints quickly

▶ Finding help for a particular problem or program

Don't bother plowing through this whole chapter for the nitty gritty: Here are the quickest ways to make Windows Vista dish out helpful information when you're stumped:

- ✔ **Press F1:** Press your keyboard's F1 key from within Windows or any program.
- ✔ **Start menu:** Click the Start menu and choose Help and Support.
- ✔ **Question Mark:** If you spot a little question mark icon near a window's top-right corner, pounce on it with a quick click.

In each case, Vista fetches its Help and Support program, newly beefed up with tables, charts, and step-by-step instructions for you to follow.

This chapter explains how to wring the most help from Windows Help and Support.

Consulting a Program's Built-In Computer Guru

Almost every Windows program includes its own separate Help system. To summon a program's built-in computer guru, press F1 or choose Help from the menu. To find help in Windows Mail and start asking pointed questions, for example, follow these steps:

1. **Choose Help from the program's menu and choose View Help (or press F1).**

   The Windows Help and Support program opens to its page dedicated to Windows Mail (see Figure 20-1). There, the program lists the topics that give people the most headaches.

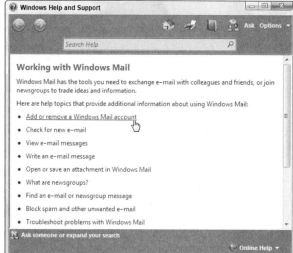

Figure 20-1:
Choose the topic con-fusing you in Windows Mail.

The Search box at the top of the screen lets you search the Help program's index. Typing a few words describing your question often fetches the exact page you need, saving you a few steps.

2. **Click the topic where you need help.**

   For example, clicking Add or Remove a Windows Mail Account tells Vista to explain more about setting up or deleting mail accounts.

3. **Choose the subtopic that interests you.**

   After a brief explanation about the topic, the Help page offers several subtopics: You can choose between either adding an e-mail account or removing one, for example. But don't miss the "See also" topics at the page's bottom. They fetch related information you may need.

4. **Follow the listed steps to complete your task.**

   Vista lists the steps needed to complete your task or fix your problem, sparing you from searching through the menus of your other problem-atic program. As you scan the steps, feel free to look at the area below them; you often find tips for making the job easier next time.

Confused about an odd term used in the Help window? If the term appears in a different color and sprouts an underline when you point at it with the mouse, click it. A new window pops up, defining the word.

 Try to keep the Help window and your problematic program open in adjacent windows. That lets you read each step in the Help window and apply the steps in your program without the distraction of the two windows covering each other up.

The Windows Vista Help system is sometimes a lot of work, forcing you to wade through increasingly detailed menus to find specific information. Still, using Help offers a last resort when you can't find the information elsewhere. And it's often much less embarrassing than tracking down the neighbor's teenagers.

 If you're impressed with a particularly helpful page, send it to the printer: Click the Printer icon (shown in the margin) at the page's top. Windows Vista shoots that page to the printer so that you can keep it handy until you lose it.

Finding the Information You Need in Windows' Help and Support Center

When you don't know where else to start, fire up Vista's Help and Support center and begin digging at the top.

To summon the program, choose Help and Support Center from the Start menu. The Help and Support Center rises to the screen, as shown in Figure 20-2.

The program offers three sections: Find an Answer, Ask Someone, and Information from Microsoft. Start with the Find an Answer section, as it summons help about these topics:

 ✔ **Windows Basics:** If you're new to computers and Windows, head here first. It walks you through the information covered in Chapter 1: Understanding the mouse, keyboard, desktop, Start menu, taskbar, files, folders, and other Windows things everybody thinks you already know.

 ✔ **Security and Maintenance:** This area offers things people put off until something's wrong: ensuring that your PC's security systems are turned on, for example; diagnosing potential problems Vista's noticed with your PC; and making sure that your PC's stocked with the latest fixes from Windows Update.

 ✔ **Windows Online Help:** Don't click here unless you're connected to the Internet, as it tells the Help program to display Vista's online Help page at Microsoft's Web site. That site's often more up-to-date than Vista's built-in Help program, but it uses more technical language.

✔ **Table of Contents:** Just as you'd expect, clicking here brings up a table of contents listing every subject. Click any subject to see subheadings, letting you branch off in the direction you're after.

 ✔ **Troubleshooting:** The spot to head when something's not working, this lets you diagnose and fix problems with networking, the Internet, e-mail, and the way your PC's parts interact with Vista.

✔ **What's New?:** Windows XP users who are curious as to why they upgraded can click here for a rundown on what's new in their particular version of Vista, be it Home Basic, Ultimate, or somewhere in between.

Figure 20-2:
The Windows Help and Support Center offers assistance with Windows and your computer.

Don't bother with the Ask Someone section. It offers Remote Assistance, helpful only when you've found that rare individual who's willing to connect to your PC over the Internet and sort out your problems. The Ask Someone section's Windows Communities choice takes you to the newsgroups, a complicated online relic from the Internet's early years. The section's last option, Contact Microsoft Customer Support Online, takes you to Microsoft's Knowledgebase, a database of Windows problems written for Internet professionals.

The Help and Support section's last area, Information from Microsoft, lists the top questions asked at Microsoft's Vista online support site. It's worth a try only on the rare chance you spot your question among the three listed.

Start your quest for help in the Search box by typing in a few keywords. Type **e-mail**, for example, to see every help topic dealing with e-mail. If Vista comes up blank, move to the Table of Contents. Find your troublesome subject, click it, and begin narrowing down the search for pertinent information.

The Windows Help and Support program works much like a Web site or folder. To move back one page, click the little blue Back arrow in the upper-left corner. That arrow helps you out if you've backed into a corner.

Summoning Windows Vista's Troubleshooters

When something's not working as it should, the Troubleshooting section of Windows Vista's Help and Support program may sleuth out a fix. Sometimes it works like an index, narrowing down the scope of your problems to the one button that fixes it. Then it displays the button on the Help page for your one-click cure.

Other times, a magic button isn't enough. If your wireless Internet signal isn't strong enough, for example, the Troubleshooter tells you to stand up and move your laptop closer to the transmitter.

To summon the troubleshooting program, follow these steps:

1. **Choose Help and Support from the Start menu.**

   The Help and Support program opens, shown earlier in Figure 20-2.

2. **Choose Troubleshooting from the opening screen.**

   The Troubleshooting icon (shown in the margin) lives in the Find an Answer section of the Help and Support program's opening screen (refer to Figure 20-2). The Troubleshooting in Windows page, seen in Figure 20-3, is ready to tackle a wide variety of problems, from general to specific.

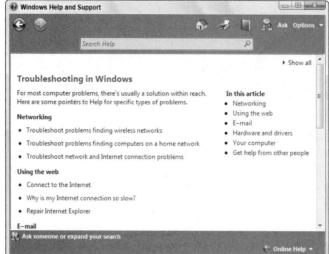

Figure 20-3:
The Trouble-
shooter
programs
help to solve
a wide
variety of
problems.

3. Click the subject that troubles you.

The Troubleshooting section offers these five topics:

- **Networking:** This topic offers help on finding wireless "hotspots" for connecting on the road, fixing home networks, and trouble-shooting network and Internet connection problems.

- **Using the Web:** Here's where to find help with Internet connections, including sharing one connection with several PCs.

- **E-mail:** This area covers Windows Mail and attachments, as well as sending pictures and video through e-mail.

- **Hardware and drivers:** When something's wrong inside your PC, Vista can show the symptoms. This area shows how to diagnose driver problems, the biggest cause of bickering between Vista and things plugged into or inside your PC.

- **Your Computer:** A catch-all section for everything else, this helps out with security and improving your PC's performance.

Click a topic, and Vista whisks you to the page dealing with that subject's most common problems. Keep clicking the subtopics until you find the one dealing with your particular problem.

4. Follow the recommended steps.

Most of the time, you'll stumble onto numbered steps that solve your problem. Follow the steps one at a time to finish the job.

Part VII
The Part of Tens

The 5th Wave
By Rich Tennant

"Well, the first level of Windows Vista security seems good—I can't get the shrink-wrapping off."

In this part . . .

No *For Dummies* book is complete without a Part of Tens section: Lists of ten easy-to-read informational nuggets. Of course, the lists don't always contain exactly ten, but you get the general idea.

The first list explains ten things you'll absolutely hate about Vista (followed by ways to fix those problems). The next list balances out the first with ten things you'll love about Vista (and how to improve them).

The last list contains tips exclusively for laptops. It explains how to change how your laptop reacts when you close its lid, for example, as well as quick ways to adjust screen brightness, volume, and turn on that built-in wireless adapter. I also throw in step-by-steps for tasks laptoppers repeat constantly: logging onto the Internet in different ways and setting the clock for a new time zone.

Chapter 21

Ten or So Things You'll Hate about Windows Vista (and How to Fix Them)

*W*indows Vista would be great if only . . . *(insert your pet peeve here).* If you find yourself thinking (or saying) those words frequently, read this chapter. Here, you find not only a list of ten or so of the most aggravating things about Windows Vista, but also ways you can fix them.

I Can't Stand Those Nagging Permission Screens

You can take either of two approaches to Vista's nagging permission screens:

▶ **Microsoft's preferred approach:** Before automatically clicking the Continue button, ask yourself this question: Did *I* initiate this action? If you deliberately asked your PC to do something, click Continue for the PC to carry out your command. But if the permission screen pops up unexpectedly, click Cancel, because something's wrong.

▶ **The easy way out:** Turn off the permission screens, as I explain in Chapter 17. Unfortunately, that leaves your PC more susceptible to viruses, worms, spyware, and other evil things tossed at your PC during the course of the day.

Neither option is perfect, but that's the choice that Microsoft's given you with Vista: Listen to your PC nag you or turn off the nags and instead trust your own antivirus and antispyware programs.

I recommend Microsoft's preferred approach — it's much like wearing a seatbelt when driving: It's not as comfortable, but it's safer. Ultimately, though, the choice lies with your own balance between comfort and safety.

I Can't Copy Ripped CDs and Purchased Music to My iPod

You won't find the word "iPod" mentioned in Vista's menus, help screens, or even in the Help areas of Microsoft's Web site. Microsoft's competitor, Apple, makes the tremendously popular iPod, and Microsoft's ignoring it in the hopes it will go away.

What won't go away, though, are the problems you'll face if you ever try to copy Media Player's songs into an iPod. You face two hurdles:

- ✔ Songs purchased from Media Player's music store, URGE, only come in a copy-protected WMA (Windows Media Audio) format, and iPods can't play them.
- ✔ Songs copied from CDs with Media Player won't play on your iPod, either. They're also stored in a WMA format.

The second hurdle has a solution: Tell Media Player to convert your CD's music to MP3 files, which *any* portable music player can play — even an iPod. Follow these steps to make the switch:

1. **Open Media Player by clicking the Start menu, choosing All Programs, and choosing Windows Media Player.**

2. **Press Alt, choose Tools from the drop-down menu, and select Options.**

3. **Click the Rip Music tab and choose MP3 instead of Windows Media Audio in the Format drop-down menu.**

4. **Click OK to save your changes.**

By ripping your music to the MP3 format, you'll ensure that your library of ripped music will be compatible with any music player you buy now or in the future. (I cover Media Player in Chapter 15.)

The Menus All Disappeared

In Microsoft's zeal for giving Vista a clean look, the programmers swept away the folder menus used for the past decade. To reveal a folder's missing menus, press Alt. The menus appear, letting you choose the option you're after.

 To keep the menus from disappearing again, click the Organize button (shown in the margin), choose Layout, and choose Menu Bar from the pop-up menu.

Parental Controls Are Too Complicated

Vista's new Parental Controls let you control exactly what your kid can and can't do on the PC. (I explain the detailed options in Chapter 10.) But if you just want Vista to hand you a synopsis of what your kid's been up to on the PC, follow these quick steps:

1. **Click the Start button, click Control Panel, choose User Accounts and Family Safety, and choose Parental Controls.**

    The Parental Controls window appears, listing each account holder's name.

2. **Click the name of your child's user account.**

    The Parental Controls Settings window appears, showing a list of buttons.

3. **In the Parental Controls section, click On, Enforce Current Settings.**

4. **In the Activity Reporting section, click On, Collect Information about Computer Usage.**

5. **Click the OK button.**

Each week or so, check out your child's activity report by following Steps 1 and 2 in the preceding steps, but, in Step 3, choose View Activity Reports. There, Vista shows you a quick, one-page synopsis of what your kid's been up to on the Net.

To zero in on suspicious areas, click your child's Account Activity area in the task pane along the left. It's all there: names of people sending and receiving your child's e-mail and instant messages, the songs and videos played, the Web sites visited, names of any downloaded programs, log-on and log-off times, the number of hours spent at the keyboard, and similar information.

The "Glass" Effects Slow Down My Laptop

One of Vista's much touted special effects, Aero Glass, may be too special to be practical. Aero Glass lets you see bits and pieces of your desktop in each window's frame. The effects also let some programs, like Vista's chess game, "float" in the air, letting you watch the game from all angles.

But the calculations required for those visual gymnastics slow down PCs that don't have high-powered graphics — and that includes many of the current crop of laptops. With Aero Glass, Windows XP's once snappy Freecell may crawl across the screen of your laptop.

Even worse, it may drain your batteries to a fraction of their battery life. If you don't like the extra burden Aero Glass dumps on your PC, turn it off by following these steps:

1. **Right-click a blank part of your desktop and choose Personalize to summon the Control Panel.**

2. **Choose Window Color and Appearance.**

   If you spot the words Open Classic Appearance Properties For More Color Options, click them. Otherwise, move to Step 3.

3. **Choose Windows Vista Basic as the Color Scheme and click OK.**

If that's *still* too slow, try choosing Windows Standard or even Windows Classic in Step 3.

To turn Aero Glass back on for impressing your friends, follow the first two steps in the preceding list, but choose Windows Aero in Step 3.

If Vista's *still* not snappy enough, right-click Computer on the Start menu, choose Properties, and select Advanced System Settings from the task pane on the left. Click the Settings button in the Performance section, choose Adjust for Best Performance, and click OK.

I Can't Figure Out How to Turn Off My PC

Windows XP's Start button offered a convenient Turn Off Computer button. Vista, by contrast, places *two* buttons in that convenient spot, and neither one turns off your PC. The one on the left puts your PC in a "low power state," and the other quickly password protects your account when you walk away for a short period.

To turn off your PC, click the arrow on the right of the two buttons and choose Shut Down. (I explain all the power button's options in Chapter 2.)

To transform the left button (shown in the margin) into a simple On/Off switch, follow these steps:

1. **Click the Start button, choose Control Panel, choose System and Maintenance, and choose Power Options.**

2. **In the task pane along the left, click Change When the Computer Sleeps.**

3. **Choose Change Advanced Power Settings. Then choose Power Buttons and Lid from the Power Options box.**

4. **Click the plus sign next to Start Menu Power Button.**

5. **On a desktop PC, choose Shut Down; on a laptop, choose Shut Down for the Power Button in the On Battery and Plugged In list.**

6. **Click OK.**

Windows Makes Me Log On All the Time

Windows offers two ways to return to life from its swirling and churning screen saver. Windows can return you to the opening screen, where you must log back on to your user account. Alternatively, Windows Vista can simply return you to the program you were using when the screen saver kicked in. Some people prefer the security of the opening screen. If the screen saver kicks in when they're spending too much time at the water cooler, they're protected: Nobody can walk over and snoop through their e-mail.

Other people don't need that extra security, and they simply want to return to work quickly. Here's how to accommodate either camp:

1. **Right-click a blank part of your desktop and choose Personalize.**

2. **Click Screen Saver.**

   Windows Vista shows the screen saver options, including whether or not Windows should wake up at the opening screen.

3. **Depending on your preference, remove or add the check mark from the On Resume, Display Logon Screen box.**

   If the box *is checked,* Windows Vista is more secure. The screen saver wakes up at Vista's opening screen, and users must log on to their user accounts before using the computer. If the box *isn't checked,* Windows Vista is more easygoing, waking up from the screen saver in the same place where you stopped working.

4. **Click the OK button to save your changes.**

 If you don't *ever* want to see the opening screen, then use a single user account without a password. That defeats all the security offered by the user account system, but it's more convenient if you live alone.

The Taskbar Keeps Disappearing

The taskbar is a handy Windows Vista feature that usually squats along the bottom of your screen. Sometimes, unfortunately, it up and wanders off into the woods. Here are a few ways to track it down and bring it home.

If your taskbar suddenly clings to the side of your desktop — or even the roof — try dragging it down: Instead of dragging an edge, drag the taskbar from its middle; as your mouse pointer reaches your desktop's bottom edge, the taskbar will suddenly snap back into place. Let go of the mouse, and you've recaptured it.

Follow these tips to prevent your taskbar from wandering:

- ✔ To keep the taskbar locked into place so that it won't float away, right-click the taskbar and select Lock the Taskbar. Remember, though, that before you can make any changes to the taskbar, you must first unlock it.

- ✔ If your taskbar drops from sight whenever the mouse pointer doesn't hover nearby, turn off the taskbar's Auto Hide feature: Right-click a blank part of the taskbar and choose Properties from the pop-up menu. When the Taskbar and Start Menu Properties dialog box appears, click to remove the check mark from the Auto-Hide box on the Taskbar tab. (Or, to turn on the Auto Hide feature, add the check mark.)

- ✔ While you're in the Taskbar and Start Menu Properties dialog box, make sure that a check mark appears in the Keep the Taskbar on Top of Other Windows check box. That way, the taskbar always rides visibly on the desktop, making it much easier to spot.

I Can't Keep Track of Open Windows

You don't *have* to keep track of all those open windows. Windows Vista does it for you with a secret key combination: Hold the Alt key and press the Tab key, and the little bar appears, displaying the icons for all your open windows. Keep pressing Tab; when Windows highlights the icon of the window you're after, release the keys. The window pops up.

 Or, if your PC has powerful enough graphics, click the Flip 3D button (shown in the margin) next to the Start button. Vista "floats" all the open windows on-screen. Click the window you want to bring to the forefront. Or, flip through them all by pressing Tab or your keyboard's arrow keys.

Or, use the taskbar, that long strip along the bottom of your screen. Covered in Chapter 2, the taskbar lists the name of every open window. Click the name of the window you want, and that window hops to the top of the pile.

In Chapter 6, you find more soldiers to enlist in the battle against misplaced windows, files, and programs.

I Can't Line Up Two Windows on the Screen

With all its cut-and-paste stuff, Windows Vista makes it easy for you to grab information from one program and slap it into another. With its drag-and-drop stuff, you can grab an address from a contact's address card and drag it into a letter in your word processor.

 The hardest part of Windows Vista is lining up two windows on the screen, side by side, to make for easy dragging. *That's* when you need to call in the taskbar. First, open the two windows and place them anywhere on the screen. Then turn all the other windows into icons by clicking their Minimize button (shown in the margin).

Now, right-click a blank area of the taskbar and then choose either Show Windows Stacked or Show Windows Side By Side. The two windows line up on the screen perfectly. Try both to see which meets your current needs.

It Won't Let Me Do Something Unless I'm an Administrator!

Windows Vista gets really picky about who gets to do what on your computer. The computer's owner gets the Administrator account. And the administrator usually gives everybody else a Standard account. What does that mean? Well, only the administrator can do these things on the computer:

✔ Install programs and hardware.

✔ Create or change accounts for other users.

✔ Install some hardware, like some digital cameras and MP3 players.

✔ Read everybody else's files.

People with Standard accounts, by nature, are limited to fairly basic activities. They can do these things:

✔ Run installed programs.

✔ Change their account's picture and password.

Guest accounts are meant for the babysitter or visitors who don't permanently use the computer. If you have a broadband or other "always on" Internet account, guests can browse the Internet, run programs, or check their e-mail. (As I describe in Chapter 13, Guest accounts aren't allowed to *start* an Internet session, but they can use an existing one.)

If Windows says only an administrator may do something on your PC, you have two choices: Find an administrator to type his password, authorizing the action; or convince an administrator to upgrade your account to an Administrator account, covered in Chapter 13.

I Don't Know What Version of Windows I Have

Windows has been sold in more than a dozen flavors since its debut in November 1985. How can you tell what version is really installed on your computer?

Open the Start menu, right-click Computer, and choose Properties. Look in the Windows Edition section at the top to see which version of Windows Vista you own: Home Basic, Home Premium, Business, Enterprise, or Ultimate.

In earlier versions of Windows, look beneath the word *System* to see the Windows version.

My Print Screen Key Doesn't Work

Windows Vista takes over the Print Screen key (labeled PrtSc, PrtScr, or something even more supernatural on some keyboards). Instead of sending the stuff on the screen to the printer, the Print Screen key sends it to Windows Vista's memory, where you can paste it into other windows.

If you hold the Alt key while pressing the Print Screen key, Windows Vista sends a picture of the current *window* — not the entire screen — to the Clipboard for pasting.

If you *really* want a printout of the screen, press the Print Screen button to send a picture of the screen to its memory. (It won't look like anything has happened.) Then click Start, choose All Programs, select Accessories, open Paint, and choose Paste from the Edit menu. When your picture appears, choose Print from the File menu to send it to the printer.

Chapter 22

Ten or So Tips for Laptop Owners

*F*or the most part, everything in this book applies both to PCs and laptops. Vista offers a few settings exclusively for laptops, however, and I cover those items here. I also throw in a few tips and quick references to make this chapter especially suited for laptop owners who need information in a hurry.

Adjusting Your Laptop's Settings Quickly

Vista offers a quick way for laptop owners to see the things that most affect their little PC's on-the-go lifestyle. Called the Mobility Center, it's a one-stop shop for tweaking your laptop's main settings. To open the Mobility Center, follow these steps:

1. **Click Start and choose Control Panel.**

2. **Choose Mobile PC and select Windows Mobility Center.**

   Windows Mobility Center, seen in Figure 22-1, rises to the screen. In the future, you can jump here quickly by holding down the Windows key and pressing X.

3. **Make your adjustments.**

   As seen in Figure 22-1, Mobility Center lets you make quick adjustments to your laptop's main settings, as described in the following list. Don't think something's wrong if you don't spot all these options on your laptop. Manufacturers customize the center's options to match each model's features.

Figure 22-1:
Windows
Mobility
Center puts
a laptop's
most
common
adjustments
on one
panel.

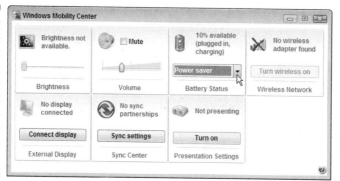

- **Brightness:** A simple sliding control lets you dim your laptop in low-light situations (or simply to save battery power) or increase the brightness when working outdoors.

- **Volume:** Tired of your laptop's annoying blast every time you turn it on? Slide down the volume level here. (Or click the Mute check box to turn it off completely, saving batteries and letting you turn it on only when needed.)

- **Battery Status:** Choose Balanced for everyday work, switch to Power Saver when working away from outlets for several hours, and switch to High Performance when plugged in.

- **Wireless Network:** If your laptop offers it, here's an easy-to-find On/Off switch for your laptop's wireless network adapter. Leave it turned off to save batteries, and turn it back on when you're ready to connect.

- **External Display:** Ever plug your laptop into a larger monitor or projector for giving presentations? Head here to set it up.

- **Sync Center:** Vista lets you keep your laptop or PC in synchronization with a compatible portable music player or cell phone, automatically updating them with each other's information. (Unfortunately, you can't sync your laptop with your desktop PC, or with an iPod.) This switch brings you to the Sync Center, where you can set up a partnership with sync-compatible gadgets and click the Sync All button for them to exchange information.

- **Presentation Settings:** This option lets you control what appears on the projector when you hook up your laptop. With the click of one button, you can turn your desktop's wallpaper into something business-safe, turn off your screen saver, adjust the PC's volume, and squelch any other distractions.

Although some buttons take you to yet more areas full of settings, the Mobility Center works well as a launching pad. It's your first stop to customize your laptop to match its surroundings.

Choosing What Happens When You Close Your Laptop's Lid

Closing the laptop's lid means that you're through working, but for how long? For the night? Until you get off the subway? For a long lunch hour? Vista lets you tailor exactly how your laptop should behave when you latch your laptop's lid.

To start tweaking, follow these steps:

1. **Click Start, choose Control Panel, and then choose System and Maintenance.**

2. **Choose Power Options and then select Choose What Closing the Lid Does from the left pane.**

   Shown in Figure 22-2, Vista offers different lid-closing settings for whether your PC is plugged in or running on its batteries: Do Nothing, Hibernate, or Shut Down.

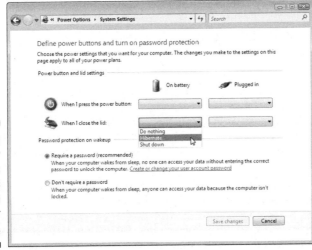

Figure 22-2: Change your laptop's reactions when plugged in or on batteries.

Generally, choose Hibernate, as it lets your laptop slumber in a low-power state, letting it wake up quickly so that you can begin working without delay. But if you'll be shutting down your laptop for the evening, turning it off is often a better idea. That option lets the laptop conserve its battery power and, if plugged in overnight, wake up with fully charged batteries.

Also, you can choose whether or not your PC should require you to enter a password when it's turned back on. (Passwords are always a good idea.)

This window also lets you choose what happens when you click the Power and Lock buttons at the bottom of your Start menu. I cover power options more fully in Chapter 2.

3. **Click Save Changes to make your changes permanent.**

Adjusting to Different Locations

PCs don't move from a desktop, making some things pretty easy to set up. You need only enter your location once, for example, and Vista automatically sets up your time zone, currency symbols, and similar things that change over the globe.

But the joy of a laptop's mobility is tempered with the agony of telling the thing exactly where it's currently located. These sections supply the steps you need to change when traveling to a different area.

Changing your time zone

Follow these steps to let your laptop know you've entered a new time zone:

1. **Click the clock in the taskbar's bottom-right corner.**

   A calendar and clock appear in a small window.

2. **Choose Date and Time settings.**

   The Date and Time dialog box appears.

3. **Choose Change Time Zone, enter your current time zone in the Time Zone pull-down menu, and click OK twice.**

If you frequently travel between time zones, take advantage of the Additional Clocks tab in Step 3. There, you can add up to two extra clocks; to check the time quickly in Caracas, just hover your mouse pointer over the taskbar's clock. A pop-up menu appears listing your local time, as well as the time in the additional locations you've entered.

Dialing a modem from a new location

I give a detailed explanation of how to connect with a dialup modem in Chapter 8. Here, I'm assuming that you're setting up a connection in a *different* city, where you must enter a different phone number, area code, calling card, or other differences. Follow these steps to connect to a dialup Internet connection in a new location.

1. **Click the Start button and choose Connect To.**

   Vista lists all previous dialup Internet connections you've added in the past — including the first one you set up.

   If you need to change the phone number, add a number that reaches an outside line, change the area code, or enter a calling card number, move to Step 2.

2. **Right-click your existing dialup location and choose Properties.**

   Vista lists the settings for your current dialup connection.

3. **Click the Use Dialing Rules check box and click Dialing Rules.**

   The Dialing Rules dialog box appears, listing the names of locations you've entered when setting up different dialup connections. The setting called My Location is the one Vista created when you set up your first dialup connection.

4. **Click New and enter the changed settings for your new location.**

   When the New Location dialog box appears, enter the name of your new location, as well as the changes required for dialing in that location: a different area code or access number, a hotel that makes you dial 9 for an outside line, or perhaps a code to disable call waiting.

   As you enter your changes, the bottom of the New Location dialog box lists the number Vista will dial to make the connection.

5. **Click OK when you finish, then click OK to exit the Phone and Modem Options dialog box, and click OK to exit the Properties dialog box.**

   Vista leaves you back at the Connect to a Network dialog box that names your dialup connection.

6. **Click Connect.**

   Vista dials the Internet number using the new settings you've entered. If you need to dial a different phone number, head to Chapter 8 for instructions on setting up a dial-up account. However, your newly entered region settings will be waiting for you there.

Connecting to a wireless Internet hotspot

Every time you connect to a wireless network, Vista stashes its settings for connecting again the next time you visit. I explain wireless connections completely in Chapter 14, but here are the steps for quick reference:

1. **Turn on your laptop's wireless adapter, if necessary.**

   You can often turn it on with a click in the Mobility Center, shown in Figure 22-1. Some laptops offer a manual switch somewhere on the case.

2. **Choose Connect To from the Start menu.**

   Vista lists every way it can connect with the Internet — including any wireless networks it finds within range.

3. **Connect to the wireless network by clicking its name and clicking Connect.**

   Your PC should connect immediately. But if your laptop asks for more information, move to Step 4.

4. **Enter the wireless network's name and security key/passphrase, if asked, and then click Connect.**

   Some secretive wireless networks don't broadcast their name, so Windows lists them as Unnamed Network. If you spot that name, track down the network's owner and ask for the network's name and security key or passphrase to enter here.

   When you click Connect, Vista announces its success. Be sure to click the two boxes, Save This Network and Start This Connection Automatically, to make it easier to connect the next time you come within range.

When you're through online, turn off your laptop's wireless adapter to save your laptop's batteries.

Backing Up Your Laptop Before Traveling

I explain how to back up a PC in Chapter 12, and backing up a laptop works just like backing up a desktop PC. Please, please remember to back up your laptop before leaving your home or office. Thieves grab laptops much more often than desktop PCs. Your laptop can be replaced, but the data inside it can't.

Keep the backed up information at home — not in your laptop's bag.

Appendix

Upgrading to Windows Vista

*N*ew computers today come with Windows Vista preinstalled — it's practically unavoidable. If you're reading this chapter, then your computer is probably still running Windows XP. If it's running Windows 98 or Windows Me, don't bother trying: Vista requires a powerful PC with cutting-edge parts.

To beef up your PC's power to get the most out of Vista, pick up another of my books, *Upgrading & Fixing PCs For Dummies*. It explains how to upgrade the graphics, add more memory, and perform other chores to satisfy Vista's craving for power.

One warning: Upgrading to Vista from Windows XP is a one-way street, because you can't return to Windows XP once you've installed Vista. Don't upgrade unless you're sure you're ready for Vista.

Preparing for Windows Vista

Windows Vista usually runs well on computers purchased within the past three or four years. Before upgrading, make sure that you've run through the following checklist:

✔ **Computer power:** Make sure that your computer is strong enough to run Windows Vista. I cover Vista's requirements in Chapter 1.

✔ **Compatibility:** Before upgrading or installing, insert the Vista DVD and choose Check Compatibility Online. When Vista takes you to Microsoft's Web site, download and run Microsoft's Windows Vista Upgrade Advisor. The program alerts you beforehand what parts of your computer may not run well under Windows Vista. You can find the Upgrade Advisor on Microsoft's Web site at www.microsoft.com/windowsvista/getready.

> ✔ **Security:** Before upgrading to Windows Vista, turn off your antivirus software and other security programs. They may innocently try to protect you from Windows Vista's upgrade process.
>
> ✔ **Backup:** Back up all your important data on your Windows XP PC.

Installing the Windows Vista Upgrade

Follow these steps to upgrade your copy of Windows XP to Windows Vista:

1. **Insert the Windows Vista DVD into your DVD drive and choose Install Now, as shown in Figure A-1.**

   Vista churns away, preparing to install itself.

Figure A-1: Choose Install Now from the Windows Vista installation screen.

2. **Choose Go Online to Get the Latest Updates for Installation (Recommended).**

   This step tells Vista to visit Microsoft's Web site and download the latest updates — drivers, patches, and assorted fixes — that help make your installation run as smoothly as possible.

3. **Type your product key and click Next, as shown in Figure A-2.**

   The *product key* usually lives on a little sticker affixed to the CD's packaging. No product key? You're stuck. You can't install Windows Vista without a product key. (If you're reinstalling a version of Vista that came pre-installed on your PC, look for the product key printed on a sticker affixed to the side or back of your PC.)

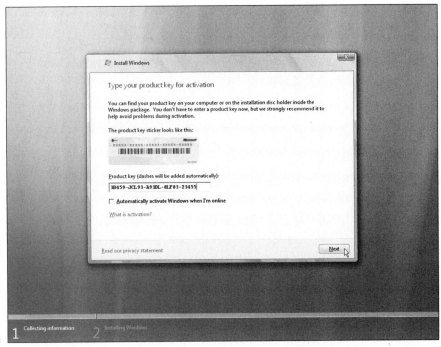

Figure A-2:
Type the
product
key and
click Next.

Don't click the check box called Automatically Activate Windows When I'm Online. You can do that later, once you know Vista works on your PC.

Write your product key on top of your Windows Vista DVD with a felt-tip pen. (Write on the side of the disc that's *printed.*) That way, you'll always have your valid product key with your disc disc.

Windows Vista's Activation feature takes a snapshot of your computer's parts and links it with Windows Vista's serial number, which prevents you from installing that same copy onto another computer. Unfortunately, the Activation feature may also hassle you if you change a lot of parts in your computer.

4. **Read the License Agreement, click the check box next to I Accept the License Terms, and click Next.**

   Take an hour or so to read Microsoft's 25-page License Agreement carefully. You need to select the I Accept the License Terms check box option before Microsoft allows you to install the software.

5. **Choose Upgrade and click Next.**

   Upgrading preserves your old files, settings, and programs. If this option's grayed out, either of two things could be wrong:

   • You're trying to upgrade an incompatible version of Windows XP. You can't install Windows Vista Home version on Windows XP

Professional, for example. See this chapter's Table 20-1 for the lowdown.

- Your copy of Windows XP doesn't have Service Pack 2 installed. To fix this, visit Windows Update (www.windowsupdate.com) and download Service Pack 2. If the site refuses, you probably don't have a genuine copy of Windows XP installed. Call your PC's vendor, be it a store or the kid down the street who built it for you.

- Your hard drive isn't big enough. Your hard drive needs up to 15GB of free space to install Vista.

When you click Next, Vista copies files onto your PC's hard drive and then installs itself. It usually restarts your PC a few times during the process.

6. Choose your country, time and currency, and keyboard layout, and click Next.

Vista looks at how your Windows XP PC is set up and guesses at your location, language, time, and currency. If it guesses correctly, just click Next. If it guesses wrong, however, set it straight on your personal information by using your keyboard.

7. Choose Use Recommended Settings.

Vista's recommended security settings keep Vista automatically patched and up-to-date.

8. If you're connected to a network, choose your PC's location.

Vista gives you options: Home, Work, or a Public Location.

Choose Home or Work, and Vista eases up on the security a bit, letting the PCs on the network see each other. If you're in a public setting, though, choose Public Location. Vista keeps your PC more secure by not letting other PCs share any of its files.

After rummaging around inside your PC for a few more minutes, Windows Vista appears on the screen, leaving you at the logon screen. But don't rest yet. Run through the following steps to complete the process:

- **Use Windows Update.** Visit Windows Update, described in Chapter 10, and download any security patches and updated drivers issued by Microsoft.

- **Make sure that Vista recognizes your software.** Run all your old programs to make sure that they still work. You may need to replace them with newer versions or drop by the manufacturer's Web site to see whether they offer free updates.

- **Check the user accounts.** Make sure that your PC's user accounts work correctly.

Welcome to Windows Vista!

Index

• E •

• F •

• T •

BUSINESS, CAREERS & PERSONAL FINANCE

0-7645-9847-3

0-7645-2431-3

Also available:
- Business Plans Kit For Dummies
  0-7645-9794-9
- Economics For Dummies
  0-7645-5726-2
- Grant Writing For Dummies
  0-7645-8416-2
- Home Buying For Dummies
  0-7645-5331-3
- Managing For Dummies
  0-7645-1771-6
- Marketing For Dummies
  0-7645-5600-2

- Personal Finance For Dummies
  0-7645-2590-5*
- Resumes For Dummies
  0-7645-5471-9
- Selling For Dummies
  0-7645-5363-1
- Six Sigma For Dummies
  0-7645-6798-5
- Small Business Kit For Dummies
  0-7645-5984-2
- Starting an eBay Business For Dummies
  0-7645-6924-4
- Your Dream Career For Dummies
  0-7645-9795-7

HOME & BUSINESS COMPUTER BASICS

0-470-05432-8

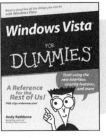

0-471-75421-8

Also available:
- Cleaning Windows Vista For Dummies
  0-471-78293-9
- Excel 2007 For Dummies
  0-470-03737-7
- Mac OS X Tiger For Dummies
  0-7645-7675-5
- MacBook For Dummies
  0-470-04859-X
- Macs For Dummies
  0-470-04849-2
- Office 2007 For Dummies
  0-470-00923-3

- Outlook 2007 For Dummies
  0-470-03830-6
- PCs For Dummies
  0-7645-8958-X
- Salesforce.com For Dummies
  0-470-04893-X
- Upgrading & Fixing Laptops For Dummies
  0-7645-8959-8
- Word 2007 For Dummies
  0-470-03658-3
- Quicken 2007 For Dummies
  0-470-04600-7

FOOD, HOME, GARDEN, HOBBIES, MUSIC & PETS

0-7645-8404-9

0-7645-9904-6

Also available:
- Candy Making For Dummies
  0-7645-9734-5
- Card Games For Dummies
  0-7645-9910-0
- Crocheting For Dummies
  0-7645-4151-X
- Dog Training For Dummies
  0-7645-8418-9
- Healthy Carb Cookbook For Dummies
  0-7645-8476-6
- Home Maintenance For Dummies
  0-7645-5215-5

- Horses For Dummies
  0-7645-9797-3
- Jewelry Making & Beading For Dummies
  0-7645-2571-9
- Orchids For Dummies
  0-7645-6759-4
- Puppies For Dummies
  0-7645-5255-4
- Rock Guitar For Dummies
  0-7645-5356-9
- Sewing For Dummies
  0-7645-6847-7
- Singing For Dummies
  0-7645-2475-5

INTERNET & DIGITAL MEDIA

0-470-04529-9

0-470-04894-8

Also available:
- Blogging For Dummies
  0-471-77084-1
- Digital Photography For Dummies
  0-7645-9802-3
- Digital Photography All-in-One Desk Reference For Dummies
  0-470-03743-1
- Digital SLR Cameras and Photography For Dummies
  0-7645-9803-1
- eBay Business All-in-One Desk Reference For Dummies
  0-7645-8438-3
- HDTV For Dummies
  0-470-09673-X

- Home Entertainment PCs For Dummies
  0-470-05523-5
- MySpace For Dummies
  0-470-09529-6
- Search Engine Optimization For Dummies
  0-471-97998-8
- Skype For Dummies
  0-470-04891-3
- The Internet For Dummies
  0-7645-8996-2
- Wiring Your Digital Home For Dummies
  0-471-91830-X

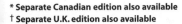

* Separate Canadian edition also available
† Separate U.K. edition also available

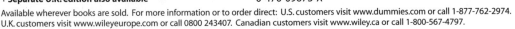

SPORTS, FITNESS, PARENTING, RELIGION & SPIRITUALITY

0-471-76871-5

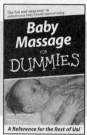
0-7645-7841-3

Also available:

- Catholicism For Dummies
  0-7645-5391-7
- Exercise Balls For Dummies
  0-7645-5623-1
- Fitness For Dummies
  0-7645-7851-0
- Football For Dummies
  0-7645-3936-1
- Judaism For Dummies
  0-7645-5299-6
- Potty Training For Dummies
  0-7645-5417-4
- Buddhism For Dummies
  0-7645-5359-3

- Pregnancy For Dummies
  0-7645-4483-7 †
- Ten Minute Tone-Ups For Dummies
  0-7645-7207-5
- NASCAR For Dummies
  0-7645-7681-X
- Religion For Dummies
  0-7645-5264-3
- Soccer For Dummies
  0-7645-5229-5
- Women in the Bible For Dummies
  0-7645-8475-8

TRAVEL

0-7645-7749-2

0-7645-6945-7

Also available:

- Alaska For Dummies
  0-7645-7746-8
- Cruise Vacations For Dummies
  0-7645-6941-4
- England For Dummies
  0-7645-4276-1
- Europe For Dummies
  0-7645-7529-5
- Germany For Dummies
  0-7645-7823-5
- Hawaii For Dummies
  0-7645-7402-7

- Italy For Dummies
  0-7645-7386-1
- Las Vegas For Dummies
  0-7645-7382-9
- London For Dummies
  0-7645-4277-X
- Paris For Dummies
  0-7645-7630-5
- RV Vacations For Dummies
  0-7645-4442-X
- Walt Disney World & Orlando
  For Dummies
  0-7645-9660-8

GRAPHICS, DESIGN & WEB DEVELOPMENT

0-7645-8815-X

0-7645-9571-7

Also available:

- 3D Game Animation For Dummies
  0-7645-8789-7
- AutoCAD 2006 For Dummies
  0-7645-8925-3
- Building a Web Site For Dummies
  0-7645-7144-3
- Creating Web Pages For Dummies
  0-470-08030-2
- Creating Web Pages All-in-One Desk
  Reference For Dummies
  0-7645-4345-8
- Dreamweaver 8 For Dummies
  0-7645-9649-7

- InDesign CS2 For Dummies
  0-7645-9572-5
- Macromedia Flash 8 For Dummies
  0-7645-9691-8
- Photoshop CS2 and Digital
  Photography For Dummies
  0-7645-9580-6
- Photoshop Elements 4 For Dummies
  0-471-77483-9
- Syndicating Web Sites with RSS Feeds
  For Dummies
  0-7645-8848-6
- Yahoo! SiteBuilder For Dummies
  0-7645-9800-7

NETWORKING, SECURITY, PROGRAMMING & DATABASES

0-7645-7728-X

0-471-74940-0

Also available:

- Access 2007 For Dummies
  0-470-04612-0
- ASP.NET 2 For Dummies
  0-7645-7907-X
- C# 2005 For Dummies
  0-7645-9704-3
- Hacking For Dummies
  0-470-05235-X
- Hacking Wireless Networks
  For Dummies
  0-7645-9730-2
- Java For Dummies
  0-470-08716-1

- Microsoft SQL Server 2005 For Dummies
  0-7645-7755-7
- Networking All-in-One Desk Reference
  For Dummies
  0-7645-9939-9
- Preventing Identity Theft For Dummies
  0-7645-7336-5
- Telecom For Dummies
  0-471-77085-X
- Visual Studio 2005 All-in-One Desk
  Reference For Dummies
  0-7645-9775-2
- XML For Dummies
  0-7645-8845-1

HEALTH & SELF-HELP

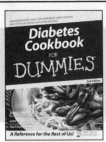
0-7645-8450-2

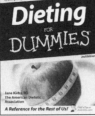
0-7645-4149-8

Also available:
- Bipolar Disorder For Dummies
  0-7645-8451-0
- Chemotherapy and Radiation
  For Dummies
  0-7645-7832-4
- Controlling Cholesterol For Dummies
  0-7645-5440-9
- Diabetes For Dummies
  0-7645-6820-5* †
- Divorce For Dummies
  0-7645-8417-0 †

- Fibromyalgia For Dummies
  0-7645-5441-7
- Low-Calorie Dieting For Dummies
  0-7645-9905-4
- Meditation For Dummies
  0-471-77774-9
- Osteoporosis For Dummies
  0-7645-7621-6
- Overcoming Anxiety For Dummies
  0-7645-5447-6
- Reiki For Dummies
  0-7645-9907-0
- Stress Management For Dummies
  0-7645-5144-2

EDUCATION, HISTORY, REFERENCE & TEST PREPARATION

0-7645-8381-6

0-7645-9554-7

Also available:
- The ACT For Dummies
  0-7645-9652-7
- Algebra For Dummies
  0-7645-5325-9
- Algebra Workbook For Dummies
  0-7645-8467-7
- Astronomy For Dummies
  0-7645-8465-0
- Calculus For Dummies
  0-7645-2498-4
- Chemistry For Dummies
  0-7645-5430-1
- Forensics For Dummies
  0-7645-5580-4

- Freemasons For Dummies
  0-7645-9796-5
- French For Dummies
  0-7645-5193-0
- Geometry For Dummies
  0-7645-5324-0
- Organic Chemistry I For Dummies
  0-7645-6902-3
- The SAT I For Dummies
  0-7645-7193-1
- Spanish For Dummies
  0-7645-5194-9
- Statistics For Dummies
  0-7645-5423-9

Get smart @ dummies.com®

- **Find a full list of Dummies titles**
- **Look into loads of FREE on-site articles**
- **Sign up for FREE eTips e-mailed to you weekly**
- **See what other products carry the Dummies name**
- **Shop directly from the Dummies bookstore**
- **Enter to win new prizes every month!**

* Separate Canadian edition also available
† Separate U.K. edition also available

Available wherever books are sold. For more information or to order direct: U.S. customers visit www.dummies.com or call 1-877-762-2974.
U.K. customers visit www.wileyeurope.com or call 0800 243407. Canadian customers visit www.wiley.ca or call 1-800-567-4797.